MUSICAL INSTRUMENT DESIGN

Practical Information for Instrument Making

Written and illustrated by Bart Hopkin

See Sharp Press
Tucson, Arizona

For information contact See Sharp Press, P.O. Box 1731, Tucson, AZ 85702-1731
or contact us via our web site: www.seesharppress.com

Hopkin, Bart.
        Musical Instrument Design / by Bart Hopkin; with an introduction by Jon Scoville.
— Tucson, AZ : See Sharp Press, 1996.
        181 pp. ; music ; 28 cm
        Includes bibliographical references (p. 177) and index (p. 179)
        ISBN 978-1-884365-08-9 (pbk.)

        1. Music Instruments — Design and construction. 2. Music Instruments — Theory.
3. Music — Philosophy and esthetics. 4. Music — Theory. I. Title.

                                784.1922

First printing — June 1996
Second printing — June 1998
Third printing — August 2000
Fourth printing — September 2003
Fifth printing — February 2005
Sixth printing — February 2007
Seventh printing — December 2010

Back cover instruments: Glass Marimba by Michael Meadows; Gourd Drums by Darrel DeVore;
Five-Bell Bull Kelp Horn by Bart Hopkin. Photo of Glass Marimba by Serge Gubelman;
photo of Gourd Drums by Bart Hopkin; photo of Bull Kelp Horn by Janet Hopkin.

Front cover design by Clifford Harper. Back cover design by Chaz Bufe. Interior design and
illustrations by Bart Hopkin. Interior typeset in Times Roman, Futura, and Arial.
Cover typeset in Avant Garde and Futura.

TABLE OF CONTENTS

ACKNOWLEDGMENTS

Most of the ideas in this book are not my own. Many are common currency, having been part of musical instrument building practice for years and years. Others I have picked up in my extensive contacts with other instrument makers, and through familiarity with their instruments and writings. These makers are knowledgeable, skilled and inventive individuals — and terribly generous too, every one of them. This book owes an incalculable debt to all who have shared their ideas and experience with me over the years. By rights the list should be much longer, but here are a few of those people:

François Baschet, Minnie Black, Wes Brown, Glenn Branca, Warren Burt, John Chalmers, Cary Clements, John W. Coltman, Bill Colvig, David Courtney, Frank Crawford, Phil Dadson, Ivor Darreg, Hugh Davies, Darrell De Vore, David Doty, Jacques Dudon, William Eaton, Rick Elmore, Cris Forster, Ellen Fullman, Denny Genovese, Reed Ghazala, Frank Giorgini, Jonathan Glasier, Robin Goodfellow, Richard Graham, Donald Hall, Lou Harrison, Colin Hinz, Sarah Hopkins, Douglas Keefe, Buzz Kimball, Gary Knowlton, Skip La Plante, Rupert Lewis, Brian McLaren, Bonnie McNairn, Michael Meadows, Tom Nunn, Nazim Ozel, Paul Panhuysen, Bob Phillips, Tony Pizzo, Nadi Qamar, Hal Rammel, Susan Rawcliffe, Sharon Rowell, Sascha Reckert, Hans Reichel, Prent Rodgers, Rick Sanford, Charles Sawyer, Daniel Schmidt, Jon Scoville, Mark Shepard, tENTATIVELY, a cONVENIENCE, Trimpin, Sugar Belly Walker, Dennis Waring, Richard Waters, Erv Wilson, Jim Wilson, Peter Whitehead.

Equally essential to the making of this book have been the people who read and criticized the manuscript prior to publication. Donald Hall, David Kreimer, Skip La Plante, Michael Meadows, Jon Scoville, Stephen Golovnin and Dennis Waring reviewed and corrected the manuscript for practical, technical and scientific accuracy. Without the assurance of their expertise, not to mention their myriad ideas and suggestions, I could not have presented much of the material contained here. Kate Buckelew, Janet Hopkin, and especially Nan Hopkin, along with the others just mentioned, provided invaluable stylistic and editorial criticism. Chaz Bufe, my editor at See Sharp Press, gave it the final polish with just the right instinct for simplifying and clarifying the language. Without their guidance, this book would have been a far more awkward and less inviting thing to read.

To all these people, my heartfelt thanks and appreciation.

To my wife, Janet, and my son, Shane, who offered boundless support and patience during the long and arduous preparation of the manuscript, my love and thanks.

INTRODUCTION

by Jon Scoville

So . . . you've opened this book, flipped through its pages, looked at its illustrations, tables, charts, and sidebars, and have seen that there's a universe of sound here for the making. And now you're sitting down with the intention of actually reading it. (In this computer-driven age, it's still the normal way our old flat-bed brains scan stuff into the corporeal PC.) But before you enter Bart Hopkin's Wonderful World of the Ways and Whys of Sound, allow yourself an imaginary journey:

Close your eyes, lean back, and imagine a group of musicians tuning up, then launching into a loud, glorious fanfare . . . with your choice of instruments, of course. Strings and brass and timpani? Sure. But how about instead a vast orchestra of saws and wobbleboards, mirlitons, rattles, marimbas, tongue drums, and tuning forks? Arising from it is a clangor and cacophony full of overtones and implications — as busy as an urban street corner, but as bright with possibility as a sunrise on a glistening sandy beach. Those waves of sound arising in your imagination, be they made by traditional instruments or by something as improbable as a balloon-mounted bar gong, are all following predictable and logical laws of acoustics (at least in this corner of the galaxy — I can't vouch for that parallel universe lurking just around the corner). This book that you hold in your hands (as you dream of new solar systems of sound) is really a guide to unfold those patterns and laws of sound, to explain some of the mysteries, and to give you the tools to create new ones.

There is an ancient imperative lodged in our DNA which asks us to make music. Our intuitive understanding of being alive on this blue planet is most poetically expressed in our songs and dances. In our instinct to organize sound and movement we fully express both the ambiguities and certainties of life. Making the instruments that make the music that makes the soundtracks to our lives is one of the ways that we reconnect ourselves with the world and with our ancient heritage. Thus we join that long tradition of (mostly) unknown instrument makers who gave birth to drums, violins, lutes, bamboo zithers, steel drums, gamelan, and the countless other instruments that produce our planet's songs and symphonies.

Yet the principles and procedures of instrument construction are often viewed as being as incomprehensible as those involved in building a car or a computer. The beauty of this book is that it gives you a Rosetta stone to understand the tools, resources, and formulas that will equip you to enter the world of instrument construction. The poetry of how your instruments will look, and, more importantly, what kind of music they will play, is left up to you. Dive in. The water is deep, but warm and inviting. The universe of sound is yours for the making.

PREFACE

This book is a guide for anyone interested in musical instrument making.

In the chapters that follow we'll survey the fundamentals of instrument design. In the process, we'll get to know the acoustic relationships that underlie familiar musical instruments, and a host of new and unusual instruments as well. My goal is that this book will help you gain an acoustical sense that will serve you well in the creation of all kinds of acoustic instruments, both traditional and innovative. This book will also fill a continuing role as a handy reference for practical information on instrument design and construction.

Musical instrument design is a vast topic. The accumulated lore about violin making alone would fill an encyclopedia. This book will not tell you how to make a violin, and it will not serve as a course in musical acoustics. What it does, that other resources do not, is gather under one cover a body of broadly applicable design principles, coupled with practical ideas and suggestions for making specific instruments. If you are interested in exploring instrumental sound, building something musical from scratch, or composing and performing with anything other than the usual commercially made instruments, then you will be glad to have the information provided here. So will anyone, for that matter, who simply wants to better understand musical sound.

Acoustical phenomena in the real world are complex. It isn't easy to describe sounds in terms detailed enough for scientific analysis. But on a broader and less exacting scale, there is a world of practical information about the behavior of sound and sounding bodies. This information may be cruder than the physicist's analysis, but it is immensely useful in musical instrument design. This book operates on the level of that broader understanding. The information contained here may be challenging for those new to the field, but my hope is that anyone, regardless of technical background, will find it comprehensible and, above all, useful.

And what about people who lack the construction skills called for in fine instrument building — is the world of instrument making beyond their reach? It is true that workshop skills will give you a head start in making ideas come to life. But many wonderful instruments can be made by complete novices, including quite a few of the instruments described in this book. You will find that musical sound is frequently right there for the taking; it is a most inviting world to explore. And beginners often show a disconcerting knack for coming up with fresh ideas and overlooked approaches. As for special equipment, while power tools are faster, you can do an awful lot with basic hand tools. After all, instrument makers since the start of time have worked with nothing more.

The early chapters of this book are devoted to principles of acoustics as they relate to instrument design. We will need to understand these in our subsequent examinations of different instruments. The succeeding chapters, forming the bulk of the book, deal with specific instrument types and their design principles. At the end are several appendices designed to codify important information and provide easy reference. Among them are a section on instrument building materials and where to get them, a chart relating wavelength, frequency and pitch name, a glossary, and much more. Here and there, alongside the main text, are separate items I have called "Sidebars." These are discussions of topics worth noting, but peripheral to the flow of the text. Scattered throughout the main text and sidebars you will find ideas and informal plans for instruments you can make.

Chapter One

MUSICAL SOUND PERCEPTION

In order to think intelligently about sound production, we need to understand certain things about how the ears and brain make sense of the sounds that reach them. This will also help us to develop better analytical listening skills, which are invaluable in instrument making.

SOME BASICS

Sound is created when something causes small, localized fluctuations in air pressure. The fluctuations propagate outward from the source as pressure waves in the atmosphere. Should there be any ears in the vicinity, the pressure waves cause movement in the sensitive membrane that is the ear drum, and, following a series of bio-mechanical and neural transmissions, the event is interpreted as sound by the brain. A single pressure pulse doesn't amount to much of a sound; it takes a series in rapid succession to give the ear something it can respond to. The arrival of a series of pressure waves causes air molecules at a given location to move back and forth with each pulse; thus the association of sound with vibration.

An important property of vibrations is *frequency*, normally expressed as the number of vibratory cycles per second completed by whatever it is that is vibrating. Think of frequency in terms of complete vibratory cycles: for a vibrating object beginning at some central point, moving to one side and back to the center constitutes a half-cycle. To complete the cycle it must continue through the center point and on to the other side, and return once again to the center point. The term *Hertz*, abbreviated Hz, is commonly used to represent cycles per second (after the 19th century physicist Heinrich Hertz). Thus, for instance, 200 cycles per second = 200Hz.

Humans ears are responsive to frequencies falling within a range extending roughly from a lower limit of about 20Hz to perhaps 16,000 or 20,000Hz for a typical young person (this upper limit drops with age). Within this range, lower (slower) frequencies are associated with low, or bass sounds,

and higher (faster) frequencies are associated with high, or treble sounds. In general, through most of the range, the human ear's acuity is quite impressive: it picks up sounds representing truly minuscule amounts of energy; and at the opposite extreme it withstands sounds carrying billions of times that energy before serious discomfort or hearing damage occurs. The ear's sensitivity is not uniform through the hearing range, however. It tapers off at both ends, and has a broad peak in the range of about 2,000Hz to 5,000Hz, corresponding to a medium-high part of the range. This means that sounds within this band sound much louder than sounds carrying comparable energy at higher or lower frequencies.

When a sound vibration occurs at a single steady frequency, you hear it as having a recognizable "note" or pitch. Pitch, in other words, is the brain's way of interpreting vibrational frequency. The ascending series of notes that you hear when someone plays a scale on a musical instrument actually represents the instrument's ability to produce sounds at a series of specific frequencies, each a little higher than the one before. (Appendix 2 at the end of this book contains a chart giving frequencies for each of the pitch names used in the standard Western musical scale.) Human ears and brains are amazingly good at recognizing steady-frequency vibrations and distinguishing one frequency from another. Frequency differences of less than one percent are easily recognized by people with no special training. This acuity diminishes toward the extremes of the hearing range.

The word "interval" refers to the perceived distance between two pitches, or how much higher one pitch is than another. People in most musical cultures seem to perceive equal musical intervals between pairs of pitches when the ratios of their frequencies are the same. The best example is the octave. The musical interval of an octave is associated with a frequency ratio of 2:1. Double the frequency of any pitch, and you get the pitch an octave above. Double it again, and the pitch is now two octaves higher than the original, while the frequency is four times as great. Just as 2:1

corresponds to the octave, a perfect fifth comprises (ideally) a frequency ratio of 3:2 between two tones; a major sixth is 5:3, and so forth. Any musical interval can be defined as a frequency ratio. The tunings chart in Appendix 2 gives ratios for all of the most important musical intervals.

TIMBRE AND OVERTONES

Most sounds in the real world are complex, and are comprised of vibrations of many frequencies. The ears do not generally hear a complex sound as a group of separate pitches at different frequencies, however, but as a single sound possessing a characteristic timbre, or tone color. That tone color results, in part, from the blend of frequencies present. In some cases the blend creates a sensation of pitchless noise. In other cases the ears and brain hear a multi-frequency sound as a single "note" or pitch, focusing on one frequency from among the many present as the defining tone.

Let's look at these phenomena more closely. We can start by describing several general vibration types.

No steady frequency present:

In some sounds no recurring pattern arises — just flurries of disordered air movement. The ear hears such unpatterned sound as unpitched noise. The noise may seem trebly or bassy, depending upon the general frequency trend. Maracas (shakers) provide one example of this sort of sound. Try shaking a maraca and humming back the note you've heard. You can't do it, because in that rush of shaker sound there is no steady, dominant frequency.

One steady frequency present:

In most natural sounds there are one or more recognizable steady frequencies present. Steady-state vibrations need not maintain the same frequency more than a tiny fraction of a second; the ear is very quick about recognizing them.

Where there is but one frequency present, the aural effect is a well-defined pitch and a timbral quality which is not unpleasant, but rather colorless. Sustained vibrations at a single pure frequency are hard to achieve by acoustic means, although some flutes or blown bottles may come fairly close. Sounds that are much closer to the one-frequency ideal can be produced electronically. Some of the beeps and boops of early electronic music are examples.

Several steady frequencies present:

If there are many frequencies present as components of a single sound from a single source, the listener usually does not get a sense of plurality, but hears the blend as a single tone having a particular timbre. The nature of that timbre depends in large part on the relationships between the frequencies within the tone. Here things become rather complex, and some key questions arise. Will the ear interpret the multi-frequency sound as having a defined pitch? What qualities in the timbral blend allow the ear to do so? And

Sidebar 1-1

WAVE FORMS

Most sounds are blends of many different frequencies sounding simultaneously. It might be difficult to envision how this actually happens physically. One can easily picture a particle of air vibrating back and forth at a particular frequency, but how can a single particle vibrate at two or more frequencies simultaneously?

To express multiple frequency vibration, the particle engages in a complex movement which can be mathematically interpreted to be the sum of the several frequencies it is supposed to be manifesting. This mathematical interpretation may seem like an artificial contrivance. (Is the complicated dance the particle is performing really the same as vibrating at multiple specific frequencies?) But this interpretive model does correspond to the ear's subjective response. Presented with a complex vibratory motion that can be shown mathematically to represent the sum of several frequencies, the ear and brain do indeed hear those several frequencies.

To aid in the study of such motions, acousticians draw graphs, plotting the pattern of vibratory movement through time. Different types of vibration yield different graphic patterns, called wave forms. The wave form for a single, pure frequency is a wavy line of very regular and smooth curvature, known as a sine wave (because it matches a graph of the sine function in trigonometry). Sounds with strong harmonics show wave forms that are more angular, but still quite regular. More complex timbral blends, with non-harmonic frequencies or added noise components, have correspondingly more complex and irregular wave forms. With highly complex wave forms it becomes difficult for the ear and brain to recognize the recurring patterns and perceive the constituent frequencies. Sounds with complex wave forms are perceived as musically confusing, noisy, or dissonant.

which factors determine what the perceived pitch will be? In answering these, we begin by defining some terms.

In a sound with multiple frequencies present, the individual frequencies are called *partials*. The lowest of those frequencies can be called the *fundamental*. Additional frequencies arrayed above are *overtones*. Overtones fall into two important categories: *harmonic* and *inharmonic*. Harmonic overtones are those that have frequencies equaling some integral multiple of the fundamental frequency. This defines a series of harmonic overtones. For a fundamental frequency f, the harmonic overtones have frequencies $2f$, $3f$, $4f$, $5f$ ... and so on indefinitely. That is the *harmonic series* (illustrated in Figure 1-3); and you will be hearing a lot about

Harmonic No.	1	2	3	4	5	6	7	8	9	10	11	12
Interval	Unison	8ve	12th	2-8ves	2-8ves + M3rd	2-8ves +P5th	2-8ves +↓m7th	3-8ves	3-8ves +M2nd	3-8ves +M3rd	3-8ves +↓aug4	3-8ves +P5th
Frequency	130.8	261.6	392.4	523.2	654	784.8	915.6	1046.4	1177.2	1308	1438.8	1569.6
Pitch Name	C_3	C_4	G_4	C_5	E_5	G_5	↓B$\flat_5$	C_6	D_6	E_6	↓F#$_6$	G_6

it before you finish this book. In their aural effect, harmonic overtones blend closely with the fundamental to create the feeling of a single tone. Inharmonic overtones (those whose frequencies are not multiples of the fundamental frequency) do not seem to blend as closely into the overall tone, giving the resulting composite timbre a spicier, edgier, or more dissonant quality.

And now, back to the question of perceived pitch in multi-frequency sounds. There are many possibilities here, and many factors at play. Here are some governing considerations:

Rule #1: In general, lower-frequency components play a greater role in establishing the perceived pitch of a tone, while higher-frequency components contribute more to its coloration. Most commonly, the lowest frequency present, the fundamental, establishes the pitch.

Rule #2: Harmonic overtones lead to a well defined pitch sense. To whatever extent the overtone frequencies can be construed as falling into the harmonic pattern, the tone will sound coherent, full, and well defined in pitch. Familiar instruments having harmonic overtones include most string instruments and the standard woodwinds and brass. The perceived effect of the composite tone quality depends in part upon which harmonics are most prominent: where the higher harmonics predominate, the tone will be brighter, as with a harpsichord; where higher harmonics are subdued, the tone will be rounder, as with a nylon string guitar.

Rule #3: In tones possessing multiple inharmonic frequency components, the perceived results are quite variable. They depend on the relative prominence of the different components, the pitch relationships between them, and the degree of crowding in different parts of the spectrum. In such cases, the ear sometimes succeeds in picking out the fundamental as the defining pitch, but hears it as part of a peculiar timbre. Sometimes the ear tracks another tone as the defining pitch. Sometimes the ear doesn't focus on any one tone as the defining pitch, and the sound is perceived as pitchless. Figure 1-2 provides examples.

Tuned carillon bells (such as the sets used in church towers) provide a wonderful example of an instrument possessing prominent frequencies *not* arranged harmonically, but still interpretable to the ear as having a single defined pitch. The tone is highly distinctive — nothing else sounds like cathedral bells — and it is one that many people find enchanting. It also can be musically confusing, in that the ear may occasionally take track the wrong overtone as the defining pitch. When you have an opportunity, try listening closely to the tone of a set of big bells, mentally isolating the pitches present, making note of their relationships, and — this is an important part of the perception of the tone — observing which overtones sustain longest, and which die out quickly.

Many "pitchless" percussion instruments are better described as having ambiguous pitch. This includes most drums, some cymbals, cowbells, triangles, and so on. With a little concentration, a listener can often pick out one or more pitches in such sounds, and these pitches, even if one tries to ignore it, take on meaning in musical contexts. In addition, it is surprising just how many everyday sounds have at least some component of identifiable pitch. To test this, try knocking, banging, squeaking, and scraping everything in a room, listening as you go for pitch among the noise. Give each item a couple of tries: sometimes the definite pitch components are elusive, but you might be surprised at how often you find them.

In the ambiguous territory between clear pitch and pure noise, a great many disorienting effects occur. There can be iridescent tones, which seem to shift pitch depending upon musical context or a change in one's perceptual predisposition. There can be tones which seem to have pitch in one musical context but degenerate into pitchless jangle in another. There can be tones for which two people disagree as to what their pitch really is. There can be tones which seem to have pitch, but which have so much pitchless noise mixed in that the resulting timbre is bizarre. There can be tones in which the components blend seamlessly, and tones in which several pitches retain a degree of individuality, sounding

FIGURE 1-2: Some characteristic vibration types and their perceived pitch and sound quality effects

Characteristic Vibration Type	Perceived Pitch & Timbre Effect	Familiar Examples
Disordered pattern; no steady vibration present	Noise over a general frequency band reflecting the general frequency trend of the vibration	Maracas; radio static; rushing wind
Steady oscillation at a single frequency	Very definite pitch; round tone lacking any piquancy	Electronic beeps and boops; ocarinas (minus edge-turbulence sound)
Fundamental plus reasonably complete harmonic series	Very definite pitch; full, clear tone; degree of brilliance depends upon relative predominance of high overtones	Strings (when properly made and tensioned); most well-designed woodwinds & brass
Fundamental plus some harmonic overtones, but not a complete series	Very definite pitch; tone quality depends on which harmonics are present	Clarinet lower register; marimba bars whose overtones have been tuned
Fundamental plus imperfectly tuned harmonic overtones	Fairly definite pitch, but perceived pitch may be slightly off the actual fundamental frequency. Tone quality somewhat rougher than it would be with true harmonics	This effect is present in most strings & winds to some degree; most pronounced in poorly made woodwinds & brass or strings that are poorly made, too stiff, badly worn, or under insufficient tension
Strong fundamental with non-harmonic partials widely spaced near the bottom	Definite pitch with peculiar or piquant tone quality depending on what the partials are relative to one another	Marimba bars with un-tuned overtones; tuned drums; carillon bells
Several non-harmonic frequencies, closely spaced near the bottom	Ambiguous pitch; one or another pitch may seem to dominate at different times; may sound chordal, or may sound muddy or jangly	Some triangles; some gongs; some scrap metal, some prepared or highly irregular strings
Many non-harmonic frequencies closely spaced	No predominant pitch; tone quality depends upon the particular mix	Well-made cymbals; some triangles; some gongs
Prominent fundamental plus lots of noise and/or inharmonic partials, with or without some harmonic overtones	Identifiable but rough pitch; pronounced timbral qualities dependent on the particular mix of components	Some snare drums; kitchen blender; some scraping sounds

gong-like or even chordal. And there can be anything in between.

The role of overtones in instrumental tone quality gives rise to an important question: Do musical instruments typically produce the same set of overtone relationships for all their sounding pitches? When the instrument moves from one note to another, does the whole family of overtones move together, retaining the same relationships? The answer is yes and no. In most cases, the overtone relationships are fairly well preserved, ensuring similar timbre from note to note. But at the same time, the relative prominence of the different overtones tends to change. Each instrument, by its nature, radiates sound particularly effectively within certain general frequency ranges. Components of the sounds that happen to fall within these ranges ring out fully, while those falling outside are de-emphasized. As different notes sound from a given instrument, different overtones are highlighted as they fall within the ranges of emphasized frequencies.

Such regions of heightened response are called *formants*. Along with overtone mix, formants are another important part of our sense of instrumental timbre. As an example, consider the violin. The violin does a particularly good job of radiating sound in two prominent ranges. Whatever mix of frequencies the string may deliver to the soundbox, the soundbox always radiates most effectively whatever part of the input happens to fall in those ranges. The resulting fullness of tone in those ranges is an essential identifying characteristic of violin sound.

The best way to illustrate how we, as listeners, are tuned in to formants is through speech. The human voice is one of the few instruments in which formant frequencies *do* undergo marked changes rather than remaining fixed. Altering the shape of the oral cavity during speech has the effect of selectively enhancing certain frequency ranges within the vocal tone, and this is the basis for the production of distinct vowels. The difference between "ee" and "ah" lies in which

A BALLOON-MOUNTED BAR GONG

Here's a simple construction that will allow you to hear and experiment with an extraordinarily rich array of partials from a single sound source. (Remember that the term *partial* refers to any of the individual tones or frequencies that make up a complex sound.) The instrument consists of a single long metal tube or bar held in a manner that allows extremely free vibration and enhanced lower frequency radiation. Thus, the struck tube reveals a rainbow of tones. Through various techniques, the player can bring different partials to the fore with each stroke, for a kind of melodic movement in both tone color and pitch.

The drawing shows the basic assembly. What can one use for the metal sounding element? Many sorts of tubing or metal bar stock can serve. For convenience and availability, I suggest a 10-foot length of 1" thinwall electrical metal conduit, commonly called EMT (widely available in hardware stores). The long tube rests on two balloons. Best is the long lumpy-bumpy-shaped sort, looking like a sausage that has been squeezed by a boa constrictor. They should be fairly large and strong. To prevent the balloons from rolling, place non-rolling objects, like wooden blocks or books, alongside them.

You sound the bar by striking it with a beater. Begin by experimenting with a variety of mallets, with the idea of finding the ones that bring out the best in the bar. Try regular percussion mallets, or household items like screwdrivers held by the blade. Look through Chapter 5, "Beaters, Scrapers & Friction Makers" for more ideas.

The key to the colorful potential of the bar is to bring out different partials and combinations of partials with each stroke. Do this, first, by striking at different locations along the bar. Different striking points excite different partials. Second, try pinching the bar firmly between thumb and fore finger of the free hand at different points as you strike, releasing immediately after. Doing this inhibits most of the tones, while allowing a few select ones to sound freely. Some pinching points kill most of the sound, for an unimpressive result. Others allow a mix of tones to come through, each mix having its own distinct pitch and flavor. Be patient, listen closely. Keep track of the combinations of stopping and striking points that produce the best sounds. After experimenting for a while, mark the striking and pinching points along the bar that you wish to remember (use colored adhesive tape, or metallic markers, or make scratches in the bar ... whatever works). You can then play a peculiar sort of bar-gong tone-color melody music, with your selected striking and pinching points providing the compositional material.

Acoustic Notes and Additional Thoughts

The rich spectrum of partials naturally exists, in potential at least, in all hard metal tubes and rods. But the full array usually remains inaccessible, because vibration is damped by whatever holds the bar or whatever it rests on. Balloon mounting overcomes the damping problem simply by being the most compliant support system imaginable. In addition, most bars in themselves lack sufficient surface area to radiate their lower-frequency vibrations effectively to the surrounding air. But the balloons provide a larger surface area: the bar transmits its vibrations to the balloon, and the balloon radiates them to the air. Low frequencies that would have been faint suddenly become more audible.

In the next chapter we will discuss more fully the acoustic principles at play in the bar gong, and you will find a follow-up discussion of the instrument in Sidebar 2-2, "Balloon-mounted Bar Gong Revisited."

Balloon-mounted bar gong.

Acknowledgments

I first encountered balloon-mounted instruments in the hands of the San Francisco builder Tom Nunn, who uses balloon mountings in connection with bar gongs and a number of other resonant metal instrument types. Tom credits Prent Rodgers with having worked out the basics of the instrument described here. Prent derived some of his inspiration from the early work of the French builders François and Bernard Baschet. It was in the 1950s that they first recognized the capabilities of balloons to serve as sound radiators, vibration insulators, and highly compliant mountings for vibrating bodies.

---

formant frequencies the speaker enhances. People are so well attuned to the differences that they effortlessly distinguish the two. You can familiarize yourself with some of the effects of different formants by singing sustained tones and altering the shape of your vocal cavity (raising and lowering the tongue, changing the position of the lips, raising or lowering the soft palate, etc.), and listening closely to the resulting tones. Try to pick out the predominant overtone components for different tone qualities. You may even acquire the skill of overtone singing — that is, bringing specific overtones so much to the fore that the ear begins to hear them in their own right, harmonizing with the fundamental, rather than merely as part of the timbral blend.

ATTACK AND DECAY; DIRECTIONAL EFFECTS

I have been emphasizing frequency blend as a primary factor in perceived tone quality. But there are others, among them the way in which a sound changes through time. For instance, how does the sound's volume vary between its moment of onset and its disappearance? This feature, the sound's characteristic rise and fall in volume, is often referred to as its *envelope*.

As an example, consider a plucked string sound. The tone begins quite suddenly at the moment of plucking, reaching its greatest volume almost immediately; it can be said to have a sharp *attack*. There follows a longish period of *decay* in which the volume gradually diminishes until it becomes inaudible. The attack is further marked by a distinct plucking sound — an unpitched noise of very short duration — which is quite different from the ensuing string tone. The purer string tone that follows is likely to start out relatively rich in high-frequency overtones; these decay more rapidly than the lower-pitched components, and so the overall tone quality becomes a bit less brilliant during the course of the decay.

Other instrumental sounds can also be described in terms of attack and decay and related factors. Although I've spent less time discussing them here, these time-change elements contribute as much as does timbre to the overall impression of tone quality.

Directional factors also contribute to perceived effect. Their results play out differently for high- and low-frequency sounds. Low-frequency sounds tend to have a room-filling quality, primarily because they spread out from their sources over a wider periphery, and find their way around obstacles more effectively than high frequencies. The fact that the human head is one such obstacle means that it is harder to locate low-frequency sounds directionally, since the sound is more likely to reach both ears equally. Higher frequencies spread over a narrower angle and don't find their way around obstacles as well, allowing more for the differential effects that the two ears use in sound location.

Through this chapter I have used the word "noise" to describe sounds that lack definite pitch. The term should not be regarded as pejorative. Steady oscillation and the harmonic series are not gospel truth. Music making has always involved plenty of pitchless sounds, from maracas and snare drums to the muffled bass drum. And an unexpected beauty lies in the in-between sounds, the non-harmonic overtone blends and the noise/pitch blends. I encourage you to cultivate an appreciative ear for these things.

As you learn to listen closely enough to make conscious what your ears already hear, you will discover that the ears' analytic capacities are great. This sort of listening awareness is valuable for anyone interested in musical instrument design and construction.

FORK CHIME

Here is another instrument that will force you to listen carefully. It combines the vibrating patterns of a tuning fork and a simple tube chime, giving rise to a complex array of frequencies. You can tune the frequencies as you make the chime (albeit roughly), and bring out different frequencies in the tone by how and where you strike.

All you need to make fork chimes is metal tubing. Aluminum or brass tubing will work well, but you can also make a fine instrument with the same steel conduit recommended for the bar gong described in Sidebar 1-2. Get enough tubing to make several chimes.

The drawing shows the design of the fork chime, with typical dimensions. Start by cutting the tube, drilling the suspension cord hole at about 22% of the length from one end, running a bit of cord through and tying it to form a loop for hanging the tube. At this point you have a simple chime; it will produce a nice tone when suspended and struck with a beater. Next, cut the slit in the opposite end using a hacksaw or sabre saw. Try to make it straight and even, but don't worry if it isn't perfect. Make the cut about 20% of tube length initially. Support the tube by the cord, and strike near the split end. A new tone emerges. It comes from the two halves of the split end engaging in the pattern of vibration normally associated with tuning forks. The chime tone is still there (though slightly raised in pitch due to the cutting), and you can hear it by striking at the center. Several other slightly quieter tones appear when you strike in different places, most of them being overtones of the basic chime and fork tones.

Spend a few moments striking the fork chime in different ways, and listen to the tones you can get. Do you like the musical relationships you hear? If not, you can change them. Cut the slits longer to lower the fork tone. Raise the chime tone by cutting a small amount of tubing from the opposite end. (If you cut a significant amount, drill a new support hole at the new 22% point). Experiment until you find a set of tones that form an attractive blend. When you have made several fork chimes with pleasing relationships both within themselves and among one another, hang them some place where you can occasionally play them as you pass by.

We will be studying the vibrating patterns of chimes and tuning forks in Chapter 4, "Idiophones."

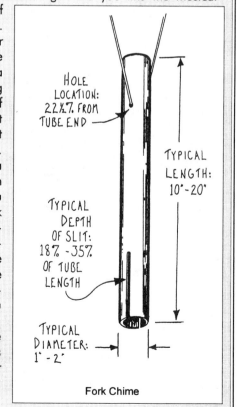

HOLE LOCATION: 22½% FROM TUBE END

TYPICAL LENGTH: 10"-20"

TYPICAL DEPTH OF SLIT: 18% -35% OF TUBE LENGTH

TYPICAL DIAMETER: 1" - 2"

Fork Chime

Chapter Two

ACOUSTIC PRINCIPLES

In the last chapter I talked about how people perceive sounds. We now turn to objects in the external world, the actual sound makers that are the subject of this book, and begin to investigate some underlying principles of musical instrument acoustics. In the process I will refer to various instruments in order to illustrate ideas, but remember that fuller information on specific instrument types appears in subsequent chapters.

BASIC PRINCIPLES OF OSCILLATION

Most sounds and most musical instruments depend on the presence of vibrations at steady frequencies. This may seem like a rather specialized requirement, but steady-frequency oscillation occurs in nature all the time. There are three factors in most natural oscillations: displacement, restoring force, and something working in opposition to the restoring force, usually inertia. For the present, we can define inertia as the tendency of an object in motion to remain in motion in the absence of any force to stop it.

To understand these factors, think of a pendulum. Pendulums move much more slowly than sound vibrations, but their principles are the same. Displace a pendulum to one side, and a restoring force (gravity) causes it to swing back toward its center rest position. But its inertia causes it to overshoot, leading to displacement in the other direction. The restoring force of gravity enters the picture again; it gradually overcomes the inertia, causing the pendulum to slow and then reverse, swinging back toward center, and then overshoot once again. Eventually, if nothing occurs to inject more energy into the system, the pendulum gradually dissipates its energy and resettles at equilibrium position, but not before having undergone a series of steady oscillations.

In sounds, the restoring force usually comes not from gravity, but from the springiness or resilience of the materials involved. In the prong of a kalimba (African thumb piano), for instance, the rigidity of the prong causes the prong to spring back after displacement. With strings it is the resil-

ience of the string and its mountings that makes it return after being pulled to one side; for drumhead membranes it is much the same. The mechanisms at work are harder to picture for wind instruments, but air, too, has innate springiness, especially when it is in a partially enclosed chamber like a bottle or wind instrument tube. The mass of the air, minuscule though it may be, plays its role in inertia.

The rules that determine frequency of vibration vary for different types of vibrating objects. But, broadly speaking, frequency depends upon two things: the strength of the restoring force, and the strength of the influences working contrary to the restoring force, primarily inertia. Since inertia is a function of mass, we'll focus on mass. Here is the general rule:

Greater restoring force leads to higher vibrational frequency.

Greater effective mass leads to lower vibrational frequency.

I have used the phrase "effective mass" to reflect the fact that the location of a given mass may make a difference because of leverage effects. An increase in mass at the end of a prong or the center of a string, for instance, lowers frequency more than the same increase near the mounting. Figure 2-1 shows how the two factors play out in various combinations, using a simple prong fixed at one end as a model.

Not every oscillation in the world is a product of the forces described here. In designing loudspeaker cones, for instance, engineers must try to suppress the natural vibration factors in order to create something that will perform as intended, under outside controlling forces. Likewise, it is possible to build musical instruments whose initial vibrations are to some degree independent of the forces described. But the vast majority of natural oscillations do follow these principles, and there are very few are the acoustic musical instruments in which they don't play a defining role.

The description given here of displacement, restoring force and inertia at work provides sufficient understanding

Musical Instrument Design   7   Acoustic Principles

FIGURE 2-1: The effects of restoring force and effective mass on resulting frequency, as illustrated in a rigidly-mounted metal prong. In each case, the prong at left will have the higher frequency.

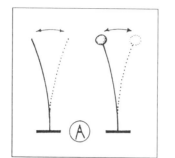

A. The greater weight at the end of the right prong increases mass without significantly affecting the restoring force of rigidity. Result: lower frequency for the prong with extra mass at the end.

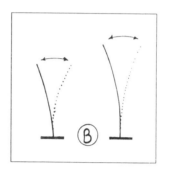

B. The left prong's lesser length means less mass, without significantly affecting the restoring force of the rigidity in the prong. Result: higher frequency for the shorter prong.

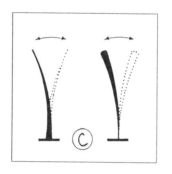

C. The left prong has greater thickness near the base, where it will have the greatest impact on effective rigidity. The right prong has greater thickness near the end, where it will have the greatest impact on effective mass, due to leverage effects. Result: substantially higher frequency for the prong that is thicker at the base.

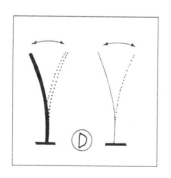

D. The greater thickness of the left prong increases both mass and restoring force in the form of rigidity. In most situations like this, the increased rigidity has a stronger effect than the increased mass, and the result is higher frequency for the thicker prong.

E. Both of these prongs have the same total mass and the same thickness over most of their length. But the one on the right has its mass located where it will make more difference due to leverage effects. Result: lower pitch for the prong with extra mass at the very end.

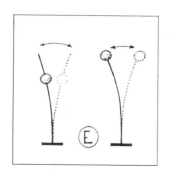

for a lot of musical instrument design work. But we can deepen our understanding by looking at the situation from another perspective. In a more sophisticated view of the same events, the simple back and forth motion of vibration can be seen as a wave of displacement running rapidly through the vibrating medium or object. Consider a rope lying along the ground. Someone holds one end and gives an abrupt vertical shake. The curved hump that scoots from the shaker's hand on down the rope is a *traveling wave*. In classic wave-like fashion, each point on the rope engages in only a small movement, up and then down again, as the hump passes. But this series of localized movements gives rise to the progressive movement of the wave as a whole.

There are two important differences between the rope and the musical wave media that we are interested in. One is that the rope's wave occurs on a large scale and progresses relatively slowly, making the wave observable. The other is that the wave in the rope dissipates all its energy along the way and at its end. If the rope were anchored rigidly at both ends and held in the air under tension, the energy would not dissipate so fast. Instead, the wave would *reflect* (bounce back) at the far end, and would then be seen running back in the opposite direction along the rope, only to reflect again at the near end, continuing in a back-and-forth movement until all its energy is dissipated. (Sidebar 3-3, "Watching Waves" describes further experiments along these lines with observable waves.)

This same sort of motion occurs in musical strings. It is also closely analogous (though harder to picture) to what happens in drumheads, music box prongs, marimba bars, wind instrument air columns and so forth. A traveling wave is somehow instigated, and it repeatedly reflects back upon itself each time it reaches a boundary. And here is the link between traveling waves and vibration: The vibration of any given point can be seen as a result of the passage at that point of the series of reflected waves, causing the point to move back and forth with the arrival of each wave front. The round trip time for each wave is constant, giving the resulting

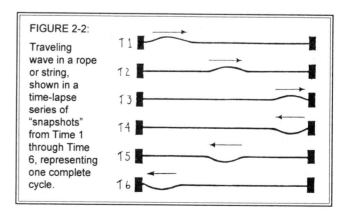

FIGURE 2-2:

Traveling wave in a rope or string, shown in a time-lapse series of "snapshots" from Time 1 through Time 6, representing one complete cycle.

vibration a steady frequency.

Vibration patterns of this sort can be called *standing waves*. Standing waves are the steady-state vibrations that arise as a result of traveling waves reflecting back and forth in a string, air column, or other medium of finite dimensions. The interacting wave fronts reinforce or cancel one another to varying degrees all along the medium at each instant to create the standing wave form. It is not intuitively obvious, but the cumulative effects of the multiple reflections can account for all the complexity of the vibration patterns we see in musical instruments, including the presence of multiple frequencies (fundamentals and overtones) in the vibrating object.

RESONANCE

Most natural vibrating systems show a preference for certain frequencies and not others. These *natural frequencies* are the frequencies at which the system will oscillate if given some sort of initial impulse and then left to vibrate on its own, as, for example, a guitar string will vibrate at a certain frequency each time it is plucked. *Resonance* is a function of this property. To illustrate, consider a tube that has one stopped end and one open end. The air in that tube has a springy quality: if it is momentarily compressed into the tube by some inward movement at the open end, increased pressure within will cause it to surge back out; in doing so it overshoots slightly, creating a relative vacuum that pulls it back in again. As this continues an oscillation of the air results just as if one had compressed and then released a coil spring.

Now let's add to this system a driver — something that will repeatedly force air in and out of the open end of the tube, driving the enclosed air at some specific frequency. As an example, we'll use a piece of wood mounted so as to act as a marimba bar. Marimba bars flex up and down at the center when struck. If one is placed over the opening of a tube a short distance away, it has the effect of pushing small amounts of air in and out as it vibrates. Like most vibrating systems, the bar has a natural frequency at which it "wants" to vibrate, and so does the air column below.

What happens with the air in the tube now if someone strikes the bar? The answer depends on the relationship between the natural frequency of the bar and the natural frequency of the air column. In the likely case that the two

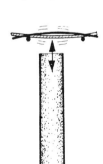

frequencies are different, the air responds minimally. The bar is trying to drive the air at a frequency the air doesn't want to go at. If the frequencies are roughly the same, however, the air joins the bar in oscillating at the frequency they now share. The intensity of the tube's response can easily be heard in the resulting sound: the bar tone is

FIGURE 2-3: Movement of a marimba bar drives air in and out of the tube below. If the natural frequency of the bar and the tube agree, a pattern of well-timed recurring reinforcement will be set up, creating a strong resonance response in the enclosed air.

greatly enhanced and augmented by the air sound from the tube. (Creating a good coupling between bar and resonance tube is one of the joys of instrument making.)

This is a good example of resonance response. The word *resonance* refers to an oscillating system's enhanced response to a driving force at or near any of its natural frequencies. It comes about because of the fact that if the driving frequency matches the oscillator's own natural frequency, the driver can consistently impart energy at just the right time and in the right direction to maximize its effect. A classic analogy is that of pushing a child on a swing. The child-plus-swing, like all pendulums, follows the rules for oscillation described earlier, and has its own natural frequency of oscillation. (That frequency, of course, is well below the hearing range.) The driver for the system is the person doing the pushing. If the pusher times the pushes so that the direction of the pushes always contributes to the swing's natural movement, the imparted energy will accumulate and the swing will go higher and higher. This the pusher does instinctively by adjusting the pushing frequency to match the natural frequency of the child and swing, one push per swing cycle. If the pusher pushes at the wrong times — pushing forward, for instance, in the middle of the swing's back swing — the two forces cancel. Then, rather than building up, the swing's motion diminishes. This inevitably happens at least some of the time if the pushes consistently come at a frequency very different from the natural frequency of the swing. If the pusher's frequency is close but not identical to the swing's natural frequency — say, just a little too fast — then some accommodation will be reached in which each swing cycle is slightly foreshortened by the too-early push. It will oscillate a little faster, but with less amplitude, as part of each push will be wasted in counteracting rather than contributing to the swing's natural movement. We can sum this up by saying that the swing shows an enhanced resonance response when driven by the pusher at the swing's natural frequency; the response diminishes rapidly if the pusher's driving frequency departs slightly from the swing's natural oscillation frequency, and drops very nearly to nothing for any pusher so witless as to push at some completely unrelated frequency.

The same sort of interaction happens with the marimba bar driver and the tube resonator. After the bar's first downward flex has initiated an oscillation in the air at the mouth of the tube, then — if the driver frequency and the natural frequency of the tube are close to matching — each subsequent downward flex comes at about the right time to reinforce the air's next inward movement, one vibratory cycle later. The recurring reinforcement perpetuates and

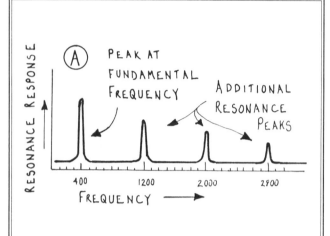

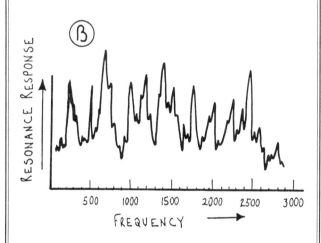

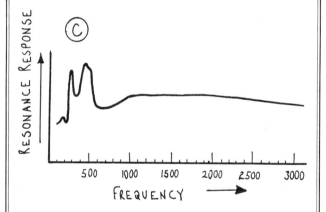

FIGURE 2-4

A. Resonance response curve for air in a tube stopped at one end.

B. A "spiky" resonance response curve, typical of many soundboards, with many narrow peaks running together to create a more generalized response.

C. Violin body resonance response curve (shown in general outline here — a more accurate curve would show many small, overlapping spikes similar to 3-4B).

increases the tube vibration.

To aid in visualizing the resonance patterns of different oscillators, one can plot resonance response curves. These are graphs of resonance response against frequency. For the marimba resonator tube, such a curve might look something like that shown in Figure 2-4A. The tube shows a very high, narrow peak at its fundamental frequency, plus several more very pronounced peaks corresponding to prominent overtones. The peaks indicate the enclosed air's strong resonance response for drivers within certain narrow frequency bands, while the wide valleys between show that the tube scarcely responds at other frequencies. Many other vibrating systems used in musical instruments, such as strings, most wind instrument air columns, marimba bars and kalimba tines, show similar curves, having narrow, well-defined and well-separated peaks with very little resonance response in between them. Some, such as globular flutes and blown jugs, show just one pronounced peak, indicating that they scarcely resonate overtones.

But the resonance response curves for many other vibrating systems look quite different. For instance, rather than showing one or more well-defined narrow peaks, they may appear as a hilly landscape. Humps in the curve may be broad rather than tall and narrow. Translated into acoustic results, a broad peak indicates that the system in question shows a somewhat enhanced resonance response over the general range of driving frequencies covered by the hump. The response is not as selective, nor is it as pronounced as a sharp spike. Somewhat similar for practical purposes is a curve that is spiky, but with so many overlapping spikes (representing many overlapping resonances) that virtually any input frequency will be covered at least to some degree (Figure 2-4B). This sort of response is typical of string instrument sound boards. For instance, Figure 2-4C is a typical resonance response curve for a violin body (shown in general outline, with smaller spikes smoothed out). The curve reveals that the violin has good general response to a wide range of frequencies, but has an enhanced response over two broad peaks in what, for the violin, comprises the lower part of its frequency spectrum. To see how this plays out, consider the violin string as driver, and the body as the resonance system being driven. The reasonably good response of the body over a broad frequency range means that the body will adequately resonate, and thus project, pretty much any pitch that the string dictates. The two peaks, meanwhile, have a profound effect in coloring the sound, and play an essential role in giving the violin its characteristic tone. They are formants (discussed in the previous chapter), emphasizing those frequencies injected by the string that happen to fall in their general area. (The acoustical causes of these two peaks in violin bodies have been extensively studied; we will learn more about the factors at play in string instrument bodies later on).

These two types of resonance response patterns — those with well-defined, separated and very pronounced peaks and those with broad, generalized frequency response — have distinct roles in musical instrument design. You need the well-defined frequency responses typical of strings, wind instrument tubes and the like, to ensure that instruments dependably and unambiguously produce their intended pitches. The violin string wouldn't do its job as a driver of precise and controllable frequency if it weren't frequency-specific. On the other hand, you need the more generalized response typical of soundboards in cases where you want to pick up, resonate and amplify not a single frequency, but a broad range of frequencies. A soundboard whose resonance response shows isolated spikes separated by deep valleys means trouble: the pronounced frequency biases will scarcely allow some pitches injected by the driver to sound, while making others disproportionately strong, and distorting still others in tone or pitch. A gentle peakiness or a great many overlapping peaks in something serving as a resonator can be valuable, in that the peaks may lend character and an attractive color to the sound.

DAMPING AND RADIATION

An important factor in resonance response is *damping*. Acousticians use the term to refer to the rate at which a vibrating system dissipates energy. The more heavily damped a vibration is, the more rapidly it spends its energy, and as a result, the shorter its duration. A vibration with zero damping would sustain itself forever without needing more input energy, but this, of course, is beyond the capabilities of mortal instrument makers. Energy dissipation can take various forms, but the important distinction for us is between 1) dissipation through radiation or transmission of the vibration, and 2) dissipation through mechanisms like friction.

Radiation (#1 above) may be to surrounding air, or it may be to other solid bodies which can in turn radiate to the air. With musical instruments, the hoped-for result is that the vibration becomes audible, as when a string transmits its vibratory impulses to a soundboard, and thence to the air. Damping due to friction (#2 above) is energy lost without contributing to sound. It can occur within the original vibrating medium, or it can occur indirectly, as when the initial vibrating object spends itself in driving some other friction-laden object. Simply stopping the strings of a guitar with one's hand works that way, providing so much frictional damping through the soft flesh that the string's vibrational energy is absorbed virtually immediately, stopping the sound.

Damping, and the related question of transmission-vs.-frictional loss, are central considerations in the functioning of musical instruments. Let's summarize their effects:

1. Heavy damping corresponds to little sustain for a given vibration, if there is not continuous additional energy input into the system. Thus, vibrations in heavily damped plucked or hammered strings die away quickly, as do vibrations in wooden vibrating bar instruments, plucked rods like kalimba tines, and so forth. On the other hand, wind instrument vibrating systems can be heavily damped without dying away, because the player continuously injects energy into the system by blowing. The same is true of members of the violin family: the string vibration is heavily damped by the player's fleshy finger on the fingerboard (witness the sound of violin pizzicato), but the player compensates by injecting energy continuously with the bow.

2. When damping is heavy and energy loss is due primarily to internal friction, then a relatively small part of the total vibrational energy goes into audible sound in the atmosphere. This makes for an inefficient sound maker, with relatively little sustain and most likely a small maximum volume level. That's why pillows make poor musical instruments: Hit a pillow as hard as you like; inject as much energy as you can. Most of that energy is lost to internal friction, and the sound is unimpressive.

3. When the damping is heavy because the system is radiating sound energy rapidly to the surrounding air, then the initial result is greater volume. (This may be contrary to your intuitive sense of the word "damping".) The greater volume is coupled with lesser sustain. In other words, if the vibration rapidly shoots off all its energy as sound radiation, the result will be a short, loud sound.

4. When damping is small, which is to say that the vibrating body releases energy only slowly, the result will be a longer-lasting sound of lesser volume. Musical instruments can be deliberately designed for greater or lesser rates of damping through energy transmission, and makers often find themselves negotiating some sort of trade-off between volume and sustain.

MODES OF VIBRATION

In Chapter 1 I spoke of the ear's response to complex vibrations involving many simultaneous frequencies. Now we can talk about how such vibration patterns arise. This kind of acoustic behavior is easiest to describe in connection with musical strings, so we will start with them. But bear in mind that these phenomena have their parallels in membranes, winds, and solid vibrating materials as well.

Within the tone of a typical musical string, a sharp-eared listener can pick out the fundamental tone along with a few audible overtones above it. (The fundamental is normally the most prominent and the easiest to focus upon, and its pitch is heard as *the* pitch of the overall sound.) Now, these multiple tones must come from somewhere; they must somehow reflect patterns in the string's movement.

The vibrating string, fastened at both ends and stretched tightly between its two anchors, is capable of several *modes of vibration*. Each mode is a pattern of vibratory movement in the standing wave. The simplest and most prominent mode, labeled as the string's first mode of vibration, is the one in which the entire vibrating length of the string flexes from side to side, assuming at the extremes of each half cycle something like the curved shape of left and right parentheses, as shown in the top part of Figure 2-5A. This first mode is responsible, it turns out, for the pitch that we hear as the fundamental in the string's tone.

Additional modes of vibration involve subsections of the string engaged in smaller movements, as shown below in Figure 2-5A. The second mode takes the form, at the extremes, of shallow S shapes. The two sides of the pattern work together at a single frequency, and so this second mode, despite its seeming dividedness, is responsible for a single pitch — ideally, an octave above the fundamental.

We can now highlight an important aspect of such vibrating patterns. In the second mode, as in all standing

Musical strings produce harmonic overtones. Normally those harmonics blend into the overall string timbre and do not stand out as separate tones. But there are ways to hear individual harmonics. The following instrument design takes advantage of a simple but elegant technique that isolates string harmonics over an extended range. It was developed by guitarist and composer Glenn Branca.

The instrument is a simple six-string board zither, with a middle bridge dividing each string into two half-strings. Under the strings on one side there is an electromagnetic pickup (such as electric guitars use). The player plucks the strings on the no-pickup side, varying the pitch with a Hawaiian-guitar-style steel slide. The vibration on the no-pickup side is scarcely audible, since the board radiates sound poorly. But any tones matching the harmonics of the half-string length will start a sympathetic vibration on the other side, to be sensed by the pickup there and amplified. Because this system does very well at isolating tones high up in the harmonic series, where the tones are close together, the player will find a vast array of pitches waiting to come forth, making for a very full musical palette. Just plucking the string and sliding the steel over its length produces a cascade of audible pitches. The tone, as it comes through the amplifier, is clean and lucid, with no plucking sound at all.

Materials

Remember to look to Appendix 1, "Tools and Materials," for sources. You can vary dimensions and the number of strings to suit your needs or taste.

One six-foot 2x4 board.

One electric guitar pickup with cable and jack.

Foam rubber, 1/8-inch thick and about 2" by 4" rectangular.

An electric guitar amplifier — or, alternatively, you can hook up to your stereo or whatever else will serve.

Two 1/8- or 1/4-inch steel rods or equivalent, 3½" long, to serve as end bridges (large nails or bolts with the heads cut off will do).

One section of 3/8- or ½-inch outside diameter metal rod or tubing, 3½ inches long, to serve as the middle bridge.

Six tuning pins, and a tuning wrench or crescent wrench to turn them.

Six 1-inch #8 roundhead wood screws.

Music wire — enough for 6 strings each about seven feet long. Use several different gauges, between about .010" (designated as #1 music wire) and .031" (designated as #13).

A "slide," meaning a hard, reasonably heavy, hand-held object to press against the strings to stop the vibration at different points. Glass and steel slides are manufactured and sold specifically for guitar players. But any hard, heavy object that feels comfortable in your hand will work.

Construction Procedure

Cut the 6-foot board. If necessary, carve out a seating with chisels or router to fit the pickup, so that the pickup with foam beneath will lie about 1/8" below the strings in the finished instrument. Drill holes at one end for the tuning

pins as shown in Figure B, small enough for the pins to fit firmly. For the most common zither pin size the appropriate hole size is 3/16". Tap the pins part way in, then screw them the rest of the way in (taking advantage of the fine threads on the pins). In the equivalent locations on the opposite side, place six strong wood screws, screwed down so that the heads are 1/4" from the board surface. Put the smaller rods for the end bridges in place and secure them with screws, epoxy or any other effective means. Mount the pickup in its seating, with the foam rubber beneath (cut to size as necessary). Use U-shaped fencing nails to fix the first few inches of cord to the 2x4, to prevent stressing the wires where they join the pickup. Attach the strings end to end, from screws to pins, as indicated in Figure D and its caption. Use the tuning pins to tighten them moderately tight, then wedge the larger rod that forms the center bridge beneath them at the midpoint. You may devise your own tuning for the strings. Plug the jack from the pickup into an amplifier and turn it on.

Playing Technique

Position the board in front of you as shown. Pluck near the bridge to your right. Move the steel slowly along the strings as you pluck, in order to hear the rainbow of harmonics that appears over a relatively short sliding distance. There's no need to pluck hard or to apply great pressure with the steel.

When you pluck the string on the no-pickup side, any harmonics having a node at the point where you place the steel will be excited, and will sympathetically excite the matching harmonic in the half-string on the other side of the bridge. The pickup there will sense it, and it will be amplified. The first few harmonics — the second through the eighth or so — sound readily, and their nodal locations are not confusingly crowded together. The higher harmonics become increasingly difficult to locate, but with practice you will be able to control them as well. To aid in locating the steel for the different harmonics, you can mark off the nodal positions on the board beneath the strings, creating a chart similar to that shown in Figure E. The locations are as follows: the second harmonic has a node at the half-string's midpoint; the third harmonic has nodes at the half-string's 1/3 and 2/3 points; the fourth has nodes at the 1/4, 2/4, and 3/4 points ... and so forth.

Acknowledgments

The German guitarist Hans Reichel has developed a "Pick-behind-the-bridge Guitar" based upon the same principle as Glenn Branca's harmonics guitar described here. While the beauty of the Branca instrument lies in its simplicity, Hans Reichel's instrument is more complex, and demanding both to make and to play — but with huge musical potential amply demonstrated in Hans' own playing.

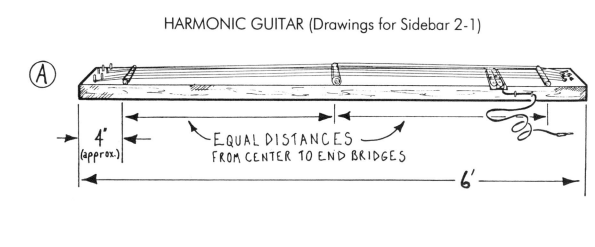

Ⓐ

4' (approx.)

EQUAL DISTANCES FROM CENTER TO END BRIDGES

6'

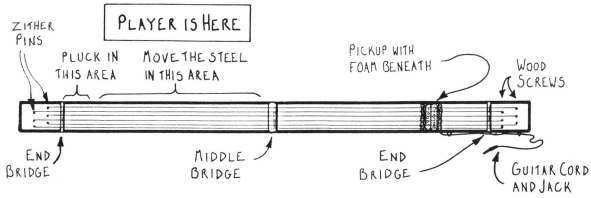

ZITHER PINS

PLAYER IS HERE

PLUCK IN THIS AREA

MOVE THE STEEL IN THIS AREA

PICKUP WITH FOAM BENEATH

WOOD SCREWS

END BRIDGE

MIDDLE BRIDGE

END BRIDGE

GUITAR CORD AND JACK

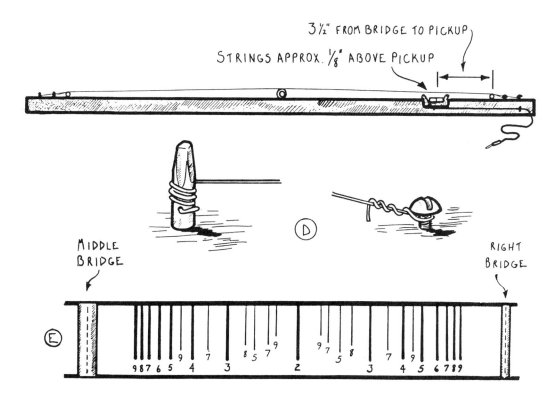

3½" FROM BRIDGE TO PICKUP

STRINGS APPROX. ⅛" ABOVE PICKUP

Ⓓ

MIDDLE BRIDGE

RIGHT BRIDGE

Ⓔ

9 8 7 6 5   9   4   7   8 5 7 9   9 7   5   8   3   7   9   4 5 6 7 8 9
          3   2

A. Oblique view. B. Top view. C. side view.

D. Attachment of the string to the tuning pin at one end, and the wood screw at the other. Make sure the string makes at least three or four loops at each end, to prevent slippage under tension. The methods shown are suitable for a steel string, which are required to drive the electromagnetic pickup on this instrument. (For nylon strings, which are more prone to slipping, pass one or more of the loops at the tuning pin over the free end of the string, and find a way to knot the string at the end with the screw.)

E. A chart of the sort that could be marked on the neck on the playing side to indicate harmonic node locations. (Only the lowest harmonic that will sound at each node location is indicated.)

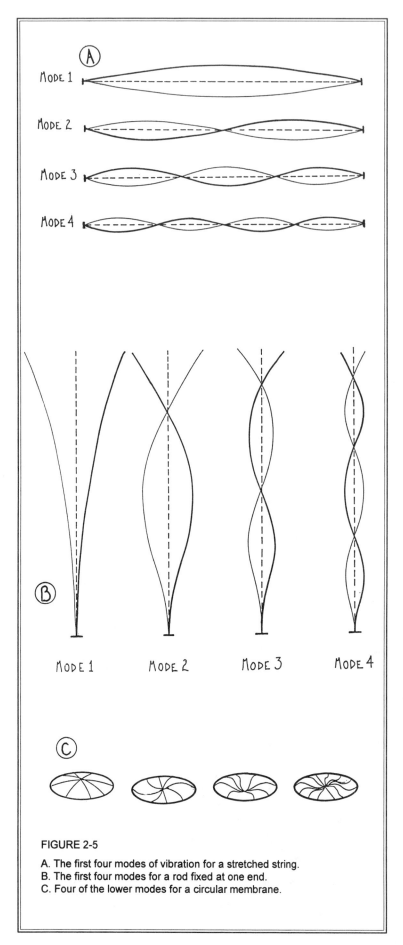

FIGURE 2-5

A. The first four modes of vibration for a stretched string.
B. The first four modes for a rod fixed at one end.
C. Four of the lower modes for a circular membrane.

wave patterns, there are points of maximum and minimum movement. The center point in this second mode is virtually immobile; it merely pivots. Points of maximum movement appear one quarter of the way from each end. These defining points have names. The point that does not move is a *node*, and the points of maximum movement are called *antinodes*. Remember the meanings of these words if you are not familiar with them already; you will encounter them many times before we get to the end of this book.

In addition to the node at the center, the second string mode has a node at each end, since these points too are immobile. The first mode, which we looked at earlier, has but one antinode (point of maximum vibration) at the center, and the two nodes at the ends.

The third mode of vibration for a stretched string takes the form of three string segments, as shown in the third drawing in Figure 2-5A. This mode is responsible for the next higher overtone, ideally sounding at the interval of a 12th above the fundamental. You can see the form of the fourth mode in Figure 2-5A as well, and you can easily imagine what the higher modes will be. One could go on with this indefinitely, but in practice the strength of the vibrational modes diminishes as they get higher. Overtones above about number 16 are significant in relatively few instruments, and in many only the first few overtones play an important role. Notice, by the way, that the string overtones form a harmonic series.

These modes of vibration don't normally occur in isolation; the string vibrates in many modes at once. It does this in a manner analogous to that described in connection with a vibrating particle of air, in Sidebar 1-1. The forces at play in the several modes operate on the string in an additive manner, augmenting or counteracting one another in varying degrees at each point along the string and at each instant in time, to produce a single complex vibration pattern. When that pattern is transmitted to the ear (via soundboard and air), the ear manages to extract the frequencies associated with the subsidiary modes that are present, and recognizes them as the fundamental and overtone pitches.

These same principles apply not only to strings, but to most instrument types. For instance, a rigid rod fixed at one end, as in a kalimba tine, manifests its first four modes of vibration as shown in Figure 2-5B. The resulting overtone pitches in this case are distinctly non-harmonic, with the second and third modes producing pitches at just under two octaves and a minor sixth, and just under four octaves and a major second above the fundamental. Circular membranes, as in drum heads, show a set of modes which are somewhat analogous to string modes, but with more variations deriving from their two-dimensional nature (Figure 2-5C). The resulting overtone series once again is non-harmonic. Fuller information on these and vibrational modes for other instruments appears in the chapters devoted to the specific instrument types.

The modes of vibration just described can be called *transverse modes*. "Transverse" here refers to the fact that the movement of any point in the vibrating object is side to side. But relative to what? Relative to the direction of travel of the traveling wave in the vibrating medium. If you look back at Figure 2-2, you'll see this effect in a transversely vibrating string: as the traveling waves move lengthwise along the string, each point in the string accommodates the wave with a lateral movement. As a practical matter, transverse vibrations are the most musically useful sort of oscillation in solid vibrating materials such as strings, bars, rods and membranes.

In addition to the transverse modes of vibration, there are *longitudinal modes*. Longitudinal vibrations are most important in air columns. (They can occur in strings, rods, and other long, thin media as well, but only rarely are they musically significant in these cases.) Longitudinal modes are those in which the predominant vibratory motion of any given point is along the same axis as the motion of the traveling wave in the vibrating material. They simultaneously manifest themselves in a complementary form, as pressure waves traveling the length of the medium, giving rise to constant fluctuations of pressure at any given point. Despite the different orientation, longitudinal mode behaviors are closely analogous to those of transverse modes. They contain well defined nodes and antinodes, and are capable of the same sort of complex patterns manifesting several modes simultaneously.

Transverse vibrations and longitudinal vibrations can cohabit in the same medium, quite independently and with little effect on one another. For practical musical purposes you can usually focus on one and act as if the other didn't exist.

Longitudinal modes are harder to picture and describe than transverse, in part because they are more difficult to observe directly. The latter part of Sidebar 2-3 may help to paint the picture. Meanwhile, let's consider as an example one wonderfully outrageous longitudinal-mode instrument. The Long String Instrument has been developed (and refined well beyond the outlines given here) by contemporary builder Ellen Fullman. Ms. Fullman was exploring the sounds she could get with very long strings, in the range of 20, 50, or 100 feet, when she noticed that an unexpectedly clear tone arose when she stroked her strings lengthwise with her fingers — in other words, when she gave them a longitudinal impulse. In doing so, she had excited a longitudinal vibration in the strings. But why should the musical tone arise at such extraordinary lengths? Longitudinal vibrations travel extremely rapidly in solid materials. In the steel of the strings, they propagate at rates of tens of thousands of feet per second. That means that in musical strings of normal lengths, longitudinal waves reflect back and forth at frequencies well above the useful musical range. But in the very long strings, the frequencies happen to fall in the heart of the musical range. Ellen Fullman's string-stroking technique is analogous to using a violin bow, but in the longwise direction. The string

Sidebar 2-2

BALLOON-MOUNTED BAR GONG REVISITED

In Sidebar 1-2, I described a balloon-mounted bar gong, an instrument producing a wondrous array of audible overtones. In the accompanying discussion I focused on the aural effects of the multiple tones. Now that we have covered a bit more ground concerning modes of vibration, we can discuss the physical basis of those tones.

Each of the bar gong's audible overtones arises from one of its transverse vibrational modes. Because the steel bar has very little internal damping, a wide range of modes sing out quite clearly, including the very high ones that would be lost in a softer material. The vibrational modes in effect here are the free bar modes (the same as in marimba bars), producing an inharmonic series (a set of overtones which does not agree with the harmonic series) with frequencies quite widely spaced near the bottom. This long bar's fundamental mode, however, is subsonic, and the second and perhaps third are, if not subsonic as well, then barely audible. As you progress further up the series the tones appear at closer musical intervals, and in the upper reaches of the long bar's copious overtone array, you get into some densely populated territory.

I recommended a special playing technique to isolate certain overtones or overtone mixes, namely, pinching the bar at selected spots while striking. How does that bring out certain tones? Pinching the bar inhibits the vibration for any mode that is active at the pinching point. But the pinching scarcely inhibits any mode having a *node* at or very near the pinching point, since the nodal point doesn't move except to pivot. Thus, by pinching the bar you filter out all modes except any that happen to have a node near the pinching point. In theory virtually every point along the bar is a nodal point for some modes, but that includes an infinity of modes that are too high to produce musically meaningful tones, so those coming through at any pinching point represent a finite selection.

You can enhance the mode-isolating effect by your choice of striking location. Any mode having an *antinode* at or near the striking point will be preferentially excited. So, pinch at the node, strike at the antinode, and you'll get the mode you want. In practice the process may be less analytical: you pinch and strike at random points as you seek out tones that you like, and mark those spots that produce the most appealing results. But now, as you do so, you'll understand the mechanisms behind the sounds.

must be attached to a soundboard or the equivalent at one end, since by itself, especially in this longitudinal mode, it doesn't move enough air to be heard. But it drives the soundboard quite efficiently, since the longways vibrations are ideal for pulling and pushing a board mounted perpendicular to the strings.

Longitudinal vibrations don't often play a primary role in string instruments, membrane instruments, or instruments using rigid materials, because of the extraordinary dimensions required. But longitudinal vibration is essential for the entire family of wind instruments. Pressure waves travel far more slowly in air than in solids, making it possible to have longitudinal mode wind instruments of reasonable lengths.

NODES AND ANTINODES: Practical Applications

For the past few pages we have been studying vibration patterns that arise in sounding bodies. Understanding these patterns is central in musical instrument design. It enables you to encourage the vibrations you wish to encourage, and discourage others. A key point to remember is that if you want something to vibrate freely in a particular mode of vibration, you must avoid inhibiting it at points that need to move for that particular mode. That means if anything must touch the vibrating thing, it should touch only at the (stationary) nodes.

Here's a practical example: Consider a rectangular metal bar such as a glockenspiel bar. When such a bar vibrates freely, it manifests a whole array of natural modes of vibration, producing a corresponding array of sounding tones. The relationships between the tones are non-harmonic — such is the nature of vibrating bars — and the resulting timbre is somewhat clangy and dissonant. One of the modes is considerably lower than the others and may be louder; the

---

WATCHING WAVES

Traveling waves are not visible in musical strings, because the motion is too fast and fine to follow. In extremely long strings, on the other hand, you can see traveling waves in action — although you can hear nothing, because the frequency is subsonic.

Get about 50 feet of quarter-inch rope, and tie it to something solid at each end, such as two trees. It should be stretched fairly tightly. Stand near one end, and pluck the rope (pull it to one side and release). You will see the traveling wave as it runs back and forth several times, reflecting from end to end. Notice that its direction of displacement reverses with each reflection: if the wave motion takes the form of an upward displacement chased by a downward displacement as the wave runs away from you, get downward chased by upward on the return. Next, shift your attention to focus on a single point along the rope. All you see now is that the single point periodically jumps, as the traveling wave passes through it. It is easy to recognize that this is a transverse wave, meaning that the direction of displacement is crosswise relative to the direction of wave travel. Each point along the rope manifests the wave as a sideways movement. The sense of travel along the rope is a cumulative effect of a series of sideways movements in progressive locations along the rope.

The rope also allows you to observe the relationship between tension and frequency in musical strings as it relates to the speed of the traveling wave. Untie one end of the rope and hold it in one hand as you pluck the rope with the other. This way you can vary the tension, simply by pulling the rope more or less tightly as you hold it. The tighter you pull the rope, the faster the transverse wave travels. The faster the wave travels, the higher the frequency with which reflected waves pass any given point along the rope — that is to say, the higher the vibrational frequency. Holding the end in your hand also allows you to feel directly the effect of each pulse as it arrives at your end of the rope, giving your hand a jerk. This must be what it feels like to

be a stringed instrument bridge.

Is there a way to demonstrate longitudinal wave motion on a similarly observable scale? This is more difficult. The longitudinal wave manifests itself as rapidly moving regions of relative compression and rarefaction of the medium, and in most materials those compressions and rarefactions are not visible. But how about springs? A traveling longitudinal wave in a coil spring appears as a region of closely spaced coils (compression) alternating with a region of widely spaced coils (rarefaction), progressing rapidly down the length of the spring. The best spring for the purpose is a long, lightweight, large-diameter one that is also fairly soft (i.e., easily stretched or compressed). Slinkies (the children's toy) do all right, but you'll do better if you can find something lighter and less droopy.

Attach each end of the spring to fixed supports far enough apart so that it is stretched but not excessively stretched, bridging the space between. There will probably be a fair amount of droop — that's OK. Give the spring a longitudinal impulse by plucking the coils in the longways direction, and you will see the wave of compression running the length of the spring, reflecting off the far end, returning, and reflecting again at the near end. You can also try holding one end in your hand, to feel the pulse when the returning wave reaches you. Now shift your attention away from the traveling wave to focus on a single coil. True to the definition of a longitudinal wave, it periodically scoots forward and back, not perpendicular to the string as with the transverse wave, but within the line of the spring-string itself. Inevitably there will be a some transverse motion in the picture as well — in fact, a long, soft spring usually ends up flopping all over the place. While this may be distracting visually, it doesn't change the rules for the longitudinal wave. The two types of motion can coexist, independent and separable.

FIGURE 2-6: First mode of transverse vibration for a bar free at both ends, shown in side view.

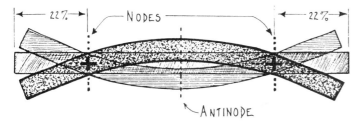

ear naturally focuses upon it as the fundamental. It involves a pattern of motion like that shown in Figure 2-6.

The bar flexes at the center; the center dips and rises while the extremes rise and dip. There are two nodes, taking the form of nodal lines rather than points, crossing the bar at a distance of about 22% of the total length in from each end.

For most people's taste we can get the most musical sound from this bar by bringing out that lowest mode, while de-emphasizing the higher, non-harmonic modes in order to reduce the clang. To do this, consider that whatever holds the bar will inevitably damp the vibration to some extent. We want to minimize damping on the fundamental mode. A simple way to do this is to rest the bar on two narrow, parallel strips of foam rubber spaced so that the nodes for the fundamental mode lie over the foam. For other modes, meanwhile, the nodes do not lie over the foam, but appear in different locations along the bar. The foam contacts the bar in places that need to vibrate if those other modes are to express themselves, so they are at least partially damped. You can hear the result in the tone of the mounted bar: the un-damped fundamental sounds clearly, but the overall tone quality is noticeably less clangy. A closer listen reveals that in the moment of attack the tone actually has a fairly strong complement of higher partials. They provide a certain definition to the start of the tone, but due to being damped by the foam, those higher modes die out rapidly, leaving the sustaining fundamental.

This kind of thinking applies not only to sounding bar instruments. Good-sounding metal tubular wind chimes, for instance — those having rich tone, good sustain and minimal clang — generally have their hanging supports running through holes at the upper of the two nodes, about 22% from the end. Or consider this: Why can a percussionist hold a triangle at the corner with relatively little damping of its sound, even though holding it anywhere along one of the straight sides kills its tone immediately? It's because the corner forms a node for the desired modes. Related principles apply in wind and string instruments as well, though the mechanics aren't always as obvious.

For another application of the same principle, let us return for a moment to the metal bar. The usual way to start it vibrating is to strike it with some sort of beater. It makes quite a difference where you strike the bar: 1) If you hit the bar in the center, the fundamental tone is strong and clear. 2) If you strike at the nodes over the mountings, the fundamental almost disappears. At the same time the upper partials, though weakened due to the discriminatory mounting system, seem more prominent since they are no longer buried by the

sound of the stronger fundamental. 3) Finally, when you strike at one or the other end, the fundamental returns almost as strong as with the center strike.

Well, it makes sense, doesn't it? If you want a particular mode to ring out, you do well to introduce energy at a point where that mode can use it. Giving an impulse at a nodal point, a point that doesn't vibrate for a particular mode, does little to stimulate that mode. Introducing energy at a point of fuller vibration has far greater effect.

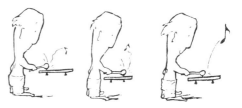

Once again, these principles don't apply only to metal bar instruments. For instance, the point at which a string is plucked makes a big difference in its sound. Imagine a string plucked exactly at its center point. That string will produce a strong fundamental, but the second and all higher even-

Sidebar 2-4

MORE ON HARMONICS

I introduced the idea of harmonic overtones in Chapter 1 when we were talking about timbre. In addition to its timbral effects, harmonicity also has acoustical implications of a mechanical nature.

Harmonicity can be seen as a kind of agreement between the modes of vibration within a vibrating body, such as a string or air column. If the overtones are harmonic, the second mode vibrates at twice the frequency of the fundamental, completing two cycles in the time it takes the first to complete one. They repeatedly arrive at the same point together, and the two reinforce one another. Mode 3 completes three cycles for each cycle of mode 1 for a similar reinforcing effect, and so on up the series. Vibrating bodies with harmonically related modes of vibration tend to be more responsive, having better sustain and a subjectively richer tone than those that do not. When harmonics are detuned, the sounding body may not sing or ring out as well. As a familiar example, you can hear the effect of detuned harmonics in dull-sounding, stretched and worn-out nylon strings. The effects also appear in wind instruments, where a particular note may speak less willingly if it lacks reinforcement from well-tuned harmonics.

This is not to say that harmonic musical instruments are superior in some musical sense to those with inharmonic partials. Inharmonic timbres have their own character, and it would be a boring world if we didn't have them around to color the music.

numbered modes will be scarcely present in the tone. Why? The center point is a node for the even-numbered modes (to see this, look back to Figure 2-5a). Kinetic energy introduced there is useless to them. By contrast, a string plucked very near one or the other fixed end will be strong in the upper partials, giving it a more brilliant tone. That's because the energy is introduced relatively near a node (namely, the end point) for the lowest modes, whereas the same impulse is nearer to where the action is for the higher modes, with their shorter subsidiary vibrating segments.

This line of thought has yet another application. You can take advantage of the position of the antinode not only in the energy-input process, but also in the instrument's energy output. Consider once again the metal bar, and imagine that you want to bring out the fundamental mode, and have tuned an air resonator tube to that mode's pitch. The antinode for that mode happens to be the very center of the bar — that is where it vibrates with the greatest amplitude. If you are smart, then, you will center the bar over the resonator, putting it in the best position for the desired mode to drive the air within. One more example: Suppose you are attaching a lightweight contact microphone to a hanging chime. Where along the chime should you locate it? At the point where the mode you most want to hear is at its strongest — the antinode for the desired mode.

PHASE RELATIONSHIPS

We have seen that most sounds in the real world are complex, comprised of many simultaneous vibrations. Another aspect of this complexity is that most musical instrument sounds involve the simultaneous action of not one, but several vibrating surfaces. For instance, a guitar string vibrates; it causes the soundboard to vibrate. The outer surface of the soundboard causes the air immediately in front of the guitar to vibrate, while the inner surface of the soundboard drives the air within the sound chamber for another, separate, air vibration. Furthermore, in its second mode, the string itself actually vibrates in two separate half-string vibrations, the two halves moving in opposite directions. The soundboard too has multiple subsections engaged in quasi-independent vibrations. And this list of semi-separate vibrating components could go on. Yet this situation is not as chaotic as it seems, because all these vibrations, in theory at least, are at the same frequencies as the driver (the string). But there are some important implications. Consider this one:

The external face of the soundboard pushes outward to create a pressure pulse in the surrounding air as part of each cycle. At the same instant, as part of the same action, the inner surface of the soundboard pulls away from the air enclosed in the chamber, creating a rarefaction (region of reduced pressure). By means of air flow through the soundhole, this rarefaction is communicated almost instantaneously to the outer air. A half cycle later, the roles of the inner and outer soundboard surfaces are reversed. The inner and outer surfaces thus continually work against one another, with the sound coming out of the soundhole precisely counteracting the sound coming directly off the front face. Just how their interaction plays out is rather complex, but it is a fact that the total volume of the guitar is reduced by this contrary action. The guitar has a beautiful tone arising from the blend of the direct soundboard sound and the air chamber resonance — but it is purchased at the cost of this loss of acoustic efficiency.

When two simultaneous vibrations of the same frequency move in opposite directions like this, they are said to be *out of phase*. The phrase refers to the fact that the two vibrating bodies are at opposite phases of their vibratory cycles at any given instant.

This illustrates one reason why two sound sources producing the same tone at the same volume are not twice as loud as one, and ten are not nearly ten times as loud. It is highly improbable that ten sources sounding the same frequency will be exactly in phase with one another for a listener at a given location. There is always at least some cancellation due to sound waves arriving at the listener's ear out of phase. Identical or near-identical sounds arriving from multiple sources do possess, subjectively speaking, a certain richness or fullness lacking in single-source sounds, but they are not as much louder as one might expect.

When two vibrations in the same medium are close in frequency but not identical, another phase-related effect comes to the fore. The two may start out in phase, reinforcing one another, but with the faster one completing each cycle more quickly, they gradually pull out of alignment, until they are out of phase and canceling. As the process continues, they keep moving in and out of phase, alternately canceling and reinforcing, to create in the cumulative effect a continuous rise and fall in volume, a sort of gentle tremolo. This phenomenon is called *beating*. You can experiment with the effect using any pair of vibration sources with which you can produce controllable pitches near the same note. Try playing two strings on a string instrument, starting with them at the same pitch and then very slowly sliding one ever-so-slightly sharp.

The rate of beating depends on how close the two frequencies are. With identical frequencies there is no beating; when they differ just slightly the beating is slow; with greater differences the beating becomes faster until at a certain point it becomes too rapid to distinguish separate beats.

Beating phenomena are at the heart of chorusing effects. When two violinists, for instance, play the same pitches in unison, they never really play precisely the same pitches. They constantly slip microtonally sharp and flat of one another, bringing the beating effects into play. The beating is not steady; it constantly shifts speed and intensity as the pitch difference between the two sources varies, and this is, to most ears, an attractive effect. It's really nothing extraordinary; it's simply a part of the richer sound of ensemble playing. When an entire string section plays in unison, the same interactions take place but in such abundance that individual manifestations tend to obscure one another, and the overall effect is smoother. Electronic chorusing effects operate on the same principles: a shiftingly de-tuned version of the original signal is mingled with the original to create irregular beating. We'll talk about applying these ideas to acoustic instruments in Chapter 10, "Special Effects."

IMPEDANCE, TRANSMISSION AND RADIATION

We come now to the subject of sound energy, and how it is stored in a vibrating object, transmitted to other objects, and radiated to the air. These questions are important for musical instruments having solid vibrating bodies (such as string instruments and percussion of all sorts) that must somehow communicate vibrations to the surrounding air. They are not so important for wind instruments, since for them the sound energy is delivered directly to the air itself, and transmission from one medium to another is not an issue.

Just how loud an instrument is, or could be under the best of circumstances, is dictated in part by how much sound energy the initial vibrating body can absorb. Heavier objects can sustain more vibratory energy than light ones; so can objects which can vibrate at large amplitude without damage to themselves or their mountings; and so can objects which are stiff enough to spring back forcefully in response to an initial displacement. Musical strings, despite their other advantages, make an effective bad example here: The average string is simply too light to hold a great deal of energy. Plucking a string harder and harder, going crazy and plucking it ferociously hard, doesn't add much volume beyond a certain point. There is only so much energy the little guy can absorb. As a result, it is difficult to make a loud string instrument. The exception here helps to demonstrate the rule: the loudest non-electric string instrument is a grand piano. Grand piano volume is achieved by using strings much more massive, and at far higher tensions (enabling them to spring back with great force), than other string instruments could possibly endure.

Vibrating bodies made of thick, solid, massive materials can absorb and then release a great deal of energy. Consider a large metal gong. You can hit the thing hard with a heavy mallet; it absorbs the blow and converts it into vibratory energy within itself without damage. All that sound energy within the gong is then available to be converted into pressure waves in the air that listeners can hear.

But the ability to absorb and hold large amounts of vibrational energy does not ensure a loud instrument. An object may have this capacity, but do a very poor job of communicating its vibrating energy to the surrounding air. Heavy, solid metal rods, for instance, can hold a very strong vibration, but without the assistance of some external radiator their sound may be anemic, especially in the lower frequencies. There are two reasons for this. One is that they don't have enough surface area to move much air. The other is that with massive vibrating objects, a large amount of energy can take the form of a vibration of small amplitude. The aforementioned rod, then, might be vibrating with lots of energy, but not enough amplitude to have much impact on the surrounding air.

And so we come to the matter of vibration transmission. You can make the rod sound louder by using it as a driver for a secondary sound radiator, which will in turn do a better job of driving the air. That secondary radiator must have a lot of surface area, and it must be lightweight and compliant relative to the rod so that the rod can drive it easily. Because the vibrations in a heavy rod are so strong, it is not hard for such a rod to drive most radiators, given the right sort of mounting. Strings, by contrast, are more exacting in their requirements. Typically they can effectively drive only a lightweight radiator, such as the thin, springy softwood soundboards of guitars and violins, the drumhead-like soundboards of banjos and their kin, or unconventional super-light radiation surfaces like balloons or styrofoam.

The measure of how well a given initial vibrating body will drive a given secondary resonator is *impedance*. You can think of impedance roughly as an indicator of a vibration's concentration of energy. High-impedance vibrations condense a great deal of vibrating force into what may be a relatively small amplitude vibration. Consider tuning forks:

The two prongs of a tuning fork vibrate in a complementary lateral motion, in which they alternately flex toward one another and then apart, at some set frequency. The handle of the fork is also vibrating, as you can verify by pressing the end of the handle against a table top: the table top then acts as a soundboard driven by the fork, and the sound becomes much louder. If you grab the ends of the tines, they are immediately damped out and stop vibrating. But why doesn't holding the handle of the tuning fork (as you have probably been doing all along) kill the vibration in the same way? The answer is that the handle is engaging in a lower amplitude, but much stronger vibration — so strong that not only does the hand not damp it, it can even impose its will upon the table top. The prongs, meanwhile, vibrate at larger amplitude, but with a relatively weak vibration. Not only are they easily damped by the hand, but if you try pressing them against the table top, all you hear is a moment of clatter followed by silence — the table top easily wins the battle of wills.

The intense, lower amplitude vibrations in the handle of the fork are high-impedance vibrations. Larger amplitude, weaker vibrations such as those in the tines are low impedance. Generally, high impedances are associated with larger masses and greater rigidity; low impedances with lesser masses and greater flexibility. (The relatively large amplitude and low impedance of the tines is associated with their willingness to flex). An easy way to get a sense of the impedance of a vibrating object is simply to touch it: low-impedance vibrations are easily damped with the hand; high-impedance vibrations are not.

An initial vibrating body of high impedance easily drives a low-impedance body, while a low-impedance initial vibrator will have more difficulty driving a higher-impedance body. This has important implications for musical instrument design. For a secondary sound radiator, such as a soundboard, to work with any degree of efficiency, it must have lower impedance — that is, be lighter and/or more flexible — than its driver. The higher the impedance of the driver relative to the radiator, the more rapid will be the energy transmission, and the briefer and louder the sound.

Shall we go through this one more time with another example? Consider the guitar. At the middle of the string, where it vibrates very broadly, the impedance is extremely low. Fortunately, at the bridge, where the string is attached, the comparative rigidity of the anchoring compresses the same vibrating energy into much smaller amplitude, and thus considerably higher impedance. This enables the string to drive the bridge and the attached soundboard. Still, given the lightness of guitar strings, it only works because string instrument soundboards are made relatively low in impedance, being both light and somewhat flexible. Just how light and flexible can be varied according to the sound one wants to achieve: Flamenco guitars are deliberately made with relatively lightweight bodies and soundboards, to facilitate rapid delivery of energy from the string to the sound radiator, resulting in a loud, percussive tone with relatively little sustain. This is in keeping with the musical style. At the opposite extreme, most electric guitars (which can achieve great volume by other means) are made with heavy, solid wood bodies. The result is a far slower delivery of vibrational energy to the body of the instrument, and far longer sustain. The volume, in the absence of amplification, is quite small.

Chapter Three

TUNING SYSTEMS AND PITCH LAYOUTS

Before moving on to descriptions of specific instrument types, we need to consider two more topics. One is tunings, meaning scale and pitch relationships. This bears directly on the choices that builders make regarding what pitches are to be available on a particular instrument, the reasoning behind those choices, and the process of tuning the instrument to those pitches. The second topic is the spatial layout of the pitches on the instrument. For some instruments the physical nature of the instrument dictates the pitch layout to a large extent, and the maker has little choice. But for others the design of the interface between player and instrument is an open question, and an important one.

TUNINGS

The piano, guitar, and most other western instruments are made to produce a set of twelve pitches in each octave, collectively called the chromatic scale. It would be easy to think of this set of twelve as the entire gamut of pitches available for use in music, but that would be false. The range of possible pitches is a continuum, and between any two frequencies there are other frequencies. Most listeners can easily distinguish musical intervals far smaller than the piano's smallest interval, the semitone. So there is no reason not to make music with pitches other than those of the standard chromatic scale. And in fact people do this all the time. Non-western musics commonly use other tunings. "Outside" pitches appear in plenty of western music as well, the most conspicuous examples being in blues and its derivatives (for instance, "bent" notes on the guitar).

Musical instrument makers have to deal with this matter of tunings and tuning systems, as they decide what pitches their instruments are to produce. Many makers stick with pre-existing tunings, such as the western chromatic scale, and so have

no need of further analysis. Some base their pitch choices on instinct and the untutored preferences of their ear, without reference either to existing models or technical analysis. Some enjoy working with arbitrary or random pitch sets. And some devise new but carefully rationalized tuning systems. Many makers regard the matter of tuning as an essential aspect of the character of the instrument and the creativity of its maker.

To fulfill this last ideal, it is good to develop an understanding of tuning systems both conventional and exotic, and the rationales behind them. This can easily become a matter of intense study — the subject of tuning systems is a large, complex, and often arcane one. I won't provide a complete exposition of the topic, but in what follows I will provide a general overview as it relates to instrument design. Readers who wish to avoid the technical stuff, and who are content to work with random tunings or tuning by instinct alone, may choose to skip the sections on just intonation theory and equal temperament theory that follow.

Underlying Concepts: Just Intonation & Temperaments

Over the last two centuries and some, a particular form of the chromatic scale has very much been the predominant tuning system in western music, especially in formal music circles. This is the scale known as *12-tone equal temperament*. Not only is it the standard tuning for pianos and electronic keyboards, but it also dictates the spacing of frets on guitars, the tuning of commercially manufactured marimbas and xylophones, and so on. Most wind instruments are designed to reproduce the same scale, although they are usually a bit more flexible in practice; while instruments with slidable pitch like violins, trombones and slide whistles are, by their nature, not restricted to any particular scale.

Twelve-tone equal temperament is a system in which the octave is divided into twelve equally spaced intervals, providing twelve equidistant pitches before reaching the octave above on the thirteenth. To one who has been playing music in twelve-equal all his or her life, it may seem perfectly natural that there should be a single uniform intervalic unit — the equal-tempered half step, equal to 1/12 of an octave — by which all other intervals can be measured and constructed. It certainly is convenient. But scales need not be built around equal intervals, and in fact they rarely were before the relatively recent (historically speaking) introduction of 12-tone equal temperament. The scale systems that humans seem to have naturally gravitated toward, in most cultures and through most of history, have employed irregularly sized intervals between the scale steps. To understand this, we need to review some basics of intonational theory, and to come to terms with the distinctions among *just intonation, temperaments* like twelve-equal, and other intonation systems.

Recall that our ears interpret musical intervals in terms of ratios. For example, one hears the interval of a major third between any two pitches whose fundamental vibrational frequencies form the ratio of 5:4. It matters not what the actual frequencies are; as long as they are in that ratio, the interval will be heard as a major third. This kind of ratio-based perception seems to form the underlying basis of many, perhaps most, of the tuning systems that have evolved around the world. In such tuning systems, the frequencies of the pitches in the set all bear simple ratio relationships to the frequency of the tonic pitch around which the tuning is built. For instance, the frequency ratios for the seven pitches plus octave of the most basic form of major scale, each relative to the tonic, are 1:1, 9:8, 5:4, 4:3, 3:2, 5:3, 15:8, 2:1.

Tunings based on simple ratios like this are called *just* tunings, or are said to be in *just intonation*. (To clear up a common misconception: just intonation refers not to a single specific tuning; it refers to any tuning which meets this general description.) Many such tunings exist, although 12-equal is not one of them. Some just tunings have come into being because musical theorists invented them. Others — and these include many of the most important tunings historically and world-wide — have arisen naturally in various music cultures, and have been found upon analysis to be comprised of simple ratios. With the intervals of just tunings, the basic harmonies have what could be described as a smooth or restful sound. Twelve-equal, by contrast, possesses a certain roughness, especially in music of any complexity.

In just tunings, the scale steps inevitably fall in such a way that the spaces between the steps are irregular; no uniform intervalic unit exists. Is this a problem? It never was perceived as such for who-knows-how-many centuries. But following the Renaissance period, there emerged in European high-culture music a growing interest in enriching the harmonic flavor of the music by modulating from key to key. This is difficult in tunings with asymmetric interval spacings, because to get the desired scale steps in each new key requires additional pitches that aren't in the original key, and the number of pitches called for quickly multiplies to an unmanageable number. It becomes impractical to build an instrument that produces many pitches.

One solution to this problem is simply to accept the limitation: build an instrument in one key and always play in that key, or modes thereof. Another is to add enough additional notes to allow for playing in perhaps just two or three additional keys. A third option is to find any cases where pitches in the new key almost match those of the original key, and use a single compromise pitch for both. This process — tuning certain pitches to compromise values to make them functional though not perfect in more than one key — is what is called *tempering*. Tempered scales are not just; the temperings throw off the theoretically ideal simple ratios. But they typically are imitative of just tunings, designed to approximate the just ratios as closely as possible while still allowing some flexibility in changing keys.

Many different tempered scales were suggested and used in Europe in the 17th and 18th centuries. Most were not equal; the distances between the scale steps varied slightly from one to the next. When the idea of a twelve-tone *equal* temperament first gained prominence during the 18th century, many musicians, tuners and instrument builders were reluctant to use it. Their objection was that compromise values for certain important intervals — the thirds and sixths — were more seriously mistuned than seemed acceptable. With the passage of time, this flaw has been increasingly forgiven and twelve-equal increasingly accepted as a standard. It has reached the point today where most westerners regard twelve-equal's thirds and sixths as perfectly normal. You can get some sense of the size of the discrepancy between just and tempered intervals by looking at the charts in Appendix 2, "Frequency and Tuning Charts."

The difference in sound between the two tuning types might seem a subtle one. But the change from the variegated interval spacings and harmonies of ratio-based tunings to the uniformity of equal temperament was culturally and philosophically significant. As western material culture moved into an age of mass production, the technology of interchangeable parts was applied to the building blocks of music as well. Something gained, something lost.

Just intonation and equal temperament are the two most important approaches to scale construction. But they are not the only possible approaches, and one doesn't have to follow them. There are plenty of musical pitch sets in use around the world that don't lend themselves to analysis in keeping with either line of thought, and theorists and composers have occasionally come up with other scale-logics. You, as an instrument maker or a musician, are free to develop and use whatever scale resources you wish, regardless of the reasoning or lack of reasoning behind them. And despite all the theory in the next couple of pages, there is nothing to prevent you from falling back upon your ear, unaided by mathematical analysis, as the best and final arbiter of just what sorts of tunings you most enjoy and wish to incorporate into the instruments you build.

Just Intonation — Theory

In the hands of some theorists the mathematics behind just tunings becomes rather intricate, but in most applications it comes down to simple arithmetic. Let us imagine ourselves constructing a just tuning from scratch. The first step is to define the tuning as a set of frequency ratios. We saw an example of such a set a few paragraphs ago, when I defined pitch relationships of a basic just major scale as 1:1, 9:8,

5:4, 4:3, 3:2, 5:3, 15:8, 2:1. How do you come up with such a set? Perhaps by following a pre-existing standard, such as some historical scale you have encountered, or something created by another theorist or composer. Alternatively, you might do a little experimenting to come up with something you find appealing to the ear and intellect. The chart in Appendix 2 provides a lot of background information on basic just intervals and pitch sets.

Whatever you settle on, the set of ratios is entirely relative: it tells you what the intervals are between the scale degrees, but it does not give you any specific pitches. So the next step is to select a frequency for the base pitch, or tonic. In the abstract, this choice is essentially arbitrary. You could choose A at 440Hz, because it is an accepted pitch standard; or, for a lower starting note, start an octave or two down at A-220 or A-110. Alternatively you could choose, say, the low G at 49.0Hz, or the C at 32.7Hz, for the tonic. Or, to be practical, you could choose the lowest pitch that sounds well on the instrument that is to play the scale.

Once you have established a tonic frequency, you can begin a process of simple multiplication to establish the frequencies of the other pitches of the set. For this example, let's take G-49.0 as the tonic, and the just major mentioned a moment ago as the set of ratios:

Tonic:	1/1 * 49.0 =	49.00Hz
Major 2nd:	9/8 * 49.0 =	55.12Hz
Major 3rd:	5/4 * 49.0 =	62.25Hz
Perfect 4th:	4/3 * 49.0 =	65.33Hz
Perfect 5th:	3/2 * 49.0 =	73.50Hz
Major 6th:	5/3 * 49.0 =	81.67Hz
Major 7th:	15/8 * 49.0 =	91.88Hz
Octave:	2/1 * 49.0 =	98.00Hz

That's one octave of the scale. You can find the second octave frequencies by multiplying the values for the first octave by two (recall that 2:1 is the ratio for the interval of an octave, and multiplying any frequency by two thus gives the octave above). Find the third octave by multiplying by two again, and so forth. (The octave duplication process applies only if you want the same pitches to repeat in the upper octaves. This is usually but not necessarily the case.)

Equal Temperament — Theory

Now let us go through the same processes with equally spaced tunings. We have spoken specifically about 12-tone equal temperament, but in fact you can have equal tunings with any number of divisions per octave. Each produces its own array of intervals, and each has its own characteristic

Rational Vs. Radical Approaches in Tuning Theory

sound. Usually, though not always, people use equal temperaments as approximations to just scales, favoring those that fortuitously happen to contain intervals closely approximating the just intervals they wish to hear. The standard 12-tone equal temperament is somewhat imperfect in this regard, matching some of the desired just intervals quite well and some not so well. But twelve has he great advantage that it is the smallest equal temperament number that does anything like a decent job of it. Other equal temperaments containing pitches closely matching important just intervals include 19, 24 (the quarter-tone scale), 31, and 53 (see Appendix 2 for more on some of these).

And what of all those other equally spaced systems, the ugly ducklings which don't happen to approximate important just intervals? While these have not been explored as much, there are composers who have taken an interest in them. Some enjoy the fact that such scales are without familiar reference points — no recognizable fourths or fifths or thirds — so the listener simply has to accept and appreciate the exotic intervals as they are, rather than trying to mentally resolve them into something familiar. It's an ear-stretching experience. Scales of 7, 10, 11 and 13 tones have been used with this effect in mind. Each has its own distinctive flavor or mood.

Equally-spaced tunings require a mathematical approach that is different from what we saw with just intonation. Here's how it works:

By definition, each step in an equal temperament must be higher than the previous by a constant interval. This means that the frequency for each step must be multiplied by the same factor to get the frequency for the next successive step. (This factor works just like the frequency ratios in just intonation, but it is expressed as a decimal for reasons having to do with its mathematical derivation.) After multiplying by that factor repeatedly to get the frequency for each scale step in succession, you should reach the octave, at twice the original frequency. These requirements can be summarized in a formula that yields a value for that factor: Where C is the constant factor, and the scale is to have n equal divisions per octave, then $C = \sqrt[n]{2}$. (That is, C = the nth root of 2). Thus, for 12-tone equal temperament, the factor is the 12th root of 2, equal to an irrational number that can be shortened to 1.05946. Knowing this, you can find the frequencies for each step of 12-equal from a starting tone of, say, A above middle C at 440Hz by repeatedly applying the factor, as follows:

A = 440Hz.

A# = 440.00 * 1.05946 = 466.16Hz.

B = 466.16 * 1.05946 = 493.88Hz.

C = 493.16 * 1.05946 = 523.25Hz.

… and so forth. If this works properly, you should reach the octave, at twice the original frequency, or 880Hz, after twelve multiplications by the factor. If you continue the series of multiplications above, you will find that this is the case.

For other equal temperaments you can find a similar constant factor, following the same reasoning to arrive at its value. Sidebar 3-1 provides a chart listing the values for a range of equal temperaments. Armed with this information, you can calculate the frequencies for any equal-tempered

SCALE FACTORS FOR EQUAL TEMPERAMENTS

Here is a list of the scale factors for equal temperaments of 5 steps per octave through 24, plus 31, 36, 41 53 and 72 (the last five have been advocated by various theorists because they contain close approximations to just intervals). The factor C is the constant by which the frequency of each scale degree must be multiplied to obtain the frequency of the next scale degree. 1/C is the inversion, useful for calculating descending scale degrees, as well as fret placement on string instruments and tube lengths for simple cylindrical wind instruments. The values given here are based in this general rule:

For any n-tone equal temperament,
$C_n = \sqrt[n]{2}$ (C = the nth root of 2)

Tones per Octave	C	1/C
5	1.1487	.8706
6	1.1225	.8909
7	1.1041	.9057
8	1.0905	.9170
9	1.0801	.9259
10	1.0718	.9330
11	1.0650	.9389
12	1.0595	.9438
13	1.0548	.9481
14	1.0501	.9517
15	1.0473	.9548
16	1.0443	.9576
17	1.0416	.9600
18	1.0393	.9622
19	1.0372	.9641
20	1.0353	.9659
21	1.0336	.9675
22	1.0320	.9690
23	1.0306	.9703
24	1.0293	.9715
31	1.02261	.97789
36	1.01944	.98093
41	1.01705	.98324
53	1.01316	.98701
72	1.009674	.990419

TUNING AIDS

Here is a rundown of devices that are used to aid the ear in tuning pitches accurately.

Quartz Tuners

These little electronic tuners are handy and practical. Some models are dedicated for use with particular instruments, but it is the general-purpose ones that most builders will be interested in. The better ones function in either of two modes: 1) Through an internal speaker, they produce specified pitches over a range of several octaves to serve as an audible reference pitch for tuning purposes. 2) They provide a visual readout indicating the pitch of a sound "heard" by the tuner. The sound is input to the tuner through a built-in internal mic, or from an external mic, pickup or electronic source. Quartz tuners are generally designed with 12-tone equal temperament in mind. They operate flexibly enough that you can use them for other tunings as well, but with less convenience.

Not surprisingly, the readout function doesn't work well for noisy and non-harmonic sounds, giving ambiguous readings or no reading at all. Here is a trick that may help in some cases: Study the physical body of your sound source as it vibrates, searching for some region that, taken alone, produces something closer to a pure tone. The ideal spot would be an antinode for the mode that you wish to bring out. Place your microphone as close as physically possible to that spot when you take your reading.

Stroboscopic Tuners

Strobe tuners work by means of an optical effect using a light flashing on a patterned rotating disk at the frequency of the input sound. Prior to the advent of quartz tuners, strobe tuners were the preferred electronic tuning tool. Some people still prefer strobe tuners, because they don't simply give you a pre-packaged result: they are a subtler and more manipulable tool, with better capabilities for interpretation and analysis of the sound and its overtone content.

Oscilloscopes

With an oscilloscope you can observe the composite wave form from two simultaneous pitches on a screen. With practice you can learn to recognize the waveforms for desired intervals, and tune the input pitches for those intervals. The process requires know-how, and it works best for simple just intervals and sustaining, harmonic, noise-free tone qualities. As with strobe tuners, oscilloscopes allow greater opportunities for interpretation and analysis than do quartz tuners.

Tuning Forks

Tuning forks provide a reference tone of known pitch and frequency. A-440 forks are common. Rare now, but still available through piano tuners' supply houses, are complete sets of 12 equal-tempered semitones.

Pitch Pipes

Pitch pipes are usually made with free reeds, like those in harmonicas, tuned to certain pitches to provide reference pitches. Their actual sounding pitch varies with wind pressure, moisture on the reed and so forth, and they are not dependable.

Monochords

"Monochord" is the name given to a simple one- or two-string instrument designed not primarily for music performance, but rather as a tool for studying intervalic relationships. You can use a monochord to sound any interval of your choosing, which is valuable in realizing unorthodox tunings. Sidebar 4-3 contains notes on monochord making.

scale, based upon whatever starting pitch you choose. You need only go through the series of multiplications by the factor for the temperament in question, just as we did for 12-equal above.

Mechanics of the Tuning Process

We have been discussing the abstract building blocks for scales. How to apply this information to the construction of particular instruments varies from one instrument type to another. For some instruments, there are calculable correlations between the dimensions of the sounding elements and the resulting frequencies, so that builders can do their advance planning and computation, build the instruments accordingly, and get the desired scales from them. With others, the correlations are not simple and predictable, and builders must work much more by ear and instinct, trial and adjustment. You will find fuller information on these processes in the chapters devoted to the specific instrument types. But there are some aspects of the process which are common to all instruments, and we will look at them now.

If you are electing to tune by ear and instinct rather than replicating some prescribed scale, then the tuning process is a primarily intuitive one of exciting a sound, listening to the pitch, and adjusting it according to the ear's preferences (tightening a string, shortening a marimba bar, etc.), perhaps intermittently referring for comparison and context to the other pitches on the instrument, until you arrive at the sound that strikes you as right.

If, on the other hand, you are following 12-equal or some other prescribed scale pattern of your choosing, then you need some sort of tuning guide — something to help you hear when the sounding element you are tuning is at the desired pitch. There are several approaches to this. One is to use the rather subtle listening techniques developed by piano tuners. These involve specialized applications and we won't review them here. Another is to buy or make special tuning equipment. In recent years electronic tuners have come on the market that are accurate, easy to use and moderately priced. These and several other tuning aids are discussed in Sidebar 3-2. A third approach — a common and reasonable one for anyone new to the game and lacking special equipment — is to tune by comparing pitches from the new instrument to those of some existing instrument whose tuning you have decided to duplicate. If you have decided to stay with twelve-tone equal temperament for your instrument, you can use a well-tuned piano, guitar, portable electronic keyboard, or whatever else you can get your hands on. Play the intended pitch on the reference instrument, then compare the pitch of the instrument being tuned. Make adjustments to the latter as necessary until you are satisfied that the two pitches match; then go on to the next pitch.

If you are tuning by matching pitches, the phenomenon called "beating," described in the previous chapter, can help. Recall that two close but not identical pitches sounding together produce a continuous wavering of their combined amplitude. The closer in pitch they are, the slower the wavering, until it stops entirely when they match. To take advantage of this, sound the two tones together, and listen for the slowing of the beating as you bring the note-to-be-

tuned closer to the reference pitch. When you hear the beating stop, you know you have a match. The beating effect is easiest to hear with instruments of simple, sustaining tone quality (not too many noise components or inharmonic partials), and when the tone qualities of the two instruments are similar. Noisy, inharmonic instruments can be torture to tune even for someone with an experienced ear.

Tuning by comparing to a reference pitch is always a good listening exercise. Some people have an inborn knack for hearing whether the note-to-be-tuned is above, below or right on the reference pitch. Others find it difficult. Everyone improves with practice.

PITCH LAYOUTS, GESTURE, & ERGONOMICS

Think for a moment about pianos and their keyboards. The standard piano produces 88 different pitches, comprising something over seven octaves' worth of 12-tone equal temperament. The player accesses those 88 notes by means of the keyboard, which has the keys laid out in the familiar two-tiered linear arrangement of white and black keys. This particular keyboard configuration came into being through an evolutionary process roughly spanning the middle ages. It has since come to serve as the norm for keyboard instruments in European music and through much of the rest of the world where European-derived musical styles have had an impact. But it is certainly not the only possible pitch layout. Any number of other arrangements for the keys are possible, and, indeed, many have been used in different times and places.

Here is an example. It doesn't involve piano keyboards, but the underlying issues are the same. In the south and central African nations where the practice of kalimba making and playing are highly developed, the most common arrangement for the layout of kalimba tines does not follow a keyboard-like, linear, scale-wise logic. Instead it has the lowest-pitched prong protruding at the center of a row of

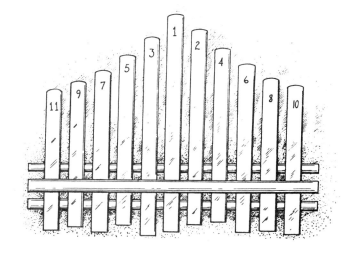

FIGURE 3-1: Non-linear pitch layout on a kalimba. The numbers indicate the sequence of pitches in ascending order. (This illustrates a simplified version for conceptual purposes; traditional instruments in southern Africa usually follow a slightly different arrangement.)

MAKING A MONOCHORD

Monochord is the name given to a simple zither designed not primarily for musical performance, but for studying intervalic relationships. Typically there are two identical strings, tuned to the same pitch. The two can be stopped anywhere along their length by small movable bridges, altering the effective string lengths. Beneath the strings is a calibrated ruler, to aid in locating the bridges for specific proportions of the string lengths. Working from the inverse relationship between string length and frequency (*f* is proportional to 1/L), you can determine the frequency ratio between the two strings: it's simply the inversion of the string length ratio. So you can use the monochord to hear any ratio you want, be it a familiar one or something unusual. Since the time of Pythagoras, monochords have been used for teaching, for research, and as an aid in creating musical scales. Here are a few suggestions for anyone wishing to design and build a monochord.

While accurate intonation is essential for a monochord, great volume and exquisite tone quality are not. With that in mind, you can design your monochord as an easily-constructed rectangular zither. For convenience, give it an active string length (bridge to bridge) of one meter. This will allow you to use a meter stick, glued to the surface of the soundboard under the strings, as the string length calibrator, inviting easy ratio calculations based on 100 centimeters. Reasonable overall dimensions for the box might typically be 6" wide, 2" high, and 44" long (this allows for the 1-meter string length). The front and back can be 1/8" plywood. The sides should be moderately thick (about 3/8"), to allow for tacking and gluing of the front and back. The two end pieces should be hardwood at least an inch thick to hold the tuning pins securely. For simplest-possible arrangements for tuning pins and end bridges, look back to the harmonics guitar plan in Sidebar 3-1. (For more on string instrument and string instrument bodies, look ahead to Chapters 8 and 9.)

A common problem with monochords is that the movable bridges lift the strings slightly from their natural positions. This deflection causes changes in tension which throw off the simple relationship between frequency and string length. To avoid this, some monochords use pinching bridges. They are designed to grab the string from above and below, stopping it securely yet without deflection. In one such instrument that I made, I used clothespins (the spring-loaded type) as the pinchers. To anchor the clothespin-bridges to the soundboard, I mounted them on very strong magnets, and attached steel strips to the soundboard alongside the meter stick beneath the strings. The magnetic clothespin-bridges can be placed anywhere along the steel strips; they hold securely yet can be moved easily. For such a design to work well, the clothespins must have strong springs, the magnets must be very strong, and the height of the clothespin-bridge must be just right.

For strings you will need about 10 feet of music wire in the general range of .014" or .018" diameter (designated as sizes #5 to #7). Adjust the open string pitches by means of the tuning pin, tuning both to the same pitch at moderately high tension. The specific pitch is your choice. Frequently you will choose to leave one string open (bridgeless) as a fundamental for comparison, as you move the bridge on the other string to different locations for various intervals.

To change pitches more rapidly without having to move bridges, you can use a steel slide, Hawaiian guitar style. This will be less accurate intonationally, however, as the pressure of the slide will inevitably deflect the string downward a bit.

The earliest monochords had one string (thus the name). Later, two became the norm. But you can include more. Having many strings allows you to hear all the tones of a chord or scale without having constantly to be resetting bridges. Such an instrument is called a Harmonic Canon.

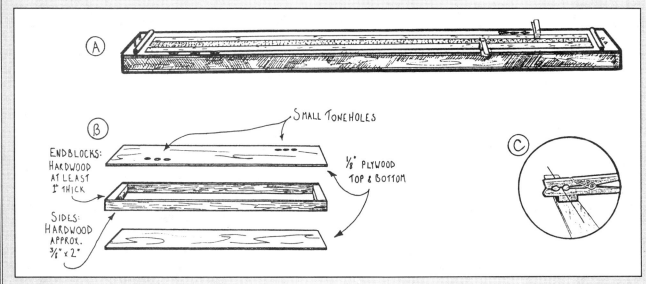

A. A simple monochord, with the magnetic pinching bridges shown stopping the strings. The two strings are anchored with zither pins at one end, and wood screws at the other. Bridges at each end are made from sections of metal rod, glued or held in place by nails. B. The construction of the box. C. The magnetic-clothespin pinching bridge. For the clothespin to close firmly over the string at the indicated location, it may be necessary to remove a little wood from the usual closure point near the tip.

CONTEMPORARY AND HISTORICAL KEYBOARDS IN EUROPEAN MUSIC CULTURE

The layout of the standard keyboard — the familiar pattern of five raised black keys and seven white keys to the octave — was never invented or planned in any clear sense. It came into being in an evolutionary process spanning several centuries. The earliest keyboard-like mechanisms were sets of broad, flat sliders protruding from the fronts of the organs of Greek antiquity. By the Middle Ages the norm was a set of seven sliders or levers comprising the diatonic octave, lying in a single even row. Beginning around the thirteenth century, progressively more levers appeared to accommodate chromatic tones, with the additional keys distinguished from the original diatonics by their placement in a second row above. By the fifteenth century, an arrangement much like the present one had become widespread, with the seven below and five above — but still, at that time, in the form of rows of levers. In the course of the fifteenth and sixteenth centuries this evolved into the bed of ivory and ebony that we see today.

Over the years, meanwhile, other layouts were proposed. Most were designed to accommodate the additional pitches required for modulation in just intonation. Like the design shown in Figure A, they often involved subdividing some of the white keys front to back to get two in the space of one, and finding ways to incorporate additional raised black keys at different levels.

In the present era, performers, builders and theoreticians have continued to propose alternative keyboard designs. Some, like the 19-tone arrangement shown in Figure B, still adhere closely to the standard arrangement. In fact, this 19-tone layout has been promoted for the fact that it fits seamlessly into the existing system, making it a logical next step. Other contemporary systems depart more radically from the existing standard. One important idea has been to use two-dimensional arrays. This brings more keys into a smaller area, allowing the player to reach more tones with less stretch. It also allows a more sophisticated approach to pitch relationships, since one can work with vertical and diagonal spatial parameters as well as horizontal. A pioneer in this area was R.H.M. Bosanquet (1841-1912), whose Enharmonic Harmonium sported a dense geometric forest of protruding levers. Among those working with two-dimensional pitch arrays today is Erv Wilson, whose designs have been incorporated in instruments by several different builders. One of his designs appears in Figure C.

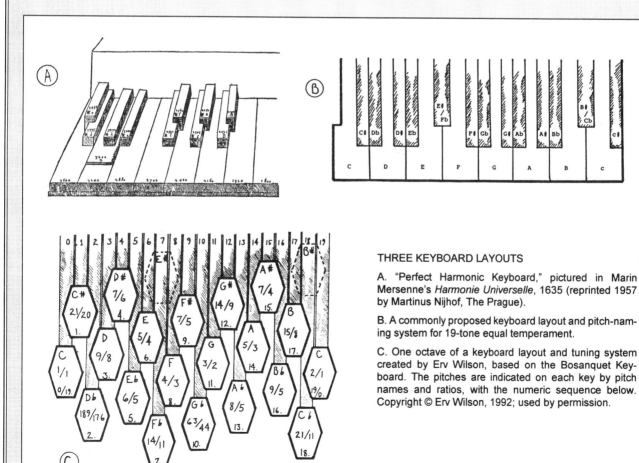

THREE KEYBOARD LAYOUTS

A. "Perfect Harmonic Keyboard," pictured in Marin Mersenne's *Harmonie Universelle*, 1635 (reprinted 1957 by Martinus Nijhof, The Prague).

B. A commonly proposed keyboard layout and pitch-naming system for 19-tone equal temperament.

C. One octave of a keyboard layout and tuning system created by Erv Wilson, based on the Bosanquet Keyboard. The pitches are indicated on each key by pitch names and ratios, with the numeric sequence below. Copyright © Erv Wilson, 1992; used by permission.

keys, with the progressively higher notes proceeding left-right-left-right to either side from there. (This description is somewhat simplified, and it ignores local variations, but it will do to illustrate the idea.) This arrangement puts the highest-pitched prongs at the two extremes. Adjacent keys are a third apart.

This layout is well suited for its intended musical context. In the usual playing position, the prongs are plucked primarily with the two thumbs, as the hands support the body of the instrument. With the scale ascending left-right-left-right, rapid scalewise passages are easily executed by alternating thumbs. Harmonies in thirds, which play a prominent role in the musical style, are easily realized by simultaneously striking adjacent prongs with the thumb.

A similar arrangement is used on one of the prominent West African instruments, the kora (a many-stringed harp-lute). It works beautifully in this case as well, for many of the same reasons. (And if you think kalimba music is heavenly, then you should listen to some good kora music.)

All this is to introduce the idea that, in designing an instrument, you may find yourself with a choice as to how the instrument's pitches are to be laid out spatially. We have seen that the question is a relevant one for keyboards, kalimbas and koras; it is also important for marimbas, tube drums, zithers, and a host of other instruments with arrays of independent sounding elements. For some other instrument types the choice is not quite so free, being at least partially dictated by physical constraints. In wind instruments, for example, the positioning of the pitches under the player's hands is usually a matter of tonehole placement, an area in which the maker has only limited options. Yet even within these constraints, a carefully planned fingering arrangement can easily make the difference between a friendly, playable wind instrument and an awkward, uncooperative one.

The most important issue here is ergonomics — the degree to which the instrument accords itself to the human body and its natural patterns of movement. And there are other considerations: Pitch configurations often serve not only as a physical interface, but also as a conceptual tool for the player. Keyboard players learn (consciously or unconsciously) to conceive musical relationships in terms of positioning on the keyboard. Players of other instruments — kalimba, or guitar, for instance — do the same, even when the physical layout of the pitches does not match the keyboard's simple grid. Several contemporary theorists have created alternative pitch arrays designed to reflect their own underlying musical logic. Many of these designs are primarily of theoretical or analytical value, but some have been built into playable instruments. Sidebar 3-4 has examples.

Beyond affecting the ease of playing, the configuration of the pitch elements establishes what kinds of musical patterns will be characteristic to the instrument. Piano music sounds "pianistic," and guitar music is "guitaristic," in large part because of the nature of the physical interface between the player and the instrument. This may seem like an innocent enough observation, but he nature of the playing movements is a key to the character of the instrument as a thing of human musical expression. It is one of the essential elements in musical instrument design.

These ideas can be incorporated into the word *gesture*. Gesture has its physical aspect in the movements one makes to play an instrument. It has a musical aspect in the characteristic turns of phrase, the sorts of note clusters, or the rhythmic patterns that seem to fit the instrument most naturally. The two aspects are very much intertwined.

Here is an explicit case of the role of gesture in music. In 1946, the American composer, theorist and instrument designer Harry Partch built an instrument he called the Diamond Marimba. It was a resonated marimba with the bars laid out in a diamond-shaped configuration, following a theoretical grid Partch had developed to represent important pitch relationships. The layout of the bars naturally gave rise to certain sorts of characteristic playing motions and resulting musical patterns. Writing about this some years later, Partch said, "The inevitable downward arpeggios, or sweeps, of the Diamond Marimba caused me to wish for a twin instrument, one in which the arpeggios would inevitably and automatically sound upward" (*Genesis of a Music*, 1974). Almost twenty years after creating the Diamond Marimba, to realize his wish, Partch built his Quadrangularis Reversum, with the pitch relationships of the bars inverted.

Finally, there are considerations of kinesthetics and aesthetic effect. Important questions for any instrument are, is the playing position a natural one, a comfortable one, one that lends itself to musical enjoyment and expression? Are the movements involved attractive? Is the visual effect funny, beautiful, dramatic, graceful, odd, boring? Do the stance and movements convey a sense of musicality or a sense of awkwardness?

In recent years our musical culture has suffered an impoverishment in the area of gesture, due to the increasing use of computers and synthesizers. Whatever their other merits, purely electronic instruments have tended (with some notable exceptions) to be gesturally bland. By contrast, many of the new and unusual acoustic instruments described throughout this book are unique in their gestural qualities, both physical and musical. As you design and build instruments, I encourage you to give some thought to these matters. The player's movements in performance are very much a part of the color and character of any instrument. Playing techniques that may not be facile or that don't lend themselves to the performance of complex music may still produce a rich result when you consider what it feels like to play the instrument, what it is like to see the instrument played, the characteristic musical patterns that the instrument invites, or the directness of contact between the player and the sounding elements.

Chapter Four

IDIOPHONES

And now we move into the investigation of specific instrument types. In order to get a handle on the wide world of possible instruments, we will divide them into broad categories, and study them one at a time. The question of how to categorize musical instruments is a matter of endless debate among people who study such things. For the purposes of this book, we will follow the broad outlines of what has become the most widely used grouping among western scholars, the Sachs-Hornbostel system (described in Sidebar 4-1).

The Sachs-Hornbostel system begins by dividing musical instruments into four fundamental categories, based upon the nature of the primary vibrating body. The largest and most diverse of these groupings is the *idiophones*. Idiophones are defined as sound sources in which the initial vibrating material is solid, and vibrates by virtue of its own rigidity. The vibrating body is not held taut like a string or a drumhead, nor does the initial vibration take place in the air itself as with wind instruments; rather, an idiophone is just a solid chunk of rigid material that makes a noise when something excites it into vibration. The chair that I am sitting in is an idiophone — strike it, scrape it, squeak it, and it produces an idiophonic sound. So are bells, gongs, triangles, kalimbas, xylophones and innumerable other sound makers.

Many idiophones are played with beaters of some sort, and a few use bows. Beaters and bows are discussed in Chapter 5, "Beaters, Scrapers and Friction Makers," and you can think of that chapter as an important adjunct to this one.

There are many different sorts of idiophones. To bring order to the unruly throng, we will take as our central theme the nature of the vibration pattern within the initial vibrating element in each instrument. Freely vibrating bars such as marimba bars, for instance, have characteristic patterns of vibration. The same patterns appear in freely vibrating rods and tubes, as well as hanging chimes, and so we will group all of these together, and discuss them first. Music box combs, kalimbas, and other instruments with vibrating tongues form another group, along with their various relatives, and we will consider them second. Bells, cymbals and musical glasses form a third group. The list goes on through a few more basic types. Toward the end of the chapter this approach will break down a bit, as we come to an ad hoc, catch-all grouping of instruments whose vibrating patterns are too irregular or idiosyncratic to fit neatly into the main categories. We begin now with the vibrating bars.

FREE-BAR INSTRUMENTS:
MARIMBAS, CHIMES, AND THEIR RELATIVES

Let us start with an image of a rudimentary free-bar instrument. This will serve as a sort of prototype, allowing us to identify salient features so that we can study those features more closely later. Imagine a xylophone consisting of a series of wooden bars, each one a little shorter than the last. The bars are supported, with their ends slightly over-hanging, on two horizontal cross pieces set on legs. The bars don't rest directly on the cross pieces, but on strips of foam rubber padding running along the top of each cross piece. Dabs of hot glue adhesive keep the bars in their places on the foam pads. You play the instrument by striking the bars with percussion mallets.

OK, what are the essential elements here?

1) First, the bars. For this prototype I suggested wooden bars; in fact, almost any reasonably rigid material in an elongated form could have served. Metal bar instruments, for instance, appear in many parts of the world. There are similar instruments which use round metal rods or hollow metal tubing instead of flat bars, since such forms follow the same vibrational patterns as flat bars. Other possibilities include glass, stone, plastics, bamboo, and ceramics, to name a just few. See Appendix 2 for more on specific materials.

2) The second essential element in the prototype free-bar instrument is a means for getting different pitches from the different bars, allowing for a range of available notes. The prototype achieves this by having the bars cut to different lengths. This is the simplest and probably the most common approach in free-bar instruments. Another alternative would be to vary the bars' thickness, but this requires a bit more sophistication — we will discuss that shortly.

MUSICAL INSTRUMENT CATEGORIZATION SYSTEMS

Grade school children have long been taught that there are four categories of musical instruments: woodwinds, brass, strings and percussion. This categorization evolved in conjunction with western orchestral music, and it works well as a descriptive tool in that context. But as a systematic taxonomy, it is incoherent. The categories are illogically named and defined, and the criteria for classification are inconsistent, with the result that some instruments seem to go in multiple categories while others fit nowhere.

More logical instrument classification systems do exist. Devising taxonomies has been a favorite intellectual exercise among organologists over the years, and there are traditional musical instrument categorizations in non-western cultures as well. The most widely used approach among scholars in the west has been the Sachs-Hornbostel system, created in 1914 by German organologists Curt Sachs and Erich M. von Hornbostel, based on ideas originally proposed by Victor Mahillon in the 1880s. Their system, in its rough outlines at least, is used in the organization of this book.

The Sachs-Hornbostel system begins with four broad classifications. Each of these is divided into several subclassifications which in turn are divided into still finer groupings. Increasingly specific instrument types are delineated as one proceeds through as many as nine strata of classification. The first criterion of categorization for all instruments is the nature of the initial vibrating body. Sachs and Hornbostel recognized four basic types:

1) Idiophones: The initial vibrator is solid material which vibrates by virtue of its own rigidity (it is not stretched).

2) Membranophones: The initial vibrator is a stretched membrane, such as a drum skin.

3) Chordophones: The initial vibrator is a stretched string.

4) Aerophones: The initial vibrator is air, either enclosed in a chamber or free.

Since Sachs and Hornbostel's time a fifth group has been added by general consensus:

5) Electrophones: The initial vibration is that of electrons in a wire.

The Sachs-Hornbostel system has most definitely proven itself useful for organizing and conceptualizing the world of existing musical instruments. But it is not the final word. There are plenty of instrument types that stand in defiance of the classifications, either because they contain elements that would place them in more than one category, or because they simply don't fit the existing descriptions. As an example, how would you classify an instrument sounded by droplets falling into a pool of water (one of the most musical sounds I can imagine)? Perhaps we need another primary grouping:

6) Hydrophones: The initial vibrator is liquid.

3) There is a system for supporting the bars. The mounting must hold the bars in a way that inhibits their vibration as little as possible. In the prototype we minimized unwanted damping, as well as rattling, by seating the bars on a compliant foam pad. The spacing of the supporting cross pieces is equally important: Ideally, the two support pieces are just far enough apart that the bars rest on their nodes (points of minimal vibration) for their first mode of vibration, rather than on their vibrationally active parts. This minimizes damping for that first mode. As we will see as we go along, there are many other forms of mounting that achieve the same effect, but the essentials in each case remain: utilization of a compliant means of support rather than a rigid one, and placement of that support at nodal points for the desired modes of vibration.

4) Finally, there is a means for exciting the bars into vibration. The prototype uses percussion, which is the most common approach for free-bar instruments. On the other hand, some free-bar instruments have been designed to be played by friction, using violin-like bows. Free-bar instruments of metal can also be played by scraping, if the surface of the bar or rod is somehow roughened or serrated. The scraped sound is unusual, and rather pretty.

Over the next several pages we will look more closely at these essential components of free-bar instruments. Let us start now with the primary one, the bars. Figure 4-1 shows the first several modes of vibration for a free bar. The accompanying chart contains information about the frequency relationships between the modes, and locations of their nodes. In reading this diagram and chart, keep in

CLAVES

Latin American clavès are free bar instruments too. A set of clavès consists of two cylindrical sticks of heavy hardwood (often rosewood), typically a little over an inch in diameter and eight inches long. The player holds one clavè loosely cupped in one hand, in a way that allows support roughly at the nodes for the first mode. The other clavè is used to strike the first, for a very clear, short, high-pitched tone. Clavès are often made in pairs of unmatched pitch, for a choice of sounding pitch.

If you can get a 1" dowel of any heavy hardwood, you have practically got clavès ready made. Just cut the two lengths. Even common, softer woods produce a recognizable clavè sound, but lacking the brilliant ring that percussionists seek.

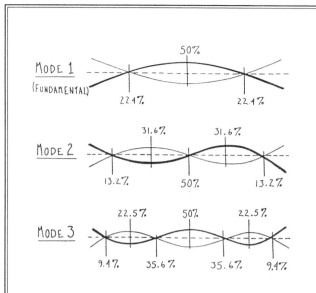

MODE 1 (FUNDAMENTAL)
50%
22.4%   22.4%

MODE 2
31.6%   31.6%
13.2%   50%   13.2%

MODE 3
22.5%   50%   22.5%
9.4%   35.6%   35.6%   9.4%

FIGURE 4-1: The first three modes of vibration for a bar, rod or tube of uniform shape, free at both ends. Locations for the antinodes are given by the numbers above the bar; locations for the nodes are given below. The percentages indicate distances from the nearest end relative to total bar length. The following chart gives frequencies and intervals relative to the fundamental frequency, identified as f1.

MODE NUMBER	FREQ. RELATIVE TO MODE 1	PITCH RELATIVE TO MODE 1
Mode 1	f_1	(Unison)
Mode 2	$2.756\ f_1$	1 8ve + a very sharp 4th
Mode 3	$5.404\ f_1$	2 8ves + a sharp 4th

mind certain facts about the shape of the vibrating bar:

1) These forms and figures hold true only for a bar, rod or tube that is uniform over its length in shape, rigidity and mass. If the bar is thicker in some places than others, or if other irregularities are present, the nodes will be in different locations and the frequency relationships between modes will be altered.

2) The patterns shown in the diagram and chart apply to rods and tubes as well as flat bars. But there are some differences between flat bars and cylindrical forms. When tubes or rods are truly cylindrical, then the direction of the strike makes no difference; the vibrating patterns are the same whether the impulse comes from the top or side. With flat bars, the player normally strikes the broad face. A sideways blow to the narrow edge would bring out a different set of vibrational modes and resulting pitches.

3) Flat bars that are very wide relative to length can manifest additional sets of modes associated with lateral vibration or twisting motions. With especially broad bars, these modes may prove distracting by falling in the same general frequency range as the intended fundamental, sometimes actually sounding louder.

Range

One of the first questions you will need to address if you intend to make a free-bar instrument is that of range. You'll want the instrument to have sufficient volume, attractive and reasonably uniform timbre, and unambiguous pitch over its playing range. There is no better way to check out potential range than direct experimentation with the bar material and sizes you intend to use. Make a number of sample bars over a large spread of lengths (and thicknesses, if that is an option) and note the compass over which they work well.

Several factors immediately come into play which pose limitations at the two extremes. In the upper end of the range, you will find a lessening of volume and a general impoverishment of tone beyond a certain point as you make the bars shorter and higher pitched. At the lower end, you will find that as the bars become quite long relative to width they tend to manifest upper modes of vibration more strongly than the

Sidebar 4-3

MAKE A DRIFTWOOD MARIMBA

This is something everyone should do at the beach, like building sand castles. Find two straightish pieces of wood two to four feet long. Lay them alongside one another, a little out of parallel, so that bars can be laid across them. Find two sticks to use as beaters. Anything reasonably solid that seems comfortable in size will do; later you can look for other more carefully chosen beaters to bring out the best in the completed marimba. Begin auditioning driftwood pieces to serve as sounding bars. An easy way to test a piece of wood for its musical properties is to toss it in the air and strike it near the center in free fall. Select those pieces that work well in terms of clarity of tone, volume, and pitch relationships. When you have plenty of bars, assemble the instrument by laying the selected bars across the two cross supports. In their non-parallel arrangement, you can place a set of bars on them in graduated order from longest to shortest, in such a way that each bar rests roughly at the nodes, with between a fifth and a quarter of each bar overhanging at each end.

Then play. Since the sounding bars are not fastened down, they will dance around, and get out of position after a while. You can stop then, put them back, and play some more. Any driftwood marimba you make will have its own musical personality, based on the pitch relationships and tone qualities of the selected bars.

fundamental. With especially long, thin bars, the upper partials come to dominate the tone. Then the ear no longer focuses on the fundamental, but tries to arrive at a sense of pitch based on one or another of the upper partials.

If the musically usable range is acceptable for your purposes, then no more need be said. But if you want more range than what your chosen bar material initially yields, you still have options. At the upper end, you can try a narrower bar. This reduces cross-vibration problems, allowing for clearer pitch. It also diminishes volume. At the lower end, there are several ways to enhance the fundamental and de-emphasize the upper partials. One is to use soft, heavy beaters. Another is to use thicker, wider bars, bringing the length/width ratio back in line for the longer bars. Another is to bring out the fundamental in the low bars by using some sort of an added resonator. We will discuss that later in this chapter.

You may occasionally want to build an instrument's sound around some tone other than the fundamental, bringing out the 2nd or 3rd mode as the predominant pitch. The workable range in that case will be the range of lengths over which the desired overtone predominates, or can be made predominate with help from you.

Tuning the Bar

Note that the chart in Figure 4-1 provides information on pitch relationships between modes, but does not give information on how to predict absolute pitch. There are formulas for predicting actual sounding pitches for free bars, but they involve marshaling complete information on the density of material in the bar as well as its inherent rigidity. In practice it is simpler and more accurate to cut a sample bar and determine pitch by listening. In many cases, once you have the pitch for a sample bar, you can then predict the pitch of other bars mathematically.

Here is how to predict the pitch of other bars based upon the pitch of a sample bar. This approach will work as long as all the bars are the same thickness, and are regular in cross sectional shape over their length. (If you use bars of different thicknesses, you will either need to cut a new sample for each thickness, or get into more demanding mathematics). The key to the process is this rule: sounding frequency (in the ideal) is inversely proportional to the square of the length. As an example, this means that if you have two otherwise identical bars, one of which is half as long as the other, the short one will vibrate at four times the long one's frequency, producing a tone two octaves higher. You can derive from this a set of relations that are summarized in the following chart. Generalized formulas (allowing you to come up with figures for intervals not given here) are given in Sidebar 4-4.

To produce a new bar with this pitch relative relative to a sample bar...	...the new bar must be this long relative to the sample bar:
1 octave higher	0.7071
1 octave lower	1.4144
1 Semitone higher	0.9715
1 Semitone lower	1.0293

These relationships hold regardless of which mode of vibration you are bringing out.

For truly uniform bars, such as high quality manufactured metal bars or tubes, the numbers generally come quite close to the mark in actual practice. You can calculate how long the bar should be to produce a certain pitch, cut the bar precisely to that length, and often get a result requiring no further tuning. The mathematical predictions are slightly less accurate for lower quality manufactured bars and tubes, and much less dependable for bars of wood or other natural materials. Still, the calculations will at least enable you to make an educated guess, cut the bar to that length, and then fine tune as necessary (we will discuss methods for fine tuning shortly).

With this background, let us describe a sensible procedure for making a set of bars for a tuned bar instrument in (let us say) 12-tone equal temperament. Cut a sample bar to a length that you guess will give you something close to your intended lowest pitch. If the bar turns out to be too short and the resulting pitch too high, put that bar aside to use later, and try again. If the bar is long and low, gradually shorten it, repeatedly testing for pitch as you go, until it reaches the desired pitch. You have now established a basis from which to work. Calculate the expected length for the next bar, a semitone higher, by multiplying the length of that first bar by the "semitone-up" factor of .9715 (from the chart above). Cut the new bar to that length; fine tune if necessary. Then use the corrected length for the next calculation. You can proceed through the entire intended range this way, with a

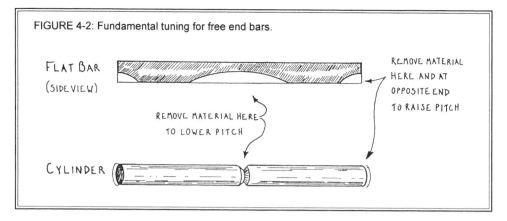

FIGURE 4-2: Fundamental tuning for free end bars.

FLAT BAR (SIDE VIEW)

REMOVE MATERIAL HERE TO LOWER PITCH

REMOVE MATERIAL HERE AND AT OPPOSITE END TO RAISE PITCH

CYLINDER

minimum of wasted effort and material.

Several times now I have spoken about fine tuning bars that were not cut exactly to pitch in the first place. Here are procedures for doing so. The reasoning will be apparent if you followed the discussion of the effects of mass and rigidity in Chapter 2, especially Figure 2-1. I will assume that you are tuning for the bar's first mode of vibration (as is usually the case). If the sounding pitch is slightly below the desired pitch, you need to reduce the mass of the parts of the bar that move the most. You must do this in a way that does not reduce the rigidity of the parts of the bar that flex, which would have a contrary effect. If you glance back at Figure 4-1, you can see that there are three regions of generous movement in the bar's first mode — the center and the two ends. Removing mass by shaving off material at the center would have the unwanted effect of simultaneously reducing rigidity, so instead remove some material at the ends of the bar. You can do this by simply shortening the bar. Alternatively, you can shave some material from the underside of the ends of the bar. This reduces the mass there without altering the length, which might be preferable for visual reasons.

If the bar's sounding pitch is too high, you need to reduce the bar's rigidity in the areas that flex. Looking again at Figure 4-1, you can see that the main region of flex in the first mode is the center. Removing material here to reduce the rigidity would at the same time amount to removing mass in one of the areas of generous movement, tending to raise the frequency. That's OK: the frequency-lowering effect of reducing rigidity outweighs the opposite effect of the lost mass. So you remove material from the underside of the bar at the center to lower the first mode sounding pitch.

I have suggested removing the material from underneath the bar. The reasons for this are primarily aesthetic — it is more attractive to conceal the irregular surface where the dirty work was done. But if the sounding elements are not flat bars, but cylinders, it is preferable to remove material symmetrically all around. The advantage here is that the cylinder then retains its characteristic ability to produce the same pitch regardless of the direction of the impulse.

The tuning procedures described here work well for wooden bars. They are OK for metal rods if you happen to have a grinder. For metal tubes they are not so great. You cannot very effectively reduce the rigidity of a tube by grinding at the center, short of grinding most of the way through the metal. To lower the pitch of a too-high tubular bar, you can drill several small holes symmetrically around

the periphery at the midpoint to weaken it there, or perhaps you can find a way to add weight to the bar ends. Or, perhaps best, dispense with the idea of lowering the pitch once the tube is cut. Tubes cut too long can be brought up to pitch by shortening; tubes cut too short can be put aside for use as higher notes.

It is traditional with wooden marimbas to deliberately cut the bars short, and lower them to pitch by cutting away a great deal of material under the center of the bar. Removing 1/2 to 4/5 of the total bar thickness at the center is typical. This produces what is usually thought of as a mellower tone by increasing sustain and altering the pitch relationships of the fundamental and the overtones. Normally the underside is shaved out in a smooth, wide curve. You can have a similar pitch-lowering effect, although with less elegance, simply by cutting a single saw kerf under the center.

Overtone Tuning

Look once again at the chart in Figure 4-1. Notice that the overtone pattern in uniform bars is decidedly inharmonic, with the second partial appearing at a somewhat sharp eleventh above the fundamental, the third at two octaves and a slightly sharp fourth. That second partial can be particularly distracting, especially in the lower notes. As a builder, you can respond to this inharmonic situation in one of three ways. 1) Accept the bars' natural inharmonicity as part of the sound — after all, it does have a certain curious appeal. 2) De-emphasize the inharmonicity by striving to highlight the fundamental (or other desired mode) and suppress other modes as much as possible. You can do this by using a fairly soft beater to strike at the center of the bar, choosing the right length-to-thickness ratio for a bar of the intended pitch, and using the right sort of resonator (more on that later). 3) Alter the overtone relationships to bring them into some preferred tuning. This you can do by re-shaping the bar. Let us look at this last idea more closely.

Overtone tuning is often done for wooden bars, and it works for solid metal bars as well. It is not normally done for tubes, glass and ceramics. (There are ways it can be done for those materials, but they are rather specialized.) For low-pitched bars — those whose tuned pitch is to be below about C_4, perhaps — the fundamental plus the next two partials are prominent enough to be worth tuning. For a couple of octaves above that, you can tune for the fundamental plus one more partial (the third partial in this region is less significant in the tone, and extremely difficult to tune anyway). For high-pitched bars there is no need to tune beyond the fundamental.

When you retune the overtones, you are creating a new and presumably preferable overtone mix for the bar. What should that new mix be? Different schools of thought have arisen. Some xylophone makers have included octave-displaced fifths and even thirds in the mix (an approach most suitable for mid- to upper-range bars). I favor an all-octaves

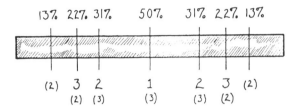

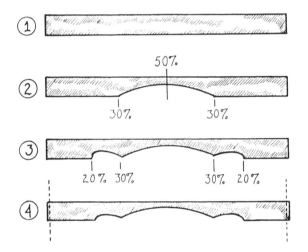

FIGURE 4-3: Locations of the antinodes for the first three modes of vibration in a free bar, showing where to thin the bar to lower the pitch for each mode. Numbers above the bar give the locations as a percentage of total bar length; numbers below the bar indicate which modes will be lowered by thinning at each location. Numbers in parentheses indicate modes which will be lowered to a lesser degree at each location. If you scallop deeply at the center, the other antinode locations will migrate slightly toward the ends of the bar. The locations given here will need adjustment in that case.

FIGURE 4-4: Marimba bar overtone tuning (one approach). This tuning yields second and third modes at 2 and 3 octaves above the fundamental. In order to hear the pitches of the different modes as you go through this process, strike near an antinode for the mode you wish to hear. Use harder, smaller mallets for higher modes and a softer, heavier mallet for the fundamental.

1) Start with a bar cut to a length such that its unscalloped fundamental pitch is about an octave and a 6th above the intended final pitch.

2) Make a long, arching scallop at the center to a depth of 2/3 of the bar thickness, starting at points 30% of the distance in from each end. This should bring the fundamental down something over an octave, still a bit above the desired pitch. The 2nd and 3rd modes will also drop substantially.

3) To further lower the second and third modes, begin scalloping in the regions between 20% and 30% from each end. To bring the 2nd mode down more, deepen the scallop more near the 30% mark; to bring the 3rd mode down more, deepen more near 20%. During this process the fundamental will drop a bit more as well. If need be you can lower the fundamental with no effect on mode 2 and lesser effect on mode 3 by slightly deepening the scallop at the very center.

4) If you're lucky you'll be able to bring all three modes down to the desired pitch together. If you overshoot — that is, if you bring all three into octave-agreement at a pitch below the intended pitch, you can slightly shorten the bar at both ends to bring it up to pitch. The overtone tuning relationships will hold reasonably true if you don't have to come up more than a semitone or perhaps a whole tone. Farther, and you'll end up having to go back and try to correct the overtone pitches again.

tuning, with the second overtone tuned two octaves above the fundamental and the third another octave above that. The resulting tone works very well musically: no extraneous pitch information is added to the mix, and the bars clearly sing the same melody on three pitch levels. It can be almost like having three instruments in one, since you can deliberately select which overtone will sound most prominently by selecting different beaters and striking in different locations.

Overtone tuning proceeds according to these rules: To lower the pitch of any one of the bar's overtones, remove material from the bar at the region of greatest flex for the mode of vibration that causes the overtone. That point of greatest flex will be found at the antinode, midway between the nodes for that mode. Removing material from points progressively farther away from the antinode has less lowering effect on the mode in question, until you get to a node, at which point it has no effect. By removing material at selected locations, you can bring down each overtone in turn by suitable amounts, until you arrive simultaneously at the desired fundamental pitch and overtone pitches.

Sounds simple enough. But in practice it turns out to be a tricky business. The problem is that the effects always overlap. Tuning for one mode always affects other modes at least to some extent. The operation becomes a fine balancing act. Figure 4-3 gives antinode locations for the first three modes, and Figure 4-4 shows the steps of an overtone tuning approach that I have used successfully. Be sure to practice on inexpensive wood (but free of knots), since you can easily destroy a good piece of wood in the process.

Finding the Nodes

For mounting purposes, and often for tuning purposes, you need to be able to find the vibrating bar's nodes — or at least come reasonably close. If the bar is uniform in shape, rigidity and density over its length, you can use the chart in Figure 4-1 to calculate node locations. For bars of non-uniform materials, the calculated results are less dependable. A deep center scallop, for instance, tends to move the nodes toward the ends of the bar somewhat. In such cases, you can turn to empirical means for determining node and antinode locations for each individual bar.

The most direct methods for locating nodes and antinodes involve varying the points of bar support, striking at different locations, listening, and feeling. Rest the bar on two padded supports and try some exploratory tapping. Placing the supports under nodes for the mode you want to hear will let that mode sing out; supports elsewhere will damp it. Striking the bar at an antinode for the desired mode brings it out most prominently; striking at a node scarcely lets it sound.

If the bar is a flat one, you can try this old-favorite technique for node location: lay the bar on a soft, padded surface. Sprinkle a fine, dry, powdery substance on it, like sawdust, salt, or talcum powder. Repeatedly strike the bar in such a way as to excite the desired mode of vibration. The particles will tend to dance off of the most vibrationally active areas, and gradually collect at areas of less motion, which is to say, at the nodes.

Resonators & Radiators

Some free bars can by themselves produce an adequately loud sound. Others require assistance to get their sound out into the world. Radiation is poorest in bars with little surface area, especially at low frequencies. Air chamber resonators below the bars are a good way to provide a needed low frequency boost. The paragraphs that follow provide basic information on air resonators as they relate to free bar instruments. It will also be worth your time as well to read Chapter 6, "Aerophones," for a fuller understanding of air resonances.

An air resonator may be deliberately tuned to resonate the pitch of an individual bar, or it may be untuned. Untuned air resonators for free bar instruments usually take the form of an open trough below a row of bars. The trough will not have well-defined resonance peaks, but it will, ideally, give a broad low-frequency boost, and so add to a general feeling of substance and depth.

Those air resonators that are deliberately tuned to resonate a particular pitch usually take one of two forms. Most common is a tube, closed at the lower end. The natural resonance frequency of the air column enclosed in the tube is tuned to roughly match that of the bar above it. For very low frequencies such as appear on some bass marimbas, the tubes would have to be unmanageably long, so another form is used: Helmholtz resonators. Helmholtz resonators take the form of vessels rather than tubes, and can produce a good air resonance at low frequencies without having to be too large in any one dimension.

Any rigid material can be used for tube resonators, from beautiful bamboo to inexpensive plastics. The ideal diameter is the width of the bar. For the stopped end, it is best to have some sort of movable, air-tight stopper. This allows you to tune the resonator by varying the effective air column length. Tune the resonator to the bar at the time the two are first introduced to each other, and adjust the tuning later if, as sometimes happens, atmospheric conditions or other factors call for retuning. Figure 4-5 shows a stopper design.

The resonator tube, in the most common arrangement, hangs below the bar. You can use any number of hanging or mounting systems, and I will cover some of the options shortly. It is a good idea to make the distance between the tube and the bar adjustable. That distance affects tuning and other resonance characteristics. You will usually find the best resonance with something like a half inch or an inch of space between the two.

Here's how to cut the resonator tube to length and tune the enclosed air column to the bar. First, look at the frequency and wavelength chart in Appendix 2. It gives wavelengths for a range of pitches. If you know the pitch or frequency of the bar in question, you can determine the wavelength for the bar's note. As a first approximation, the length of the resonator tube should be 1/4 that wavelength. But to allow room for tunability, cut the tube a few inches longer. Insert a stopper near one end of the tube. Now, to hear the tube's resonance pitch, blow over the edge of the tube, or bonk the tube edge-on on the floor, or use some other means to excite the air in the tube. Adjust the stopper until the air pitch is close to that of the bar. Now hold the tube under the bar. By repeatedly striking the bar and adjusting the stopper position and the tube/bar spacing, you will be able to arrive at settings for the richest resonance. The resonance is strongest when the tube's air resonance pitch is just below the bar pitch. Hearing the effect of that coupling with a bar and tube of your own making is a great joy.

Because the overtone relationships in the bar and those in the tube follow different patterns, they will be in agreement only at the fundamental; the tube will not resonate the bar's overtones. This means that the presence of the resonator helps to bring the fundamental into prominence in lower bars whose sound otherwise would be dominated by upper partials. (An exception: One or more overtones in overtone-tuned bars may agree with those of the resonator. The resonator will still greatly enhance the fundamental.)

For very low-pitched bars, the required lengths for tube resonators become impractically long. And so we turn to Helmholtz resonators. Helmholtz resonators are vessel-like or globular bodies enclosing a mass of air that is open to the atmosphere through a single relatively narrow opening. They can be tuned either by altering the total volume of the chamber (less volume → higher resonance frequency), or altering the size of the opening (smaller opening → lower resonance frequency). Since altering the overall chamber size usually isn't practical, the common approach to tuning Helmholtz resonators for free-bar instruments is to have some arrangement for altering the opening size.

Some African marimbas use Helmholtz resonators in the form of gourds throughout the mid and lower range. In western instruments, Helmholtz reso-

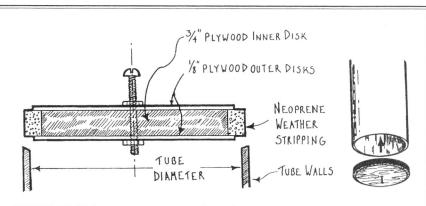

FIGURE 4-5: A tube stopper design — suitable for marimba bar resonator tubes as well as tunable stopped tubes for other purposes. The machine screw through the center provides a handle for adjusting stopper position (it also holds the whole thing together and covers the hole made by the circle cutter if one was used to make the disks). The disk diameter, including the weather strip, should be slightly larger than that of the tube it's intended for.

nators are normally reserved for very low-pitched instruments. In such applications, the resonators cannot be fat all the way around, since a full set of such big round-ish things wouldn't fit under the bars. Instead, people make big rectangular or tear-drop-shaped flat-sided boxes of about the maximum width to fit under each bar. Such boxes, large in two dimensions and smaller in one, still behave "globularly." The low-frequency vibrations that occur inside these things are so intense that they can actually flex the side walls if the walls aren't impractically thick and heavy. Makers have learned to prevent this by placing cross struts within the chamber, in the form of dowels here and there bridging the space between the two walls and preventing their flexing in opposite directions.

With tubular chimes, whether they are suspended vertically like chimes or mounted horizontally like marimba bars, you can try this simple and clever approach to air resonance: let the air within the chime itself serve as a tuned air resonator. The enclosed air column, once properly tuned, will very noticeably improve both volume and tone quality, especially for lower-pitched chimes. There are various ways to tune the air column. The simplest approach was developed and patented by Charles Sawyer. Here's how it works. For reasonably proportioned chimes, the fundamental resonance frequency of the enclosed air column typically falls well below the fundamental of the chime itself. To bring up the air resonance, a stopper can be inserted into the tube, shortening the air column. In fact, since the desired stopped air column length is normally less than half the tube length, stoppers can be inserted from each end, creating two tuned, stopped air columns, as shown in Figure 4-6M. The stoppers must be rigid and smooth-surfaced enough to form a solid end-stop for the enclosed air, yet not so heavy or rigid as to significantly damp the chime in its vibrations. Ideal for the purpose is a slightly oversized plug cut from styrofoam. The tuned air columns won't do their job, however, if the open ends of the chime have the normal right-angle end-cut. There is no mechanism by which air is forced in and out at the opening, and so no resonance is set up. To create such a mechanism, cut the tube ends at an angle. Then, as the ends of the tube vibrate up and down, the overhanging ends catch the air, creating localized pressure fluctuations at the opening. Those pressure variations are enough to set up the resonance. The procedure, then: Cut and tune the tube, with the angle cuts at the ends. Make stoppers of styrofoam, and force one in from each end. Push them in a bit at a time, intermittently blowing over the edges at the ends and listening for air resonance pitch. When the stopper is located so that the air resonance pitch at each end matches the chime fundamental pitch, the tuning is done. Mount the chime by whatever means you may have in mind, strike it at the center, and listen for the enriched tone.

Air resonators are not the only means for adding body to the tone of free bar instruments. Consider the question in its most basic form: there is a vibration going on in this bar; how can you bring it out into the air? A simple answer would be to increase the surface area of the bar, allowing it to push more air itself. Perhaps you could simply attach something very light but with lots of surface area to the bar. Or you could put the bar in direct contact with something of large surface

Sidebar 4-5

BALLOONING FOR MODE SELECTION

Here is a sidelight to the use of balloons as sound radiators on vibrating bars: You can attach the balloon at different points along the bar to bring out different modes of vibration. Attach the balloon at a node for a given mode, and the balloon scarcely amplifies that mode. Attach it at an antinode for a given mode, and that mode sings. If, for instance, you want to emphasize the fundamental and de-emphasize an obtrusive mode 2, attach the balloon at the center of the bar. The center is mode 1's antinode, but a node for mode 2. If you want to bring out the second mode instead, try attaching balloons at a point about 28% of the way along each bar. This will de-emphasize mode 1, since it happens to be near the mode 1 node at 22% (see the chart in Figure 4-1). But it will bring out mode 2, since it's quite near the mode 2 antinode at 31%.

I made an instrument using this principle for the lower half of its range, which was designed to bring out the second mode. It used 3/8" steel rods hung at a 2nd mode node (13% of the distance from the end), with a balloon tied to each bar at 28% from one end, as suggested above. It worked pretty well, sounded nice, and was especially fun to show off and explain to people, with its chimes all decked out with multi-colored balloons. But I found I hadn't the patience to blow up and tie on 15 or so balloons each time the old ones deflated. The instrument sits idle today, decked with flaccid balloon remains.

area, much as a musical string can be attached to a soundboard. The difficulty here is that whatever contacts the bar will add damping and is likely to inhibit the tone. The approach can work, but only if whatever it is that contacts the bar is very light and/or yielding compared to the bar itself.

Well, then, what has the requisite qualities of being extremely light and having relatively large surface area per unit weight? We have already encountered two materials that meet this description: inflatable balloons, and styrofoam. You can rest the bars directly on balloons (as we did with the bar gong described in Sidebar 1-2; see also Figure 4-6J); or you can simply tie balloons to the middle of the bars. The balloons not only improve lower frequency radiation; but they also provide a mounting with a minimum of damping. With balloon mounting, one needn't worry about supporting at the nodes. The balloons are so compliant that the vibration is scarcely inhibited no matter what the point of contact.

Styrofoam is even better as a sound radiator. You can lay a steel rod across the open top of a styrofoam ice chest, strike it, and hear its inner vibratory life in full bloom. You can even, within limits, fine tune the frequency-specific radiation characteristics of the styrofoam by trimming the size of the ice chest: a small ice chest does not project the low frequencies as well as a large one. As long as the bars are fairly heavy, styrofoam gives relatively little damping, even when the support points don't exactly coincide with the nodal points. (It does not work well, however, for light bars or tubes, or with support points far from the nodes.) Another approach: if you are working with especially heavy metal bars or other high-impedance materials conventionally mounted, try attaching small, light styrofoam radiators directly to the ends or center of the bars. Sections of styrofoam egg cartons or styrofoam cups work well for this, or, on a larger scale, try the lid of a small ice chest. But if the styrofoam body is large relative to the bar, you will find that you have purchased greater volume at the cost of increased damping, giving faster decay and a shorter tone.

Similarly, you can attach various papers or foils to overhang the ends of the bars (as in Figure 4-6N), once again increasing radiating surface area with minimal increase in mass. If you experiment a while, you will find you can get some odd and interesting effects this way, due to frequency biases in the paper (which shift according to how you flex it) and rattles that may arise between bar and paper.

For more on these topics, see Chapter 8, "Resonators and Radiators."

Mounting Systems

Over the years countless free bar mounting systems have appeared. Since there is no mystery to it, anyone can devise a system to suit his or her purposes, as long as it respects a few basic considerations: 1) The system should be rattle-free. 2) The system should allow supports at or near the nodes. 3) The point of contact between bars and mounts should be loose and/or padded rather than tight and rigid. 4) The arrangement should prevent the bars from dancing around too much and touching one another or getting out of position. Figure 4-6 shows several possible approaches.

Chimes

Since most of this section has focused on horizontal marimba-like arrangements, we will devote a few paragraphs to suspended chimes, such as wind chimes.

Chimes typically are suspended by strings. Support systems for chimes are shown in Figure 4-6 A and B. Usually only one support point is needed, and if the maker is smart that support point will be one of the nodes for the mode of vibration he or she wishes to emphasize in the tone (usually the fundamental mode with a node at 22% of the total length). The only time a second support point may be needed at the lower node is if there is a problem with the chime swinging excessively when struck. It is a good idea then to make one or both supports out of an elastic cord, to hold the chime in position but still allow some play.

Orchestral chimes, sometimes known as orchestral bells, tubular bells, or tubular chimes, are sets of tuned metal tube chimes typically several feet long, with a sound reminiscent of large cathedral bells. They hang vertically, with their tops (which are covered with a metal cap) in an even row, making it convenient to strike them at the top with a rawhide mallet. This striking at the end brings out all the vibrational modes without favoring the fundamental. The result is a complex blend of non-harmonic partials having a bell-like quality. The ear does not focus on the fundamental as the defining pitch, but instead postulates a different fundamental based upon the relationships between certain prominent overtones.

There is a pitch-control option for hanging metal chimes (as well as bells and gongs) which is not an option for horizontally mounted bars: water dipping. If a vibrating body has sufficient impedance — meaning it is sufficiently massive and rigid to have a vibration which is forceful even if not large in amplitude — it will be able to sustain its vibration even when partly submerged. At the same time, the water adds inertia, slowing down the vibration and lowering pitch. If you slowly dip the lower end of a vibrating chime in water, you will hear the pitch drop. You can use water dipping as a tuning mechanism, or just as an unusual and very pretty textural effect. Dipping can be done by hand, or you can design dipping mechanisms.

Chimes made of metals produce clear pitches with long sustain times. Tubes of various brasses, bronzes or copper are often used; also increasingly common is aluminum, which produces a mellow tone with relatively subdued partials. Chimes made of glass and ceramics are usually less distinct in pitch and have less sustain. Bamboo and other hard, brittle woods may be used for their light, clinky sound; they have almost no sustain in this application.

The degree of sustain makes a big difference in the aesthetic effect. The continuous harmonious wash of large, aluminum tubes is always attractive, while the sparse, delicate clinking of bamboo is equally appealing in quite a different way. If you choose long-sustaining metals, then the pitch relationships between the chimes become an essential element in the aesthetic effect. So does the relative presence or absence of upper partials (which are likely to be non-harmonic). You will want to keep the question of upper partials in mind as you decide how long your longest chime should be relative to its diameter, since long, thin chimes tend to have prominent overtones.

Wind chimes may sound either by hitting each other, or by means of a separate striker. A striker can be a horizontal disk hanging in the center of a set of chimes, with some kind of tail hanging below to be pushed about this way and that by the wind. The advantages of the separate striker are: 1) You can make the separate striker of a chosen mass, hardness and shape to bring out just the tone you want from the chimes. 2) The separate striker allows for the sounding of individual chimes, whereas when two chimes strike one another, both sound with each strike. The sounding of individual chimes is valuable if you seek a more melodic effect, as opposed to a general ongoing textural blend. 3) The separate striker allows for a striking point near the center of each bar, tending to bring out the fundamental — whereas when bars strike one another they're likely to make contact near their ends, making the non-harmonic partials more prominent.

Another consideration is the physical spacing of the chimes and striker. Closely spaced wind chimes tend to sound frequently, while with widely spaced chimes the time intervals between strikes are longer. The mass of the various elements and the degree to which they move in varying winds affect this as well. The aesthetic question here is, do you want something that continuously tinkles away in the slightest breeze, or do you want something that gives you time to hear each note before the next one comes along?

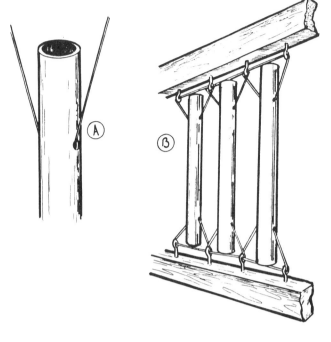

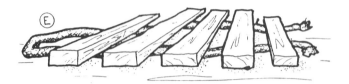

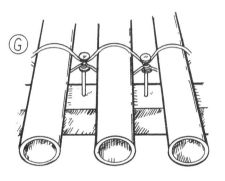

VELCRO SEWN ONTO WEBBING HOLDS
TO VELCRO STRIPS ON UNDERSIDES OF BARS

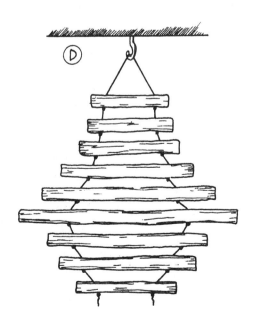

FIGURE 4-6 SOME OF THE MANY POSSIBLE APPROACHES TO MOUNTING FREE BARS

A. Chimes are typically suspended by a cord passing through one of the two nodes for the fundamental.

B. In cases where the chimes might swing excessively, you can add another support at the lower node. Use elastic cord for one or both of the support cords. This holds the chime taut without inhibiting the vibration excessively.

For marimba bars the most common arrangement is to build some sort of frame with cross pieces slightly out of parallel so as to fall under the nodes of a set of progressively longer bars. The bars can then be rested on the cross pieces by any of several possible means, some of which are shown in the following illustrations.

C: Hammock-style suspension can be both effective and attractive. The inset shows an approach in which the bars are held to straps on nylon webbing by Velcro.

D. A hanging Venetian blinds arrangement. In this illustration, the ropes pass through holes drilled at the nodes, with knots below each bar to hold it in place.

E. Here is the simplest method: the bars are rested on a soft rope or strips of foam, or some other sort of padding strip, directly on the floor or a table top. Alternatively, you can attach strips of foam, such as adhesive-backed insulation foam, directly to the underside of each bar at the nodes. Reflected waves from the surface below may significantly enrich the sound, or may significantly deaden it. By adjusting the height of the pads, you can bring out the best in each bar. Lower- pitched bars require greater heights above the surface (taller pads). If you place the bars in order of ascending pitch as close together as possible without touching, the partially enclosed air chamber formed beneath will further enrich the sound, especially enhancing the tone of the lower bars.

F. Here the bars are supported by ropes passing through holes drilled at the nodes, with knots to prevent their touching one another.

G. 1/8" shock cord — a stretchy cord available at mountaineering stores — passes over and under the bars (or tubes, in this case). In between it loops around supports in the form of double-headed nails.

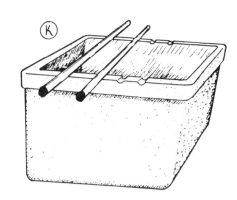

BAR
RESONATER TUBE
THREADED ROD

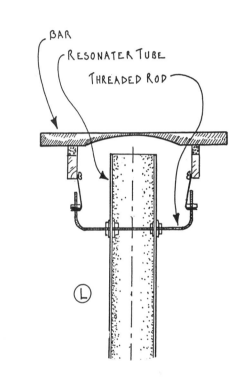

STYROFOAM PLUGS

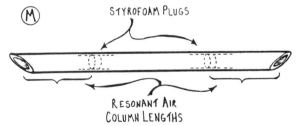

RESONANT AIR
COLUMN LENGTHS

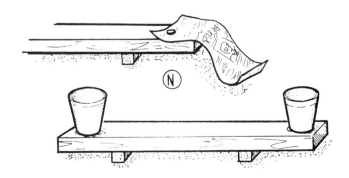

H. You can fix the bars to their supports by means of Velcro, with a Velcro loop strip attached to the underside of the bar, and a Velcro hook strip running the length of the pads beneath. This system makes it easy to remove and add bars.

I. Here the bar is held to a padded frame by a screw running through at the nodes. It should run through an oversized hole, and the shaft must be padded with soft surgical tubing or something similar.

J. Balloons may seem inelegant, and they lack permanence, but they sound great. You need blocks at the sides of the balloons or some other means to prevent rolling. Supporting at the nodes is unimportant with balloons.

K. Like balloons, styrofoam serves not only as a bar support, but also as a sound radiator. It's especially effective with heavy bars, such as solid steel cylinders, whose fundamental would otherwise be inaudible. Such heavy bars can rest directly on the styrofoam. Shallow grooves cut in the rim, as shown, will keep the bars in place but may add damping; other methods such as a dab of hot glue or a tab of adhesive tape may do the job. Supporting at the nodes is not essential, but it is worthwhile to experiment with different positionings. Lighter bars in direct contact with styrofoam tend to be less effective; in this case try adding an intermediate layer of padding.

L. How to support the resonator tubes below the bars? Again, any number of designs are possible. Here is one I have found effective. A 1/4" threaded rod passes through the resonator tube, and is bent up through 90 degrees near each end. (Position the rod through the tube, with its nuts in place, before bending it.) At each side a rigid wire running down from the frame loops around the threaded rod. A nut above the wire loop holds it in place, and makes the resonator height adjustable. The holes where the rod passes through the tube should be sealed — gaskets in the form of faucet washers can take care of that.

M. Charles Sawyer's design for using the air column of the chime itself for added air resonance in tubular chimes, as described in the main text.

N. Another approach to increasing the volume: attaching additional surface area radiators to the bars. The loose paper shown in the upper drawing yields a highly variable and interestingly distorted sound. The styrofoam cups increase both radiation and damping, yielding a loud, penetrating tone of brief duration.

RODS FIXED AT ONE END:
KALIMBAS, TONGUE DRUMS AND OTHERS

And now, on to the instruments with tongue-like appendages that can be struck, plucked or bowed to produce a definite pitch. The most prominent representatives of this family are the lamellaphones, known by one or another of their African names including *sansa*, *mbira* and *kalimba*. Other members of the family include tongue drums and music boxes with mechanically plucked "combs."

The essential element here is that long protruding thing, variously called a tongue, prong, lamella, tine or rod. It differs from the bars we have been studying in that it is not free at both ends, but rigidly fixed at one end to the body of the instrument. Plucking or striking the free end causes it to swing back and forth in a vibration whose frequency depends on the mass of the portion that swings, and the rigidity of the portion that flexes. This configuration gives rise to a characteristic set of vibration patterns and overtone relationships unlike those of free bars. The fixed end also calls for very different sorts of mountings. They must be rigid, massive and firm, offering a solid anchor at one end to support the free vibration at the other. Conveniently, the rigid mounting provides the means for the tongue to drive a soundboard. Since the tongues on most of these instruments are much smaller than a typical marimba bar, lacking the surface area to move much air on their own, a soundboard helps them radiate their vibrations to the atmosphere.

Figure 4-8 shows the vibration patterns for the first three vibrating tongue modes, along with their resulting frequencies. Notice that the relative frequencies shown here hold only for rods or bars that are uniform over their length in rigidity and mass. For irregularly shaped prongs, similar vibration patterns hold, but the nodes and antinodes are displaced, yielding different overtone frequencies.

Fundamental Tuning

The principles behind the tuning of vibrating tongues were illustrated in Figure 2-1 back in Chapter 2. The basic ideas are these:

1) If you add mass where there is a lot of motion (which means, near the end of the tongue) you lower the frequency. You can do this by lengthening the tongue, or by affixing glue, wax, solder, or anything else that will stick to the end.

2) If you remove mass where there is a lot of motion (again, near the end), you raise the frequency. You can do this by shortening the tongue or thinning the end.

3) If you reduce rigidity in a region where there is a lot of flex (near the base of the tongue), then you lower the frequency. You can do this by thinning the tongue near the base.

4) If you increase rigidity in a region with a lot of flex (again, near the base), then you raise the frequency. You can do this by substituting a thicker tongue. (If the length is unchanged, the effect of the increase in rigidity will outweigh the effect of the increase in mass at the end.)

In the description of the Baschet instruments at the end

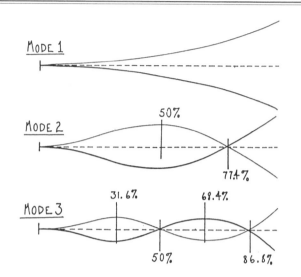

FIGURE 4-7: The first three modes of vibration for a rod fixed at one end. Locations for the antinodes are indicated by the numbers above the bar; locations for the nodes are below the bar. The percentages indicate distances from the fixed end, as a proportion of the total bar length. Frequencies and intervals relative to the fundamental appear in the chart below. The node and antinode locations, pitches and frequencies given here apply to flat bars, as well as cylinders and other related shapes. But they hold true only for rods or bars that are uniform over their length in thickness, density and rigidity.

MODE NUMBER	FREQ. RELATIVE TO MODE 1	PITCH RELATIVE TO MODE 1
Mode 1	f_1	Unison
Mode 2	$6.27 f_1$	2 8ves + a flat minor 6th
Mode 3	$17.55 f_1$	4 8ves + a flat major 2nd

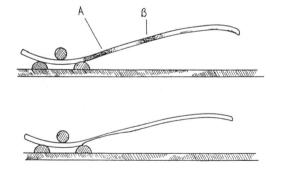

FIGURE 4-8: Kalimba prong overtone tuning. Thinning at region A lowers the fundamental more than the 2nd mode. Thinning at region B lowers the 2nd mode more than the fundamental. With luck you can put the 1st and 2nd modes three octaves apart simply by lowering the fundamental through thinning near the base, for a final bar shape something like that of the lower drawing. Reducing thickness at the base to about 1/2 of the original thickness is usually sufficient, lowering the fundamental pitch a little over a fifth. Lengthening or shortening the rod after that (as is often done as a means of tuning the overall pitch) will throw off this relationship, but usually fairly negligibly; at worst it's not hard to correct by a little more filing.

of the "Friction Rod Instruments" section later in this chapter, you will find information on one more, rather specialized tuning technique.

Overtone Tuning

In the chart in Figure 4-7, notice that the overtones on tuned tongues of uniform dimensions are non-harmonic. This is a serious consideration with kalimba-like instruments, with their relatively long, thin tongues, often of metal, since their tone may be rich in overtones. It is less important for tongue drums of wood, bamboo and most other materials, whose tone tends to be strongly dominated by the fundamental. With any material, you can make the fundamental more prominent and increase sustain by creating a tongue shape with more mass toward the end or, equivalently, thinning it near the base (which also, of course, lowers the pitch). This is analogous to center-scalloping a marimba bar.

And, as with marimba bars, you can take the process further and deliberately retune the overtones on tuned tongues. Some African kalimba makers practice overtone tuning, and a few makers elsewhere have gotten wise to it.

The principles are exactly the same as those used in overtone tuning for marimba bars. For each overtone mode, file away material to thin the prong at the points of maximum flex for the mode in question, to lower the mode's pitch. Thankfully, the process is much easier for kalimba tines than for marimba bars. Here is a quick rundown:

First of all, notice that the second partial (the next above the fundamental) is found way up at about two octaves and a sixth above the fundamental. The third is just over four octaves above. That third partial is so high that we can ignore it for most purposes. The second, however, is a significant contributor to the sound of rods in the mid and lower ranges. And at an octave-displaced sixth, it can definitely be a distraction. You can re-shape the rod so as to narrow the interval between fundamental and overtone to two octaves, or widen it to three. Widening it to three is a little easier (though perhaps not as musically satisfying); Figure 4-8, with its caption, shows how to do this.

Kalimbas

Kalimbas consist of a set of tuned individual prongs, usually but not always made of metal, mounted on a board of some sort. (As I noted before, such instruments are called by many names; I use "kalimba" as a generic simply because it seems to be the best known in the West among many local African names.) It is usually played by plucking the prong ends, but some makers have created mallet kalimbas as well. The prongs can be made of any material that is rigid enough to sustain the vibration. Hard woods and bamboo have often been used; they lack the sustain of metals and so create a light, percussive effect. African kalimbas are usually made with mild steels (which are relatively soft), for a full, warm sound. Spring-tempered steel, which is very hard, will yield a brighter sound. Flat bar shapes are most common for the prongs, but cylindrical shapes can also be effective. The maker has the option, as well, of hammering round shapes flat on an anvil. A common procedure, following Shona tradition, is to flatten more toward the plucked end, creating an elongated fan shape. See Appendix 2, "Tools and Materials," for ideas on where to get materials for kalimba tines.

Figure 4-9 shows several methods for mounting the prongs on the soundboard. You can devise any number of other systems, as long as they meet a couple of criteria: 1) The mounting must be tight, strong, and durable. It undergoes a great deal of stress under normal playing, and the prongs easily work loose and rattle, and/or come untuned. 2) The prong positioning should be adjustable for tuning purposes. Tuning in kalimbas is usually achieved by sliding the prong farther in or out, so that more or less of the prong overhangs the bridge, in effect creating a shorter or longer prong.

For instruments designed to cover a large range, the longer, lower-pitched tongues should be thicker than the high-pitched ones, keeping the length-to-thickness ratio in line so that upper partials don't come to dominate the long tongue tone. The shape of the very end of the prong where the plucking takes place also has its effect on tone. A gently rounded end makes for a pluck that does little to excite upper partials. The tone is rounded rather than brilliant, and the upper partials are less obtrusive than they might otherwise be. For a kalimba with a wide range, you can provide the lower prongs with rounded ends by bending the tips downward, and leave the upper ones un-bent or only slightly bent. Beware: a sharp-ended prong can be very hard on the player's fingertips.

Kalimbas work well over a very large range. I have made a kalimba-like instrument reaching all the way up to D_6 with clear, well-defined tone (although the tone quality is rather different from typical kalimba sound, and the tiny prongs are murderously difficult to tune). At the other extreme are the big marimbulas and rumba boxes that appear here and there in Latin America and the Caribbean. Jamaican rumba boxes are true bass instruments, full of an oomph as satisfying as a string bass — more satisfying in a way, because their effect is actually more bassy and rhythmic. Although their volume is usually not impressive, they can work wonderfully carrying the bottom in an ensemble. I made one with a decent-sounding range down to A_1 (a fourth above the string bass low E), which I pluck forcefully with heavy wooden picks to provide more volume and definition.

How massive should kalimba prongs be? The very high prong mentioned above is a 1/32" diameter piece of spring-tempered steel rod less than 1/2" long. For the lowest notes on the rumba box just described, I used a similar spring-tempered steel rod of about 5/32" diameter (but thinned at the base), in lengths ranging up to about 8" (sounding length). For ranges in between, you can select the best prong thicknesses by common sense, instinct and experimentation. You will find, in the process, that this is not simply a question of how massive the prongs are in themselves, but rather how massive they are relative to the soundboard. A prong that is too heavy relative to whatever supports it does not sustain a vibration well; it rocks its mounting with an exaggerated motion and dies. The result, in an extreme case, is a dull thud. At the opposite extreme, a prong that is very light relative to its mountings may set up a nice vibration within itself, but fail to drive the soundboard enough to produce much volume. While a typical kalimba tine may not seem very massive, it is far more rigid at the base than, say, a

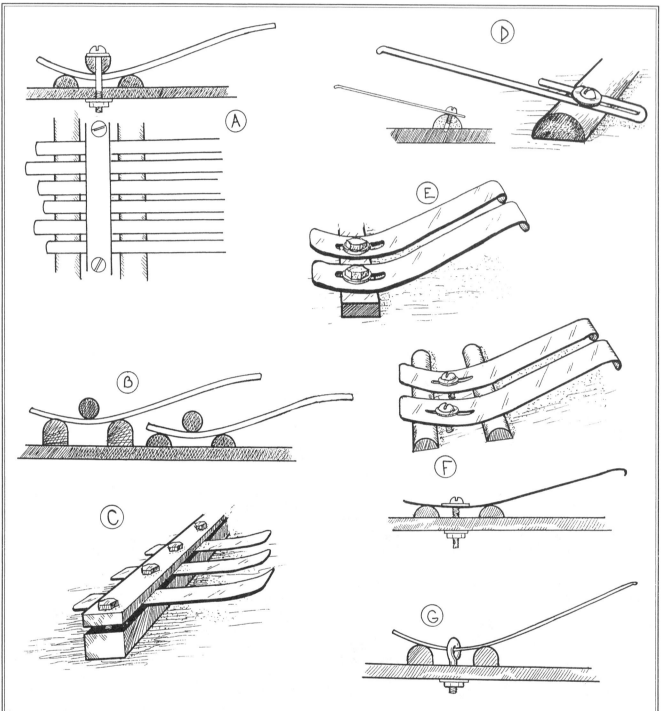

FIGURE 4-9: Some of the many possible approaches for mounting kalimba tines.

A. Variations on this arrangement are the most common form. The prongs are held down firmly between two bridges by a cross bar over the prongs between the bridges. This allows sliding the bars in and out to alter their vibrating length for tuning purposes. The cross bar must be extremely rigid and held down very firmly; if it bows outward then some prongs will be loose. It may be necessary to have additional tie-downs between the prongs, instead of only at the ends. Sometimes the rear bridge is omitted, so that the rear side of the prong presses down directly against the soundboard.

B. An arrangement similar to A above, but with two tiers.

C. This approach often appears on rumba boxes or marimbulas of the Caribbean. It is dependably sturdy, especially if the lower half of the bridge is a steel bar with threaded holes to receive the bolts from above.

D. Having individual hold-downs for each prong alleviates many potential problems. Figures 4-10 D, E, F and G show possible methods for doing so. The method shown in D is suitable for specially bent cylindrical prongs, not for flat bar-like ones. In this picture the screw threads directly into a bridge in the form of a hardwood half-round. Since threads in wood may strip with repeated tightening and loosening, threading into a steel bar as in 4-10 E is preferable.

E. Similar to 4-10 D, but suitable for wide, flat tongues. Ideally, the bridge here will be a steel bar with threaded holes to receive the bolts from above.

F. A tuning arrangement similar to 4-10 E, but without the threaded steel bridge. The disadvantage of this approach is that you need access to the inside of the instrument to do the tuning.

G. Like 4-10 F, but suitable for cylindrical prongs.

musical string. As a result, it can drive a soundboard more forcefully than you might expect, and so demands a heavier mounting and soundboard than you would find in a string instrument in the same ranges. For more on this, see Chapter 8, "Resonators and Radiators."

Also, remember the common sense rule that the lower the pitches you wish to project, the larger the surface area you need in order to project them. You might get away with a soundboard of less than a square foot for a kalimba in the upper ranges, but for a rumba box to have a good effect you will need a surface of at least, let us say, about 20" x 24" to push those long wavelengths and give it a fat bottom sound. Bigger still is better — think, for comparison, of the size required to project the sound of a string bass. Many kalimbas employ a sound chamber — that is, an enclosure covered with a soundboard having a soundhole, analogous to the body of a guitar. The air resonance of the enclosure greatly enriches the tone, especially for the lower frequencies. Again, see Chapter 8, "Radiators and Resonators."

With kalimbas, the maker has a great deal of freedom regarding how the pitches are to be laid out. Traditionally kalimbas have used variants of the left-right-left-right pattern, ascending outward from the center, discussed in Chapter 3. Linear scalewise patterns have also been used. For an arrangement reminiscent of western keyboards, you can create a two-tiered mounting system.

Jaw Harps

The instruments commonly called Jew's harps — another plucked prong instrument — are found in many forms worldwide. Aside from the name they have no special association with Jewish culture, so we will stick with the ethnically neutral alternative term, "jaw harp." The essential element is a prong, usually flat-ish in shape and several inches long, made of wood, metal, or bamboo. It is held in a small, hand-held framework. The player holds the jaw harp in front of his or her mouth, and either plucks the prong, or plucks the body near the base of the prong in a way that excites the prong. The prong excites the air in the oral cavity, and the player can, by changing the positioning of the tongue and lips, bring out a wide range of overtones. A good player can create lively melodies of overtones over the continuing drone of the prong's fundamental.

Key elements in jaw harp design: The whole assembly should be light and convenient for hand-holding, but the framework must be more massive than the prong, to provide counterpoise. The prong is typically at least two inches long, ranging up to perhaps six inches. It should be flat and wide, rather than round, in order to push the air effectively. It also should be fairly flexible. If it is too strong and rigid, the instrument's tongue tends to dominate the sound with its fundamental. A more flexible prong, being weaker in the fundamental, allows the overtones to stand out more, as they should. There seems to be an ideal range in which the fundamental is fairly low, and the prong seems a little flimsy, but the overtones resonate well. Some jaw harps have multiple prongs tuned to different fundamentals.

The framework that supports the prong provides a resting point for the player's teeth or lips, with clearance for the prong in between. The prong should be perfectly parallel to

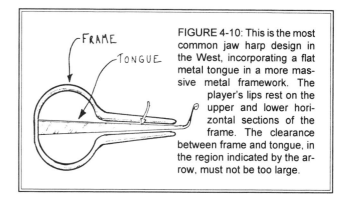

FIGURE 4-10: This is the most common jaw harp design in the West, incorporating a flat metal tongue in a more massive metal framework. The player's lips rest on the upper and lower horizontal sections of the frame. The clearance between frame and tongue, in the region indicated by the arrow, must not be too large.

the sides of the frame, with very narrow clearance (see Figure 4-10).

Jaw harps can be made all of a piece, with the prong and the framework cut from the same piece of material. Most bamboo instruments are made this way. Or they can have a separate prong attached to a framework, as with most metal versions. The prong must protrude from the frame far enough to make plucking easy.

Many jaw harp players incorporate blowing and sucking as well as plucking into their technique. Blowing tends to bring out the fundamental, as the vibrating tongue forms a gateway through which the air passes in pulses at a frequency determined by the prong's vibration. In this mode, the prong functions in a manner similar to the free reeds we will be discussing in Chapter 6, "Aerophones."

Tongue Drums and Boos

Tongue drums are related to log drums or slit drums found (more rarely, these days) in many parts of the world. Log drums take the form of hollowed logs with an open slit cut in the surface. Striking with a beater near the slit produces an idiophonic sound from the wood, enriched by air resonance from within. In this simplest form there is no tongue, but in some more sophisticated versions the slit is replaced by an H-shaped cut over the hollow. That shape creates two tongues, and striking the tongues produces a richer sound, with more distinct pitch. In recent years, builders with more access to the lumberyard than to the natural tree trunk have replaced the log with a rectangular box, and developed forms with many tongues. The tone of these instruments, a sort of bubbly "thook," can be immensely appealing.

Typical size for a tongue drum might be 18" by 10" by 6" — but they vary widely. The woods used to make the sides and bottom are not terribly important. Their main function is to provide the structure and define the enclosed air chamber. They also provide mass and counterpoise for the tongues, so it is a good idea to use fairly thick material, like nominal 1" board. The wood for the top is more important. As with marimba bars, you can make a decent-sounding tongue drum with soft woods, but hard woods will give a better result. Denser woods and springier woods, like the expensive tropical tonewoods, are usually assumed to produce the best instruments. But don't follow the herd on that — see if you can be the one to discover which temperate zone wood will do just as well. Very large diameter bamboo works wonderfully, and has the added convenience that it is its own enclosure — you don't have to build a box.

As a general rule, the tongues should lie along the grain for strength. Many makers use scroll saws to cut the tongues in their top pieces in fanciful shapes. The reasons for this, one suspects, are visual rather than acoustic. But you will do well with shapes that make the ends of the tongues larger than the bases, putting more mass toward the end and more flex in the base.

Lots of tongue drum makers let the tuning of their tongues be random. They simply cut some tongue shapes that appeal to them and then enjoy whatever tones result. Tongue drums are, in fact, tunable, by following the rules given earlier for rods fixed at one end. To facilitate the tuning process, you can attach the top of the drum to the sides, but leave the bottom off until tuning is complete. This allows you to tune by removing material from the undersides of the tongues. Try to remove material by cutting or filing in the direction of the grain, not across the grain. Tongue drum tuning, however, is a problematic process, especially for drums with several tongues. The vibrating tongue drives the whole top of the drum rather forcefully, since the connection between the tongue and the board from which it is cut is quite rigid (compared, for instance, to the flexible junction of a string and soundboard). That vibration is communicated through the top to other tongues. The resulting interaction between tongues can play out many ways depending upon their frequency relationships, but much of the time the interaction has the effect of deadening and/or detuning the individual tongues. A similar problem arises frequently with other monolithic idiophonic instruments as well — for instance, it is a factor in the design of Trinidadian steel drums.

So how to get around the problem? Lowering the pitch by doing some undercutting near the base of each tongue makes the connection between each tongue and the rest of the top less rigid, lessening the problem. Making tongue shapes with large heads and narrow bases has the same effect. You can also place tongues tuned to close intervals far apart on the drum or, better, stick with tunings that don't require tongues tuned to close intervals on the same drum. Since each drum normally only has a few tones anyway, this is not an onerous restriction.

Then again, the ultimate solution would be to make one tongue per drum. You could then make a set of drums to create a complete scale. If you follow through with this very reasonable idea, you arrive at something very much like the family of instruments called boos, which we will discuss shortly.

Air resonance from within the chamber is a factor in tongue drum tone. Tongue drum makers normally do not deliberately tune air resonances, but leave the total amount of opening area small (no large holes in the body of the drum), which ensures that the air resonance will be quite low, hopefully enhancing the bassy sound of the wood. If you make tongue drums with just one tongue, then you can consider tuning the air resonance to the tongue pitch — see Sidebars 4-6 and 4-7 for more on that.

Tongue drums need not be made of wood. Several makers have made tongue drums of metals — some of them extraordinarily beautiful to see. Their tone is quite musical, although, in my opinion, it is less distinctive and doesn't have the same appeal as wood. Rigid plastics can work as well.

Boos are an important variation on tongue drums. Harry Partch gave the name *boos* to a set of vibrating tongue instruments he made of bamboo; I am taking the liberty here of expanding the term to include a host of similar instruments made from other materials.

A boo consists of a long, narrow, hollow chamber, such as a segment of bamboo, which is open at one end. In the upper wall of the chamber a tongue is made by cutting two slits extending in from the open end, as in Figure 4-12. Boos are usually made in tuned sets, mounted in a row on a framework for ease of playing. The great thing about boos is that, because each tongue has its own air chamber, the tongue and the air resonance can be tuned to one another. The tuned air resonance strengthens and enriches the tone, just as do the tuned tube resonators below a marimba bar.

Any rigid tubular material can be used to make boos. The most convenient diameters are between about two and six inches. Bamboo, of course, is great. People have also used metal as well as plastic pipes. (ABS plastic pipe is preferable in this application to PVC. Remember to look to Appendix 1 for notes on where to get what.) Boos of square cross section work well too: some makers have used square metal pipes, and some of the nicest non-bamboo boos have been

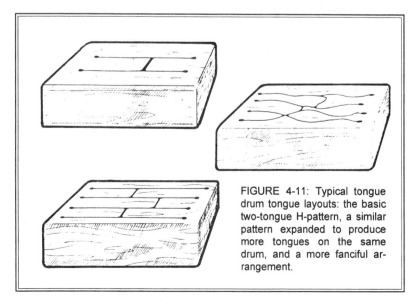

FIGURE 4-11: Typical tongue drum tongue layouts: the basic two-tongue H-pattern, a similar pattern expanded to produce more tongues on the same drum, and a more fanciful arrangement.

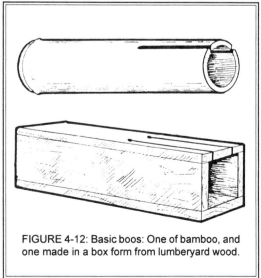

FIGURE 4-12: Basic boos: One of bamboo, and one made in a box form from lumberyard wood.

BOO TUNING

Here is a procedure for tuning boos so that the tongue and air resonance pitches agree. While the specifics differ, the principles apply to adjusting air resonances in other similar instruments as well, but with some modifications — see Sidebar 4-7 for more.

Boos typically take the form of a tube-like enclosure (though the shape may be rectangular), stopped at one end, enclosing what can be thought of as a short air column. The tongue is formed by cutting two parallel slits from the open end. With a very short tongue, the air resonance pitch for the tube-like enclosure will generally be well below the tongue pitch. Lengthening the slits that form the tongue lowers the pitch of the tongue. At the same time it has an effect similar to shortening the tube, raising the air resonance. The idea is to lengthen the slits to just the point where the two match — and, hopefully, to arrive at that matching point right at the desired pitch. Begin by selecting, cutting or making a tube, stopped at one end, of the right size to land at about the right pitch in the end. For bamboo, this will be one with a natural air resonance

about a 4th or 5th below the desired pitch, since the air resonance usually rises that much by the time the tongue slits are cut to their final length. (You can check the air resonance pitch at any time by blowing over the edge of the tube or tumping it edge-on on a solid surface). Depending on the material and its thickness, coupling will typically be achieved when the tongue is somewhere between 1/3 (for lower tones) and 1/2 (for higher tones) the overall length of the tube. With this in mind, begin by cutting the slots to a point a little short of 1/3 the length, leaving the tongue pitch a little high and the air resonance a little low. Cut the slots farther from there a tiny bit at a time, checking the two pitches frequently. The goal at this point is to get the air resonance right, at a touch below the intended pitch for good coupling. The tongue can then be fine tuned down or up to the correct pitch by removing material from the underside of the tongue near the base to lower its pitch or near the tip to raise it.

---

built in the form of elongated, open-ended wooden boxes.

You can lower the pitch of a boo by lengthening the tongue, which is to say, by extending the slits alongside the tongue. In the same process, the air resonance pitch rises, as the lengthening of the slots has the effect of opening the tube over part of its length. The process of bringing the two into agreement at the desired pitch is described in Sidebar 4-6.

Once you have created a tuned set of boos, you will need to devise a framework to hold them in playable position. The challenge here, as with many percussion instruments, is to hold them in a manner that is sufficiently firm to withstand

FIGURE 4-13: Woodblock (A and B) and Temple Block (C). Notice in the woodblock cutaway side view (B) that the cut-out doesn't go all the way through the block, and there is usually a complementary cut-out on the opposite side. Note also the unequal thickness in the top and bottom overhanging sections — this gives the block two alternative tones.

repeated blows, but which does not transmit the dull thud of the blow to the framework and floor. Padding in the mounting is in order. You can read more about this at the end of Chapter 5, "Beaters, Scrapers and Friction Makers."

Temple blocks and wood blocks are smaller forms of slit drums. They are similar to the instruments just discussed in that they all involve an air chamber within an enclosure of woody material, producing an idiophonic percussion sound enriched by air resonance.

The easiest slit drum to make involves no more than taking a single joint of moderately large diameter, hard bamboo, stopped at the end by the natural blockages, and cutting a slit in the side, perhaps a quarter or half inch wide, over a portion of the tube length. Strike the slit along its edge with a stick or mallet, for a bright, loud "thock!" You can also make slit drums using hollowed wood instead of bamboo, or build them up box-like. The standard percussionist's wood block takes a slightly different form, as shown in Figure 4-13. The tone is very dry, with less of the richness of air resonance. Temple blocks are similar in principle, but use a hollowed-out rounded shape, as the drawing shows. There is no easy way to hollow out such a cavity, so they are usually made of two or more pieces hollowed separately and then glued together, with the outside carved or otherwise shaped. The tone again is a loud, sharp, but rich, clearly pitched "thock!" sound.

Friction Rod Instruments

Many instrument makers have found bowing to be an effective means for exciting the vibration in a metal rod fixed at one end. You can bow with a normal violin or bass viol bow, or with bows specially made for the purpose. At its best the resulting tone floats forth with an ethereal beauty. It can also be shrill and screechy. Bowed rod instruments

---

MAKING A TUNED SET OF BAMBOO TONGUE DRUMS

You can use the air-resonance tuning principle described for boos in Sidebar 4-6 to make a lovely sounding tuned set of bamboo tongue drums. Materials: several joints of large bamboo, minimum diameter about 2½".

(For sources of materials, see Appendix 1.) For each tongue drum, cut a joint of bamboo so that both ends are stopped by the natural blockages. You will cut a tongue with an opening at the end, as shown in the drawing. After cutting the tongue, bring it down to the desired pitch by gradually lengthening it. Unlike the boos discussed above, the slits created by the cutting of the tongue will not bring the air resonance pitch up sufficiently to agree with the tongue pitch. That's because of the different body form: the bamboo tongue drum has no open end and doesn't behave acoustically like a tube. So you bring the tongue drum air resonance up to the desired pitch by another means: making the enlarged opening at the end of the tongue, as shown. The larger this opening, the higher the air resonance pitch. Gradually enlarge it until it is just below the tongue pitch (test it by blowing over the edge). You should then hear the tongue tone take on greater volume and richness.

Important: As soon as you finish, give the bamboo a couple of coats of polyurethane or other moisture-proof finish, inside and out if possible, to prevent splitting.

The bamboo tongue drum will sound good with a superball mallet or similar moderately soft beater.

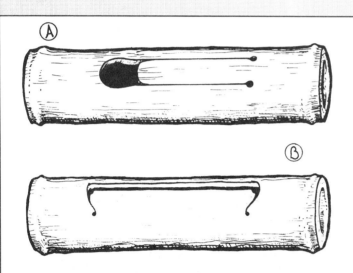

Bamboo tongue drums. The long-tongue version shown in A will produce a mellower tone, reminiscent of bubbling water. From an acoustical-mechanical point of view, this instrument is almost identical to the boo shown in Figure 4-12, but the air resonance may be slightly richer. The short, wide tongue version in B produces a shorter, sharper sound.

Sidebar 4-8   A DESIGN A FOR NAIL VIOLIN

The drawing here shows an exploded view of a nail violin made by the contemporary builder Michael Meadows. He offers this brief description:

The thick side piece is laminated soft maple or sycamore (good nail-holding ability), 1½" high, covered with a veneer of walnut on the outside. A ¹/₁₆" strip of walnut was steam-bent for the curvaceous back. The top and bottom are koa wood, ⅛" thick and 10" across, with the edges overhanging the sides ⅛". The bottom is the same shape as the top, but with a hand-hold cut in near the back. I used a variety of finish nail sizes from #10 to #4. Each size has an optimum pitch range of about a major 3rd. Scope these out to suit your choice of tunings. With the instrument assembled, drill for each nail hole stopping 1/4" or so short of how deep you've figured each nail should go. The bit used for each nail hole should be slightly undersized. If the pitch is sharp on any nail, filing at the very base — in a circumscribing sort of way — will lower the pitch. Too flat? Pound it in some more.

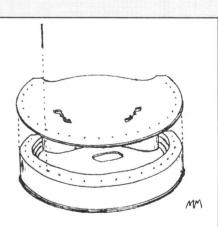

Nail violin (drawing by Michael Meadows). In this exploded diagram one sample nail is shown; in the finished instrument nails would be set in the holes all around the rim.

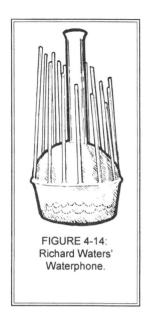

FIGURE 4-14: Richard Waters' Waterphone.

have been made with very small rods, as with the 18th century nail violin. More recently, several builders have worked with rods in the range of about 1/8" to 1/4" in diameter, extending in length up to several feet.

For long metal rods, the fundamental is likely to be subsonic, but quite an array of overtones appear within the hearing range. A typical bow stroke will bring out one or another of these in relative isolation. You can, with luck, select which overtone will sound by stroking the rod at different points along its length, and with different bowing angles or degrees of pressure. This takes a great deal of bow control as well as familiarity with the instrument. With small rods, as on nail violins, upper partials play less of a role. The fundamental is in the hearing range, while the overtones are off in the stratosphere. Yet you still sometimes get unwanted squealing.

Let me give a little more description of specific types, starting with the nail violin. The body of a nail violin is usually a flat, zither-like wooden soundbox perhaps a foot or eighteen inches across, with curved sides, often semicircular in shape. A set of nails, graduated in length, is set into the wood around the curved periphery, near the edge. Due to the relatively high impedance of the rigid nails, they are usually anchored in the heavier side walls of the sound chamber rather than in the soundboard itself. The reason for the curved shape of the chamber walls is the same as for the arching of violin bridges: the straight bow, by playing along a tangent to the curve, can selectively play one nail at a time. There may be a sort of rail along the periphery just outside the row of nails upon which the bow can ride, ensuring that the bow contacts the nails at the right height above the soundboard. The nails can be tuned by driving them in to varying depths, or by filing near the base or top. The tone is whistle-like. See Sidebar 4-8 for more on nail violin making.

Instruments incorporating larger bowed rods need a still heavier and/or more rigid mounting. Perhaps the best known currently of the heavier bowed rod instruments is the Waterphone, first created and patented in 1968 by Richard Waters (Figure 4-14). A middle-sized Waterphone uses bronze rods something over an eighth of an inch in diameter and ranging in length from about four inches to a foot. The rods rise upright from the periphery of a stainless steel, vase-shaped vessel, brazed in place. Individual rods can be bowed tangentially, as with the nail violin. The stainless steel vessel — this is the remarkable thing — contains a small amount of water. It moves about as the instrument is played, causing shifting resonances for an extraordinary, otherworldly tone.

Some of the most ingenious friction rod instruments ever conceived are those of the Parisian brothers, Bernard and François Baschet. Let me describe a representative one of their instruments here, the Cristal. (What follows is actually a generalized description of a type that has taken many forms over the years.) The Cristal, in its broadest outline, consists of four functional elements or systems: 1) a friction system for generating a vibration; 2) a tuned vibrating body which imposes its frequency on the vibration; 3) a high-impedance transmission system, which carries the vibration from the tuned vibrator to 4) a sound radiator.

The friction component is a set of upright glass rods, fairly light in weight and typically less than a foot high. The player strokes them with wetted fingers to excite a friction vibration. The tuned elements are lengths of threaded metal rod, mounted horizontally on a heavy metal crossbar so that they protrude to the front of the instrument. As shown in Figure 4-15, the glass friction rods are attached directly to the threaded metal rods. The point of attachment is about one third of the rod's length from its mounting, which is near the

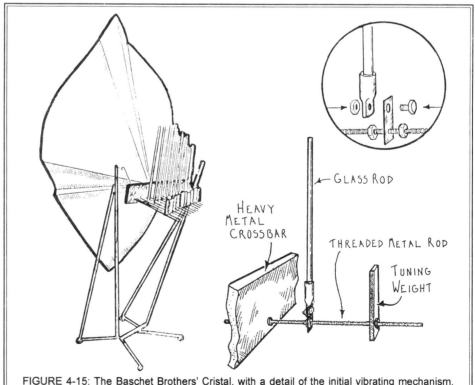

GLASS ROD

HEAVY METAL CROSSBAR

THREADED METAL ROD

TUNING WEIGHT

FIGURE 4-15: The Baschet Brothers' Cristal, with a detail of the initial vibrating mechanism. (There's one such assembly for each note in the instrument's range.) The inset shows the attachment of the glass rods to the threaded rods.

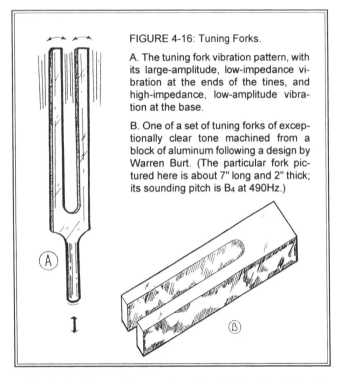

FIGURE 4-16: Tuning Forks.

A. The tuning fork vibration pattern, with its large-amplitude, low-impedance vibration at the ends of the tines, and high-impedance, low-amplitude vibration at the base.

B. One of a set of tuning forks of exceptionally clear tone machined from a block of aluminum following a design by Warren Burt. (The particular fork pictured here is about 7" long and 2" thick; its sounding pitch is B$_4$ at 490Hz.)

antinode for the rod's second mode of vibration. It is this second mode that the Cristal is designed to bring out. In addition, there is a tuning weight rising from the threaded metal rod, adjustably located at about two thirds of the its length. This two-thirds point is near the natural location of a node for the desired second mode. The tuning weight further reinforces the rod's inclination to emphasize the second mode. Additionally, adjusting the position of the weight will, within limits, force a shift in the de-facto node location. This allows it to serve as a tuning mechanism: shifting the weight toward the end of the threaded rod lowers the pitch.

The Cristal has one of these assemblies — glass friction rod, metal rod and tuning weight — tuned to the appropriate pitch for each note in its range. The vibrations in the tuned metal rods go into the heavy metal support bar. Attached to the bar are additional rigid rods which transmit the vibrations in turn to a large sheet-metal sound radiator, reminiscent of a giant speaker cone. The radiator moves plenty of air, and gives us something to listen to.

TUNING FORKS

The vibration patterns that arise in tuning forks can be seen as a special case — a double version — of the fixed rod patterns we have just been studying. Tuning forks have two matched prongs rising from a single stem. When the fork is excited, the two prongs vibrate laterally in opposition, moving in toward one another and then out away from each other. Their patterns of movement, including overtone modes and the resulting frequencies, are the same as those for rods fixed at one end. The lateral movement of the tines translates into a low-amplitude, high-impedance longitudinal vibration in the stem (see Figure 4-16A). When the two prongs are not perfectly matched, the tuning fork will still function, but with some loss of efficiency, producing a single compromise frequency.

The low-amplitude, high-impedance vibration in the handle of the tuning fork can be used to drive a soundboard or similar radiating surface. Alternatively, you can design a tuning fork to have lots of surface area in the prongs, lessening the need for a soundboard. An easy way to do this is make a tuning fork from a section of metal tubing. Simply slit a metal tube over part of its length, creating two equal halves, as was done in the Fork Chimes described back in Sidebar 1-3. The longer the slit, the longer the prongs and the lower the tone.

Other options for tuning fork making :

You can bend a metal bar or rod into a U shape. If you use a good, rigid metal and make a bend with good uniformity, you may get decent results this way, especially if you give it a strong mounting of some sort. A better approach is to get metals that have been cast or machined to a bifurcated shape. The Australian/American composer Warren Burt has obtained excellent, pure-toned, long-sustaining results by machining blocks of aluminum (Figure 4-19B). Or you can use appropriately shaped pre-existing metal objects — U-bolts and various other items you find in hardware stores and scrap metal yards. You can tune a fork either by shortening it to raise the pitch or grinding near the base of each tine to lower it.

Several makers over the years have created instruments using tuning forks mounted on soundboards and struck with hammers — some keyboard-controlled, and some struck directly.

BELLS, CYMBALS AND GONGS

There is a distinction between bells and gongs: Bells have a node at the center, and an antinode near the rim. Gongs have a node near the rim and an antinode at the center. You support a bell at the center, where it is not vibrationally active, and strike it near the rim to excite the vibration. Gongs are supported near the rim, and are struck at the center. Cymbals, in keeping with this delineation, are a form of bell. So are musical glasses, whether struck or played by finger friction around the rim, because they follow the bell's patterns of vibration. Many vibrating bodies can function either way, depending upon how they are held and where they are struck.

Bells and gongs are by nature inharmonic. Where the overtones actually fall in any given case depends on the distribution of mass and the curvature of the form.

Bells

There are really two distinct idiophonic forms that are commonly called bells. One is the familiar bell shape, opening out to the air at one end. The other is an enclosed shape, spherical or roughly so, with smaller slit-like openings somewhere in the body of the bell. Sleigh bells are a familiar example of the latter. In what follows we will concern ourselves primarily with the open bell form.

The largest bells, such as some big cathedral bells, may produce over a hundred discernible overtones. The most prominent tones usually come from the modes shown in Figure 4-17. In small bells, these lower modes are quite dominant. The one labeled T2 is usually strongest, allowing

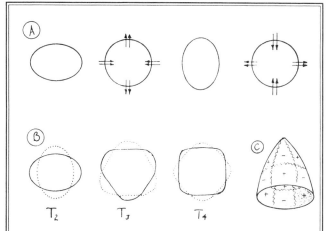

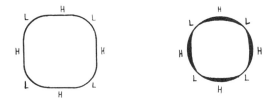

FIGURE 4-17: Bell modes.

A. Sequential representations of rim shape (exaggerated for clarity) for the lowest of the transverse modes in bells. Arrows show direction of movement, through one complete cycle.

B. Rim shape for a series of three transverse modes, each shown at two extremes (solid and dotted lines).

C. An example of the sort of multi-dimensional higher modes that become audible in large bells.

FIGURE 4-18: Rim shapes for tuning bells to multiple fundamentals. These two shapes — one involving variation in thickness and one involving a non-circular form — create a situation in which the rim has different effective rigidity depending on the orientation of the primary mode vibration. Striking at the locations marked H excites the bell in the more rigid orientation to produce a higher pitch. Striking at points marked L excites the lower pitch.

it be heard as the fundamental pitch in most small to medium-sized bells. With its complementary equal and opposite movements, the T2 mode can be seen as analogous to a three-dimensional tuning fork.

Over the centuries bell founders working with very large bells have responded to the inharmonicity of bells in two ways: First, a bell shape has been developed which brings the pitches of the five most prominent partials into more manageable, though still not precisely predictable, relationship. By casting bells in this shape to begin with, the desired overtone relationships are at least approximated. Second, founders have learned to tune those five overtones relative to one another after casting, much as the overtones in a marimba bar can be tuned. They do this by careful reshaping, removing metal from the inside surface of the bell along concentric rings in key regions. The most favored tuning that has evolved, interestingly enough, is an inharmonic one, involving a minor third along with a fifth and a couple of octaves. The T2 mode provides what is called the "hum tone," relatively quiet initially but longest sustaining among the tones. An octave above that is the most prominent tone, and the one that listeners normally perceive as the identifying pitch. Interestingly, bell founders have learned that greater precision in tuning of the octaves does not lead to a bell tone which people prefer. Part of the charm of large bells lies in a certain somber quality, and that quality is diminished when the relationships among the partials become too predictable.

Back to bells of more manageable size: With smaller bells, you can usually tune for T2 as the defining pitch. Removing mass near the rim — e.g., shortening the bell — raises the pitch. Making the bell less rigid by removing material nearer the base, where the flex is greatest, lowers the pitch. Adding mass near the rim, as, for instance, by attaching bolts near the rim, also lowers pitch, but it should be done symmetrically all around.

You can also tune a bell to produce two distinct tones in the T2 mode, depending upon where the bell is struck. (The art of tuning bells for multiple fundamentals was first cultivated in China long ago.) The trick is to remove material from selected points along the rim as shown in Figure 4-18, rather than thinning uniformly all around. This creates regions of different degrees of rigidity depending on the orientation of the T2 vibration. You can achieve the same effect by bending the rim into a non-circular shape, or by adding substantial weight at four points evenly spaced around the rim.

Bells are usually made of metal, to provide a clear tone and long ring time. The alloy known as bell metal, used in European carillons, is a bronze consisting of about four parts copper to one part tin. Other metals, of course, are used in other sorts of bells. Bells have also been made from wood, clay, stone and glass. You can find bell forms in all sorts of everyday items, particularly bowls and glasses. A trip to a scrap metal yard or a well-stocked second-hand store will turn up many bells that didn't know they were bells. Several people have found that large old artillery shells, as well as oxygen tanks and similar compression tanks cut in half, have excellent tone. Clay flower pots, suspended upside down from the hole in the base, yield an attractive non-metallic bell tone. So do large glass jugs. Cut them in half (easier said than done) and suspend them upside down from the center, being sure to try both the top and bottom half for a nice bell tone. Many makers experienced in ceramics have fashioned their own bells from clay. You can also make metal bells from heavy sheet metal, cut to the appropriate pattern (if you do this, you can work out your pattern with a paper model), bent to shape and soldered, brazed or riveted along the seam. If you have the equipment and know-how, you will find that hardening the metal by heating and quenching improves the tone.

Many traditional cowbells have rectangular rather than circular rim shapes. This changes the vibrational pattern and the resulting sound entirely, since the flat sides vibrate quasi-independently. Most cowbells are made from sheet metal as described above, rather than being cast.

Cymbals are very wide, shallow bells, designed to produce such an array of high overtones that the sound is all crash and sizzle. According to traditional lore, fostered by commercial interests, cymbal making is a mysterious art involving ancient family secrets; the uninitiated cannot make a decent cymbal. Actually you can have a lot of fun experimenting with cymbal sounds in your home workshop. You will have the best luck with fairly thin sheets of very hard metals. Bell metal is traditional, but I have had good results with stainless steel. Forget softer steels, aluminum, etc., unless you want more bong than hiss. You may find that a particular piece of metal sounds good left entirely flat. Otherwise, you will get into the business of cold-hammering to create the shallow dish shape. This can best be done by first creating some sort of shallow concave mold into which to hammer the metal. Use a heavy ball-peen hammer directly on the metal, or better, hold the ball-peen head against the metal and strike the flat head with another hammer. *Wear safety goggles*, gloves and ear stops; cover the face of one hammer with an intermediary material such as a leather covering to prevent metal-against-metal chipping. Incidentally, I have sometimes found that the best cymbal-like sounds come from the gong modes rather than the bell modes — in other words, consider hanging a flat-ish sheet of hard metal like a gong from points near the rim and striking near the center. Also, for lots of extra sizzle, add rattles in the form of loose rivets or small pieces of wire passing through holes in the cymbal (this is described in Chapter 10, "Special Effects").

Beaters and clappers: Some bells have internal clappers, in the form of weights hanging within and striking the sides of the bell when swung. Others use a hand-held external beater. Different sorts of beaters produce very different tone qualities, and finding the right beater can make all the difference in bringing out the best in a bell. Experiment.

Musical Glasses and Glass Harmonica

For centuries people have been making music with wine glasses, as well as with glass and ceramic bowls. From an acoustic point of view, these are inverted bells vibrating in the normal transverse bell modes. You can sound them by percussion with light sticks, or the friction of a moistened finger circling the rim (try this on a wine glass sometime if you never have, listening for a whistle-like tone). The Indian *Jaltarang* is a set of ceramic bowls, played by percussion, and tuned by the addition of water in varying amounts to the bowls, which lowers the pitch.

Most sets of musical glasses in the European tradition are nothing more than a collection of regular wine glasses, played by fingertip friction. Some people simply set them on a table. Some find ways of strapping them down or otherwise fixing them in place. Most sets are water-tuned, but there are also sets that need no water. For the most part, such pre-tuned sets are found, not ground. Some glass players audition hundreds of different glasses in search of ones fortuitously producing the desired pitches. Within limits, however, glasses can be fine-tuned by grinding, removing material from the rim to raise the pitch. The contemporary glass harmonica maker, Gerhard Finkenbeiner, lowers the pitch of slightly sharp glass bowls by a process known as acid etching: immersing the bowl in hydrofluoric acid solution for a specified period of time thins walls by a precise amount. Thinner walls lead to lower pitch.

Glass harmonicas are mechanized sets of musical glasses developed by Ben Franklin in 1761. He nested a graduated set of tuned glass bowls in a row on a horizontal spindle operated by a treadle, thus bringing the rims in closer proximity and making possible the performance of more complex music. In later years motors have replaced the treadle arrangement; automatic moistening systems have been added, and a few other improvements have been made. Glass harmonicas use stemless glass bowls which are blown specifically for the purpose, with holes at the center for mounting.

Contemporary makers have created a variety of other forms. Two examples: the German maker Sascha Reckert's glasses actually are glass tubes, cut to length, mounted vertically at the nodes and functioning acoustically not as bells but as free bars. Cris Forster's set of tuned wine glasses are mounted in a two-dimensional array on a vertical board and motorized so that each glass rotates separately, shimmering in the light.

Miscellaneous additional notes about musical glasses: Inexpensive imported hand-blown glasses are the best bet for finding a wide range of pitches, since they are less uniform than mass-produced glasses. A glass with irregular wall thickness may give two microtonally close notes; sounding together they will produce a mild beating which can be pleasant. Quartz glass is the preferred glass for top-quality instruments, followed by lead glass. Soda-lime (the most common glass) is less resonant but will produce a workable instrument. Glasses speak better with newly polished rims; polish the rims of older glasses with a buffing disk to improve the response. For optimal playing results, fingers should be clean and free of oils, and the water you dip them in should be hard; glasses may not speak with soft water. A drop of vinegar in the water may help.

Gongs

Gongs, in their simplest form, take the shape of a flat disk, suspended or otherwise mounted somewhere near the edge and struck near the center. More elaborate gongs may be slightly convex rather than perfectly flat. They often have bosses, which are button-like raised portions in the center, and rims turned back around the periphery.

Like those of bells, gong vibration patterns tend to be complex, having several sets of many modes that don't fall in a single linear sequence. Many large, lower-pitched gongs have no single predominant tone and aren't perceived as having definite pitch. With smaller gongs and some large gongs, however, it is quite possible to bring the lowest mode to the fore to provide a defining pitch.

Factors affecting gong pitch: The larger the diameter,

FIGURE 4-19: A depiction of a normally flat disk at one vibratory extreme in the lowest gong mode, with a nodal ring indicated by the dotted line. The pitch can be raised by adding a boss at the center, folding the periphery back to form a rim, or making the gong smaller or thicker.

MAKING A TUNED GONG SET

The most rewarding material for small gong making — the easiest to work with and with the prettiest tone — is aluminum. You can make lovely gongs from an aluminum disk, simply by raising a small boss in the center. Reinhold Banek and Jon Scoville describe this sort of gong in their book *Sound Designs*, and what follows here owes a great deal to them.

(Be sure you've read the section on gongs in the main text to give yourself some understanding of the principles involved.)

Begin with a trip to a scrap metals yard. Disks of aluminum, in suitable diameters ranging from about 6" up to 14" or more, often lurk in odd corners there. If aluminum proves unavailable, you can try steel disks. They produce good results as well, but they are harder to work. If disks are not available, try rectangular sheets. Take up prospective gongs and drop them, tapping them at the center in free fall, to get some sense of their sound. Pick up several disks, to make gongs at different pitches.

If you do not find any disks, you may end up cutting disks from rectangular sheets — a potentially difficult task, in the absence of specialized tools. On the other hand, you can also try making gongs in a square shape, or hexagonal shape, or any other shape you may come across, as long as the form is not so long and narrow as to behave acoustically like a bar rather than a gong.

The gongs can be suspended by loops of cord through 1/8" holes as shown in the figure. The holes should be near nodal points for the modes you want to sound most clearly. For the fundamental mode, there is a nodal ring somewhere between about 60% and 80% of the distance from the center to the edge (its actual location depends upon the size of any boss, the existence or non-existence of a rim, and so forth.) For our purposes, holes at 70% of the center-to-rim distance will suffice. In each gong-to-be, drill the two holes as shown in the drawing. Ease the edges of the holes, using a countersink bit, to give them a slight bevel — this will reduce wear on the support cords. Cut pieces of strong cord 1½ the disk diameter in length, loop them through the holes, and tie them.

With the right sort of beater, the disks will produce a pleasant enough tone just as they are. But you can tune them, and bring out the fundamental for a clearer pitch, by raising a small boss at the center of the gong. Hammering a small boss in a previously un-bossed gong brings the pitch up considerably, for both the fundamental and most of the higher modes. Progressively enlarging the boss continues to raise the pitch but more and more slowly. Adding the boss will allow you to raise the pitch a maximum of a fifth or sixth, typically, above that of the original flat disk.

Make the boss by hammering over some sort of concave mold. A large, flat, thick piece of wood with a cavity carved out in the middle will serve. Use a heavy ball-peen hammer directly on the center of the gong, or, for more control, hold the ball end of the hammer against the gong and strike it with another hammer. *Wear gloves, safety goggles and ear muffs*; protect the face of one hammer with an intermediary material such as a leather covering to prevent metal-against-metal chipping. As you proceed, check the pitch frequently (since you've already attached the cords, you can hear the pitch by simply holding the gong by the cords and tapping at the center.) You will find that the breadth of the boss is more important for pitch purposes than the depth, and easier to control. Gradually enlarge the boss until you arrive at the desired pitch.

The drawing shows a simple system for hanging gongs; it allows gongs to be added or removed from their framework with minimum effort. Use moderately soft beaters, and strike the gongs at the boss.

A final note: Raising the boss doesn't raise the pitch of all the overtone modes equally. It tends to raise the fundamental more than the others. This means that the overtone relationships within the tone change as the fundamental is tuned, creating changes in timbre. With luck, or perhaps a skill born of experience, you can try to bring the two or three most prominent tones into an attractive relationship.

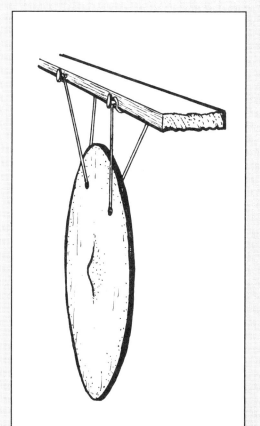

A nipple gong, shown with a simple suspension system that allows for easy hanging and removal of individual gongs on a frame. Note that the support piece is broad enough that the support cords angle well out and away from the gong.

the lower the pitch; the thicker (= more rigid) the material, the higher the pitch. All three of the usual shape modifications — adding or enlarging a boss at the center, making the gong more convex, and folding the periphery back to form a rim — have the effect of making the form more rigid, and raising the pitch. They may also help bring out the fundamental, making for a clearer sense of pitch. Of the three, adding a boss is easiest and most controllable, so it is a good place to start in simple gong making. Look to Sidebar 4-9 for more on gong making, tuning, and mounting.

Gongs have traditionally been made from bronzes similar in make-up to bell metal. After casting, they may be further shaped or tuned by cold-hammering or filing. Most readers of this book, not having the wherewithal to do their own metal casting, will find it practical to start with sheet metal, and proceed from there by hammering. With steel or bronze, hammering work-hardens the metal, improving the tone. You can successfully make non-traditional gongs from any number of materials, including most available metals. I have found aluminum, with its characteristically gentle tone and its easy workability, to be especially rewarding. Steels are a bit more clangy, and they are harder to work, but will still yield appealing results. One of the keys to creating a good-sounding gong is to use metal of an appropriate thickness relative to the intended gong's diameter. A too-thin gong will be weak in the fundamental. Just how thick a gong should be for a particular diameter depends upon the type of metal used, the presence or absence of boss, rim or general concavity, and the maker's taste.

Most gongs sound best with moderately heavy, soft beaters. They can also often be played by friction, using a bow at the edge. Gongs respond very well to water-dipping techniques for pitch bending, as described earlier for chimes.

While most gongs are designed for deep tones, you can also use them for cymbal-like sounds with a splash of closely-spaced high frequencies. Best for this purpose are thin sheets of a hard, rigid metal like stainless steel. Cymbal gongs can perfectly well be left flat and un-bossed, and non-circular in shape. (Adding a boss and/or rim may bring some lower-frequency bonging tone to the metal.)

SAWS AND WOBBLEBOARDS

Sheets of metal often show different resonant frequencies depending on how they are flexed. Thus, if you strike or bow a piece of metal and then flex it as it continues to ring, the pitch will bend. The resulting sound may strike listeners as beautiful and mysterious, or comical, depending on the circumstances. Musical saws take advantage of this effect; so do wobbleboards, and so do the flexatones found in many a percussionist's trick bag.

Musical Saw

The musical saw may be a regular carpenter's saw, or it may be a modified saw form designed specifically for music. The player sits, holding the handle of the saw between the legs and grasping the far end with one hand (see Figure 4-20A). With the other hand, the player either bows the edge of the blade, or strikes the blade with a medium-soft mallet. The flex of the blade determines the sounding pitch. The playing is easier if you attach something like a C-clamp to serve as a handle at the end of the blade.

The blade-flexing pitch control system is trickier than it first appears. The blade must be flexed not into a simple arc, but into a double curve, forming a shallow S-shape. The critical area is the region where the direction of curvature reverses — the unique strip with no curvature shown in Figure 4-20B. By altering the flex, the player can shift the location of this strip up and down the blade. The player must bow or strike near that point, even as it moves. Here is what is happening: The saw blade manifests essentially the same vibration pattern as the marimba bars we studied earlier. But the orientation of the vibration is not along the blade, but across it, as shown in Figure 4-20C. When the blade is flexed, the curvature increases the rigidity in this crosswise direction to a point where vibration is inhibited. But in the region of no flex the blade remains freer to vibrate, so the vibration centers there. The length of this vibrating segment, and thus its pitch, is determined by its location along the blade. If the no-flex strip is near the narrow end of the blade,

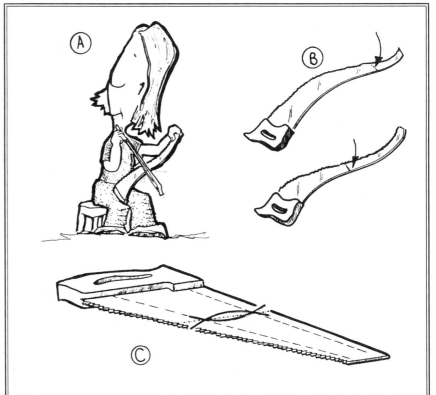

FIGURE 4-20: Musical saw. A. The standard playing position. B. The bowing or striking point, where there is no curvature as the curve reverses direction, shown for two different saw-flexes yielding two different pitches. C. The lateral vibration pattern, with the nodal lines over the saw's length shown as dotted lines.

the vibrating segment is short and the pitch high. If nearer to the handle where the blade is broader, it is longer and the pitch lower. The art of saw playing is the art of flexing the blade so as to position the region of no flex just where the cross dimension is long enough to produce the desired pitch.

Made-for-music saws are usually longer than carpenter's saws and narrower at the small end to increase range. They are thinner and made of softer steels than the hardened tool steel of carpenter's saws, to make flexing easier and to improve control. Typical dimensions for the blade of a musical saw might be between 26" and 32" long, between .035" and .040" thick, a little over 1" wide at the tip, and about 7" wide at the handle. Since the saw teeth are irrelevant to the sound, made-for-music saws are toothless.

Wobbleboards

I have borrowed the term "wobbleboard" from Reinhold Banek and Jon Scoville, who devote several pages to the topic in their book, *Sound Designs*. A wobbleboard is a rectangular sheet of flexible material that, like saws, produces bendy pitches depending on how the material is flexed. The sound has a lovely bubbly quality. Wobbleboards may be made of any flexible sheet material; metals are usually the most fun. They can be played by bowing at the edge, by striking almost anywhere with a fairly soft, medium-heavy mallet (but see the comments below about handles and damping), or by flexing. Flexing works this way: most large, semi-rigid sheets possess at least some small degree of warpage or curvature. If you hold the sheet at the edges and wobble it back and forth so that the center flexes from one side to the other, that little warpage means that the sheet doesn't glide smoothly back and forth. Rather, at the mid point it abruptly pops through. That popping sets up a vibration in the sheet. If by some fluke you end up with a sheet having no natural warpage, you can add some by bending the sheet *ever so slightly* along the long dimension.

It might seem natural to think that wobbleboards operate on principles similar to musical saws. That turns out to be true only up to a point. The first clue that there are differences lies in the fact that wobbleboards produce saw-like glissandos, yet they don't possess the saw's narrowing toward one end. What causes the pitch to rise and fall? Here is my theory. Wobbleboards are generally much wider than saws, and made of thinner, more flexible metals. A marimba bar-like strip vibrating in saw-like fashion across the wobbleboard would lack sufficient rigidity to vibrate effectively. Flexing the sheet has the effect of increasing rigidity, making for a more sustainable vibration and bringing the natural frequency up into the hearing range. No S-curve is needed for the wobbleboard; a simple curve provides the requisite increase in rigidity, with the degree of curvature controlling the pitch.

Wobbleboards can vary greatly in size and shape. An important consideration is the overall rigidity of the unflexed sheet. Thinner (less rigid) boards sound sloppy and tinny; boards that are too thick are hard to flex and

they lack range and volume. Great big boards, such as sheets of 1/8" plywood, produce a low, thunderous sound without well-defined pitch. Go to a scrap metals yard, or anywhere else where you might find lots of sheet materials in a variety of sizes and thicknesses, and experiment.

Sometimes you can improve the sound of a wobbleboard by fixing the right amount of mass at the ends. Conveniently, the added mass can take the form of handles. This is especially valuable for percussion playing, since hand-held wobbleboards tend to sound poorly under the mallet due to excessive damping. Just adding handles in the form of C-clamps may help. Too much added mass may have the reverse effect, inhibiting the vibration.

Related to wobbleboards are floppy metal sheets suspended by cords at the corners, sounded by striking or shaking. The sound usually has less defined pitch than a wobbleboard. Very large suspended sheets, known as thundersheets, have been used for theatrical sound effects.

If you find a sheet you like and plan to use it regularly as a wobbleboard or thundersheet, round the corners and/or lap the edges to avoid scratching and cutting.

INSTRUMENTS WITH IRREGULAR VIBRATION PATTERNS

Imagine a trip to a scrap metal yard in search of sonorous scraps. You will find plenty of rods, bars and tubes, and other regular and symmetrical forms whose acoustic behavior we have discussed. But you will also find irregular shapes — odd configurations made for some forgotten purpose — whose acoustic behavior cannot be predicted based on the simple models we have studied. All I can say about this endless diversity of form is to try each one as it comes along. Try different support and striking points, and try striking with different sorts of beaters. To hear an object without the damping caused by holding it, toss it in the air, if it is small enough, and give it a tap in free fall. Complex shapes may have several regions of vibration and multiple subsidiary vibrating patterns, each with its own node and antinode locations. Some forms turn out to be disappointing in their sonic response. Some turn out to be rewarding. Experiment.

Rasps, Rattles, and a Million Others

There are a number of instruments among the percussionist's standard equipment designed to produce a rush of irregular noise, with not a trace of perceptible pitch. A particularly effective way to do this is with a flurry of separate sounds coming together in a single swish. These include shaken things like maracas, shekeres, and sleigh bells, as well as scraped instruments like guiros and similar things with rough or ridged surfaces. In addition to these, there are a million other small, unpitched idiophone types, from slapsticks and coconut shell horse hoofs to sproingy springs and tin can pop tops, each having its own special flavor. I won't try to list them all here. Just know that they are out there to be found and played and enjoyed.

Chapter Five

BEATERS, SCRAPERS, & FRICTION MAKERS
(Also, Some General Notes on Mounting Systems)

This chapter is devoted to things that you can use to start vibrations. They include mallets, sticks, bows, scrapers, and squeakers. At the end of the chapter are some notes on mounting systems for non-hand-held musical instruments. We start with —

MALLETS AND STICKS

I use *mallet* to describe percussion instrument beaters with distinct heads, and *sticks* to describe those that are headless, or nearly so. Mallets and sticks are highly specialized tools. The right beater will bring out an instrument's most satisfying sounds, while many highly musical bodies are completely unmusical under the wrong beaters. To find the best beater for a given application, nothing beats trial and error. But there are some guidelines:

1) Beaters with small striking surfaces excite high frequency vibrations preferentially; larger striking surfaces muffle the high and bring out the low frequencies.

2) Likewise, beaters with hard striking surfaces bring out high frequencies preferentially; softer striking surfaces muffle the high and bring out the low frequencies.

3) Heavier mallets favor low frequencies. More generally, mallet weight should be appropriate to the mass of the vibrating body; heavy mallets will overdrive and possibly damage light or fragile vibrating bodies.

4) Mallets with fuzzy surfaces damp high frequencies.

In addition, the duration of the beater's contact with the vibrating surface is important. In most cases it should be virtually instantaneous, especially if you want to bring out high frequency vibrations. The duration of contact depends in part on playing technique, but also on the degree of bounce in the beater. This is a function of both the bounciness of the head and the resilience of the handle.

Mallet Handles

Mallet handles are typically about 14" long, but that can vary. Their thickness and weight should be proportional to the weight of the mallet head, giving a feeling of control and balance. You can make a handle out of whatever material does the job. With mallets of light or moderate weight, springy materials like thin bamboo do nicely, providing the needed bounce. But the best materials for flex in the shaft are not always the best for sure and comfortable grip. To get around this, you can make mallets with stepped handles, having thicker and more rigid material toward the handle end, leading to something thinner and more flexible toward the head. You might use, for instance, a 1/2" wooden dowel of six or eight inches for the hand grip leading to a 1/8" spring steel rod of six or eight inches, with the head at the end. For extremely heavy mallets, forget about flex; just look for whatever material is strong enough and has the right weight and thickness to create a controllable and well-balanced mallet.

Mallet Heads

Most mallet heads are spherical, but they can also be disk-shaped, or other shapes. An advantage of disk-shaped mallet heads is that tape, cloth, and other flat coverings sometimes used to wrap the head can conform to the surface shape. For lightweight mallets, heads of a single solid material work fine. For heavier mallets it is often good to have multiple layers, with softer, lighter materials toward the outside, and progressively heavier, harder materials toward the center. This makes for a mallet that is massive, yet soft and resilient in its surface characteristics. The resulting tone is, ideally, uniform across the dynamic range — heavy strokes produce a tone quality that is not radically different from that of light strokes. Mallets that are harder on the outside, but compress through a softer layer underneath, produce a lot of surface noise and are inconsistent in tone quality.

Simple mallet heads can be made from a number of readily available materials, such as —

Superballs: For a versatile medium-soft beater, you can hardly do better. Superballs come in small and medium sizes, rarely over 1½". You can affix them to a mallet handle by drilling a slightly undersized hole and inserting the end of the handle with glue. Superballs are also good for drawing out friction sounds, as we will see later. The best adhesive for attaching superballs seems to be superglue.

Other balls: Most other rubbers are softer, lighter, not as resilient, and generally not as effective as superballs. But they come in handy for larger, heavier mallets, since superballs don't seem to exist in large diameters. A rubber imitation softball, for instance, at something over 3" in diameter, has its uses. Other, harder balls, such as real softballs and hardballs, have their uses as well.

Drawer pulls: Spherical wooden drawer pulls can be had in a range of sizes at hardware stores. The make a decent lightweight, hard beater.

Thread spools: These are useful as a core for overwrapping with cloth-like materials that wouldn't conform well to a spherical head (we will talk more about overwraps in a moment).

Inner tube: You can get a medium-soft, medium-light cylinder or disk-shaped head by wrapping several rounds of bicycle inner tube around the end of a wooden or metal stick. Or cut it into long, narrow strips and wrap more randomly for a spherical head. The more wraps, the bigger, heavier and softer the head.

Synthetic rubbers: Neoprene rubbers are available from specialized industrial supply outlets. The hardness of the material is indicated by the *durometer* scale: a rubber with a durometer reading of 50 is good for a soft mallet such as a bass marimba mallet; something closer to 85 is good for a harder mallet such as a xylophone mallet. Synthetic rubbers come in stocks of different forms, such as rods and sheets of varying thicknesses. They are also available in liquid form, for pouring into a mold.

Yarn: Winding a nice, symmetrical ball shape in yarn onto the end of a stick is harder than it looks. The result is a fuzzy, not-too-soft, very lightweight beater. Wrapping a few layers of yarn over a spherical inner core of other material is a bit easier than building up the entire head of yarn.

Felt: You can wrap strips of felt or other thick, fluffy fabrics around the end of a stick in a manner similar to the bicycle inner tubes mentioned above. The result depends on the material, but it is similar to yarn.

Nuts and Bolts: On rare occasions where you want a small, hard, heavy beater, you can use a long bolt (the head of the bolt forms the head of the beater), or a large nut screwed onto the end of a wood or metal handle.

Hard rubber and rawhide: the hard rubber or rawhide hammer-shaped mallets used in woodworking shops also serve well as heavy, medium-hard beaters for some applications.

Frequently you will want the density and firmness of one of the harder materials mentioned above, but with a softer surface. Here are some options for creating a softer outer layer:

Rubber coating: There is a product called Plasti-dip, made to give tool handles a non-slip, insulating surface. It is a liquid plastic; you dip the tool handle in it and hang it up to

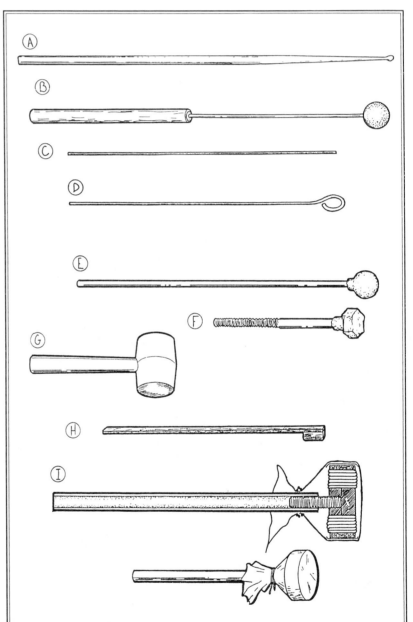

FIGURE 5-1: Sticks and beaters of various sorts

A. Wooden drumstick. B. Mallet with stepped handle. C. A light metal rod beater. D. Light metal rod beater with looped tip. E. Wooden knob mallet with rubber surface coating. F. Bolt with rubber surface coating. G. Furniture maker's rubber mallet. H. Wooden beater for hand-hammered strings. I. An example of an extra heavy, multiple-layered gong mallet. The layers, progressing from the core outward: large bolt head and nut, several rounds of bicycle inner tube, 1/8" dense foam rubber, duct tape overwrap to hold it all together, and cloth overwrap. The 14" handle of rigid plastic tubing was chosen primarily because it happened to be the right diameter for the bolt to thread snugly into it.

dry. If you take a wooden drawer pull mallet and give it one dip in Plasti-dip, you will have a slightly less edgy mallet. If you give it another dip after drying, you will have softened it a bit more. You can go up to about five dips before the head starts to get misshapen and droopy. For a unique combination of density and hardness, and yet a softened surface, try dipping large bolt heads.

Moleskin: *Dr. Scholes' Moleskin* is a soft, thin felt on an adhesive rubbery backing, intended as a foot comfort product. It makes a good slightly padded surface for mallet heads.

Cloth: For spherical head shapes, simply drape the cloth or leather over the head, and gather and tie it at the neck. The folds that appear in the cloth don't usually cause much problem. The cloth wrap looks nice with a colorful ccllar tie and the skirt that forms below, and it covers up any rough-looking inner work. For disk-shaped heads, you can wrap the outer surface of the disk with cloth or leather.

Adhesive tapes: There is a form of electrical tape made of a softer rubber than the standard PVC electrical tape. You can layer it over the end of a thick dowel or heavier cylindrical mallet end to achieve the desired thickness and softness. Similarly, many layers of duct tape will provide a medium-soft, medium-heavy head.

Sheepskin: An overwrap of wool-covered hide provides a soft, fuzzy surface.

Weather stripping: A layer of 1/8" adhesive-backed neoprene foam rubber weather stripping makes an effective and convenient soft outer layer for a heavy mallet.

For a very big, very dense mallet, you may want many layers of progressively softer materials. The materials I used in creating a successful hockey-puck-shaped gong mallet are shown in Figure 5-1 I.

Sticks

There is a standard form for commercially made drumsticks, with a slight taper toward one end culminating in a tiny carved bulb. This shape lets the stick bounce well when it strikes. Drummers take advantage of the bounce in performing rolls and such. Trap set drummers use these sticks all the time, on all the instruments in the kit, primarily because it would be impossible to play with fluidity if one were continually changing beaters for the different instruments. But the sticks are optimized for use on the snare drum.

In many special applications, small beaters consisting of a short, light metal rod are ideal. You can use anything from coat-hanger wire to brazing rod. Makers should round off or loop the ends of such beaters to prevent injury. Cymbals, agogo bells, triangles, and other metals display a brilliant clarity at low volume under such beaters.

FRICTION DEVICES

People tend to think of bows in connection with string instruments, but bowing works well with many idiophones as well. Free bars, rods fixed at one end, cymbals and bells — any of these may respond well to bowing. Bowing devices

---

come in a variety of forms, although for most purposes violin bows and their kin work as well as any of the alternatives.

Conventional Bows

Most bows are made with horsetail hair running end to end and held more or less taut on an arched stick. Modern orchestral bows are actually arched slightly backward, with spacers at each end to hold the hairs away from the stick, designed this way for reasons having to do with balance and control (Figure 5-2B). Orchestral bows are rather long — a couple of feet and more — allowing for long strokes. Shorter bows are easier to control, and really tiny bows, like six inches to a foot long, perhaps used in pairs (one in each hand) are just the thing for some instruments where longer bows would be too awkward. Despite a lot of tradition about specific types of wood producing the best bows, many different woods and other materials, including plastics, have been used to make successful bows.

The horsetail hairs (or equivalent) can be affixed at the ends by any form of attachment that works. Each hair has the "bite" needed to excite the string when it pulls in one direction and not the other, so it's necessary, when stringing with horsetail, to reverse every other hair and lay them in opposite directions. Professional violinists rehair their bows frequently as the bite of the hair wears down with extensive use. The ideal degree of tautness in the hair varies from instrument to instrument and playing style to playing style, though it is usually moderately firm but not stressed. Orchestral bows have means for adjusting the tautness. On other bows the tautness is achieved by flexing the bow inward before attaching the hair, and letting the bow's springiness hold the hair taut (Figure 5-2A). Still other bows have the hair deliberately left slack, and leave it to the player to hold it tight as part of the bowing hand's grip. Having the hairs in a flat ribbon arrangement is better than giving them the form of a round cord, because it allows for different playing angles and different amounts of contact. At a sideways tilt, an increase in pressure brings increasing amounts of hair in contact with the vibrating object.

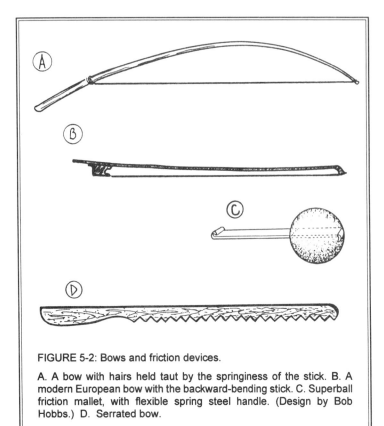

FIGURE 5-2: Bows and friction devices.

A. A bow with hairs held taut by the springiness of the stick. B. A modern European bow with the backward-bending stick. C. Superball friction mallet, with flexible spring steel handle. (Design by Bob Hobbs.) D. Serrated bow.

Why horsehair? Because it works well, it is a good length and thickness, and, historically, it has been widely available. Horses don't seem to mind parting with a few tail hairs, I have found. If you have equestrian friends with gentle steeds, you can seek permission to cut or pull a few (but gently). Stand off to one side rather than directly behind! With horsehair, as with all bowing materials, it is necessary to increase the bow's grab by rubbing it before playing with rosin. Rosin packaged especially for bows is sold at music stores.

Other bow-stringing materials are considered less desirable, but they do work. Some cheap bows are strung with strands of fiberglass, or fine strands of nylon monofilament line (sold as thread at fabric stores). In fact, any strong thread will do. Very fine threads are usually preferable, yielding a more even and refined sound. Generous applications of rosin are especially important for synthetics. Plans for a simple folk-instrument bow appear in Sidebar 5-2.

Unconventional Bows

Some instruments — especially mechanical string instruments and some oddball historical keyboards — use continuous bows. They take the form either of rosined wheels or looped bands of some flexible material running between pulleys. In the hurdy-gurdy (a European chordophone, now rare) a rosined wheel, usually made of pear wood, sounds several strings continuously and simultaneously. The player operates the wheel by means of a crank protruding from the front of the instrument. The height of the bridges is such that the strings just contact the wheel as it turns. (A veneer of pear wood circling the rim of the wheel is better than a solid disk of pear wood, because that way the grain is consistent

against the strings as the wheel turns.) In the Violano Virtuoso, a mechanical violin-playing instrument from the first decades of the 20th century, the strings were played (quite convincingly, believe it or not) by motor-driven, automatically-rosined celluloid disks.

Hard materials like sticks, bamboo and such have also sometimes served as bows, aided either by rosin or water, occasionally with passable results. To make a tiny, rigid bow, bowed piano composer Stephen Scott has glued horsehair onto the flat sides of popsicle sticks, and applied rosin.

Friction Mallets

A mallet head with sufficient traction can excite a stick-slip vibration in almost any flat, thin surface, including drum membranes, window glass, sheet metal, and wooden veneers. Superballs make the best mallet heads for the purpose. A key element in any successful friction mallet is the handle. It must have a great deal of flex, to allow the ball its myriad tiny jumps as it stick-slips its way across the surface. For this reason, what's best for a percussion mallet isn't best for a friction mallet. Figure 5-2C shows a mallet design specialized for friction, created by percussionist Robert Hobbs. The short, highly flexible handle allows the player to control the amount of firmness of pressure by holding the mallet closer to or farther from the ball. The method of attachment prevents the head from slipping off due to the constant pulling.

Fingers and Gloves

In many applications, direct stroking by moistened or rosined fingers is adequate to set up a stick-slip vibration. Or special rosined gloves may be worn. Hand stroking seems to work best when longitudinal vibrations are called for. The Baschet instruments with their glass friction rods (described in the last chapter) work this way; so do most friction drums (see Chapter 7), and so do a number of stroked metal rod instruments, as well as the longitudinally played Long String Instrument mentioned in Chapter 2.

SCRAPERS

The most familiar scraped instrument is the Latin American guiro, traditionally made from a gourd with ridges filed into the surface along the side, and scraped with a short stick or switch. But many other scraped instrument forms are possible. Scrape sounds have distinctive character; if I were in charge, there would be more scraped instruments in the world.

Generally, the most effective scraper is something that gets the thing to be scraped vibrating, without making too much noise itself. Often the best material from this point of view is a simple metal rod, thick or thin, depending on the application. Broad, flat scrapers tend to add too much of their own sound to the mix. A small switch, such as a stick of bamboo or similar material with one end split into several sticklets, can produce a distinctive sound in some applications.

Another type of scraper is the serrated bow, in the form of a stick with a series of notches which can be dragged across a string or the edge of a cymbal or other idiophonic sounding body (Figure 5-2D). Combs and similar multi-fingered objects can be used the same way.

MOUNTING SYSTEMS

Before ending this chapter I want to address a different topic — one of concern for many different instrument types, including various idiophones, membranophones and percussion aerophones, as well as a few chordophones. Instruments need to be supported somehow when they are played. Some can be hand-held, while some require stands or housings or some other form of external mounting. A good mounting system has these qualities: it holds the sounding elements in a playable position; it possesses the right degree of mass and rigidity; it is sturdy; it is rattle-free; it doesn't inhibit the musical vibration; it doesn't radiate unwanted noise or transmit it to the floor; and (least important or most important?) it looks nice. Meeting these requirements can often be frustratingly difficult, although doing so is primarily a matter of common sense and basic shop skills.

Whenever possible, the best mounting system is the human body. Instruments that can be hand-held, held on the lap, or rested on the knee always seem to do well. The human body is most adaptable; people always seem to find ways to position things to provide the optimal amount of surface contact, flex and rigidity.

The other advantage of human bodies is that they seem to do better than anything else at holding things firmly, while providing insulation. Imagine that you have some vibrating object that you need to hit hard to bring out its sound. If you set out to build a mounting for this object, you will naturally want to make something strong and firm, to hold the object well. But when you strike hard, the force of the blow is transmitted all through the rigid mounting and radiated from it to the air. Worse, the blow is also transmitted through the mounting to the floor, where it radiates as a heavy thump.

Sidebar 5-2   A SIMPLE ALL-PURPOSE BOW

The drawing below shows a small, home-buildable bow using thread or fine monofilament nylon line. I have given specific dimensions here, but you can easily modify the design to suit your purposes.

The ideal wood for the bow is springy but not prone to splitting; maple is good. For the hair, use fine monofilament nylon thread, cotton thread, or any similar strong thread, available where sewing supplies are sold. For hardware: two eye bolts at 2" and 2½", plus one wing nut and one cap nut to fit. And don't forget the bow rosin.

You can cut the hardwood to the shape shown in the drawing, or assemble a similar shape from smaller pieces very strongly glued together. Drill the two 3/16" holes for the eyebolts (access to the one at the handle end will be difficult; depending on your drill, you may need to use an extra-long bit). Bend the eyes of the eyebolts very slightly open as shown in the inset in the drawing, to allow for slipping the thread into the eyes. Put the 2" eye bolt through the hole at the handle end and tighten on the cap nut as shown. Put the 2½" eye bolt through the far end, and thread the wing nut down about 3/8". Tie the thread at one end to one of the eyes, and loop the line back and forth, through the eyes. Continue looping until you have two parallel flat strips about 3/8" wide. Tie off the line to one of the eye bolts. Rotate the eye bolts, if necessary, so that one of the strips of bow hair (thread) faces outward, ready for playing. Tighten or loosen the wing nut if needed to adjust the bow hair tension. Rub the thread generously with rosin, and the bow is ready to use.

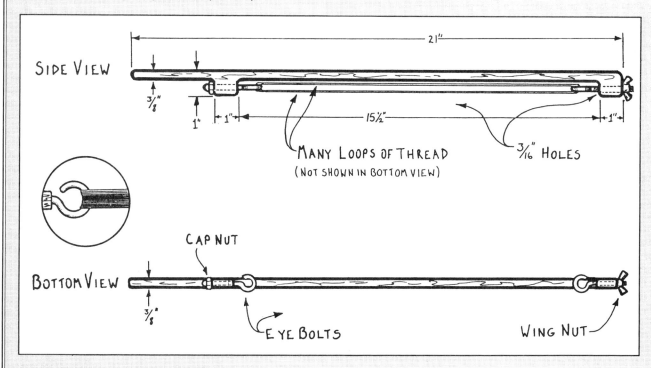

This problem rarely arises if the mounting is a human being: you can hold the object firmly in your hand or on your lap, and your body will absorb a good jolt without transmitting unwanted thump to the air, the floor, or the chair you sit upon.

The point is, insulation is a central consideration in making instrument mountings. The sounding body must be able to vibrate freely, insulated from unwanted damping effects. And it should also be insulated so as not to transmit unwanted vibration, like a thud from a beater's blow. For low-impedance vibrations, like those originating in strings or in the air itself, these considerations rarely present a problem. Such vibrations require little force to get started — no heavy blows — and once started they lack the strength to drive things they aren't intended to drive. But heavier initial vibrators often need special insulation systems. Stroked or bowed rods, for instance, may produce strong enough vibrations to rattle their whole mounting system and whatever it contacts. There are several ways to provide needed insulation.

One is padding. Padding may be inserted between the initial vibrator and its mounting structure, or between mounting structure and floor, or both. The amount of padding varies with the application. Padding may take the form of rubber washers on the screws or bolts that hold the sounding elements, or sections of soft latex tubing (surgical tubing) placed over nails that secure vibrating bodies. You may need strips cut from a heavy blanket between vibrator and mounting, or imitation fur, or foam rubber in various thicknesses. In some cases the best answer might simply be to rest sounding elements on big pillows on the floor.

Another amazingly effective insulator is one we have seen before: balloons. Nothing allows for freer vibration for the sounding element, and nothing transmits less to other solid bodies. The disadvantages of balloons are 1) they tend to be unstable (they wobble a lot); 2) there's no easy way to attach things to them; and 3) they frequently need to be replaced.

A third approach to insulation is to suspend vibrating bodies by cords or coil springs. Slightly stretchy cords are better than inelastic ones in many applications.

A few quick but important final points: In designing mountings, consider the primary direction of radiation from the sound elements relative to the player and listeners. Remember that some sounding objects need clearances — space around the vibrating surfaces or near aerophonic openings — to sound well. Reflections from flat surfaces near and parallel to a vibrating body sometimes reinforce the tone, but sometimes cause cancellations and weaken the tone. It is often beneficial to design mountings so as to leave room for later adjustment of overall height, important clearances, or any features with close tolerances.

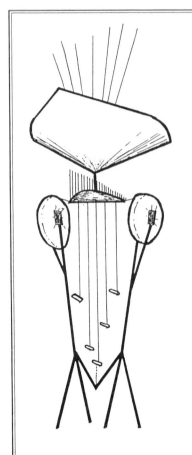

FIGURE 5-3

Manflower, an instrument created by François and Bernard Baschet, uses both balloons (in the form of inflated cushions) and cords in the mounting system, for insulation and freedom of vibration. Height: comparable to a standing person.

Chapter Six

AEROPHONES

And on we go to the wind instruments. Aerophones are musical instruments in which the initial vibration takes place not in some solid material, but in the air itself. The most familiar aerophones enclose a body of air in a hollow tube of some sort, as with flutes, clarinets, or trumpets. A little less common are aerophones having non-tubular air chambers, such as ocarinas, the egg-shaped Chinese *Hsun*, or the jugs from which jugbands get their name. There are also aerophones that have no enclosure, but simply impart a vibration directly to the surrounding atmosphere, such as harmonicas, sirens, and bullroarers (three very different approaches, all to be described more fully later).

In one sense, winds are the simplest of all instruments: what could be more straightforward than exciting a sound directly in the air? But the principles governing wind instruments are the most subtle of all the instrument types. In this chapter we will start out by describing a simple flute. Then we will take that flute through a succession of metamorphoses to illustrate various facets of wind instrument design. Things may get a bit abstract along the way, but with luck our friend the simple flute will help keep our feet on the ground. To make the going smoother, I have removed some of the more technical information from this chapter, and placed it in Appendix 5, "More on Air Columns and Toneholes."

Imagine that you are going to make a flute. (For instructions on making a simple flute similar to the one described in the following, see Sidebar 6-1.) You start with a section of plastic tubing, let's say, 17 inches long, with an internal diameter of three-quarters of an inch and tube walls

an eighth of an inch thick. Most flutes are played by blowing over a blowhole in the side of the tube near one end, so you put a 3/8-inch hole an inch from one end. You stop the same end with a cork, shoved a half inch into the tube, as shown in Figure 6-1. To get a range of pitches, you drill six more 3/8" holes along the tube to serve as toneholes. That completes the instrument. To play it, you hold it pressed just under the lips and blow a fine stream of air across the blowhole, covering and uncovering the toneholes to get different pitches.

Now, what are the essential elements of this flute?

1) Something to excite the air into vibration. That is what the blowhole is for. The vibrations come from air turbulence arising when the air stream from the player's lips strikes the edge of the blowhole, creating what is called an edgetone.

2) Something to control and enrich the edgetone. This is the job of the tube — or, more accurately, the enclosed column of air with its natural resonance frequencies. Without the air column, the edgetone would be capricious in pitch and poor in tone quality. When the edgetone excites the resonances of the air in the tube, the resonances impose their frequencies on the turbulence at the edge, reducing the capriciousness of pitch. They also help to radiate a far richer tone.

3) Something to allow the player to produce different pitches. That is what the toneholes are for. Opening and closing them modifies the effective length of the air column, altering its resonant frequencies, and so changing the sounding pitches.

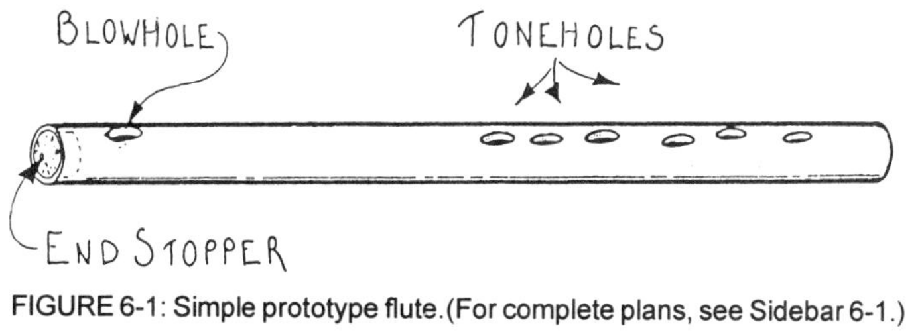

Not every wind instrument has a blowhole, a cylindrical air column, and a set of toneholes. But most wind instruments do have elements to fulfill each of these three functions — something to excite the vibration in the air, something to control it and add resonance, and something to modify the resonances in order to alter the pitch. Our approach, for the bulk of this chapter, will be to study the possibilities for each of these essential elements.

FIGURE 6-1: Simple prototype flute.(For complete plans, see Sidebar 6-1.)

EXCITING THE VIBRATION

Edgetones

Our simple flute, as well as other flutes, panpipes, some organ pipes, and several other wind instrument types, produce their sounds by means of edgetones. An edgetone comes about when a narrow air stream is directed over an edge or blade that divides the stream. An air-flow pattern tends to arise at the edge where minute pressure fluctuations direct the air first more to one side, then more to the other, in rapid succession (see Figure 6-2). On either side of the edge, the effect is like a series of quick pulses. If the edge is surrounded by open space, then the frequency of alternation is likely to be unsteady, as with howling wind sounds. But if the edge happens to be the opening of a wind instrument tube, the situation is more controlled. The bulk of the air flow alternately heads into the tube and then to the outside. Air column resonances can then coerce the airflow pattern into agreement with the tube's natural frequency.

Our prototype simple flute is the sort known as a sideblown, or transverse, flute. The player holds the flute horizontal, with the flute extending out to one side and the blowhole in front of the lips facing up (Figure 6-4). The edge of the hole opposite the player's lips is the playing edge. The near end of the tube must be stopped for the tube to sound (thus the cork in our prototype). With flutes like this, it is the player's job to focus and direct the air stream by blowing through pursed lips in just the right way to bring about the edgetone effect. The air stream must be narrow and focused, and the angle of incidence and the velocity of the air stream are important factors. Learning to produce a clear tone takes some practice.

Here are general principles for sideblown flutes: The distance from the stopper to the center of the blowhole is an important factor in range and tone quality. Typically, the best tone will come about when the distance roughly equals the internal diameter of the flute tube. It is a good idea to use an adjustable stopper, so you retain the option of fine tuning the stopper position by trial and error. A slightly oval blowhole, providing a larger, flatter blowing edge opposite the player's lips, is better than a circular hole. A typical blowhole size for

Here are steps for making a simple sideblown flute like the prototype flute described in the main text. The dimensions and hole spacings are taken from Mark Shepard's excellent booklet, *Simple Flutes: Play Them, Make Them*. I have used these dimensions and found them to be quite accurate, yielding an instrument with little need for subsequent fine tuning. Notes for making a fipple flute of similar tuning and dimensions appear on the following page.

SIDEBLOWN FLUTE IN G

Materials

One 3/4" cork (wine bottle size), and 16 7/16" of 3/4" internal diameter tubing, preferably 1/16" - 1/8" thick. Plastic tubings such as the PVC or ABS plastics available in hardware store will work well, but see the notes in Appendix 1 regarding possible toxicity.

Construction Procedure

Cut the 3/4" tube to 16 7/16". Tap the cork into one end, to a depth of 1/2", as shown in the drawing. To form the blowhole, drill a 3/8" hole in the side of the tube 1" on center from the corked end. Ream the hole out slightly so that you end up with an oval shape, about 1/2" in the long dimension, with the long dimension along the line of the tube. Smooth and de-burr the edge. Drill the fingerholes, starting with #6 (farthest down the tube). They will be 3/8" holes, spaced as in the following chart. The location values represent the distance from the center of each tonehole to the center of the blowhole.

Hole Number	Hole Location	Sounding Pitch
1	6 3/8"	F#
2	7 17/32"	E
3	8 25/32"	D
4	10 7/16"	C
5	11 3/16"	B
6	12 25/32"	A
Open end	15 7/16"	G

These hole spacings roughly follow the tube length percentage recommendations for standard pennywhistle fingering given in Figure 6-24. (Read the caption for that figure for information on fingerings as well.) Remember that the holes need not be in a straight line down the tube; it makes fingering easier if some are offset to one side or the other to accommodate the natural fall of the fingers.

After the holes are drilled, fine tune if necessary by enlarging a given hole to raise its pitch or reducing it (by back-filling with autobody filler, epoxy glue or bee's wax) to lower its pitch.

The stopper position recommended above is probably optimal. But you can try adjusting its position relative to the blowhole to improve the tone, make it easier to sound the upper octave, or improve the tuning in the upper octave.

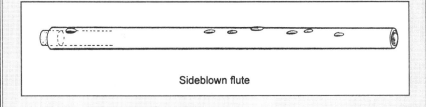

Sideblown flute

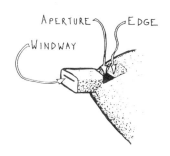

FIGURE 6-3: Fipple and edge arrangement, shown here on a globular flute.

Sidebar 6-1   SIMPLE FLUTES (Part 2)

FIPPLE FLUTE IN G

This is the fippled version of the flute appearing on the preceding page.

Materials:

One 1"-long, 3/4"-diameter cork (wine bottle size), and 16 9/16" of 3/4" internal diameter tubing — see notes on tubing materials above.

Construction Procedure

Flatten one side of the cork by cutting and/or sanding, to create a sloped flat surface along one side, as shown in Figure B. Tap the cork into the 16 9/16" tube to where the end is flush. This will leave a narrow windway between the tube and the flattened part of the cork. Now cut the beveled opening in the tube, to form the aperture and edge. Make the angle cut as in Figure C, and end it with the vertical cut at 1" from the tube end. Carefully de-burr the edge as need be; then blow through the windway to check for tone. If you don't get a clear tone, try adjusting the cork to shift the air stream angle over the edge. If after some effort you still can't get a clear tone, try making another cork with a slightly different bevel.

To complete the instrument, make the toneholes. The arrangement is the same as that described for the sideblown flute on the preceding page, with all measurements taken from the center of the toneholes to a point in the opening at the end of the windway, 1/8" from the vertical cut.

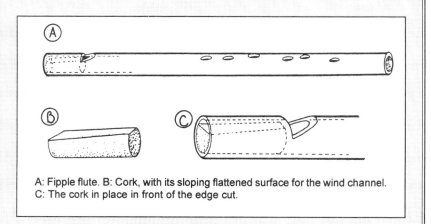

A: Fipple flute. B: Cork, with its sloping flattened surface for the wind channel. C: The cork in place in front of the edge cut.

FIGURE 6-2: Edgetone mechanics. At the start of the tone, the major part of the air flows to one side of the edge. This results in a pressure buildup on that side, which deflects the air stream and forces the majority of the air flow over to the other side. This causes a pressure buildup there; the process then reverses and the cycle repeats.

flutes in the middle ranges is just under 1/2" across the long dimension. Blowholes should be moderately deep — 1/8" or more — so if your tubing material is extremely thin, the flute might benefit from an overlay of thicker material in the region of the blowhole to increase hole depth. The edge should be free of nicks, burrs or other irregularities. A slight inward slope to the playing edge, so that the angle of the edge is a bit less than 90 degrees, may improve response. The size of the blowhole affects tuning of all the notes, with a larger hole raising the pitch.

Another configuration for our simple flute, rather than having the blowhole at the side, would be an end-blowing form (Figure 6-5). In end-blown flutes the player blows directly over the open end of the tube. Sometimes the blown edge is altered in shape — notched, beveled or rounded — to improve tone production. (A playing-edge angle of about 30 degrees, some makers have suggested, is optimal.) The Japanese shakuhachi, and the Middle Eastern ney, are important examples of endblown flutes. In the West, end-blowing is most often used with tubes stopped at the far end, or with globular chambers such as bottles or jugs. End blowing is the standard approach with sets of panpipes, which are almost always made with stopped tubes.

The third common edgetone arrangement is the fipple. Fipple flutes are those that use a narrow air channel, rather than the player's lips, to focus the air stream and direct it over the edge (Figures 6-3 and 6-6). Familiar fipple flutes include the recorder family, the referee's whistle, and most ocarinas. Some of the most beautiful and exotic instruments in the world are the complex fipple flutes of pre-Columbian Central and South

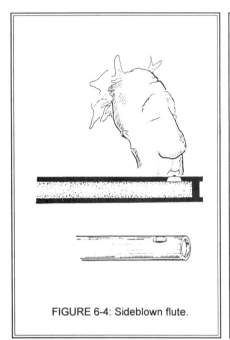

FIGURE 6-4: Sideblown flute.

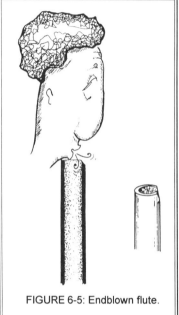

FIGURE 6-5: Endblown flute.

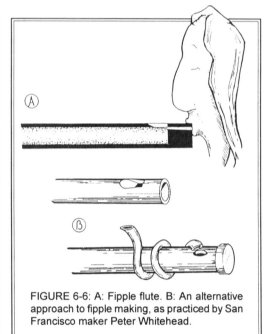

FIGURE 6-6: A: Fipple flute. B: An alternative approach to fipple making, as practiced by San Francisco maker Peter Whitehead.

Sidebar 6-2

PANPIPES

Panpipes are tuned sets of stopped pipes held together in a raft-like row. You play them by end-blowing, sliding the panpipes back and forth in front of the mouth in a motion similar to harmonica playing. The sound is a breathy flute sound, but having (in the hands of a good player) a distinctive "chiff" in the attack for each note. The pipes of a typical instrument range from perhaps three or four inches long to ten or twelve. Much longer panpipe sets are used in the Andes, some Pacific islands, and southern Africa. The longer ones are harder to play.

Panpipes are very easy to make. For the tubes, look for an internal diameter in the range of 1/2". Tube walls should not be too thin — bamboo or various available plastics might be about right. Bevel the blowing ends of the tubes. (A bevel of 45° or more on the side of each tube opposite the lips, where the air stream strikes, usually works well.) The tubes should be cut a little longer than they need to be for the pitches you want, and a stopper inserted and adjusted to give the desired pitch. (We'll be discussing tuning for air column tubes as this chapter proceeds.) The stopper can be anything that forms a dependably leak-proof seal — cork, for instance. But I recommend making a snug-fitting slidable stopper, which will allow easy tuning and re-tuning of the pipes. You can make it using a double-headed nail, shortened and wrapped at the head end with a 1/8" layer of closed-cell neoprene foam weather stripping as shown in the drawing. Make the nail long enough so that the unwrapped end protrudes below the end of the tube, providing a handle for making adjustments.

In some traditional panpipes, the pipes are held together in a row by wrapping with cord or leather thongs. Or they are strapped to a board or stick across the back side of the row, usually in scalewise order. Some makers have simply glued the row of pipes together, and some have set the lower end of the pipes in a solid base of some sort. You can also make panpipes from a single piece of solid wood, with the holes drilled to varying depths.

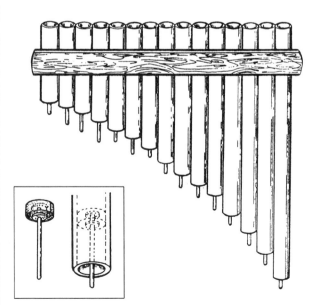

Panpipes. In the inset, a sliding stopper arrangement made from a double-headed nail with neoprene rubber weather strip wrapped between the heads.

America. Fipple-and-edge making is an art, a craft and a science. Sidebar 6-4 has information on fipple and edge design.

Reeds

The edgetones just described are one of many possible ways to excite the vibration in our simple flute. Reeds are another. Wind instrument reeds work by converting a steady stream of air into a series of rapid pulses by means of some sort of air-gating mechanism. The steady air stream usually comes from someone's lungs, and the gateway is the reed that alternately blocks and un-blocks an opening through which the air must pass. The pulsing generates a vibration in the surrounding air, yielding the audible tone. If the air-gate leads into a wind instrument tube, then the resonances of the air column can come to dominate the reed just as they dominate an edgetone. The reed accommodates its pulsing frequency to the tube's preferred frequencies, and you get a controlled tone with all the resonance of the air chamber.

A reed may literally be a piece of cane, or it may be made of other material, such as springy metal. Clarinets, oboes and harmonicas are familiar examples of reed instruments. For analytical purposes, we can regard trumpets and trombones as reed instruments as well, because the trumpeter's buzzed lips likewise form an air-gating system. Let's look at the possibilities one at a time.

Single and Double Reeds

Single reeds, sometimes called beating reeds, appear on instruments of the clarinet and saxophone families, and a great many related instruments around the world. The beating reed is positioned over the opening in a mouthpiece as shown in Figure 6-7.

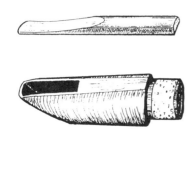

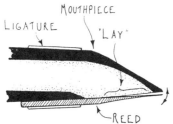

FIGURE 6-7: Single reed and mouthpiece (clarinet or saxophone), showing the reed, the mouthpiece and a cutaway view of the two together. The "lay," which is the degree of curvature of the face of the mouthpiece just under the reed, is one of the crucial factors in tone and playability. The ligature is a steel band circling the mouthpiece that holds the reed in place.

FIGURE 6-8: Beating reed of a sort used in pipe organ reed pipes. Notice the tuning wire, making it possible to adjust the vibrating length of the reed.

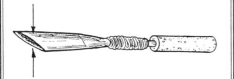

FIGURE 6-9: Double reed. The arrows indicate the way the two halves flex to close the air passage.

When air under pressure tries to flow into the tube, the reed repeatedly slaps shut against the rim of the opening, then swings open again to let more air through, so that the air enters the tube in pulses.

The reeds normally used with clarinets and saxes are cut from the stalk of a species of cane called *Arundo donax*. They are cut to a particular shape, as shown in Figure 6-7, to obtain the desired qualities of lightness and springiness. They're made to different sizes for different instruments, and in different "strengths," meaning thickness and corresponding rigidity or softness. The playing technique for single reeds is rather subtle, and best learned from a teacher.

Classical saxophones and clarinets use similar mouthpieces, onto which the reed is strapped. Players of these instruments will tell you that the mouthpiece is the heart of their instrument; the remainder of the tube, with all its fancy keywork, pales in importance by comparison. Essential elements of the mouthpiece are the shape of the internal chamber, and the *lay*, which is the facing over which the reed slaps down to close (identified in Figure 6-7). Subtle changes in these elements can make a big difference in sound and playability.

The makers of clarinet and sax mouthpieces have, over the years, achieved an exquisite degree of refinement in their art. And so, if you choose to create a single-reed instrument of your own design, one of your options is to borrow the mouthpiece and reed from an appropriately sized member of the clarinet or saxophone family.

You can also make a beating reed from scratch. Sidebar 6-5 has suggestions.

Most pipe organ reed pipes use a type of beating reed made of metal, as shown in Figure 6-8. Notice the tuning mechanism, which allows for lengthening or shortening the active portion of the reed, permitting the best possible resonant coupling with the pipe. Much cruder beating reeds of plastic are sometimes used in children's toys, party noisemakers and such; often you can remove the little plastic reed assemblies in order to apply them to your own purposes.

Double reeds are the sort used on oboes and their kin. Rather than having a single tongue beat against an opening, double reeds are made in two halves which beat together. The arrangement of the two reed halves for double reeds is such that they need to be affixed to a rather narrow tubular duct, called the staple. Because such a narrow tube of any length would not function well acoustically, double reeds are usually used on conical tubes that start out small at the mouthpiece end and grow larger over their length.

Classical double reeds are made from the same cane as single reeds, but cut and configured differently, as you can see in Figure 6-9. For the oboe, as shown here, the end of the staple is covered in cork, and it fits snugly into the small end of the conical musical instrument tube. The arrangement is slightly different for the bassoon. If you are interested in making a double-reed instrument you may find that your best bet is simply to buy a ready-made reed at a music store — or perhaps to buy the cane and staple, and then convince an experienced oboist to show you the tricks of reed making.

Some historical double reed instruments have a "wind cap," which is a perforated cap over the reed. The player seals his or her lips over the cap, and the lips do not touch the reed. Such reeds, which must sound without pressure from the lips, are made flatter than other double reeds, with a narrower opening between the halves. Similar reeds appear in bagpipe chanters.

Membrane Reeds

In some of the islands of Indonesia, an instrument is made as a children's toy and for sale to tourists. It uses a unique arrangement which I call a *membrane reed*. The membrane reed is easy to make with commonly available materials, and it works well.

In keeping with our use of the word "reed," a membrane reed functions

MAKING SINGLE REED MOUTHPIECES

There are several ways you can make your own single reeds.

1) You can work with a curved strip of metal. Figure A shows an easily made form. It is crude, with a coarse sound, but it works. When I tried this I used a strip of stainless steel for the reed; other non-corrosive springy materials might do as well. The degree of curvature of the reed (which corresponds to the "lay" of a conventional mouthpiece) is important in the playing response, and worth experimenting with. Notice also in this design that the reed can in effect be tuned: you can vary the effective length of the reed by adjusting the location of the tie that holds the reed. You need not tune the reed to a specific note, but the reed's general preferred frequency range is an important factor in bringing out the best response in the coupled system of the reed and air column.

2) You can make an *idioglottal* reed. This wonderful word refers to reed instruments in which the reed is of a piece with the body of the instrument, a tongue carved from the wall of the tube itself by three slightly beveled cuts, as shown in Figure B. The bevel allows the tongue to beat against the angled walls rather than flexing through and inward. Either bend the reed outward slightly, or else remove some extra material from the cuts, so that the reed does not lie against the tube walls in rest position. In my minimal experimentation in this area, I managed to create a working idioglottal reed from a section of flexible black plastic pipe. The tone was muddy, but it did speak. Where the art of idioglottal reed making is more advanced, bamboo or similar rigidly springy grasses are used to form the tube and tongue. I have watched the ever-versatile maker Ben Hume carve such a reed; in his experienced hands it took only a few minutes to produce something that spoke readily and with an admirably refined tone.

3) You can make something closer to a standard clarinet or sax mouthpiece, but in a more home-buildable form. The process is simpler than you might expect, although it may take some effort to get the subtle curvature of the lay just right. You will need to have experience playing clarinet or sax, or enlist the help of someone who does, to assess when the lay is just right and the reed is playing well. I recommend using commercial clarinet or sax reeds, at least initially.

You can follow this approach to make an instrument with an integral mouthpiece, simply by making the mouthpiece cut at one end of your main instrument tube. Or you can use a shorter section of tubing to make a detachable mouthpiece, as is done with standard clarinets and saxes. An appropriate tubing is not too thin-walled — 1/8" thick or a little less is good. Good diameters are from 7/16" up to about 5/8". Tubes within this range are suitable because they can accommodate pre-cut commercial reeds, from the rather narrow clarinet reed up to the larger reeds for the lower members of the sax family.

Cut the tubing at an angle as shown in the first drawing in Figure C. The angle can be any-where from about 16 to 30 degrees; a midrange angle of about 22 degrees is fairly typical. This angle does seem to have some effect on tone quality, with broader angles yielding a mellower tone. Sand the surface of this cut perfectly smooth and straight. Then sand a bit more, to impart a slight, uniform curvature toward the tip, as shown in the second drawing. This shaping is rather subtle, and slight variations make a big difference in playing. The upper part of the mouthpiece cut should remain flat to hold the base of the reed, with the curvature affecting only the last 3/4" or so. The gap that the curvature creates between the tip of the reed and the surface of the mouthpiece should be between about 1/32" and 1/16", perhaps a shade more for larger instruments.

To test your work, moisten a reed, strap it on, and blow (or get your reed-playing friend to blow). You can easily strap on the reed using a rubber band as shown in the third drawing. (You can devise a more elegant reed-holding system later, if you wish.) If the reed slaps shut and stays closed, allowing no air to pass, then your curvature is too shallow; the gap is too small. If it doesn't close at all and air simply rushes through the gap, the curvature is too deep and the gap too wide. If it squeals rather than producing a steady tone, the gap may be too small, the reed may be too dry, or there may be some unevenness somewhere. Remove the reed, go back to the sandpaper, do some re-shaping, and try again.

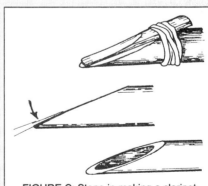

FIGURE A: A homemade beating reed made of stainless steel or other non-corrosive springy metal (shown in two possible orientations). The player places his or her whole mouth over the section of the tube that holds the reed, and blows.

FIGURE B: An idioglottal reed, with an end-on view showing the sloped walls of the reed as formed by the cut.

FIGURE C: Steps in making a clarinet-type single reed mouthpiece
1. Make the angle cut at the tube end, and sand it smooth.
2. Give a slight back-curvature to the last 3/4" or so of the cut surface.
3. Strap the reed in place.

as a pulsing air-gate system. The essential element is a small membrane stretched over what would otherwise be the open end of the tube. Figure 6-10 shows one of several forms that such a reed can take. (The Indonesian version is different, and more complex.) The cut-off neck of a balloon is stretched over the open end of the tube. Holding the mouth of the balloon in his or her mouth, the player stretches the balloon neck to one side and down over the rim. When the player blows, the air squeezes its way between the balloon rubber and the tube rim, and into the tube. And it does so in pulses: the balloon rubber lifts to allow a burst of air through, then comes back down under its own elastic pull. The pulsing rate accommodates itself to the natural frequency of the tube. In short, the system behaves exactly as a wind instrument reed should. You could easily put a balloon membrane over the end of our prototype flute, and it would sing for you.

Membrane reeds have one troublesome characteristic. You can't predict wavelength based upon tube length. The

---

Sidebar 6-6 — MAKING A BIG MEMBRANE REED

(See illustrations on the following page)

Membrane reeds, as described in the main text of this chapter, work well over a range of sizes from moderately small to quite large. The plan given here is for a large membrane reed. At this scale, the instrument is rather clumsy and not well suited for melodic playing, but it produces a big, bottomy sound, wonderfully gratifying in a crude sort of way; and it shakes your whole head as you blow. Since these instruments are inexpensive and easy to make, you may want to make several in different sizes.

Materials

4'- diameter tubing. You can use inexpensive thinwall plastic drain pipe. Length can range from about eighteen inches to five feet or more.

Very big round balloons. Those intended to inflate to 18" are good. Get a supply of at least six or eight.

Mouthpiece: See Figure E (next page) to get a sense of what is suitable for the purpose.

1/4" vinyl tubing — about 14" (the translucent sort; available at hardware stores).

Optional (for tonehole instruments only): 1/4" x 1/2" neoprene closed-cell adhesive-backed weather stripping.

Construction Procedure

Cut a section of 4" pipe to your chosen length, with a level and unwavering cut. Three feet is a reasonable length for an initial effort. Cut a piece of 1/4" vinyl tubing long enough to circle the rim of the big tube. With a sharp utility knife, slit the vinyl tubing longways and seat it over the rim of the big tube as shown in Figure B (next page). Glue the vinyl tubing in place (hot glue works well); tape the point where the ends join tightly with electricians tape to ensure that the ends stay in line with each other.

Cut off the end of the balloon and slide the balloon over the top of the big tube, as in C and D. You can hold the balloon in place with rubber bands. (A single rubber band of the very large size designated as 105 works great.) Slip the mouth of the balloon over the mouthpiece (see Figures E and A), and fix it in place with small rubber bands.

What you have now is a simple big membrane instrument of the sort shown in Figure A, which you can play as described below. You can stop here and enjoy the instrument as is, or add a tonehole to increase its range.

Big membrane tube pitch is very flexible, so precise calculation is not needed for tone hole size and placement. For a three-foot tube, try a 2½" hole centered at 8¼" from the far end — this will give a tone about a minor third above the whole-tube tone. After cutting the hole, take about 10" of 1/4" x 1/2" dense neoprene rubber weather stripping and cut it in half longways, leaving two 1/4" x 1/4" strips. Using the adhesive backing, create a raised padded rim around the periphery of the hole with one of these strips, as shown in F. With the weather strip as a gasket, you can how cover the hole leaklessly with your hand.

If you want to add more toneholes, you'll probably have to get into oversized levers and keypads (as I did, with some success, on one such instrument). But I leave the design of such things to you.

Playing Technique

Take the mouthpiece in your mouth. Holding the ledge of the mouthpiece behind your teeth, you can pull back on the balloon neck, as shown in Figure A. Stretch the neck slightly down and away, so that it rides against the tube rim. Now blow.

Stretching the balloon neck tighter raises the pitch; loosening it will cause pitch to drop until the tone droops into nothingness. Placing fingers directly on the membrane close to the edge also raises the pitch. The maximum range depends on tube length: with a long tube, you can get a range of a fourth or fifth; with shorter tubes you can get more.

If you have added a tonehole, hold the tube near the top with the left hand to control balloon-neck stretching and do any membrane-pressing. Cover and uncover the hole with the right hand.

Acoustic Notes and Further Thoughts

The large balloon-membrane forms a semi-rigid stopped end for the air column within the tube. Stretching the membrane by pulling tighter on the balloon-neck makes it more rigid, which has the effect of raising the tube's resonant frequency. Pressing the membrane with a finger does the same, just as with the balloon flutes described later in this chapter. Stretching, in addition, raises the membrane's own natural frequency — the frequency at which it wants to flap up and down like a drumhead — and this too contributes to the pitch-raising effect.

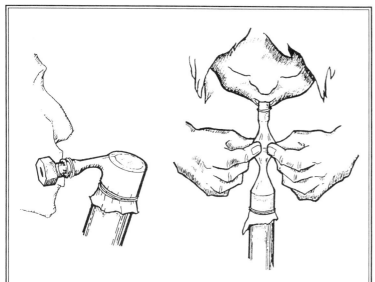

FIGURE 6-10 (left): A simple membrane reed arrangement. The part in the player's mouth in this drawing is a plastic plumbing fixture, held behind the teeth, allowing the player to stretch the balloon neck without the mouthpiece slipping out of the mouth.

FIGURE 6-11 (right): A simple form of labial reed, using a balloon neck and tube.

softness of the membrane covering the tube end alters the natural resonance frequency of the tube. Stretching the membrane more tightly raises the pitch considerably. For different physical reasons, producing a loud tone by blowing hard usually flattens the pitch. Thus, membrane reeds tend to be intonationally unstable. Yet if the player can gain control over these factors, they allow for a lot of flexibility and some highly expressive effects.

Plans for making a big-tube membrane reed — a wonderful sounding instrument — appear in Sidebar 6-6.

Labial Reeds

Here is an odd one. *Labial reeds* are air-gating systems that operate by forcing air through a pair of normally closed lip-like diaphragms. In fact, they operate much like the human lip-buzzing described below, but without the human lips. (The term "labial reed," like several others used in this book, is not in standard usage; it is simply what I came up with since no other term seems to exist.) A familiar example of a labial reed would be the squeal of balloon whose air is allowed to escape slowly through a pinched neck. It should be possible to attach such a system to a tuned air column, so that the column dictates the

BIG MEMBRANE REED (Drawings for Sidebar 6-6)

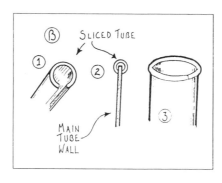

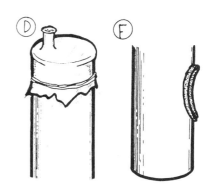

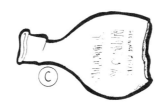

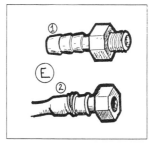

A. Big membrane reed in playing position.

B. The 1/4" vinyl tubing eases the edge of the 4" tube over which the membrane passes. 1) Vinyl tubing with slit cut in it; 2) cutaway view of the vinyl tubing in position over the main tube; 3) the end result, vinyl tubing glued in place.

C. Balloon with the end snipped off.

D. Balloon membrane stretched over the tube end.

E. The mouthpiece. 1) A commonly available plastic plumbing fixture that will do the job nicely. Other items of similar size and shape might do just as well. 2) The plumbing fixture with the balloon neck held on by a rubber band or equivalent; notice that the threaded section of the fixture has been removed.

F. Weather-strip foam gasket around the rim of the big tonehole.

pitch of the reed and controls the squeal (see Figure 6-11). But I know of no musical instrument that uses a labial reed. I have done just a little experimenting with this system without great results; I include it here with the thought that someone may pick up the idea and follow it through to greater success.

Lip-buzzed Instruments

By placing one's lips against the opening of a tube and buzzing through them — making what without the tube would be a "raspberry" or "Bronx cheer" sound — one can produce a clear, well-defined tone. Bugles, trombones, French horns, shell trumpets, wooden alphorns, shofars made of ram's horn, the elephant's tusk Oliphant, and a host of other instruments are played this way. The technique amounts to using a "lip reed" — namely, an air-gating system similar to that of other reeds, but using the player's lips as the gate.

Lip reeds differ from other reeds in this important respect: with other reeds, you can control the rigidity or tension of the reed only minimally, by lip pressure and positioning. But you can control the tension of your lips over a wide range. This means that you can bring out many different notes by means of lip tension alone. For instance, blowing into a tube whose natural resonances form a harmonic overtone series, a skilled player can play through the first several tones of the series. This is what buglers do, when they play melodies composed entirely of tones from the lower part of the harmonic series. With the help of three or four valves you can fill in the notes between the available tones of the series, and play complete scales.

Well made brass instruments do not require players to blow into the unadorned end of a tube. They use a mouthpiece. Brass instrument mouthpieces serve two purposes: First, they give the player something comfortable to press his or her lips against, providing physical support that encourages the right sort of buzzing for the size and range of the instrument. Second, they provide enhanced resonance over a broad, moderately high range. As a result they add to the brightness of the overall sound.

If you are making a lip-buzzed instrument of your own, you may choose to use an existing brass instrument mouthpiece. They come in a range of sizes, from the big, heavy, sousaphone mouthpiece to the very small one for the French horn. Though the results may not be as impressive, you can also make your own mouthpiece. Sometimes — with clay, wood, conch shell or dried kelp — you can form the mouthpiece from the same material as the main tube. Otherwise, dense, hard, non-corrosible materials are your best bet. You can benefit by studying existing mouthpiece shapes.

Free Reeds

Free reeds are used in harmonicas, accordions, the family of Asian mouth organs that includes the Japanese sho, and countless other instruments. Free reeds provide one of the smallest ways there is to make a fairly big musical sound, as the pocket-sized harmonica nicely demonstrates. Free reeds differ from the other reed types we have been seeing in this important respect: they don't need a coupled air column to tell them what pitch to produce. Each free reed is designed to produce a single specific pitch on its own. For that reason free reeds are used in different ways than other reeds. For instance, it wouldn't work well to attach a free reed to our prototype flute body. Instead, instruments using free reeds usually employ an entire bank of reeds — one free reed for each note in the instrument's range — with, in most cases, no attached air column.

The free reed's gating system works in a manner that can be compared to a swinging door, of the kind that swings through to both sides without any stop. The reed-door, in this analogy, is a strip of some flat, springy material, sized so that it just fits in an opening without quite touching the edges. When air is forced through the opening, the reed flexes in and out to create the pulsing effect. The frequency is determined by the reed's own natural vibrating frequency, offset somewhat by aerodynamic factors. You can expect it to sound close to or somewhat below the frequency at which the reed vibrates when plucked.

Free reeds are tunable and re-tunable following the principles discussed in Chapter 4 regarding vibrating tongues, also illustrated in Figure 2-1. The rules, in their simplest form, are: 1) decreasing rigidity of the reed by thinning it near the base lowers the pitch; 2) decreasing mass at the end by thinning there raises the pitch; 3) increasing mass near the end by adding material there lowers pitch.

You can borrow free reeds from existing instruments, and put them to your own purposes. Harmoniums are the best source, since the reeds are usually of good quality and cover a wide range of pitches. Also, each harmonium reed is set in its own small frame, easily removed and replaced. I give this advice reluctantly, though, since beautiful old harmoniums, until recently quite common at modest prices in antique shops and junk stores, are now becoming rare. Alternative sources include harmonicas, pianicas and accordions, but these are less useful because they usually have entire banks of reeds set in a single mounting block, rather than being separately removable.

Alternatively, you can try your hand at making your own free reeds. Here are some suggestions: Use a springy, non-corrosive metal for the reed itself. Brass is traditional; stainless steel also works well. The reed must not be too massive relative to its mounting; if the reed drives the mounting noticeably when it vibrates, then the mounting is not sufficiently heavy or firm. The reed should just about fill the opening it covers, with just enough clearance to swing through without

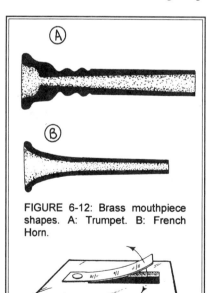

FIGURE 6-12: Brass mouthpiece shapes. A: Trumpet. B: French Horn.

FIGURE 6-13: A free reed. The reed flexes through the opening, alternately opening and closing the hole in the process.

catching. Free reeds are not usually set within the opening, but in front of it, as shown in Figure 6-13. The reed will sound with the wind direction that pushes the reed into the opening. Free reeds are often given a slight bend or twist, as if to leave a little passageway for the air to sneak through even when the reed is at rest — perhaps it helps to have some initial flow-through to start the tone.

Corrugaphones

Here is one more means for exciting a vibration in an air column, apparently unknown until recently. Instead of there being some sort of vibration-inducing mechanism at one end, in *corrugaphones* the vibration-inducing process takes place over the full length of the tube. This calls for a special form of tube, ringed over its entire length with evenly spaced lateral ridges. This happens to be characteristic of various types of corrugated flex-pipe, such as the gas heater hose found at hardware stores. When air rushes through a corrugated tube, it sets up a standing wave as it bumps over the ridges. (See the "Basic Principles of Oscillation" section of Chapter 2 if you need to review the idea of standing waves.) The frequency is determined jointly by the speed of the air and the spacing of the ridges, and the practical result is that pitch rises as air speed increases. But the tube does not produce a continuous upwardly sliding glissando as air speed increases. Instead, standing waves are set up only at the resonant frequencies of the tube, with the tone jumping from one resonance to the next as air speed increases. In other words, you get a harmonic series.

One form of corrugated-tube instrument has become fairly common: *Whirlies* (known by several other names as well) are the corrugated plastic tubes, usually a little over an inch in diameter and about three feet long, that sometimes appear in toy stores. You sound them by holding one end and whirling the tube overhead, generating a flow through the tube as air is forced out the far end and drawn in the near end by centrifugal force. The tone is unusual and evocative — a deep, breathy sort of "ooooo," rising and falling through the tones of the harmonic series, made more intriguing by the gestural aspect of the whirling.

Whirlies require a larger air flow than human lungs can supply because of their large diameter. You can play smaller-diameter corrugated tubes by blowing. The most playable of widely available types is 3/8" gas heater hose. No special mouthpiece or embouchure is necessary to play a corruga-horn; just blow, or suck — harder for higher notes (to get faster air speed); softer for lower. With tubes of suitable lengths and diameters, the range extends well up the series, where the available tones are close together and you can, with practice, play quite melodically. For a less exacting player the tube can produce very pretty glissandos and special effects.

Interestingly, the range of a corrugated tube is determined more by its diameter than by its length. Lower notes become available with larger diameters. If the length of a particular tube is such that its fundamental resonance frequency falls below the available range for its diameter, the tube won't produce the fundamental, but it will still generate the portion of its harmonic series that falls within the range limitations for its diameter.

Plans for making a multiple corrugahorn, a lovely instru-ment, appear in Sidebar 6-7.

AIR COLUMNS AND CHAMBERS

So far in this chapter we have been considering the many ways for exciting the vibration in wind instruments, from the edgetone of our prototype flute to various types of air-gating mechanisms. Now it is time to move to stage two: a study of wind instrument air chambers, and how they serve to control and enrich the initial vibration.

Air chambers used in musical instruments can be divided into two categories: tubes and vessels. Tubes form an elongated air column, as with flutes, trumpets, and the like. Vessels enclose a more three-dimensional body of air, with no one dimension excessively dominating the others. For acoustic purposes, vessel-shaped chambers are often labeled *Helmholtz resonators*, after the physicist who first studied their properties. Examples are bottles and jugs, the egg-shaped Chinese *hsun*, and similar globular-shaped instruments. The two forms — tubes and vessels — operate by different acoustic rules. We will begin with vessels, because their acoustic behavior is simpler.

Helmholtz Resonators

Globular air chamber resonances are strongly dominated by a single frequency. The tone contains little in the way of partials, and as wind instruments they cannot be made to produce anything analogous to an upper register. For various physical reasons they don't work as well in connection with reeds, but they do well in resonating edgetones, as with ocarinas (which are globular fipple flutes). Helmholtz resonators also work well as external resonators for non-wind vibrating systems such as marimba bars.

Three variables affect the resonance frequency:

1) The volume of the chamber. The larger the chamber, the lower the pitch.

2) The size of the opening. The smaller the opening, the lower the pitch.

3) The depth or thickness of the opening. Making the hole taller (or making the neck longer, in the case of jug-like shapes) also yields lower pitch.

In most cases, the most convenient way to alter the resonances in a globular chamber is by varying the opening size. You reach the lower limit in range for a given vessel when the hole becomes so small that there is not enough open surface area to move much outside air, and as a result the sound becomes too quiet. The upper limit is reached when the opening becomes so large that the springy effect of the enclosed air becomes too diffuse, the resonant frequencies become ill-defined, and the body of air simply doesn't oscillate very well. The maximum available range you can achieve from a single resonating chamber this way is typically not much more than an octave.

There are many ways to control pitch through varying aperture size. The most convenient for ocarinas and their kin is simply to use toneholes that can be covered and uncovered with the fingers. Lifting a finger to open a tonehole increases the cumulative aperture size, thus raising the frequency. The

Corrugahorns, as described in the main text, take advantage of the harmonic series whistle produced by blowing through a corrugated tube. Since, in its lower ranges, the intervals between the tones of the series are fairly large, it makes sense to bring several corrugated tubes together, tuned to different fundamentals, so as to fill in the gaps. To make a multiple corrugahorn you will need:

4 feet of 3/8" gas heater hose, a semi-rigid but flexible corrugated metal tubing (often having a coating of non-metallic gray) available at hardware stores.

One two-liter plastic soda pop bottle.

Two 1" hose clamps.

A small piece of hardwood board or high quality 3/4" plywood (5" square is adequate).

Cut the bottom 2/3 or so off the pop bottle, such that the cut is an inch into the cylindrical section (see the drawing). Cut the hardwood or plywood to form a disk of a diameter to match the pop bottle, so that the disk fits snugly into the opening where you made the cut. Drill four 7/16" holes through the disk, evenly spaced, 1" in from the edge. Insert the disk in the pop bottle. Force it in tight; glue and/or tack it if necessary.

Now cut and tune the tubes. You can tune them as you wish; but let me suggest tuning them over a range of a fourth between C_6, at a tube length near 12 ½", and F_6, near 9 ³/₈". Those pitches represent the tubes' lowest sounding pitch, which is actually their 2nd harmonic. The first harmonic does not sound at these lengths with this tube diameter, but a generous array of additional harmonics is available above. (See "Acoustic Notes" below for more on this.) Cut the tubes initially with a hacksaw. You can fine-tune with more hacksaw work, or a grinder, or hand files. WARNING: Cutting and grinding will generate fine metallic dust. Wear goggles and a breather. Carefully blow away any filings before putting the tube to your mouth to test the tuning, and *don't test the pitch by inhaling* — exhale only. Once you have cut the four tubes and tuned them to your satisfaction, file the ends to remove any burrs.

Insert the tubes into the holes in the disk, twisting each one in like a screw (the corrugations are like threads). You can adjust the tuning of the tubes slightly at this point by screwing them in farther to raise the pitch; out more to lower it. That done, bend the tubes so that the ends of the two longest are beside one another, and the ends of the two shortest are beside one another. Slip a hose clamp over each pair, and slide it down along the tubes about 3".

The playing technique for this instrument is described below. Read through to get the basic idea; then arrange the tube ends and hose clamps in a comfortable playable position. Tighten the hose clamps, and the corrugahorn is complete.

Performance Technique

Hold the instrument with the top of the cut-off pop bottle in your mouth, and your thumbs resting against the hose-clamp screw housings. Cover the four tube ends with four fingers. Then lift the finger for the tube that you wish to sound, and blow. Air will flow through that tube only, and it will sing. Blow harder for greater air speed, and the pitch will jump to a higher harmonic. Between the four tubes with their harmonic series, you can play a complete diatonic scale over an octave, and a greater diversity of pitches through the next octave. In addition to monophonic melodic playing, you can experiment with lifting two fingers at once, and you can produce a wealth of exotic effects by lifting and replacing fingers very rapidly, or by shifting air speed rapidly so as to whirl up and down through the harmonic series.

Acoustic Notes and Other Thoughts

If you make this instrument with longer tubes, you will not get a significantly wider range, but you will have more tones within the range available from each tube. The tube lengths for the suggested tuning were chosen because, given the 3/8" diameter, these lengths will controllably sound the 2nd through about the 6th harmonic. If you tune them properly, that yields a scale like the following chart:

	Tube #1	Tube #2	Tube #3	Tube #4
2nd Harm.	Do	Re	Mi	Fa
3rd Harm.	Sol	La	Ti	Do
4th Harm.	Do	Re	Mi	Fa

... and so forth.

I've used do-re-mi-fa in the example above. You could distribute your pitches differently within the tetrachord. An arrangement I found particularly attractive in the playing is the Phrygian C - Db - Eb - F.

Acknowledgments

Among the many people who have worked with corrugahorns, Frank Crawford must be acknowledged for developing the idea and researching the underlying acoustics. The idea of using multiple tubes and end-stopping them comes from Richard Waters.

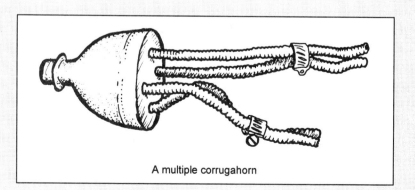

A multiple corrugahorn

acoustic principle here, however, is somewhat different from the way toneholes function in tubes. Hole location — an essential factor in tubes — is of relatively minor significance in globular chambers, except in so far as it relates to ease of playability. Look ahead to Figure 6-24B for a sample ocarina tonehole chart.

Tubes

The prototype simple flute with which we opened this chapter was a cylindrical tube open at both ends. (One end was stopped with a cork, but the blowhole nearby functions as an opening at that end. For the moment we will ignore the toneholes.) This open-ended cylindrical form is just one among many possible tube shapes. It is easy to imagine others — flaring shapes, narrow cone shapes, lumpy-bumpy shapes, and so forth. But from among the many, only a few are commonly used in wind instruments. The reason is that a typical tube has resonance peaks at several frequencies. For most possible tube shapes, these resonance peaks form an inharmonic series. There are just a few types in which the resonances form a harmonic overtone series. The most useful of these are the cylinders and the cones (usually, for wind instruments, very thin, elongated cones).

Wind instrument designers generally prefer well tuned harmonic overtone series in their instruments for two reasons. One is that if the series is true, then when the instrument sounds its fundamental tone, the overtones above join in the overall vibration, reinforcing it and creating a tone that is strong, stable and rich. In the absence of this cooperation between the fundamental and overtones, the tone may be weak and unstable. The second reason is that many wind instruments make use of the higher resonances to provide the notes in the upper ranges, and if the resonances are out of tune, so will be those notes.

In actual practice, most existing wind instruments do deviate from the ideal cone and cylinder shapes, for a variety of musical and acoustical reasons. Yet each of the standard wind instruments remains grounded in one or the other bore shape, and each retains enough of the shape to manifest its most important acoustic characteristics.

With that in mind, let us look at the acoustic behaviors of the two basic forms. There are actually three types to be considered: 1. Cylindrical, open at both ends; 2. Cylindrical, closed at one end; and 3. Conical (by definition, closed at one end). Each has its own characteristic patterns of wave motion and vibration. We won't analyze them in detail here, but we will outline the practical results.

Cylindrical tubes open at both ends

Included here are most flutes, including our prototype, since the flute's blow hole acts as an open end. Also included are some percussion aerophones (more on them later), and several other types. Figure 6-14, with the caption that accompanies it, explains the first three vibrational modes for open-ended cylinders, and provides formulas for calculating the approximate resonant frequency for each mode. Two important observations: 1) The cylindrical tube open at both ends resonates a complete harmonic series. 2) In its fundamental mode of vibration, the tube encloses one half of the sounding wavelength (approximately). Knowing this allows you to calculate the frequency for a given tube length, or,

conversely, to calculate the length required to produce a given frequency — see the figure caption for details.

Cylindrical Tubes Closed at One End

These include stopped flutes such as slide whistles, most panpipes and many organ pipes, some percussion aerophones and many tuned marimba resonator tubes. It also includes those reed and lip-buzzed instruments that are cylindrical over most of their length, such as the clarinet family. These latter groups fit the stopped-end description because lips or reed form a barrier at the end of the tube.

Figure 6-15 shows the first three modes of vibration for such tubes. Notice that in this case, the overtone series is harmonic, but it is not complete. The vibration patterns support only the odd-numbered tones. The absence of resonances to support the even-numbered harmonics contributes noticeably to the timbre of such instruments. The characteristic sound is sometimes described as dark or hollow, best exemplified in the lower register of the clarinets.

Notice also that the stopped tube encloses not a half of the fundamental wavelength, as the open tube did, but a quarter. Thus, if we were to stop the far end of our simple prototype flute (ignoring the toneholes for the moment), its sounding wavelength would be twice as long, and its tone an octave lower at half the frequency. This property makes closed tubes economical for achieving lower pitches: you can produce a given pitch at half the tube lengths that open tubes require.

Conical Tubes

True conical tube instruments are rare, since a complete cone would come to an end at a single point, rather than at, for instance, a mouthpiece-shaped body of air. But many instruments approximate a conical form closely enough to take advantage of some of its acoustic properties. These include reed instruments such as oboes, and lip-buzzed instruments such as French horns. As with cylindrical tube instruments, a reed or buzzing lips can take the place of the closed end of a complete cone, and so support wave forms similar to those that would arise in the complete cone. The cone angles of conical musical instrument tubes are not large. The largest among standard instruments is found in the saxophones at 3 or 4 degrees, ranging down to about 0.8 degrees for the bassoon.

Although the internal mechanics are different, for our purposes conical bores behave much like cylindrical tubes open at both ends. The resonances cover a complete harmonic series, and wavelength is approximately twice the tube length.

From the information in Figures 6-14 through 6-16 and their captions, you can determine approximate wavelength and resonant frequencies for any given tube length. You can then figure the resulting pitches, by referring to the chart in Appendix 2. In practice, though, various peripheral factors affect the final result. Their cumulative effect is usually to make the tube behave as if it were slightly longer than its physical length. Appendix 5 provides additional information, should you want to make more precise calculations.

Additional Factors in Air Column Behavior

The end of a wind instrument tube, where the enclosed

FIGURE 6-14: The first three modes of vibration for a cylindrical tube open at both ends. Stippled areas represent regions of maximum variation in air pressure and minimum air movement, while the double-headed arrows represent areas of maximum movement and minimum variation in pressure. In the following formulas, f = frequency; v = the speed of sound (343.5 meters/second or 1127 feet/second is an acceptable value); and L = tube length. The formulas given here derive from the principle that frequency is inversely proportional to wavelength.

Mode 1 (the fundamental) encloses approximately 1/2 of the sounding wavelength within the tube, to produce an approximate frequency of $f_1 = v/2L$.

Mode 2 encloses approximately one wavelength, for an approximate frequency of twice the fundamental frequency, or $f_2 = v/L$. The sounding tone is about an octave above the fundamental.

Mode 3 encloses approximately 1½ wavelength, to produce an approximate frequency of three times the fundamental frequency, or $f_3 = v/(2/3)L$. The sounding tone is about a twelfth above the fundamental.

Mode 4 (not shown) would enclose two full wavelengths for a frequency four times the fundamental, at $f_4 = v/(1/2)L$. Higher modes continue the pattern, with the generalized frequency formula $f_n = nv/2L$, where n is the mode number. The sounding tones proceed up the harmonic series, at two 8ves, two 8ves and a 3rd, two 8ves and a 5th, and so forth above the fundamental.

The end correction and other factors discussed in Appendix 5 throw these results off slightly.

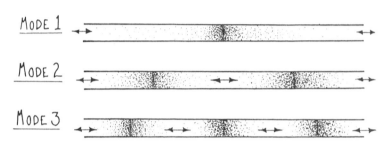

FIGURE 6-15: The first three modes of vibration for a cylindrical tube closed at one end. Stippled areas represent regions of maximum variation in air pressure and minimum air movement, while the double-headed arrows represent areas of maximum movement and minimum variation in pressure.

Mode 1 (the fundamental) encloses 1/4 of the full wavelength within the tube, to produce an approximate frequency of $f_1 = v/4L$.

Mode 2 encloses 3/4 of the wavelength, to produce an approximate frequency of three times the fundamental frequency, or $f_2 = v/(4/3)L$. The sounding tone is about a twelfth above the fundamental.

Mode 3 encloses 1¼ wavelength, to produce an approximate frequency of five times the fundamental frequency, or $f_3 = v/(4/5)L$. The sounding tone is about two 8ves and a 3rd above the fundamental.

Mode 4 (not shown) would enclose 1¾ wavelengths for a frequency seven times the fundamental, at $f_4 = v/(4/7)L$. Higher modes continue the pattern, with the generalized frequency formula $f_n = (2n-1)v/4L$. The sounding tones proceed through the odd-numbered components of the harmonic series, at two 8ves and a very flat 7th, three 8ves and a 9th, and so forth above the fundamental.

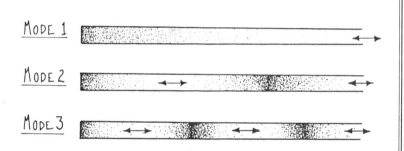

FIGURE 6-16: The first three modes of vibration for a conical tube. Stippled areas represent regions of maximum variation in air pressure and minimum air movement, while the double-headed arrows represent areas of maximum movement and minimum variation in pressure.

Although the internal waveforms look different, the frequency and wavelength calculations for conical tubes come out identical to those for cylindrical tubes open at both ends:

Mode 1 (the fundamental) encloses 1/2 of the full wavelength within the tube, to produce an approximate frequency of $f_1 = v/2L$.

Mode 2 encloses one full wavelength, for an approximate frequency of twice the fundamental frequency, or $f_2 = v/L$. The sounding tone is about an octave above the fundamental.

Mode 3 encloses 1½ wavelength, to produce an approximate frequency of three times the fundamental frequency, or $f_3 = v/(2/3)L$. The sounding tone is about a twelfth above the fundamental.

Mode 4 (not shown) would enclose two full wavelengths for a frequency four times the fundamen-

tal, at $f_4 = 4v/2L$. Higher modes continue the pattern, with the generalized frequency formula $f_n = nv/2L$. The sounding tones proceed up the harmonic series, at two 8ves, two 8ves and a 3rd, two 8ves and a 5th, and so forth above the fundamental.

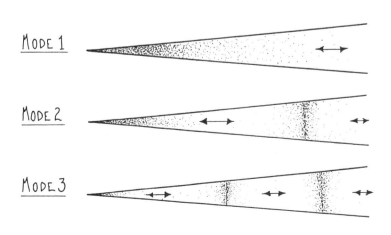

air meets the outer air, is a critical point. A large opening is good for sound projection, since it creates a lot of "surface area" for radiating the sound. The sound that radiates into the room from a small opening will be restricted, even when the internal wave is quite strong. You can increase the size of the opening, and thus increase radiation efficiency, by adding a flaring bell to the end of the tube. The presence of a bell affects the tuning and relative prominence of the overtones. Brass instrument makers have learned to compensate for these effects, but the factors involved are rather subtle. Estimating the effective tube length for a tube with a belled end is difficult, but it is safe to act as if the tube effectively ends at some point mid-bell. On woodwinds, open toneholes can also have the effect of increasing radiation efficiency by creating a larger cumulative opening and thus more radiating surface area.

Short, fat air columns are generally poorer in overtones than long skinny ones. At the extremes, excessively fat pipes will not speak at all, and excessively slender ones tend to break up into harmonics rather than produce the fundamental. You can see this effect at work in the ranks of a large organ: the thickest pipes are the ones called "flute pipes," which are characterized by a strong fundamental and relatively weak higher overtones. The ones called "string pipes" are much more slender, and they show prominent harmonic overtones.

But unlike the organ with its many pipes, most wind instruments use a single pipe designed to produce multiple pitches. Our prototype flute, for instance, sometimes acts like a short pipe producing a high note (when many toneholes are open), and sometimes acts like a long pipe producing a low note (when most holes are closed). In designing such instruments, keep in mind that every time you open a tonehole, slide a slide or open a valve, you are changing the length/diameter ratio for the instrument.

Is there an ideal length/diameter ratio one can strive for? Mark Shepard, in his *Make a Flute!* booklet, has suggested a standard ratio of about 23 to 1 (overall length, all toneholes closed) for his midsized flutes. (At 17" long and 3/4" in diameter, the prototype flute comes very close to this). But as the example of the organ above indicates, people will select different ratios as they seek different tone qualities.

The cross-sectional shape of an air column has relatively little acoustic consequence. Instead, cross-sectional area is the important consideration. An air column which is square in cross section, and of uniform dimensions over its entire length, behaves very nearly the same as a cylindrical pipe of the same cross-sectional area. A straight-sided square pipe which increases in cross section at a uniform rate behaves like a conical pipe.

It is also generally assumed that as long as

The effects of bends in wind instrument tubes are negligible if all bends are gentle and gradual.

Sidebar 6-8

UNIFORM TONE QUALITY ACROSS A RANGE OF TUBE LENGTHS

Here is a question concerning length/diameter ratio for tubes, and how it affects tone quality: How can one best retain the same general tone quality in a family of pipes of different lengths, such as a rank of organ pipes, or a set of recorders in several sizes? The obvious answer would be to retain the same length/diameter ratio across the range. It turns out, though, that the ear hears the lower pitched pipes in such an arrangement as relatively dark, and the higher ones as relatively bright. To create greater unity of timbre, the lower pipes should be a bit thinner relative to length, creating a slightly richer harmonic spectrum. A rule of thumb developed by organ builders over the years has been to make tube diameter one and two thirds as large for each doubling in length.

the cross-sectional area retains the intended value, it doesn't matter how the tube may curve and snake around — a cylindrical pipe will still behave acoustically like a cylindrical pipe even after bending, as long as there are no sharp angles or kinks. This convenient assumption isn't quite true. A perfectly straight tube has some acoustic advantages. The problems associated with bends should be negligibly small, though, if all bends are reasonably gentle and gradual.

MATERIALS FOR WIND INSTRUMENT TUBES AND VESSELS

Wind instrument tubing materials that are light and/or yielding will damp air resonances within the tube to some degree, and lower the resonance frequencies slightly. Walls made of rough or porous materials also have noticeable damping effects. Circular cross-section shapes for tubes are good for rigidity, while flat-walled tubes may show greater damping if the walls are not sufficiently heavy, due to flex in the tube walls. Increased damping leads to poorly defined resonance peaks, especially in the high frequencies, creating a sound that is less bright.

There is a lot of traditional lore about which materials are best for wind instruments. In practice, however, any reasonably heavy, hard, smooth and rigid material will sound much like any other such, and have the same potential for producing a good-sounding instrument. (Different materials, however, will have different qualities in durability, rot or corrosion resistance, etc.) Extremely hard reflective materials are not necessarily the ideal: people sometimes prefer the mellower tone of somewhat damped resonances.

Here are suggestions for tubing materials. There are, of course, many possibilities beyond those listed here. For more on these materials and their availability, see Appendix 1, "Tools and Materials."

Bamboo and other vegetable stalks

The best natural material for cylindrical tubes is bamboo. The cane reed, *Arundo donax*, also works well. Some other hollow reeds and vegetable stalks may suffice, although most break easily, or absorb water and become soft. Most of these materials are naturally cylindrical or very nearly so, but you can sometimes find a section of expanding bore near the base of a stalk.

Wood

Nonporous hardwoods work best for instrument tubes. There are several ways to make the bore in what would otherwise be a solid piece of wood. Drilling requires a very long bit and a special jig to ensure that it doesn't wander to one side. If you have doubts about undertaking such a job yourself, consider getting a well equipped woodworker to do the job.

Another approach is to carve an open semicircular groove in each of two half-pieces, and then join the pieces to create the bore. This approach calls for fewer specialized tools but requires time-consuming precision work. Alternatively, you can assemble a box-like square-bore tube from four pieces of wood. In either case, use a high grade, marine-quality wood glue to join the parts. While drilling yields a cylindrical bore, you can create conical or other bore shapes with the carved-halves and box-building approaches.

A third approach is to have some termites eat a hollow through the core of the wood, as with the Australian didjeridu.

Plastic

Plastic tubes are available at hardware stores and plastics outlets in a range of sizes. Many plastics are inexpensive, and they are generally easy to work. Disadvantages: In mouth-blown wind instruments, they have more problems than other materials with water condensation, making it necessary for players to stop to swab their instruments frequently. And, of course, they are unattractive, unclassy, and difficult to paint or otherwise decorate. As well, some common plastics are considered mildly toxic (see more on this in Appendix 1).

Metal

For cylindrical bores, a wide variety of prefabricated metal tubings are available. If you have metal-working skills and equipment, you can try making a conical tube out of sheet metal, either by making a sort of spiral wrap or proceeding as if you were making a very long, narrow funnel with a seam along one side. The tube-shaping techniques used in commercial brasswind manufacturing plants are not do-able in most home workshops.

Ceramics

Clay can be molded to any shape, and a few creative builders have made eye-catching wind instruments with it. You can create conical and cylindrical forms as well as globular, not to mention the highly irregular shapes that the material seems to invite. Wind instrument makers have found that an instrument in clay can be played, very gently, when the clay is in the partially dried state sometimes described as "leather hard." After initially shaping the instrument and then setting it aside for a period of time to reach this condition, the maker can test it, and make fine adjustments as needed before firing.

Kelp

Bull kelp (*mereo cystis* or *macro cystis*) is a seaweed found all along the West Coast of the U.S., which dries to form a conical tube of up to, at the largest, six or eight feet. There is a bulb at the large end that can be cut off at the right point to leave a flared opening. The walls of the dried tube are thin and brittle, but it makes instruments of clearer sound than you might expect, with beautiful form.

Conch shell

Another gift from the sea that provides a natural conical bore is conch. Conch shell trumpets have been played in many Pacific island countries, as well as South America and Southern Asia. They produce warm, full, and far-carrying tone. To make the mouthpiece for a conch trumpet you must grind down the tip with a heavy abrasive to form a mouthpiece shape.

Animal horn

Steer horn and ram horn are naturally hollow and form an excellent conical bore.

Tubing designed specifically for musical instruments

You can always use tubing from existing musical instruments, especially for a hard-to-find conical bore. Pillage tubing sections from a junked instrument, or purchase new tubing from instrument manufacturers.

Sometimes you may want to add a flaring bell to the end of an otherwise straight-sided cylindrical or conical tube. (Doing so will usually improve volume and tone, but may throw off the overtone tuning.) For this purpose you may choose to appropriate the bell from a commercially manufactured brass instrument, and somehow attach it to the end of your existing tube. Simply adding a straight-sided funnel to the end of the tube is less effective acoustically, but it will still improve volume and may brighten the tone quality. Many gourd varieties have flared sections which can be attached to a tube end to create a bell. You may be able to fashion a curvingly flared bell out of wood or clay or Sculpy™ (a hand-moldable plastic for kids), or who knows what. The ideal is to have the flare fan out through a full 90 degrees of curvature.

Materials for vessel Flutes

For globular forms, try bottles and jugs, rigid plastic containers, coconut shells (halved for cleaning and then rejoined), or short lengths of large diameter tubing. You can shape hollow forms from wood, doing the work in two halves and joining them. Many ocarina makers work with clay, because of its infinite shapability. Eggshells are an excellent option: You can make a functioning ocarina with a fipple attached to a goose egg shell. Better yet are larger eggshells. Ostrich eggs can be worked with drills and files, and they make a beautiful, rich-toned ocarina in conjunction with a fipple made of clay or shaped wood.

PITCH CONTROL FOR WIND INSTRUMENTS

We have spoken about the many ways to excite an aerophonic vibration, and we have spoken about the resonant air chambers, both tubular and globular, that control and enhance those vibrations. Now it's time to talk about means for controlling and altering the air chamber resonances in order to get a range of pitches. The prototype flute from the start of this chapter had toneholes to do the job. In the coming pages we will study how toneholes work, and consider a range of other approaches, both conventional and unconventional.

Most air-column instruments use variations in effective tube length to produce different resonant frequencies. Before talking about specific means for doing that, let's look at an overview of the tube-length/sounding-pitch relationship. Being at home with this relationship will enable you to work intelligently with the pitch-control mechanisms that follow. These relationships apply to simple tubes without toneholes.

At the most basic level, the relationship between tube length and frequency is a simple inverse relationship: the longer the tube and the resulting wavelength, the lower the frequency and the resulting pitch. Doubling the tube length approximately halves the frequency, lowering the pitch by an octave.

In working out the tube lengths needed to produce the pitches you want, you can take either of two approaches.

1) You can take a relative pitch approach, calculating the appropriate ratios between tube lengths. First determine the frequency ratios for the intervals you want in the scale, then invert those ratios to get air column length ratios. An example: suppose you have a tube one meter in length which is to sound your tonic pitch. For a second scale degree at 9/8 the tonic frequency (that's a major second above in pitch), you need to shorten the effective sounding length by the inverse ratio: 8/9 x 1 meter = 88.9 cm. For a third degree at 5/4 the tonic frequency you need 4/5 x 1 meter = 80 cm, and so forth, on through the ratios of your chosen scale. The preceding ratios imply a just intonation approach. If you are working with equal temperament, the relevant numbers are: decrease the length by just under 6% to raise the pitch an equal-tempered semitone; increase it by the same factor for a semitone lower. This percentage value reflects the fact that a pitch rise of one twelve-tone equal-tempered semitone corresponds to an increase in frequency by a factor of 1.05946. (Review Chapter 3, "Tunings and Pitch Layouts," and Appendix 2 for more on this.)

2) You can take an absolute pitch approach, finding the tube lengths required to produce the wavelengths and corresponding frequencies you want. First determine the frequencies for the pitches you want to hear, and look up the wavelengths for those frequencies. Then determine the tube lengths necessary to produce those wavelengths, based on whether the tube shape you're using encloses one half or one quarter of the wavelength. An example: Suppose you want to have a cylindrical tube open at both ends that will produce the note C_4 as its fundamental. On the frequency/wavelength chart in Appendix 2, you find that the wavelength for this pitch is 131.3 cm. You know from Figure 6-14 that the fundamental wavelength for an open cylindrical tube is approximately twice the tube length; so for a wavelength of 131.3 cm you need a tube half as long, or 65.6 cm. (Review Figures 6-14, 6-15, and 6-16 if necessary. See Appendix 2 for frequency-wavelength conversions).

The inverse relationship between tube length and frequency is never precise, and in practice, though you can come close, it is difficult to predict exactly what a complex air column's resonant frequencies will be. Appendix 4, "More on Air Columns, Toneholes & Woodwind Keying Mechanisms," provides further information that will allow you to refine your calculations. Still, when you design and build a wind instrument, you can usually expect to do at least some after-the-fact fine tuning.

On the other hand, you may choose to do no predictive calculation at all in planning tube lengths, tonehole placements, and the like. There are wind instrument makers who work this way, simply making holes or cutting tube lengths in keeping with some innate sense of proportion. When the combination of luck and instinct are right, the tonal results can often enough be fresh and pleasing.

Whether or not you use predictive calculation for wind instrument tuning, there is one practical way to refine the process, and that is the use of prototypes. Once you have succeeded in making one well tuned specimen, you can then make others like it with confidence in the tuning, if you can replicate the dimensions of the original exactly. Alternatively, you can use an existing well tuned instrument from another maker as your prototype, and copy its proportions as faithfully as possible.

Those things said, let us look at some of the specific pitch control methods available for winds.

The simplest means for getting many pitches out of a single wind instrument is to have a multitude of pipes cut to different lengths for tuning to different pitches. Panpipes, for instance, have a separate tube for each note; pipe organs have that and more.

The majority of wind instruments, however, use just one tube for many pitches. Perhaps the easiest way to obtain multiple resonances from a single tube is to make use of the tube's natural harmonic overtone series. With this approach there's no need to alter the tube physically; you just bring different harmonics to the fore to act as the sounding pitch. This is how the corrugahorns discussed earlier work. You can achieve a similar effect with any simple wind instrument having a relatively long, narrow tube, since the standing waves in such tubes break up into harmonics easily. To make a harmonics flute out of our prototype simple flute, you would need only to eliminate the toneholes and greatly extend the length. Several builders have done this with fipple flutes, and become adept at playing them. With a recorder mouthpiece affixed to a longer-than-usual tube without toneholes, you can produce a wide range of harmonics by varying wind pressure. Here's one more trick: if you use soft tubing such as flexible plastic hose for the instrument body, you can selectively bring out harmonics by pinching the tube at a pressure node/displacement antinode for the desired mode. The results are imprecise and the tone is sort of soggy, but the kookiness of the technique gives it a certain appeal.

Other wind instruments achieve a range of pitches by providing some means to vary the natural resonance frequencies of a single chamber. Most often, this is a matter of varying the effective length of a tube. I know of one maker, Robin Goodfellow, who achieves this in the most literal fashion. She makes an oboe-like instrument out of a soda straw. On this, with impressive speed and surprisingly good intonation, she plays an ascending scale by snipping a section

A MORE PLAYABLE SLIDE WHISTLE

Slide whistles are difficult to play with good intonation, because the available pitches are not marked in any way and they are not discrete; instead there is an undifferentiated continuum of pitch to slither around in. That is true of many other instruments, like trombone and violin. But with the violin the player develops a strong kinesthetic sense of the neck and its topography. The trombone is a bit more like the slide whistle in its uncharted sliding, but, because of the size difference, slightly inaccurate slide placement produces a greater detuning on a typical slide whistle than on a trombone. Furthermore, professional musicians spend years learning to play the trombone and the violin in tune; nobody does that with a slide whistle.

So here is a way to make slide whistles easier to play in tune. You can make these modifications on an existing, store-bought slide whistle, or you can build them into a slide whistle you make from scratch. First, mount the slide whistle on a stick which extends beyond the body of the whistle as far as the farthest extension of the slide (see

Figure A). Attach a flexible blow tube of about two feet to the slide whistle's mouthpiece. This enables you to lay the slide whistle and attached stick in full view before you on a table, while playing through the blow tube. Now you can mark off the slider stopping locations for the pitches you want to hear, directly on the stick. Playing by eye and ear together, you will suddenly become a far better slide whistle player.

I did this with a commercially manufactured slide whistle in the alto range, and another whistle of my own construction in the baritone range. For a good store-bought slide whistle I recommend the chrome-plated instrument made under the brand name American Song Whistle (from American Plating Company, Chicago, IL) and sold, at very reasonable cost, in many music stores and school music supply catalogs. My baritone whistle is too large by far to play on the lap, so I play it in an upright position, a little like a string bass, with the blow tube running down to the mouth of the instrument near the floor.

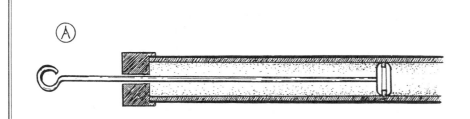

A: Calibrated Slide Whistle.

B: The calibration stick.

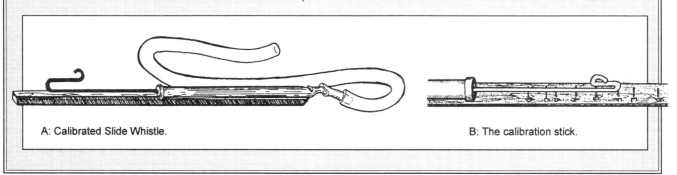

FIGURE 6-17: Slide whistle elements. A: Slide mechanism, in cutaway view (the blown end of the tube would be to the right). The fairly long channel through which the slide passes in the end-block at left helps prevent the stopper from pressing unevenly on one side of the tube.

B: A sliding stopper, with a groove around the periphery to serve as a reservoir for grease.

off the end of the straw with a pair of scissors for each new note. Unfortunately, the technique works only for ascending lines.

More practical methods for altering effective tube length include the toneholes on the prototype flute with which this chapter began, as well as the slides and valves used in brass instruments. We will consider these now, along with a few additional approaches that will probably be new to you.

Slides

There are two types of wind instrument slides: sliding

stoppers, such as are used on slide whistles; and open-tube slides, such as are used in trombones. Sliding stoppers provide a movable stopped end to the tube. They cannot be used with instruments in which it is necessary for air to flow *through* the tube, since the stopped end doesn't allow any outflow. This pretty well limits their use to flutes, where flow-though is not required.

It is my opinion that slide whistles, sometimes called Swannee whistles, are one of the great under-rated instruments of the world. Played well in a melodic style, they

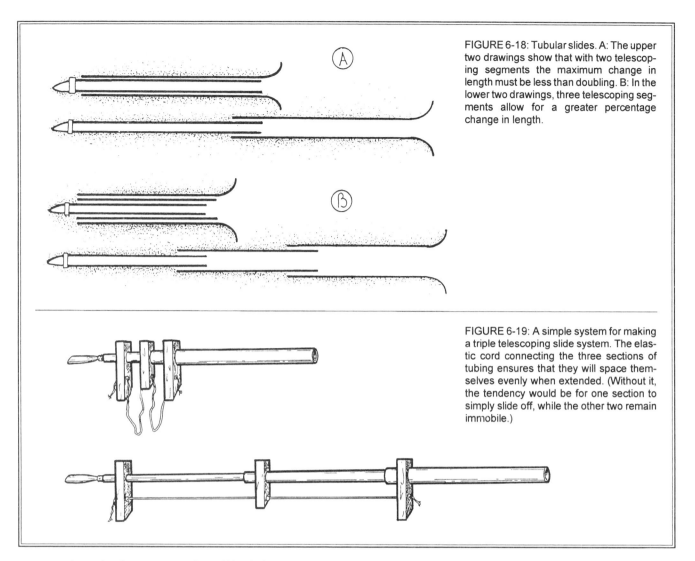

FIGURE 6-18: Tubular slides. A: The upper two drawings show that with two telescoping segments the maximum change in length must be less than doubling. B: In the lower two drawings, three telescoping segments allow for a greater percentage change in length.

FIGURE 6-19: A simple system for making a triple telescoping slide system. The elastic cord connecting the three sections of tubing ensures that they will space themselves evenly when extended. (Without it, the tendency would be for one section to simply slide off, while the other two remain immobile.)

possess a haunting beauty. A typical slide design appears in Figure 6-17. The maker's challenge is to have the stopper fit in the tube snugly enough to form a leakless seal, but not so snugly that the sliding action is unplayably stiff. A generous dose of lithium grease on the stopper helps on both fronts: it improves the seal and eases slidability. If you use a disk of some hard material to form the body of the stopper, rim it with a gasket of soft but firm material like dense foam rubber.

Open-tube slides can work where sliding stoppers cannot, in through-blowing winds like reeds and lip-buzzed brass. They have an important physical limitation of their own, though: the greatest change in length you can achieve from two telescoping sections of tubing is something less than a doubling of length, as illustrated in Figure 6-18A. This means that the maximum possible pitch change is less than an octave. That's OK for trombones, because trombones overblow the fifth. To achieve an ascending scale, after playing through the available sliding range in the first register the trombone player can jump to the next register a fifth above, re-extending the slide and continuing without a break. But for instruments like flutes or clarinets, which overblow the octave or the twelfth, you cannot shorten the tube enough to fill the entire gap between the low tone and the first available second register note.

To get around this problem, you could make a tube in several telescoping segments as in Figure 6-18B. In practice,

problems of irregular tube shape and potential leakage compound themselves with the increase in the number of sliding segments. Such an instrument can still work well if you manage to find or make several sizes of thin-wall tubing manufactured to very close tolerances for telescoping. Figure 6-19 and its caption illustrate a simple design for multiple telescoping tube sections.

Practical notes on making workable tube slides: the key to easy, leakless sliding is finding or making tubing in sizes that fit perfectly one inside the other. The tubes — or, at least, the inner ones — should be as thin-walled as possible, so that there isn't a large change in air column diameter at the point where one tube ends and the other continues. Finding well-fitting tubing sets at regular metals outlets may be difficult, but some hobby shops have brass tubing in a range of close-fitting diameters. Alternatively, you can purchase tubing made specifically for trombone slides from one of the band instrument manufacturers, or you can use the slides from an old trombone. Other, non-musical items may also provide suitably fitted tubing pairs. Peter Schickele, a.k.a. P.D.Q. Bach, has made slide oboes using adjustable music stand uprights. Lubrication between the inner and outer tubes is valuable. The grease recommended for sliding stoppers is too viscous in this application — look instead to a light oil.

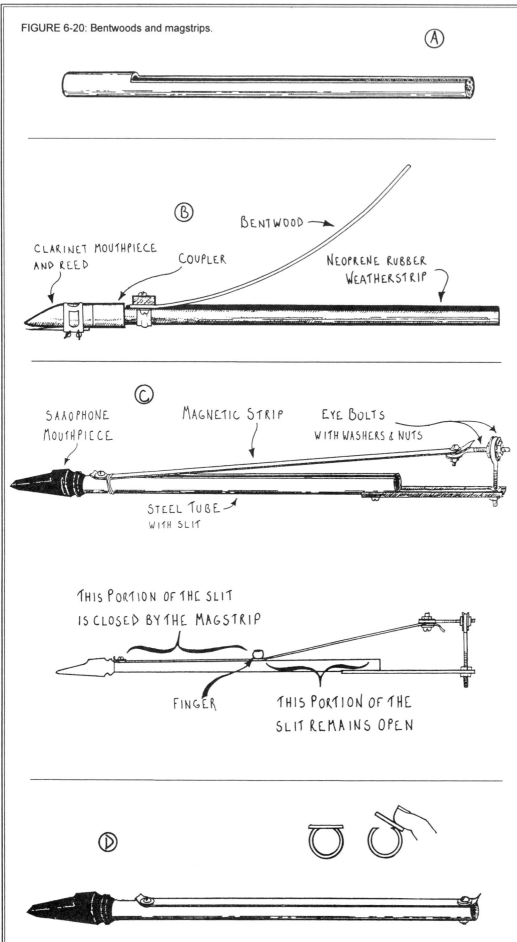

FIGURE 6-20: Bentwoods and magstrips.

Ⓐ

Ⓑ

BENTWOOD

CLARINET MOUTHPIECE
AND REED

COUPLER

NEOPRENE RUBBER
WEATHERSTRIP

Ⓒ

SAXOPHONE
MOUTHPIECE

MAGNETIC STRIP

EYE BOLTS
WITH WASHERS & NUTS

STEEL TUBE
WITH SLIT

THIS PORTION OF THE SLIT
IS CLOSED BY THE MAGSTRIP

FINGER

THIS PORTION OF THE
SLIT REMAINS OPEN

Ⓓ

A. Tubing for a bentwood clarinet with the slit cut in the top. Plastic tubings of moderate wall thickness — around 1/8" or a little less — work well. Don't make the slit by making two parallel vertical cuts, but rather by making a single horizontal cut to slice off the upper surface of the tube. This leaves a flat surface on which to attach the gasket-like padding strips described below.

B. A completed bentwood clarinet. The foam rubber strip runs along the ledge on both sides of the slit. It serves as a sort of gasket, ensuring that when the bentwood is pressed down, it will seal leaklessly. It can be made from a strip of 1/8" x 1/4" neoprene rubber weather strip sliced in half to make two strips each 1/8" wide. Be sure to use the resilient neoprene rubber type, not the less expensive, more compressible weather strip. The coupler (a piece normally used to connect two sections of plastic pipe) replaces the clarinet's barrel joint. It may have to be re-sized by enlarging the interior at one end to accept the clarinet mouthpiece.

C. The magstrip design described in the text. The system for holding the far end of the magnetic strip, using two eye bolts, is a little crude looking, but it has the advantage of being adjustable both vertically and horizontally. The lower drawing shows how pressing the strip causes it to cover the upper portion of the slit. Flexible magnetic strips are available from American Science and Surplus, listed in Appendix 1.

D. An alternative magstrip design. Here the magstrip lies flat over the slit, so that the slit is closed over its entire length. In the inset, showing an end-on cutaway view, you can see that pressing a finger on one side of the strips will lift the other side, opening an air space. The opening appears only in the region where the finger presses; the remainder of the slit remains sealed.

Bentwoods and Magstrips

Bentwood is the name I use for another bendable pitch control method I have used with great success. It works equally well on flutes and through-blowing instruments, and even, though more awkwardly, on conical instruments (impossible with either kind of slide just discussed). And it is fairly easy to make. After I came up with the idea I checked in a patent library to see if I could find anything else like it, and indeed I discovered that several similar mechanisms have been patented at various times, although hardly anyone ever seems to have made much use of them.

The idea is this: You start by making a wind instrument tube with an open slit, a half inch or less wide, running the length of the tube from the far end to a point just short of the mouthpiece (see Figure 6-20A). Attach a long strip of stiff but flexible material, extending out over the slit but curving up and away, as shown in Figure 6-20B. If you press this strip down, it covers more and more of the slit. In the process, the effective tube length increases, just as if you were covering up a series of toneholes. You can play melodies or continuous glissandos simply by pressing the bentwood down along the slit to varying degrees.

You can play some pretty wild stuff on a bentwood clarinet, but the arrangement does not lend itself to crisp articulation and precise pitch. Roller coaster glissandos are more the norm. So I later developed magstrips, an alternative version which, though less dramatic from a gestural point of view, allows for more controlled playing. As shown in Figure 6-20C, magstrips incorporate a ribbon-like strip of flexible material held taut over the open slit, angling slightly up and away. Using a finger to press this strip down at any point along its length will close the upper part of the tube. The seal of that closure would be problematically leaky, were it not for this feature: The instrument is made of steel tubing. The flex-strip over the slit is made of rubberized magnetic material (the same stuff sometimes used for business logos stuck to the sides of commercial vehicles). The magnetism is weak, but it is enough to cause the upper part of the strip to slap down over the slit leaklessly when the finger presses.

Valves

In most of the standard lip-buzzed instruments, commonly called brass instruments, the sounding pitch is controlled in part by altering tube length through the use of valves. (The player does the other part of the job by changing registers through lip tension.) Valves do what they do by diverting the sound wave through an extra segment of tubing when the valve is pressed, creating a greater total air-column length and a correspondingly lower pitch. A standard valving arrangement and set of tube length relationships has evolved which serves for most members of the brass instruments family. The basic idea can be seen Figure 6-21, and typical added-tube-length percentages can be found in the figure's caption.

The valving mechanisms used in brass instruments must be made to very close tolerances, and for most mortals it is not possible to make them outside of a metal shop with specialized tools. The best option available for adding valves to a homemade instrument is to borrow the valving mechanism from a commercially manufactured brass instrument which has been junked, or buy a valving mechanism from one of the band instrument manufacturers. The sections of tubing leading into and out of the valve mechanism are usually removable, so you can replace the original tubing with tubing segments made to suit the purposes of your instrument. One limitation in using a pre-existing set of valves is that you are forced to use tubing diameters that match those of the valving.

But why bother with valves in the first place? Why not use toneholes such as the woodwinds use, since they are far easier to make? The answer is that lip-buzzed instruments with side holes yield relatively weak and poorly defined tones as the air column resonance fails to sufficiently dominate and control the buzzing lips. In the past there have been lip-buzzed instruments with side holes, such as the *serpents* that were used in Europe three or four hundred years ago, as well as some keyed bugles of the last century. Revivals of these instruments have shown that skilled players can coax beautiful sounds from them, particularly from well made keyed bugles.

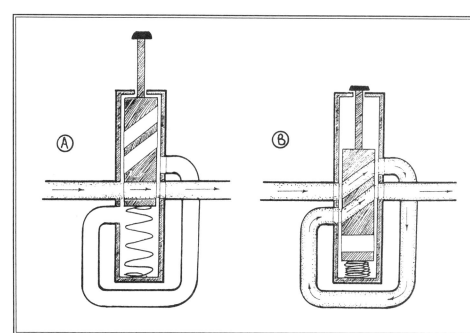

FIGURE 6-21: Diagrammatic view of a brass instrument valving mechanism. A: With the valve unpressed, the sound wave bypasses the detour. B: With the valve pressed, the sound wave is directed through an extra excursion, increasing the tube's effective length.

A standard valving arrangement uses three valves. The first adds about 6% more tubing to the total length, lowering the sounding pitch by a semitone. The second adds something over 12%, to lower it by a whole tone. Valves 1 and 2 together lower the pitch by a minor third. The third valve adds about 21%, an amount calculated to drop the pitch about a minor third relative to the increased tube length with valves 1 and/or 2 already down. Various combinations of the third valve with the other two are used to lower the pitch by intervals up to a diminished 5th.

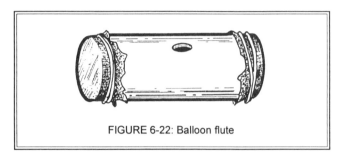

FIGURE 6-22: Balloon flute

If you do use toneholes with lip-buzzing, the fewer and the larger the toneholes are, the better the results will be.

Multiple Bells

In some early brass instruments, valving systems were used to send the air from a mouthpiece tube into one or another of several separate horns, each with its own bell. Each horn was a different length, to provide a different wavelength and pitch. Those were wonderful instruments to see, with a bouquet of bells rising from the single stem. From an acoustic point of view, such a design has some advantages over the single bell. Many-belled brass instruments never became widespread because it entails more work and expense, not to mention more weight and bulk, to provide six bells for a single horn when the job could be done almost as well by one. But for a home builder working with a lightweight, inexpensive and plentiful tubing material, such as dried kelp, the multiple-bell approach might be an attractive option. For such an instrument, you could work with a set of valves appropriated from some existing brass instrument, attaching the several bell segments to the outgoing tube opening from each valve.

Varying the Size of the End Opening

With wind instruments using short and fat, unflared tubes, you can alter the pitch by covering and uncovering the end opening to varying degrees. You can try this experimentally, using the mouthpiece from a recorder (remove the lower sections of the recorder tube), and holding the palm of your hand over the open end. Fully covered, the mouthpiece pipe produces the lowest available tone, and with the end wide open you get the highest. The available range between the two depends on the size of the opening. It is difficult to control pitch accurately, so the technique is more useful as a special effect than as the basis for a definite pitch instrument. But it is an attractive effect, with some of the feeling of a hooting owl or bird call.

Varying Tube Wall Rigidity

One of the factors affecting an air chamber's resonant frequencies is the rigidity of the walls and end-stops. The more yielding they are, the lower the resonance frequencies. Most wind instruments purposefully use highly reflective, virtually unyielding walls. But wind instruments with walls of variable rigidity are feasible. The ideas that follow come from Prent Rodgers, the builder who has done the most to explore the possibilities. His balloon flutes are wonderfully easy to make.

Prent's idea was to use relatively short, thick tubes,

with rigid side walls but highly yielding ends (see Figure 6-22). To make the tube ends, he uses balloon-rubber membranes stretched over the two openings. The player controls rigidity by pressing his or her fingers on either or both end membranes. Lightly touching one of the membranes near the center causes the tube's pitch to jump, typically, by about a whole tone. Touching the other membrane raises it again. Pressing harder increases the effect. (In addition to increasing rigidity, pressing harder has the secondary effect of pushing the membrane inward, reducing tube volume and further raising the pitch.) You can have lesser pitch rises by touching the membrane near the edge with varying degrees of pressure. Maximum range for such instruments is typically about a sixth, although sometimes you can get an octave and more.

The standard balloon flute takes the form of a side-blown flute (but short and fat, so that it functions more as a globular resonator than a tubular resonator), with the blow hole set at the center of the tube rather than the usual location near one end. Balloon flutes work well in very small sizes, like about two inches long, up to a maximum of perhaps a foot.

Toneholes

For many wind instruments, toneholes are the easiest and most practical pitch-control systems. They are especially suited for small instruments. With large instruments, ergonomic difficulties arise: how to stop holes that are too large to cover with a finger, and how to bring widely spaced holes within reach of the hand. A glance at any of the larger classical woodwinds, with their elaborate key-and-lever mechanisms, will tell you that these problems are not insoluble, but they certainly do complicate matters.

Toneholes do what they do by shortening the effective vibrating length of a tube, causing the air within to vibrate at a higher frequency. If the tonehole diameter happens to

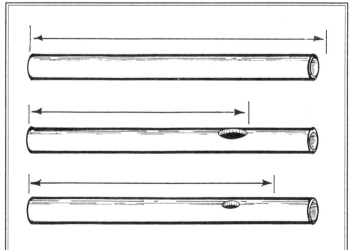

FIGURE 6-23: Effective tube lengths resulting from toneholes of different sizes. Top: No tonehole; effective length is full tube length plus a bit more due to the end correction. Middle: Tonehole as large as tube inside diameter; effective tube length equals the distance to the center of the hole plus a bit more due to the end correction. Bottom: Smaller tonehole; effective tube length ends somewhere between the tonehole and the end of the tube.

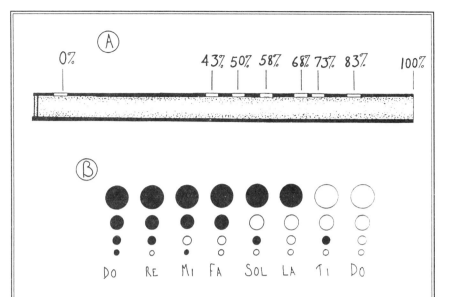

FIGURE 6-24: A. Standard Pennywhistle Fingering. The hole spacings given here opened in sequence will yield a major scale. By means of cross fingerings (covering one or two holes below the first open hole) they yield all of the chromatics as well, except the minor second. By uncovering or half-covering the highest hole while closing those below it, you can throw the tube into its second register at the octave, to extend the range upward several more tones. All spacings are from the centers of the holes. These hole spacings will work for flutes over a wide range of lengths, assuming that the bore is uniformly cylindrical. Recommended bore diameter — 11/16" for shorter flutes to 1" for longer (ideally, a length-to-diameter ratio of about 23:1); recommended hole size 3/8" for smaller bores to 7/16" for larger bores. Larger or smaller holes will throw off the tuning. Some fine tuning by adjusting hole size may be necessary after holes are initially made. (From Mark Shepard, *Simple Flutes: Make Them, Play Them*.)

B. A standard 4-hole fingering pattern for ocarinas (blackened circles represent covered holes). With additional cross fingerings not shown here, you can obtain all the tones of a chromatic scale except the minor second and minor third. Notice that the holes become successively larger. This is to achieve a suitable percentage increase in total open area with each new hole. Hole locations are of negligible importance — you can locate them according to ease of fingering. (Hole sizes not drawn to scale).

be as large as the tube diameter, the resulting pitch is roughly the same as what the pitch would be if the tube were cut off at the tonehole location. But toneholes aren't usually that large. The effect of a smaller hole is to shorten the wavelength within the tube as compared to a hole-less tube, but not as much as if the tube were cut off at that point (see Figure 6-23). You can raise the pitch at an existing hole by enlarging the hole, or lower it by finding some way to backfill and reduce the size. Increasing the depth of the hole (by using thicker-walled tubing or building up the rim) is like reducing hole size in its pitch-lowering effects; making the hole shallower raises the pitch just as increasing the size does.

Like large tube ends, large toneholes make for better volume, because they afford more open area from which the sound can radiate. In addition, larger holes will contribute to a tone quality which is richer in higher partials. For these reasons, large variations in hole size on a single instrument leads to an inconsistent timbre from one note to the next.

In making a tonehole wind instrument, you may be able to do your hole placement and tuning by instinct, trial and error, and subsequent fine tuning, dispensing entirely with preliminary calculations. This is especially true for instru-

ments with relatively few holes — say, less than five or six. Start with the lowest tonehole and work upwards. Make a small hole at what you guess will be the best location to produce the intended pitch, then toot and listen for the actual pitch. Given the small hole size, it should be low. Gradually increase hole size to bring it up. Then proceed to the next hole, and the next and the next. Each new tonehole added above affects the pitch of the existing lower ones (see Appendix 5 for an explanation of this), but with luck the effect will be negligible, or at least small enough to be corrected by a second round of fine tuning.

If you prefer to work in a more controlled manner, then you will want some guidelines for deciding where to drill the holes in the first place. There are several approaches.

1) Follow a standard pre-existing pattern for tonehole placement, such as the widely used pennywhistle fingering given in Figure 6-24. Or, copy from an existing instrument. If you do the latter, you must be sure that your instrument's tube matches that of the prototype in all dimensions.

2) Make a series of instruments with identical tube dimensions. Make your mistakes and attempted corrections on the first; incorporate your best results into the second. Continue your refinements through a third and fourth and fifth if need be.

3) Use your knowledge of acoustics to estimate, as well as possible, what the locations should be, knowing that you can later fine tune through adjustments in hole size and depth.

Option three is in many respects the ideal approach, but it requires some effort. It is extremely difficult, even for physicists who study these things, to predict with precision

The Scientific Approach to Tonehole Placement.

what pitch will result from a given tonehole size and location. But you can make rough predictions that will place the toneholes close enough to the ideal location so that later fine tuning can bring them in line. Appendix 5 contains guidelines to get you going with this.

Register Holes

If the player can force a wind instrument to sound in an upper register, the instrument gains a lot of range without requiring a whole new set of toneholes. The instrument is said to be playing in an upper register when the air column's fundamental mode of vibration is somehow inhibited, and a higher mode comes to the fore to act, for sounding purposes, as a new fundamental. Sometimes the trick of forcing the instrument into a higher mode of vibration is all in the embouchure: air flow angle, wind pressure, lip placement or pressure, and oral cavity size work together to excite the enclosed air preferentially in one mode or another. With more sophisticated instruments, the choice of register is made more stable by an additional special hole called a register hole. Appendix 5 tells how to create a register hole.

Tonehole Making — the Practical Side

Making toneholes for small wind instruments is a fairly straightforward business. Here are some pointers.

You can make wind instrument tone holes by drilling or burning. Makers working with bamboo often use burning, because bamboo splinters or splits easily under drilling. A practical procedure for burning: choose an old or dull drill bit of appropriate size (here serving not as a bit, but as a poker), and provide it with a sturdy, non-heat-conducting handle such as a file handle. Use a propane torch or other means to heat the end of the bit red hot. If possible, insert a close-fitting wooden dowel into the instrument tube. This will prevent burning the back wall of the tube and also reduce tear-out on the inside when the bit pokes through. Apply the poker to the appropriate spot on the tube, and burn through. Enlarge or reshape the hole if necessary by applying sideways pressure with the hot bit. Clean away carbon and other residue with alcohol; clean and de-burr the bore inside by forcing steel wool through with a dowel. Toneholes with sharply cut, angular edges create turbulence, which can affect timbre and willingness to speak — so, smooth and round the hole edges inside and out with fine steel wool, emery paper, and/or a small, fine file. Remember that bamboo splits easily, and it is good idea to put some sort of finish coat inside and out to prevent moisture loss, and perhaps to bind the tube with twine or wire after making the holes.

Procedures for drilling are similar. If possible, insert a close-fitting dowel before drilling to reduce tear-out and prevent marring the opposite side of the tube. After drilling, clean and de-burr the bore with a dowel and steel wool (or, for tough materials, just bulldoze through with the end of the dowel). For enlarging or reshaping, go to a small burr bit or grinder bit. Remember to round the hole edges to reduce turbulence.

To reduce an oversized hole, a temporary measure is simply to cover part of it with sticky tape. Better yet, as a temporary measure or even as a permanent solution, use bee's wax, which allows adjustment and reshaping. With ceramic instruments you can backfill a too-large hole by replacing some clay. In other cases some sort of filler is called for. You can use the non-runny epoxy sold as "epoxy gel," or autobody filler. Autobody filler is strong, it bonds well to most materials, and it forms a hard surface which naturally evens itself out as it rapidly dries. For backfilling substantial areas, bring out the close-fitting dowel again. Grease or wax the dowel and slide it into the tube; for good measure, grease or wax again the portion directly under the hole. Then fill over it. The dowel will support the filler in the right shape. The wax prevents sticking when you remove it after the filler has dried. With this technique you can even completely cover a misplaced hole. Another very effective means for completely filling a misplaced hole, if it is circular, is to stop it with one of the tapered wooden stoppers sold as screw hole plugs.

Toneholes to be played by the fingers should be made with the human hand in mind. When possible, locate the holes at the spots where the fingers naturally fall with the instrument held comfortably. Offset some of the toneholes a bit to one side, rather than having them all in a line along the top of the instrument, if that puts them better in position for the fingers. You can make a large-ish tonehole more coverable by making it slightly oval in shape, with the long dimension in the direction from which the finger approaches it. If your tubing material is thick, you can create an effectively larger hole without actually enlarging aperture size by undercutting (back-sloping the sides of the hole) to reduce effective hole thickness. Alternatively, you can make a concave seating for the finger on top.

Air leaks around the toneholes when they are supposed to be closed during playing can be the downfall of any wind instrument. And leaks are sneaky; they can be hard to find. A helpful leak detection tool is the leak light. A leak light is simply a tiny electric light mounted at the end of a flexible probe. Insert it into the tube of a wind instrument, turn it on and turn the room lights off, and you can get a pretty good idea of which fingers or pads are not doing their hole-covering job. Where the light slips through, there is a leak. You can purchase a leak light from band instruments repair supply houses or school music supply houses. Or, if you enjoy doing this sort of thing, purchase the components and make a little battery-operated light and probe mounting yourself.

To avoid leaks, the tube surface surrounding the hole must be smooth and free of grit, bumps or irregularities. For finger-covered holes, if the tubing material is thick enough, it sometimes helps to make a small rounded concavity around the hole, the better to accommodate the shape of the fingertip. Alternatively, making a raised rim around the perimeter can improve the seal, as the narrow rim sinks slightly into the flesh or key pad that covers the hole. There are many ways to make such a rim; some involve carving into the material of the tube (if it is thick enough); others involve either somehow raising the tube material or adding new material to form a rim. Use your ingenuity. Small holes are much less leak-prone than large ones.

Keys and Pads

With instruments on which the toneholes are too large and too far apart for the fingers to cover, it becomes necessary to create a system of pads and levers. Making simple levers to cover an unreachable hole or two on a moderately-sized instrument isn't too hard — it only requires a little mechanical design work on the part of the builder. But what about something on the level of, say, a tenor sax, with its convoluted system of levers and pads controlling every last tonehole? This requires a degree of sophistication in metal work that is beyond the reach of most home workshops. Practical notes on wind instrument keying systems for home builders can be found in Appendix 5.

PLOSIVE AEROPHONES

From a logical point of view, *plosive aerophones* (sometimes called *percussive aerophones*) should have been discussed several pages back, alongside reeds and edgetones, as one more means of exciting the resonant air within a chamber. But the plosive aerophone family is distinctive enough that I have given it a separate section. Plosive aerophones typically are instruments sounded by percussion, but whose predomi-

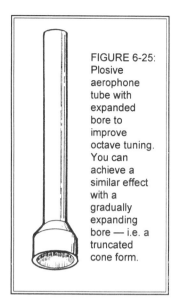

FIGURE 6-25: Plosive aerophone tube with expanded bore to improve octave tuning. You can achieve a similar effect with a gradually expanding bore — i.e. a truncated cone form.

nant tone is aerophonic. For a simple example, pick up a piece of rigid tubing, say two feet long and an inch an a half in diameter. If you clump the palm of your hand sharply down over the open end of the tube, you will hear a brief tone at the resonant frequency of the enclosed air. That is the plosive aerophone sound. There may be some idiophonic sound present as well, coming from the material of the tube itself, but in percussion aerophones, the air resonance tone should dominate.

Percussion aerophones usually involve some kind of enclosed air chamber. The chambers can take globular forms as well as tubular, and they can work well in sizes ranging from fairly small to rather huge. Let's begin with tubes.

Sidebar 6-10 describes the basics for making a simple but surprisingly effective instrument from a graduated set of end-struck tubes. Cylindrical tubes, we saw earlier in this chapter, produce different tones depending on whether both ends are open (forming a half-wave resonator to produce a higher tone) or one end is stopped (forming a quarter-wave resonator, with a tone about an octave lower). Percussion aerophones can be made either way. In fact, the same open tube can function both ways, depending on how it is played. For the closed-tube tone, clump your open hand down over the tube end so as to cover the opening completely. Don't lift your hand immediately, but keep it in place for the duration of the tone. You will have stopped the tube, and the resulting pitch will be the lower octave. If you strike in such a way as not to cover the end, lifting your hand immediately after the strike, you will hear the open-tube pitch above. You can even create an upwardly bending tone by striking so as to fully cover the end, but lifting your hand quickly as the tone still sounds, causing the tone to try to bubble up to the upper octave before its brief burst of energy is dissipated.

Inconveniently, the octave difference between the closed tube and the open tube is not a true octave. The upper tone is slightly flat (due to the open-end correction factor, discussed in Appendix 5). The discrepancy is big enough that the same set of tubes can't serve as upper and lower register in a single instrument. There is a way around this problem, suggested by the French maker Jacques Dudon. If you create a tube with a larger opening at one end than the other, the closed-tube resonance will be lower when it is the large end that is closed off. By adjusting the difference in opening sizes, you can bring the open-tube tone and the closed-tube tone into octave agreement, or experiment with other pitch relationships.

Several means for exciting a body of air by percussion have proven effective. Striking open tube ends directly with the hands works well, and so does the use of broad, flat,

---

Sidebar 6-10

A BASIC END-STRUCK PERCUSSION-TUBES SET

Any piece of appropriately sized rigid tubing makes a good end-struck percussion tube, producing a clear tone when you clump your hand over one end or strike it with a soft, flat bat like a rubber beach sandal. Tubes in diameters between about 1" and 2" sound best for playing with the hands; with a large, flat bat you can go up to 3" or 4". Larger diameters give greater volume. The pitch depends primarily on the length of the tube.

A tuned set of such tubes is an easy and rewarding instrument to make. Hand-held tubes always seem to sound best, but you can't hold more than two or three at once and leave one hand free for striking. For a larger set, leaving two hands free for beating, you need to make some kind of mounting. In designing a mounting, keep these things in mind: 1) The tubes must be spaced 2" or more apart to allow unencumbered striking of individual tubes. 2) The far ends of the tubes must not be blocked or obstructed. 3) If your set includes tubes longer than about three feet, they cannot be mounted upright without making the instrument too tall to play comfortably. Either mount horizontally, or use elbows or U-joints in an upright mounting to bend the tubes back on themselves. Gradual bends are preferable to right angles. 4) The mounting framework must be strong and rattle-free. 5) This is most important and most difficult: The mounting must be padded enough that the thump from the blow is not transmitted to the framework or the floor and radiated from there to the air, yet the tubes must be secure and stable enough that they don't get knocked out of position under the blow. There are many possible approaches here; experiment and let common sense be your guide.

MAKING A SCRAPER FLUTE

You can make an aerophone in which the air enclosed in a tube is excited by scraping the surface of the tube. For this to work, the outer surface of the tube must be serrated. It also helps if the tube is of a somewhat yielding material, so that the tube walls give a little under the scraping and agitate the air within. The sound is coarse, like the raspy singing voice of some hard-living, sentimental protest singer.

You can take either of two approaches with scraper flutes: 1) make a single tube with toneholes along the side, achieving a range of pitches that way; or 2) make a set of tubes without toneholes, but graduated in length, and mount them in a row in a framework. The instructions here are for making the single flute.

You will need 15" of 1" polyethelene tubing (flexible black plastic cold water pipe, sometimes called "poly pipe," usually sold in 100' coils). In addition, you will need two eyebolts in the smallest available size, plus four hex nuts to fit, and a small bungee cord or equivalent. There is a 12"-long, 1/8"-diameter bungee cord size that works well.

Cut a section of tubing 14^7/$_8$" long. This should give you a fundamental air resonance at A$_4$. Check by blowing over the edge, and shorten if necessary for fine tuning.

The air tone will speak under scraping a little better if you make the tube less rigid in the region that will be scraped. This you can do by squashing the tube in a vise (the squashed shape is less rigid than the cylinder). Squash it over about half its length, which will be the scraping region, leaving the squashed end opening in an oval shape, as shown in Figure B.

You can make the serrations easily with a grinder, or more laboriously with a hand file. *Wear goggles and a dust mask.* Make them about 1/4" apart on center, fairly deep but not so deep that you risk filing through the

tubing. Cover one face of the squashed end with serrations over about 6" (= 2/5) of the tube length, as shown in the drawing.

The maximum number of toneholes is 5, since one hand will be operating the scraper and not available to cover holes. You can space the toneholes to yield the scale of your choice. Here is a hole spacing that will yield a minor hexatonic scale:

Hole Number	Distance From End	Hole Diameter	Sounding Pitch
0 (tube end)	0	-	A$_4$
1	3 ^{13}/$_{16}$"	3/8"	C$_5$
2	4 ^{15}/$_{16}$"	11/32"	D$_5$
3	5 ^{7}/$_8$"	13/32"	E$_5$
4	6 ½"	5/16"	F$_5$
5	7 ^{5}/$_{16}$"	3/8"	G$_5$

The holes should not be in a straight line along the top of the tube, but displaced to one side or the other as dictated by the ease and comfort of the fingers that will be covering them in the lap playing position described below. You will end up with holes # 1 - 4 as fingerholes in a curved line off to one side of the tube, and #5 as a thumb hole off to the other. Fine tuning may be necessary after drilling these holes.

When you operate the scraper with one hand and control the fingerholes with the other, no hands are left to hold the tube securely. So you will strap it to your lap. The visual effect is comical, especially if you get up to walk with the tube still strapped around your thighs, but this mounting works well for playing purposes. One half inch from each end, drill and attach the eyebolts as shown. The small bungee cord will run from eyebolt to eyebolt, around the backs of your thighs, to hold the tube in place as you sit and play.

You can try different scrapers. I have found that steel rod of 1/4" diameter or so works well, so I use a medium-large phillips head screw driver, drawing the shaft along the ridges.

Sound the tubes by scraping or striking. Blend the two for a scrape with well-defined attack, by starting the scrape with a bit of percussion. Control pitch by covering and uncovering the toneholes with the free hand.

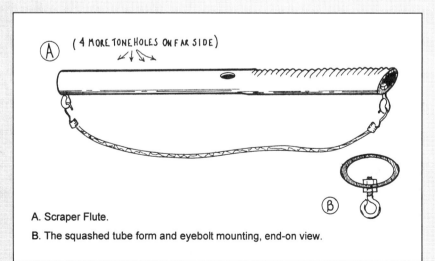

(4 MORE TONEHOLES ON FAR SIDE)

A. Scraper Flute.

B. The squashed tube form and eyebolt mounting, end-on view.

padded beaters. In Papua New Guinea players use beach thongs (the familiar rubber sandals). Others have used flat bats made of similar rubbers, but cut to different shapes and sizes.

Jacques Dudon's true-octave instrument described above is sounded by an encounter between air and water. The tube is a big one, open at both ends, with a larger mouth at one end as described above. The player dunks the large end a short distance into the drink, thus abruptly closing the aperture with a wall of water. This generates a wobbly but clear tone at the lower octave. When the player lifts it out, the tube abruptly opens again, and now the upper octave sounds. The two motions together make an appealing "goo-eenk?" sound.

Another way to excite an enclosed body of air is to strike the walls of the chamber, giving them a jolt which in turn jolts the air within. This works nicely if the walls are soft enough to give under the blow and thus communicate the impact to the air. Certain semi-rigid plastic tubings work especially well. You can also use heavy cardboard tubes, such as those used in storing bolts of fabric, if you first soften up a striking spot on the tube wall by battering the spot with beaters until it becomes yielding enough to give a clear tone.

Certain brands of caulk come in tubular plastic containers intended for use in caulk guns. Once they are empty of caulk (but for an acoustically helpful plug remaining in the nozzle), you can tune them by cutting them to different lengths. Hold them by the nozzles, one in each hand, and play by striking the sides of the tubes against your knees or a table edge while doing the rumba.

For side-struck percussion aerophone tubes, you can emphasize different modes of vibration within the tone by striking at a pressure antinode for the mode of vibration you wish to bring out. For an open tube, that means strike near the center for a strong fundamental and strong odd-numbered harmonics but relatively weak even harmonics. For a closed tube, strike nearer to the closed end to excite the fundamental and its harmonics. Review the cylindrical tube waveform diagrams in Figure 6-14, 6-15 and 6-16 for a more complete picture.

Another way to obtain an aerophonic sound from a tube is by scraping. To do this, you have to carve coarse lateral ridges along the surface of the tube, providing a scraping surface with plenty of bite. Plans for making a scraper flute appear in Sidebar 6-11. Scraper flutes produce a wonderful sound, raunchy but with a tender sort of guttural intimacy.

Tubes or globular chambers whose walls are too rigid to give under the force of a blow may still work as percussion aerophones if they can be struck in such a way that the idiophonic tube sound does not bury the air sound. Stamping tubes, played in diverse music cultures around the world, work this way. A tube of wood, bamboo or plastic (metal is likely to clank too much), stopped at one end, is tamped firmly, edge-on, closed end down, on a solid surface. Big tubes can produce a truly impressive bass tone; small tubes a lovely, light and bubbly one. Following the lead of California maker Darrell De Vore, you can add one or two flute-like toneholes to small, hand-held tubes for multi-pitch tamping. With a bamboo tube in each hand, each tube having two toneholes and three available notes, Darrell produces

music like a gentle rain.

Percussion aerophones with globular chambers give rise to different tone qualities from instruments using tubes. The globular sound is all fundamental, full and bassy rather than sharp or brilliant. There is a family of Nigerian instruments called (in English) *side-hole pot drums*. The instrument is a long-necked vase-like ceramic vessel, with a mouth at the top and an additional opening set in the side. The additional hole means that you can clump your hand down so as to fully cover the pot's mouth, and still hear the rich resonance through the side hole. In addition you can use the free hand to partially cover or uncover the side hole to modify the tone. Add to this diversity of types of strokes over the main hole and a lot of idiophonic percussion effects from the ceramic material itself, and you have a colorful source of musical sound.

SIRENS

Everyone knows what a siren is, or at least what it does, but not everyone may know how a siren works. A siren is an air-gating system, like the reeds we described earlier, but very different in function. In its most basic form, it consists of a disk with a concentric circle of evenly spaced holes, which rotates in front of a narrow air stream. Whenever one of the holes passes in front of the air stream, a pulse of air passes through. The pulsing frequency equals the number of holes in the concentric ring of holes multiplied by the number of disk rotations per second. Thus, a disk having 44 holes rotating at 10 rotations per second produces an audible tone of A4 at 440Hz.

Sirens designed for maximum noise, like fire engine sirens, have an arrangement that greatly increases volume and operating efficiency. They use two disks with identical hole spacing, one in front of the other. One is stationary. It covers the end of an air chamber kept at high pressure by the influx of air from a compressor. The other is mounted directly in front of the first, and is free to rotate. At times, in the course of rotation, the two disk's rings of holes are momentarily in line, and air passes freely through all holes simultaneously. At other moments the holes don't coincide; the two disks block each other's holes, and no air can pass through. To make the outer disk spin, its holes are drilled not perpendicular to the disk surface, but at an offset angle (alternatively, there are sloped blades just outside the holes creating a similar effect). When air rushes through the sloped holes, it drives the outer wheel like a turbine. That is why siren sounds start at low pitch and gliss upward — the pitch rises as the disk picks up speed under the force of the air stream.

Despite its wonderful efficiency as a noisemaker, such a siren is not very useful as a musical instrument, beyond a few hair-raising special effects. It doesn't lend itself to any practical pitch control system. To make a musical siren, we will go back a one-disk siren design, and develop it along different lines. For musical purposes, you need the disk to rotate at a constant speed, under the control of a motor (or treadle and flywheel, or whatever). This yields steady pitch rather than sliding pitch. To allow the instrument to produce more than a single tone, you want not just one ring of holes, but many concentric rings. Each ring is made up of a different

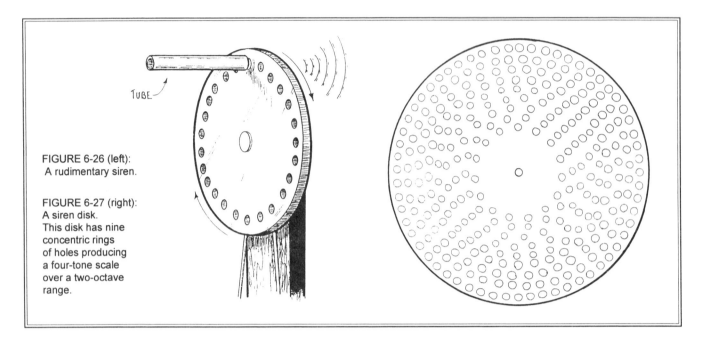

FIGURE 6-26 (left):
A rudimentary siren.

FIGURE 6-27 (right):
A siren disk.
This disk has nine
concentric rings
of holes producing
a four-tone scale
over a two-octave
range.

number of evenly spaced holes, so that each ring potentially yields a different frequency and pitch when the disk rotates. Figure 6-27 shows such a disk. For the air stream, you can use a flexible blow tube and nozzle, hand-held in front of the rotating disk, to direct the air at one or another of the rings and sound the different pitches.

The pitch relationships of the finished instrument — that is, the scale it produces — will depend upon the ratios of the numbers of holes in each ring. For instance, if one ring is to produce a tone an octave above another, it must have twice as many holes, since a frequency ratio of 2:1 corresponds to the interval of an octave. Changing the disk rotation speed will change the actual pitches produced, since it will change the pulsing frequency, but it will not change this pitch relationship. Suppose, then, that you want to create a disk that will allow you to play the pentatonic scale consisting of the tonic, a minor third, perfect fourth, perfect fifth and minor seventh. To do this, you create a series of concentric rings whose hole counts correspond to the ratios of that scale. If you consider the innermost ring with the fewest holes as the tonic, then the second ring should have 6/5 as many holes to produce the minor third above, the next 4/3 as many for the fourth above, then 3/2 for the fifth above, 9/5 for the minor 7th, and 2/1 for the octave. (The minimum number of holes in the successive rings required to achieve this particular set of ratios are 30, 36, 40, 45, 54, 60.)

One of the tricks in creating an effective musical siren is to get the air tube nozzle as close as possible to the rotating disk without touching it. This minimizes side spreading and ensures that the bulk of the air passes through the holes in discrete pulses. Even at its best this musical siren design is not loud, and volume drops considerably when the nozzle is not minutely close to the disk. To make it easier to hold the nozzle close to the disk without touching, you can have a "fence," like that on a woodworker's lathe, crossing in front of the disk. Then make the outer shape of the nozzle such that the player can ride it along the fence much as a worker at a lathe holds the chisel against the fence.

The musical siren calls for a strong but quiet motor, and speed control for the motor is a great help.

OUTER AIR INSTRUMENTS

There is another family of aerophones, sometimes called "outer air instruments," that have

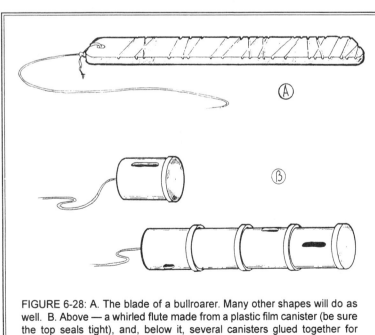

FIGURE 6-28: A. The blade of a bullroarer. Many other shapes will do as well. B. Above — a whirled flute made from a plastic film canister (be sure the top seals tight), and, below it, several canisters glued together for multiple, birdcall-like voices. The pitch is determined by the volume of the canister and the size of the opening (larger opening = higher pitch).

no reeds and no air chambers, but simply excite the air in the open atmosphere. The best known of these are bullroarers. A bullroarer consists of a blade, usually of wood, with a string attached at one end which the player whirls around in the open air. The blade rotates rapidly as it whirls, producing a buzz that varies in pitch and volume with the blade's speed of rotation. The sound is often compared to a giant insect's buzz, and it can have, to one who is open to such things, something of a hypnotic effect. The sound is monotonous, but the player's movement is dramatic.

The blade may be anywhere from 6" to as much as 30" long, and perhaps one sixth or one eighth as wide. It should be thin but not too thin, or it won't have sufficient weight to overcome wind resistance, making it hard to whirl. A quarter inch thick is usually about right. The silhouette of the blade typically is pointed at both ends but other oblong shapes, including rectangles, can work. It seems to help to have an irregular surface, with carved decorations or saw kerfs or whatever, on one side of the blade (see Figure 6-28A).

You can also make small whirled flutes. (These are not outer air instruments, strictly speaking, but they are similar in concept.) The edgetone is generated in a little canister with an edge-tone hole cut in the side. The canister is whirled on the end of a string like a bullroarer. It rotates as it whirls, exposing the edge to varying air flows and turbulences to create a shifting array of chirping and sighing sounds. Plastic film canisters and pillboxes work well; larger containers can also work. See Figure 6-28B and its caption for details.

Chapter Seven

MEMBRANOPHONES

And now the drums!

A membranophone is any instrument whose initial sounding element is a vibrating stretched membrane. That includes drums of all sorts, plus a few seemingly rather un-drumlike things. In addition to serving as the primary vibrating element in drums, stretched membranes also serve as secondary sound radiators in an extensive family of stringed instruments. The American banjo is the best-known representative in the West, but the family of membrane-resonated strings includes most African string instruments and many Indian and Middle Eastern ones as well. We will talk more about these instruments in coming chapters, but bear in mind that much of what we learn about membranes in this chapter will also be useful in understanding the banjo and its kin.

One of the great things about membranophones is that they are efficient. Membranes in themselves typically have the generous surface area required to move a lot of air. And most drumheads (though not all) are strong and moderately massive, allowing them to accept a strong impulse and respond with a loud sound, without distortion of sound or damage to the instrument. With their strength and carrying power, drums are wonderful for outdoor music. A special feature of drums is the fact that people rarely attempt to tune them with the sort of mechanistic precision one applies to, say, pianos. Yet listeners are very much affected by the timbre and pitch information inherent in different drums. As a result, drums often serve as a door to a primordial kind of tuneful listening, relatively free of learned doctrine.

As we did with the aerophones, we will posit a prototype simple drum to help guide our study. For the basic design, we will borrow (not for the first time) from the book *Sound Designs*, by Reinhold Banek and Jon Scoville, to make something similar to their tube drum. The drum consists of a goatskin head stapled over the top of an extra-heavy over-sized cardboard tube. The head is soaked in water before application; this allows it to shrink as it dries, bringing it up to playable tension. (For fuller instructions on the making of this drum, see Sidebar 7-1.)

Now, what are the essential elements in this simple drum?

1) The drumhead — in this case, the goat skin.

2) The drum body — in this case, the heavy cardboard tube.

The body serves two purposes:

a) It provides a frame over which to stretch the head.

b) It encloses a body of air which adds its resonances to the sound.

3) Means for attaching the head to the body — in this case, the staples.

And there is one more secret ingredient. It is the relationship between the drumhead, with its natural resonances, and the enclosed air below with its natural resonances. A successful drum is one in which drumhead resonances and air cavity resonances work well together. The key element in the interaction between the two is the method of attachment, which, more than anything, governs the tension on the head. It is valuable if the attachment method allows for adjustment of the tension (not possible on our prototype).

This chapter covers the above-mentioned components in this order: 1) the membranes themselves; 2) the structures that support membranes (the drum body); 3) the mechanisms that hold the two together and apply tension; and, 4) the interaction between the elements, along with the question of drum tuning. At the end of the chapter is a catch-all section to discuss further the different drum types, different methods for exciting the vibration, and so forth.

Before all that, though, one piece of business: a description of drumhoops is necessary for understanding some of what is to come. Although the head on the tube drum discussed above was held in place by staples, many drums use hoops, which hold the skin securely, distribute tension evenly, and give hold-down mechanisms something to hold on to. Some drums have just one hoop, called a *flesh hoop*. It is a ring of wood or metal, with an inside diameter slightly larger than the outside diameter of the drum body it is to go on. The edges of the drum membrane are securely wrapped around this hoop, so that the hoop provides a frame to support

DIRECTIONS FOR MAKING THE PROTOTYPE SIMPLE DRUM

To make the Banek/Scoville tube drum described in the main text, start with a section of very heavy cardboard tubing, let's say two feet long and 8" in diameter. It must be at least about 3/16" thick; thicker is better. Industrial-strength cardboard tubing like this is used as forms for pouring concrete pillars, and can be purchased at building supply centers. Paint or otherwise coat the tube to prevent absorption of moisture. Take a 12" goatskin drumhead (see Appendix 2 for supply sources), and soak it in a pan of water for an hour or more. Remove it, wipe off excess moisture, and lay it over the end of the tube with the excess skin running down the sides. Using a heavy-duty stapler, staple the skin to the tube wall all around. Position the staples around the sides in this order: 12 o'clock, 6 o'clock, 3 o'clock, 9 o'clock ... and continue in similar fashion from there to fill in the spaces, making two rounds of closely-spaced staples altogether. Keep the stress uniform, pulling the skin good and tight as you go. Set the drum aside to dry overnight. The drumhead will tighten as it dries, leaving you with a satisfyingly playable drum the next day.

To make a standing drum (one which does not require being held by the player or having a separate stand), start with a length of cardboard tubing about 4" longer than the intended sounding length of the drum — e.g., for the equivalent of a 24" drum, cut the tube initially to 28". Use a jig saw to cut out four 4" high sections around the base, so that the remaining material serves as legs, as shown in the drawing. These legs alone may have some damping effect on the drumhead's vibration, so cut four 3" cubes of foam rubber and make a 1½"-deep slit across the top of each. Slip one cube onto each "leg" of the drum, as shown in the drawing. This very generous padding will improve the resonance of the standing drum. (One disadvantage: it will also make the drum less stable as it stands).

The tone of this drum will change from hour to hour under the influences of heat and humidity. When the head becomes too slack, drying it a bit by leaving it in direct sunlight will improve the situation. But avoid prolonged sun exposure or excessively hot and dry conditions, as too much shrinkage of the head may over-strain the mounting or cause the rim of the tube to collapse in on itself to some degree. The head will then be unrecoverably slackened when conditions return to normal.

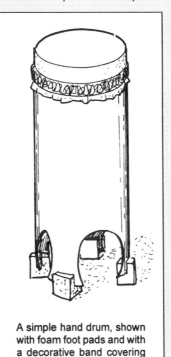

A simple hand drum, shown with foam foot pads and with a decorative band covering the staples.

the membrane. Pressing the flesh hoop down over the rim of the drum stretches the membrane over the opening. It then only takes something to hold the hoop in place — tacks, lacings, tensioning hardware or whatever — and you have a workable drum.

A more reliable approach is a double hoop system, used on most modern commercially-made drums. A flesh hoop is held down firmly over the top of the drum by a second hoop, called the *counter hoop* or the *hat*. Whatever applies tension — lacing or hardware — doesn't apply directly to the skin or the flesh hoop, but instead pulls down on the counter hoop. The making and application of drum hoops are discussed in Sidebar 7-3.

DRUMHEADS

Most drumheads, like that of our prototype, are circular in shape. Figure 7-1 shows the vibration patterns and resulting overtone frequencies for the first several modes for circular membranes. The partials, as you can see, are inharmonic.

There is no rule that says that drumheads must be circular. Square membranes have been used in various instruments, and other shapes are equally possible. For reasons having to do with wave reflection patterns in the drumhead, non-circular membranes may be somewhat less resonant than circular ones, having less sustain and more un-pitched noise components.

Some drums have a muffled quality, with little clear pitch sense. These are drums where the partials are heavily damped and don't ring clearly, as with membranes under low tension, and skins with the fur left on (as is done in some traditional drum types). Many other drums have a more ringing tone, with one or more identifiable pitches present in the tone. Often the player can control which overtones come across most strongly by the nature of the strike. Snare drums are a special case: here the sound is purposefully dominated by noise components which obscure the membrane pitch (we'll have more on snare drums later).

Drumhead Materials

The material and mass of the drumhead itself is an important factor in determining drumhead overtone response. Light, thin, and/or innately rigid membranes tend to bring out high overtones. Heavier, softer ones produce darker tones. Any number of materials can be and have been used for drumheads:

Animal skin

This, through most of human history, has been the standard material for drumheads. In

FIGURE 7-1:

Modes of vibration in circular membranes.

Circular membranes have several sets of transverse vibrational modes. One set of modes shows concentric circular nodes. These modes are characterized by symmetry all around — everything happens in circular rings. The first three modes in this set appear in Figures A, B and C. A second set differs from the first by the presence of a linear node crossing the center of the membrane in the upper modes, as in Figures D and E. Additional sets of modes not shown here follow more complex patterns.

The following chart lists overtone frequencies relative to the fundamental for the modes shown.

Mode	Frequency Relative to Fundamental	Pitch Relative to Fundamental
Circular modes:		
C1	f_1	(Unison)
C2	$2.3f_1$	Sharp major 9th
C3	$3.6f_1$	8ve + minor 7th
Bilateral modes:		
L2	$1.59f_1$	Minor 6th
L3	$2.92f_1$	8ve + ↓ 5th

The relative prominence of the modes depends upon a host of factors relating to the nature of the strike and the striker, the internal damping of the membrane, the effects of adjacent bodies of air, and so on.

clearly, especially with strokes near the rim, so that the goatskin retains a characteristically brighter sound despite the prominent low fundamental.

Natural skin drumheads are soaked in water before being applied to the drum or hoop, and then allowed to dry there. This allows the maker to take advantage of three useful characteristics of skin:

1) It retains the shape in which it dries. Thus, if the edges of the skin have been wrapped around a hoop, they will be inclined to stay wrapped around that hoop; the stiffness of the dried wrapped skin works to hold it in place. If it has been allowed to dry while stretched over the top of a drum body and pulled down the sides, it will keep the shape and fit for that particular drum.

2) The shrinkage after soaking helps to bring the head up to high tension as it dries on the drum.

3) Hide is naturally full of gluey stuff — the basis of old fashioned hide glues — that softens when the skin is soaked, and forms a bond as it dries. For non-tunable drums, like those with tacked-on heads, this helps prevent slippage. The self-adhesive property also helps secure the skin to wooden drum hoops (but not to metal, to which hide glue will not bond).

See Sidebar 7-2 for more on the processes of preparing animal hides for use as drumheads.

Synthetics

In recent decades more and more drums have been given drumheads of plastic or fiberglass. The primary advantages of the synthetics are affordability, uniformity, stability and durability. Plastic drumheads are available from music suppliers in a great range of sizes and weights. The overtones ring much more than they do with natural hide, and the fundamentals are not as rich. Commercially made synthetic drumheads come with the equivalent of a flesh hoop built in.

Fabric

Some makers have fashioned drumheads of canvas. Untreated canvas is too porous and too dispersive in its surface characteristics to work well, so canvas drumheads may be coated with something to act as a filler, which provides a bit more weight. Wood finishes may do the trick if they are not too brittle when dry. I have heard this approach recommended, but I should add that in my limited experimentation

this way representatives of many species have found a voice after death. Cow hide gives a rich tone in congas; calf skin is used for a warm tone in orchestral kettle drums. Some makers prefer muleskin, because it has a reputation (whether rightly or wrongly) for being less stretchy. Goatskin is lighter, and is used on middle-sized and smaller drums. For very small drums, pig skin, deer skin, rabbit skin, cat skin, snake skin, and heaven-knows-what-else skin have been used. Other animal membranes such as bladder have also served. Many builders and percussionists have great faith in the innate superiority of natural hide over the synthetics that have been offered as substitutes.

One might expect to routinely use lighter skins, such as goatskin, for drums tuned to higher pitches. That's a suitable approach in many cases, but not always. For instance, on some drum types, cow hide, which is relatively heavy, sounds best at extremely high tensions, yielding a relatively high drumhead pitch (this is the typically preferred conga sound). Meanwhile goat skin, which is lighter, is often set at somewhat lower tensions to bring out a particularly clear fundamental tone, substantially lower than the typical conga drumhead pitch. The overtones in the goat skin still ring

PREPARING ANIMAL HIDES AS DRUMHEADS

Not so long ago, the skinning of animals and preparation of hides were familiar activities for most people. Now, in the urban world at least, this is not so. Drum makers who work with natural hide but who do not plan to slaughter their own animals have three choices. They can purchase whole hides and do all of their own preparation and cutting; they can purchase sections of hide prepared and pre-cut to circular shapes for drumheads; or they can buy ready-made drumheads, already prepared and attached to a hoop.

Hides and pre-cut heads vary in quality. Overall skin thickness is a major factor in tone, as thicker skins favor a rounder sort of tone. Thinner skins are easier to form and to work with, and can be brought up to pitch with less strain on the drum body. In any event, the skin should be of uniform thickness and free of irregularities. The outer surface of the hide is smoother than the inner, and normally serves as the outer playing surface of the drumhead.

The hide from which drumheads are made is rawhide — that is, hide that has not been tanned. (Tanning is a process which softens the hide, making it usable as leather.) But they have been treated with a chemical to remove the hair, and run through a machine that scrapes the fat off the inside.

Heads made from animal hides, especially heavy ones like cow skin, are too stiff to work with when dry. To soften them up, the head must be soaked in cold water. Heavier heads can soak for several hours or overnight; for lighter heads, an hour or two may be enough. This causes the skin to expand and become malleable, and to take on a doughy texture. After the skin has been soaked, the next step depends upon the sort of drum to be made and the mechanism used to hold the skin to the drum.

1) *For hoopless drums*: The skin can be stretched over the top of the drum, pulled tightly down the sides, fixed there by tacking, gluing, lacing or whatever, trimmed as need be, and allowed to dry. (Some of these options are illustrated in Figure 7-4.)

2) *For hand-played drums using hoops*, such as congas: You need a skin diameter about six inches greater than the rim diameter. The soaked skin must be formed over the top of the drum, with the edges extending several inches below the rim. Some of the skin extending down the sides must then be wrapped back up around the hoop — a process called "lapping," described in Sidebar 7-3. Any excess material is carefully trimmed. The skin is allowed to dry, with the flesh hoop held in place securely but not too tightly by the hat (counterhoop) or some other hold-down method. Figure 7-5 shows how the components fit together. (Also, Figure 7-4 shows some alternatives to the traditional lapped hoop approach referred to here.) Hand-played drum skins need this special over-the-top pre-forming process because the drum hoops need to be well below the rim of the drum so that the player can strike the skin near the rim without hitting the hoop. If the drum is to be tunable, prevent the skin from gluing itself to the drum body by waxing the rim, or dusting it with chalk or talc prior to pressing the wet skin against it. After the skin has dried, it can be removed and reapplied later, or simply left on and tightened down for playing.

If you don't want to go through this process, conga heads in standard sizes can be purchased pre-formed and lapped to a hoop.

3) *For drums played with sticks*, such as snare drums: The skin can simply be lapped over the flesh hoop (see Sidebar 7-3 and Figure 7-5) without any special forming over the top of the drum. It doesn't need to be pre-formed over the top of the drum as hand-played drums do, because with stick drums it's OK — desirable, in fact — for the top of the counter hoop to be a little higher than the level of the head. The striking angle of drumsticks is such that it is easy to avoid hitting the hoop, plus with sticks you can get those good sounds called "rimshots" by deliberately hitting the hoop and skin simultaneously. After the skin has dried on the flesh hoop, the skin and hoop assembly is set over the rim of the drum body and tightened down by whatever tensioning method you are using.

As a final step, and as an occasional caretaking step as the skin ages, give the head a rubdown with oil. This keeps it supple and, for a skin which has become dry, noticeably improves the sound. Many oils will serve the purpose; I have found that mineral oil, being widely available and inexpensive, is a good choice.

with it, I have had poor results. However, I have found that rubberized cloth, such as the stuff that old fashioned "slicker" raincoats are made of, works fairly well. The tone is warm and gentle, having a reasonably full fundamental, but with far less excitement in the overtones than plastics or natural skin.

Rubber or stretchy plastics

Balloon rubber and inner tube rubber have both been used for drumheads. Their stretchiness gives them the advantage of being very easy to mount under tension. The results in typical applications are disappointing, as the soft rubber is too yielding to absorb the energy of the strike well, and has too much internal damping to sustain a vibration. But the lightness and yield of stretchy rubbers have some value when you need a membrane that is easily dominated by an associated air column. Balloon-rubber drumheads set over long, narrow tubes, for instance, will not produce great volume, but the tone is appealing. (Further discussion of tube drums appears later in this chapter.)

Rigid materials

If the material of a membrane is not stretched, but rather is rigid enough to support itself, then the instrument technically does not fit the definition of a membranophone. Be that as it may, many makers have produced drum-like instruments using diaphragms of rigid plastic, thin plywood, metal, ceramic or other materials, and many of the principles of membranophone design apply.

Weighting the Drumhead

Drumheads are normally made as uniform as possible in consistency and thickness, forming an evenly weighted flat surface on the drum. But it's not unusual to see a trap set drummer offsetting this by taping pieces of gauze or other padding to snare and tom-tom drumheads at selected off-center locations. The purpose is to reduce unwanted ring from various partials in the drum tone. By placing the dampers at selected locations, one can modify different overtones and fine tune the drum tone (albeit, often in a haphazard way). One could bring some sophistication to this process through a study of the vibrational patterns, node locations and frequencies for the several circular membrane modes described in Figure 7-1.

Another way to modify the overtone output of a drumhead is weighting the center of the head. This increases the sustain, brings out the fundamental and diminishes the overtones. One frequently sees this done to a very limited degree by the application of a thin disk of heavier material at the center of commercial synthetic drumheads. Some conga players achieve a similar effect by deliberately thinning their drumheads around the rim by sanding. A fuller application of the same idea can be seen in tablas. At the center of the tabla drum head is a rounded mound of a special gritty, pasty material applied directly to the skin. It adds mass at the center, diminishing uniformly toward the periphery, but due to its special makeup, it does so without limiting the skin's flexibility. The *shai*, as this feature is called, is one of the reasons why tablas have such clear, well defined pitch, and such long ring time.

The making of the shai is a sophisticated process and we won't go into it here, but there are ways to apply similar processes to other drum types. Any large, flat, stiff material added to increase weight will inhibit the drumhead's flex. But you can add small weights at the center of the head without such problems. I have found, for instance, that a nut or washer affixed to the center of the head can make a small drum sound deeper and richer. There are many ways one could go about attaching weights. Here is an approach that I have found easy and effective: Drill a small hole at the center of the drumhead. Put a very short machine screw (1/4" or 3/8") through the hole, and secure it with a nut from underneath.

DRUM BODIES

The body of a drum serves, first, as a framework over which to stretch the membrane. For the family of drums called *frame drums*, that's all there is to it: the body has no more depth than what is needed to provide a sturdy support structure at the rim of the membrane. The best known frame drum in western pop culture is the tambourine (the sort that has a stretched membrane, which not all do; and please ignore the jingles for the moment). A purer example is the Irish bodhran. There are many more the world over.

With deeper drums, the body encloses a volume of air beneath the drum head. The air chamber adds its own resonance to the overall sound, and at the same time influences the vibration patterns of the drumhead itself, since the two are in intimate contact. This lends a deeper, richer sound, and mitigates the effect of non-harmonic partials in the drumhead. How these effects actually play out depends very much upon the tuning relationship between the membrane and the air chamber. The enclosure also serves to partially isolate the soundwaves coming off the front surface of the drumhead from those off the back. At the same time, it gives the air-resonated sound from the back a different make-up from the un-resonated sound from the front. These factors are important, because the soundwaves radiating from each side are exactly out of phase with one another. If the sounds from the two sides are identical and if they are free to spread

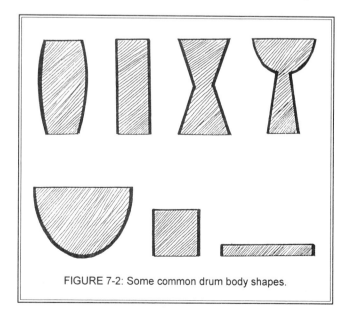

FIGURE 7-2: Some common drum body shapes.

unobstructed, they cancel to some extent, especially in the lower frequencies. The enclosure reduces the evisceration of the lower frequencies and generally yields a fuller sound.

The drum body serves one other function: its mass provides counterpoise to the vibrating drumhead, as well as to the force of the player's blow. A lightweight drum body isn't suitable for a massive drumhead, because the head needs something substantially more massive than itself to provide a stable anchor as it vibrates.

An important component in the drum body is the edge of the rim over which the drum head pulls as it is tightened. To avoid strain on the skin and distribute the stress evenly, the surface of the rim must be perfectly level. The point at which the head leaves the rim should be cleanly defined. Any slight sloping toward the inside on the surface of the rim will give rise to buzzing or rattles, or inhibit the tone by creating uneven reflection of the waves in the head. The outer side of the rim, where the strain is greatest, must be gently rounded.

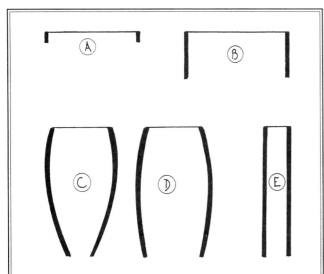

FIGURE 7-3: Acoustic effects of different drum body shapes.

A. Frame drum. Since there is almost no enclosure, there is no added air resonance. Out-of-phase waves from the front and back of the skin will tend to spread around the shallow frame and cancel, especially in the low frequencies. The result is a sound that may be loud but lacking depth. The low frequency cancellation effect is reduced if the head itself is particularly resonant and/or quite large.

B. Tenor drum. Slightly more resonance and less cancellation than the frame drum.

C. Barrel drum with narrow opening. The deep and well defined chamber provides strong air resonance for a much fuller sound. The small opening means that the enclosed air shows a fairly narrow resonance peak (strong resonance over a narrow frequency band) around a low resonant frequency. With such drums the head tone will often be much higher than the air resonance tone. In such cases the two tones can be heard separately, with different types of strokes bringing out one or the other preferentially.

D. Barrel drum with large opening. The enclosed air shows a broad resonance peak over a range slightly higher than it would be with a smaller opening.

E. Tube drum. The tube shows a strong, narrow resonance peak, probably at a frequency well below that of the small head.

If the drum body material is too thin to provide a rounded rim surface, you can add a ring of some thicker material to the top to provide a rounded rim. The added ring can also serve to reinforce a drum-body top that would otherwise be weak and subject to collapse. An easy approach is to apply flexible plastic tubing to the top as described for the membrane reed in Sidebar 6-6. A more sophisticated option for metal drums is to braze or solder a hoop of metal rod to the top of the body.

With these principles in mind, we can look at variations in drum body shape and consider the acoustic implications.

Some drums are single-headed, meaning that they have one membrane, and some are double-headed. Single-headed drum bodies are usually left open to the air at the far end. Single-headed drums which are entirely enclosed often produce unsatisfying results (an exception is very large drums, such as kettle drums, discussed below). The enclosed air, with no freedom to move, damps the drumhead's vibration, giving a dull tone; also, the air resonances have no opening through which to radiate into the room. Double-headed drums, however, may be entirely enclosed, because the flexibility of the second head gives the enclosed air the needed freedom of movement. In addition, the sympathetic movement of the second head when the first one is struck contributes to the sound communicated to the surrounding air. Yet even most double-headed drums have a hole in the side someplace, even if it's only a quarter or half inch in diameter, to allow some air flow. A larger hole in the side of a double-headed drum, providing a generous direct outlet for the air resonance tone, may also prove effective.

Kettle drums appear to contradict the earlier statement that single-headed drums need an air opening opposite the head to allow the head free vibration. In fact, orchestral kettle drums (timpani) do have a small opening in the base. Opinions differ on how the opening affects the vibration of the head. But it seems reasonable to assume that the relatively large body of air enclosed in a large kettle drum would be more yielding than the air in a smaller enclosed drum, and would inhibit drumhead vibration less. Also, while the enclosed air may restrict the fundamental, it may actually encourage some other modes, such as the one labeled L2 in Figure 7-1.

In single-headed drums with an opening opposite the head, the size of the opening is significant, as are the size and shape of the chamber. When the enclosure is short and fat and the opening wide — as with, say, timbales — then the enclosure is not really much of an enclosure, and lacks well defined air resonances. As with the more extreme case of frame drums, the skin sound will dominate. The head can be tuned to any pitch it can take, while air resonance will have little impact (see Figures 7-3A and B). At the opposite extreme, if the chamber is long and the opening narrow, as for instance with tube drums, then the enclosed air has well-defined resonances at specific pitches (Figure 7-3E). They will affect the tone very much, and their relation to the drumhead pitches takes on more importance.

Some drums have large internal chambers with relatively small openings. Congas, with their narrow-based barrel-shaped bodies, are an example (7-3 B and C). Such a chamber doesn't show a set of well-defined resonance frequencies like a narrow tube, but rather is dominated by a single broader resonance peak in the lower frequency ranges. (The word *broader* here means that there will be resonance response not limited to specific frequencies, but spread out over a wider band of frequencies.) Three primary factors influence the tuning of this broad resonance peak: 1) The larger the chamber overall, the lower the resonance frequency band. 2) The smaller the opening, the lower and narrower the frequency band. 3) The looser and less rigid the drumhead, the lower and broader the frequency band. This last factor means that the air resonance tuning is not fixed, but interacts with the drumhead tuning — a situation which makes the whole business a good deal less cut-and-dried than it would otherwise be. In congas and other long drums with high head tensions, the air resonance peak is typically well below the pitch at which the drumhead rings. That air resonance is the source of the bassy "bottom tone" of a heavy, damped stroke. It affects the quality, responsiveness and richness of the open ringing tone as well, but in a highly variable manner depending on the relative tuning of the skin and the air below. In contrast, with long drums set at lower tensions, such as the cardboard tube goatskin drum described at the start of this chapter, the drumhead fundamental is more likely to be in the same range as the air resonance, and the two will interact more closely.

There are many more possible drum body forms beyond the basic types we've just discussed. But the acoustic principles described here are primary guiding principles in drum body design. Later, we will take our level of understanding one step deeper, when we discuss drum tuning.

Drum Body Materials

The essential criteria for drum body materials are that they be sufficiently rigid and sturdy, and appropriately massive. Being readily available, affordable, and workable with common tools also helps. Here are notes on some specific materials. Remember to look to Appendix 1 for more information and notes on where to get what.

Woods

Hardwoods are more elegant, stronger, and longer lasting than softwoods. They are acoustically superior too, being more massive and reflective, but the difference in the end result between top quality woods and inexpensive softwoods is not as pronounced as you might expect. Also, the larger species of bamboo can be effective for very small drums or tube drums. The workability of wood helps when it comes to carefully shaping the rim that is the contact surface between skin and body, and attaching hardware (tuning mechanisms and such).

Barrel drums, with staves, are beautiful and make efficient use of valuable woods, but it takes some skill to make seamless, leakless joints between the staves. Some people have made drums by shaving down the sides of actual barrel staves, creating, in effect, a narrower barrel. If instead you start from scratch to make a drum with the traditional bulging shape, you will need either to steam and bend the staves, or cut them in a wide arc on a band saw, to create the outward curvature that is characteristic of barrel drums. Or you can

buck tradition by making a straight-sided barrel drum and challenge listeners to find fault with the resulting tone.

Drums are often made from hollowed-out tree trunks. I know of no easy way to do the hollowing. One way to make the task more manageable is to first split the trunk in half, then do the hollowing, and finally rejoin the halves. Sometimes, with luck, you can come across a section of trunk that has been naturally hollowed for you by a rotting process that has left the outer wood solid. I have noticed that this seems to happen a lot with ancient apple trees. With hollowed trunks, the upper rim is unlikely to form a true circle, posing problems when it comes to attaching hoops and hardware. In such cases you may choose to be content with tacked-on drumheads. Be aware that some tree species like redwood have softer sapwood near the surface; they don't make good candidates for hollowing.

Some wide, shallow drums, such as snare drums, are made by building up a strong circular shell of many thin veneers, laminated together using a circular form specially made for the purpose. For instructions on this process, see Irving Sloane's *Making Musical Instruments*. Similarly, there are some highly flexible commercially available plywoods that can be formed into a large drum shape, and stiffened by laminating on a second layer of the same material.

Cardboard

The heavy cardboard tubes suggested in Sidebar 7-1 are affordable, easy to work with, light in weight, and easy and fun to decorate. Disadvantages are that their strength is borderline — certainly insufficient for cow-hide drum heads kept at high tension — and they turn to mush if they get wet. You can increase their moisture resistance with water resistant finishes such as polyurethane.

Gourd and Calabash

Very large gourds can work well for lightweight drums, and they can be found in a wonderful variety of drum shapes, though they are fragile. Calabash are far stronger and in that regard superior, but they lack the diversity of form.

Metals

In the book mentioned a moment ago, Irving Sloane gives instructions for making a brass snare drum. He recommends starting with a half-hard 21-gauge (.029") sheet metal stock, and gives full details on working it.

Orchestral timpani are traditionally made of copper, but the demands of their fabrication exceed the capabilities of most home workshops.

For simpler, home-buildable metal drums, there are plenty of sources for metal cylinders or truncated cones of various lengths and diameters. Try buckets and small garbage cans, with the bottoms removed. And there are diverse types of tubing, ranging from relatively narrow conduit or water pipe up to drainage pipes and culverts in large diameters.

Plastics

As with metals, look for extra-heavy plastic buckets, or tubings in various sizes. Construction yards carry plastic pipe in diameters up to 12".

Ceramics

Some beautiful drums have been made of clay. Drawbacks are fragility, and the fact that clay, once dry, is no longer workable, making it difficult to attach hardware. For that reason, clay drums usually have their skins attached by lacing. Some are shaped with protrusions in the sides to hook the laces over.

ATTACHING THE HEAD

An essential question in attaching drumheads is whether the method of attachment allows the drum to be tuned and retuned after the skin has been applied. With tacked-on drumheads, even if the person who does the tacking does a great job, the skin will inevitably loosen up over time, especially under heavy playing. With natural skin you can re-tighten a bit prior to each playing by holding the drumhead over dry heat (or wetting it, if need be, to loosen it). You can even find a certain pleasure in an untunable drumhead's changeability as you hear it responding to every little change in the weather and communicating the information to you by its tone. But, with drums that are to be heavily played, it is usually worth the effort to find a mounting system that allows adjustment of the tension on the head.

On the other hand, there is an appealing aesthetic to lightly made and lightly played drums that are free of tuning gadgetry. If you are designing a drum for which all the hardware seems a burden to the organic spirit of the drum, then, I say, skip it. Play gently, and accept that the head tuning will not last forever.

Following here are notes on each of several methods of attachment:

| Sidebar 7-3 | MAKING DRUM HOOPS, AND ATTACHING HEADS TO HOOPS |

Wooden hoops can be made by laminating several strips within a circular form, just as wooden drum shells are sometimes made. The individual, thin strips are sufficiently flexible to form the circle, but ten or more of them glued like plywood make a pretty strong hoop. When doing this, make sure that the points at which the ends of the strips meet are located differently in each layer.

To make a hoop out of single thicker piece of wood, you can bend it by means of a special tool called a bending iron, or by boiling or steaming the wood until it is sufficiently pliable, then quickly clamping it over a circular mold to dry.

If you don't mind having a rather large hoop, cut a ring from plywood, as shown in Figure 7-4J. The plywood should be at least 1/2" thick for light drums, and 1" for heavier drums, and should be wide, like 1½" or 2" from inner to outer rim. In this case, instead of lapping the skin over the ring, you can simply tack or staple it to the underside, being sure to staple generously all the way around.

Wooden or metal embroidery hoops and quilting hoops, available at sewing, crafts and hobby stores, can serve as drum hoops in many applications. See Figure 7-4K for more on that.

Some wooden hoops, or at least "woody" hoops, are made from heavy vines, either single or with multiple strands twisted like a rope, which are formed into a ring when green, and then allowed to dry that way. You can also get some of the advantages of a hoop simply by using heavy, stiff rope to reinforce the periphery of the membrane.

Metal hoops can be made from bar stock of one sort or another. Metal flesh hoops are often made of square stock, in the range of 1/4" to 3/8", because the angles help hold the skin and reduce slippage. Counter hoops are usually made of a flat bar stock — perhaps 3/16" by 3/4". Hoops for commercially made drums may have more elaborate shapes to accommodate hold-downs.

Bending your own metal hoop to a perfect circle and joining the ends is difficult without special shop equipment. You may get lucky and find a barrel hoop or some other prefabricated hoop of the right diameter — another reason for instrument makers to haunt scrap metal yards.

For smaller drums, you can make serviceable hoops by cutting rings from large-diameter, thick-walled plastic or steel tubing.

The counter hoop and the flesh hoop should be the same diameter, and that diameter must be at least 1/2" larger on the inside than the rim of the drum body.

Attaching the membrane to the flesh hoop is not a concern for commercial plastic drumheads, as they come from the manufacturer with a built-in hoop. You can also buy skin heads already lapped to hoops. For those who wish to do it themselves, the standard approach, mentioned above, is lapping, which is simply wrapping the edges of the soaked skin around the hoop and letting it dry there. With thin skins or other light materials it is not hard to do. But getting a piece of tough cow skin wrap around a hoop can be seen as a challenging problem in topology or, more to the point, as a wrestling match. The soaked hide is flexible, but not all that flexible. For very tough, heavy hide, you can use padded pliers or vise grips (being very careful not to tear the skin). Wrap the skin all the way around the hoop if possible, being sure in particular that it covers the top of the hoop, where the counter hoop will press down (this allows the pressure of the counter hoop to help secure it). The cutaway views in Figures 7-5 will help you picture this. Have a generous batch of clothespins or some stronger equivalent handy to pin each section of lapped hoop as it is done, and hold it in place until it dries.

Alternatives to lapping: With thick wooden hoops, you can staple or tack directly to the hoop. With embroidery hoops or their equivalent, you can take the approach described in Figure 7-4K.

Mount-less Mounting

For small drums intended for light use, you can take advantage of the self-tensioning and self-gluing properties of natural hide to attach lightweight skins using no additional mounting mechanisms. It works best if the area immediately below the rim curves sharply inward, in a shape like those shown in Figure 7-4A. Darrell De Vore makes drums like this using hemispherical sections of large gourds, with an air hole of two inches or so opened in the back. Just soak the skin, then form it over the rim and the receding section of the drum body. It tightens and adheres as it dries, to form a surprisingly full-sounding small drum.

A similar approach — minus the wetting and drying — works with balloon rubber membranes on small tubular drums. Let the body of the balloon form a sort of sleeve to be slid over an appropriately sized opening. Start by cutting off the narrow balloon neck if necessary, then slide the balloon down over the tube until the end stretches over the opening. The traction of the latex is generally enough to hold it in place.

Tacking, Stapling or Pegging

This is the method described for the prototype drum at the start of this chapter. In place of staples, large-headed tacks can be used (Figure 7-4B), or wooden pegs can be driven through holes near the edge of the membrane and into holes in the side of the drum. Natural hide will improve the attachment through its self-gluing properties.

Some tacked drums use a single drum hoop, traditionally of some tough, woody, dried vine, to which the membrane is attached by wrapping the edges around the hoop. This hoop is pulled down over the rim of the drum, and tacks are driven through the hoop and the attached skin.

For non-stretchy and/or non-shrinking drumhead materials, tacking is not an effective method.

Lacing

Lacing allows for increasing or otherwise adjusting drumhead tension at any time. There are a thousand ways to lace drum skins; we will just look at the basic ideas here.

For double-headed drums, the lacing usually connects the two heads and tightens them by pulling them together. For single-headed drums, the lacing needs something lower on the drum body to attach to, such as pegs driven into the body, or metal hooks looped under the bottom edge. Alternatively, each lace can simply pass under the bottom of the drum and across to the opposite side. For the cord used in lacing, look for something dependably strong and as un-stretchy as possible. Avoid nylon cord or rope (too stretchy). Natural sisal rope works well.

You can make a decent laced drum without hoops by running the lacing through holes around the periphery of the skin in closely-spaced loops so as to distribute the stress widely and evenly (Figure 7-4C, D, and E). But for better results, hoops are a good idea. A simple single hoop can be used, with the laces running over the hoop and through the skin rather than through the skin alone. In this case you usually need an additional set of lacings looping around and around to hold the skin firmly to the hoop. Double-hoop systems, in which the lacings are attached to the counter hoop, are better yet.

Drum makers have developed many tricks for adjusting tension on laced drums. Several of them are illustrated in Figure 7-4F through I.

Tensioning Hardware

Drum lacing appeals to a natural aesthetic that metal hardware does not. But for strong, long-lasting drums that are to be vigorously played, many makers turn to metal tuning hardware. The principle behind hardware design is the same for most drums: several bolts or heavy threaded hooks are regularly spaced around the counter hoop. Each bolt or hook reaches down from the counter hoop to where the threaded end passes through some sort of anchor attached firmly to the side of the drum. A nut below the anchor allows the whole arrangement to be tightened with a wrench, pulling down on the hoop to tighten the skin. Figure 7-5 shows two typical arrangements. The tuning process is one of tightening or loosening the nuts or bolts, doing just a little at a time, proceeding from one bolt to the next in a star pattern back and forth across the rim, to alter the tension evenly all around.

You can get prefabricated drum tuning hardware from musical instrument supply houses. Or you can recycle from an unused drum. Or you can have it custom made by a metal worker. Or you can make your own from commonly available hardware. If you make your own, let your personal blend of common sense and ingenuity prevail, but be sure to make the system strong. Be sure also — this is important — that it doesn't get in the way of the player's stroke and that it doesn't jut out from the drum body.

DRUM TUNING

The relationship between the drumhead and the air enclosed beneath it is an essential factor in drum tone. If you have a tunable drum (one with lacings or tuning hardware; not with a tacked-on head), then you can work with this relationship by adjusting the tension on the drumhead to bring out the best in the drum. Drumhead tension affects not only the head itself, but also the resonance frequencies within the chamber. That is because the rigidity of the walls is one of the determining factors in air chamber resonance frequency, and the drumhead is one of those walls. As a result of this interdependence, you cannot simply determine the drum's air resonance pitch and then tune the head to it. You have to go through a process of adjustment to find a region where the two reinforce one another. When you do, the drum will speak with a fuller tone.

The process is not a mechanistic one; it is usually a feel-your-way kind of thing. Rarely is it a simple matter of finding a point where the fundamental resonance of the head matches the fundamental resonance of the body. The head resonances are generally too complex for that, and the air resonances insufficiently well defined. For many drums, with the head at reasonable playing tension, its resonances are too far above the main air resonance to bring the two in line anyway. The process, then, is more a matter of seeking out a tuning at which the head seems most responsive, and one which yields an attractive timbral blend. Remember that in most drums the air resonances enhance a general frequency region rather than specific notes. You can tune the head so

FIGURE 7-4 (Captions are on facing page)

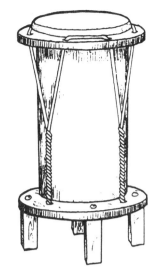

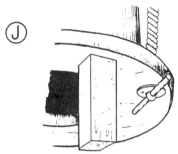

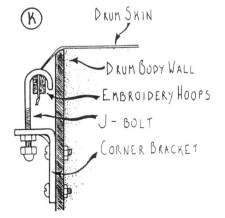

DRUM SKIN

DRUM BODY WALL

EMBROIDERY HOOPS

J-BOLT

CORNER BRACKET

FIGURE 7- 4 (continued)

DRUMHEAD ATTACHMENT METHODS

A. Mountless mounting. The skin's natural gluing properties, along with its stiffness and the receding drum body shape, may be enough to hold the head in place for lightweight, lightly played drums.

B. Tacking and gluing.

C & D. Two of the many possible drum lacing patterns.

E. Details of two methods for connecting the lacings to the drumheads. (The lower one requires an additional thong woven through the circumference of the head.) These approaches reduce the likelihood of tearing as compared to the simple loop-through lacing shown in C and D. Another way to guard against tearing is to reinforce the skin at the pass-through points by running the lace through additional pieces of rawhide, functioning like washers.

Figures 7-4F through I show adjustable head tensioning methods for laced drumheads:

F. Braces. Sliding the leather braces farther up each angled pair of laces increases tension on the head; slipping them back down releases the tension.

G. Twitching. Inserting sticks between the pairs of laces and twisting them once, twice, three times or more increases tension.

H. Shims: Inserting blocks under the laces increases tension.

I. Hourglass drums: the waisted shape of the drum allows the player to hold the drum under his or her arm and press the lacings inward by squeezing under the arm to increase tension for variable pitch during playing.

J. A drumhead mounting system developed by the author. There are two rings, which can be made of 1" plywood. The upper ring serves as a drum hoop. The hole in the ring is large enough to fit over the rim of the drum, and the drumhead is stapled to the ring on the underside. The lower ring forms part of the stand and also serves to anchor the laces. Its hole is just small enough that the bottom of the drum body rests on the ring near the perimeter of the hole. The inset shows a view of the underside of the lower ring. It illustrates how the laces pass through holes in the lower ring, where they loop over a small metal rod, such as the shaft of a nail. Turning the nail causes the laces to twist up above. The more the twist, the tighter they pull down on the head. A large washer serves as a spacer between the twist-rod and the surface of the lower ring. It provides sufficient friction to prevent untwisting.

K. Double hoops: The double hoops made to hold fabric for embroidery or quilting work can serve conveniently as drum hoops. These hoops are available at fabric stores and crafts stores, in a range of sizes. Those made as embroidery hoops are quite lightweight; hoops for quilting are heavier and stronger. For either sort, wooden ones are preferable to plastic. The hoops come in pairs, with a smaller one fitting within a larger; the larger has an adjustment screw used to tighten it snugly over the smaller. For embroidery, you place the fabric over the smaller hoop, then press the larger in place so that the perimeter of the fabric is held between the two hoops. Then tighten the screw to hold it there securely. You can do the same with a drumhead, then place the hoop and head over the rim of the drum and tighten it down by means such as those shown in Figure 7-4K.

Some considerations to keep in mind: 1) Some quilting hoops are made fairly heavy and strong, and so may be adequate under fairly high tension. But embroidery hoops are not made to take high stress, and will easily distort and break. I suggest using two pairs of hoops, one on top of the other, and using many hold-downs around the periphery — eight or more — to distribute the stress. And don't use weak embroidery hoops for high-tension drums like congas with cow-hide heads. 2) If you mount a soaked skin in the double hoops and let it dry, it will hold pretty well without slipping. But you can make it more secure still by driving tacks through the outer hoop and the skin and into the inner hoop at intervals around the periphery. Or, better, use machine screws running right through, tightened with nuts on the inside. 3) The mounting brackets on the side of the drum must be strong. If you use steel corner brackets (shown in Figure 7-4K as one convenient approach), be sure to use very heavy brackets. It may be best to get extra heavy, oversized brackets and shorten one arm with a hacksaw so that it doesn't protrude too much. 4) Speaking of which — those protruding brackets are at best awkward, and at worst dangerous. Be sure to round all corners or, better, devise a protective cover for the hardware to prevent its catching, scratching or poking. Be sure to use an acorn nut to cover the bottom of the J-bolt.

THOUGHTS ON MAKING A TUNABLE DRUM

Sidebar 7-1 describes a non-tunable drum which is quite easy to make. I have tried to dream up similarly simple approaches to making a tunable drum, but this is easier said than done. Still, this chapter contains information that will allow you to experiment with a wide variety of tunable drum designs. What follows here is an idea for anyone wanting to make a tunable drum that is not excessively difficult to build. No specific plan is given here; I've left the details to the reader. Hopefully you will be able to apply a combination of common sense and creativity to come up with a workable design based upon these notes. This sidebar refers extensively to topics discussed elsewhere in this chapter, so you will want to review the relevant passages in the main text before proceeding.

My favorite design for a home-buildable tunable drum is that described and pictured in Figure 7-4J. This design calls for two rings cut from heavy plywood. The upper ring serves as the drum hoop, with the skin, after soaking, stapled to the underside. If you are making a hand-played drum, remember to start with a drum skin at least four to six inches larger in diameter than the drum body. Form the still-wet skin over the rim of the drum body so that the drum hoop (the plywood ring) will ultimately be positioned well below the rim. Use large staples, and use plenty of them, to secure the skin all the way around. The second plywood ring is located at the base of the drum. The rope lacings anchor to it and, as Figure 7-4J shows, drumhead tension is controlled by twisting the lacings at this lower anchor point. Optionally, with short legs added, the lower ring can also serve as a stand for the drum. Remember to pad the feet; use especially thick, soft pads for low-pitched drums with lightweight skins such as goat skin.

This two-ring approach is solid enough to support high drumhead tensions, with either goatskin or cowhide drumheads. It can be used with any sort of drum body material that is strong enough to support the degree of tension you plan to apply.

Whatever you use for the body, remember to make the upper rim of the body, over which the skin passes, as even and uniform as possible. Remember too that the rim should be rounded where the skin passes over. For drum body materials that are too thin to provide a rounded rim, you can add a piece of thicker reinforcing material around the periphery of the body at the rim to allow for rounding.

With wooden drum bodies, the wet skin will likely glue itself to the rim as it dries. You don't want this to happen on a tunable drum. Prevent it by waxing the rim, or even just dusting it generously with talcum powder, before applying the wet skin.

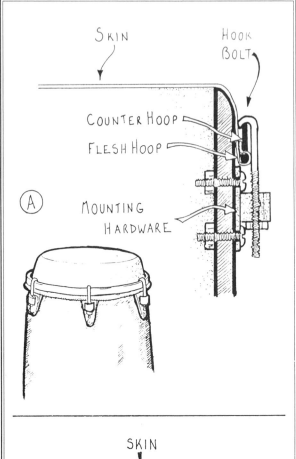

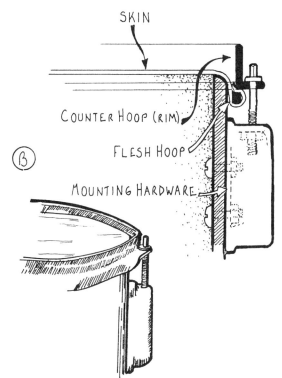

FIGURE 7-5: Drum tensioning hardware.

A. Conga drum and other hand-played drums. For hand-played drums, the rim of the counter hoop is usually set below the playing surface.

B. Snare drum, with specialized hardware for the counter-hoop and the anchor. Notice that on this stick-played drum the counterhoop rim is above the playing surface.

that it benefits from enrichment in that general region, without having to tune to a certain pitch.

Much of the time, when drummers tune their drums, they don't tune each drum to itself as I have been describing here. They tune to specific pitches that relate to the music being played. A conga drummer recording with an ensemble playing a piece in a particular key will be inclined to tune his drums to pitches that make musical sense in that key. And the results, considering the sound of the ensemble as a whole, justify the practice. But for a real drum lover, the greatest satisfaction comes from tuning a drum so as to bring out its fullest voice, regardless of specific pitch. (Long and narrow tube drums, by the way, are a special case when it comes to tuning — see the discussion under Tube Drums below.)

There is one other possible approach to drum tuning, though it is rarely used. Find a way to make the drum body's air resonances tunable. With tube drums, make the tube length variable. With barrel drums or other types, make the opening size adjustable.

One more word about tuning: an important aspect of tone lies in the balance of tensions within the head itself. Ideally, the head is tightened down in such a way that the pull is uniform all the way around the rim. Under unequal tension you may get a weak fundamental, or multiple fundamentals, and/or irritating dissonant partials. You can check the uniformity of tension on the head by striking with a series of light strokes just at the rim, progressing around the periphery and listening to hear whether the pitch varies from one point to another. If it does, redistributing the tension may help. On the other hand, the problem may be that the skin itself is not uniform in thickness or consistency.

DRUM MOUNTINGS & DRUM POSITIONING

Drums need to be held in such a way that the drumhead and the openings in the drum body are not blocked by adjacent surfaces. Reflecting surfaces such as floor or walls a little distance away from the open end have variable effects, sometimes enhancing the tone and sometimes detracting, depending on the drum tuning and the distance to the reflective surface. Altering the distance can make a difference in drum tone, as can altering the angle of the drum or the reflective surface. For drums with legs or drums which rest in drum stands, padding the feet where they meet the floor will often improve the tone. Very generous padding such as that described in Sidebar 7-1 may prove especially valuable for drums with lightweight skins (goatskin) set at low or moderate tension. With drums, seemingly more than with other instruments, the surrounding acoustic space can make a substantial difference in sound. The same drum may sound very differently played indoors or outdoors, in a large room or a small room, or at different locations within the same room.

MORE DRUM TYPES, SOUNDING METHODS, ACCESSORIES, ETC.

The remainder of this chapter is a hodgepodge of notes on different drum types, accessories, construction techniques and sounding methods. The last section is devoted to friction drums, which present yet another world of membranic possibilities.

Pellet drums

Pellet drums are membranophones sounded by pellets bounced or rolled on the membrane. Most pellet drums are small, say a couple of inches in diameter. Some have pellets within that strike the membrane when the drum is shaken, while others have small objects attached by short lengths of string to the outside of the drum, so that they bounce around and hit the membrane when the drum is twisted or shaken. With larger drums, the player can drop pellets on a drum skin from above. Many things can serve as pellets — pebbles, hard seeds, dry beans, BBs ... The key is in choosing something of the right mass for the size of the membrane. The sound often has a kind of gentle thunder or raindrops feeling. You can make a pellet drum of very appealing sound simply by dropping some dry rice grains into a balloon, inflating and tying it, and then shaking it about.

Variable-Tension Drums

There is a family of West African laced drums in which you can vary the tension on the drumhead as you play (see Figure 7-4I). Some types are called *talking drums*, because the rising and falling pitch of the drums is reminiscent of the inflections of human speech. They usually take the form of double-headed drums, and the key to the design is this: the drum body is waisted, being larger at the two ends where the skins are, and narrow at the center like an hourglass. The lacings run between the two heads, crossing high over the waist, so that there's room to squeeze the lacings inward to increase tension on the heads. The drum is normally held under the player's arm, to be squeezed by bringing the elbow in closer to the body. In this position, the playing angle is awkward unless you use drumsticks having a pronounced curve toward the playing end, and this is indeed what is traditionally done. Strong hoops and a curved, smooth rim are important for such drums.

Snares

The snare from which snare drums get their name is a cord that crosses the bottom (unplayed) membrane of the double-headed snare drum. It is tensioned so that it is not too loose, but just loose enough to rattle when the lower head vibrates sympathetically in response to the stroke on the upper head. It changes the sound entirely by adding a mess of sharp, high frequency noise components, yielding sharper definition, reduced ring time and increased perceived volume, and diminishing the sense of defined pitch. Years ago snares were made of gut string, with several strands crossing the head, and some people still prefer the warmer tone and greater sustain of a gut snare. Nowadays they're more often made with about twelve strands of a kind of wiggly wire, looking a little like a coil spring that's been over-stretched. Loosening the snare allows it to droop below the head untouching, rendering it inoperative and making the snare drum no longer a snare drum. There are commonly used snare-tensioning hardware devices nowadays, mounted on the side of the drum, that simply snap the snare on or off. In the old days a

Sidebar 7-5

COFFEE CUICA

You can make a remarkably effective cuica-like instrument from a coffee can. The can should be metal, and it should be the sort that comes with a plastic lid for re-sealing after the top has been removed with a can opener. You will also need a bamboo skewer or similar smooth stick about 1/8" in diameter and 8" long, a scrap of chamois or cotton rag a few inches square, and some duct tape.

Remove both ends of the coffee can with a can opener. Reinforce the center of the plastic lid by centering a 1/2" square of duct tape on each side. Drill the center point of the plastic lid with a 1/16" bit. Push the skewer through the hole so that about 1/2" protrudes on the outer side of the top. Fix the stick there by wrapping several rounds of 1/2"-wide duct tape around the stick, snug up against the lid, both inside and out. Put the plastic top on the can, so that the stick extends through the interior of the can and out the opposite end a bit.

To play: wet the scrap of rag. Hold the can with one hand. With the other, reach into the can and lightly pinch the stick with the wet rag between thumb and forefinger. The plastic lid groans and burbles when you rub the rag up and down the stick. Vary the pitch by altering the pressure or speed of your rubbing. Greater pressure causes the stick to push or pull harder on the plastic lid, increasing its tension and raising its natural frequency.

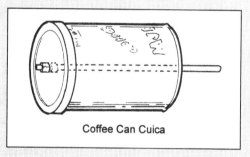

Coffee Can Cuica

Acknowledgment: I first saw this wonderfully simple instrument in the hands of Mary Buchen.

screw-tensioning mechanism (of a sort that wouldn't be too hard to make in a home workshop) was commonly used. The degree of tension on the snare makes a difference in the duration and snappiness of the resulting sound. While the upper head on a snare drum (called the batter head) must be strong, the snare head should be light to make it responsive.

Tube drums

Tube drums differ from other drum types in that they are often made in tuned sets of many drums. (Other drums may come in tuned sets but rarely of more than about six drums — two or three is typical for timpani, conga and tom toms). Tube drums are suitable for making in multiples for two reasons: they are easy and inexpensive to make, making the manufacture of multiples feasible; and they generally have clearer pitch than other drum types due to the well defined resonances of the tubes. Typical tubing diameters are between two and six inches. Lengths range from perhaps six inches for a narrow drum (anything shorter will not yield well defined air resonances) to several feet. Plastic, metal, and bamboo tubing have been used. The drumheads are best made of fairly light material, such as lightweight plastics or animal skins. Balloon rubber membranes make for an inexpensive and easily-made drum, with a lovely light, bubbly tone. Balloon drums are poor in volume, and they don't last long. Then again you might be surprised; under modest tension, balloon drumheads can remain playable for a couple months or more.

Tube drums can be tuned to prescribed pitches. The perceived pitch is usually the air resonance pitch. (The air resonance frequencies of the narrow tubes are more strongly defined than the air resonances of fatter drums.) The tiny drumheads, meanwhile, are generally tuned much higher than the air resonances. In the overall mix, the air column resonance stands out in the tone and provides the sense of pitch, while the drumhead tone adds excitement and definition to the stroke, and higher frequency color to the overall timbre. Tube drum tuning is achieved in part by using tubes of varying lengths, and partly by adjusting head tensions. (Head tension, as mentioned before, affects not only the tone of the membrane itself, but the resonance frequency of the air column below.) With skin or plastic heads and adjustable head-tensioning hardware, the tuning operation is a painstaking one, but manageable.

With tube drums having balloon heads, the situation is a little different. They are usually tuned simply by stretching the balloon membranes tighter or looser over the tube opening and letting them stay put by friction. Deliberate tuning is possible within limits, but difficult and frustrating. On the other hand, a randomly tuned array of 10 or 15 balloon-drum pitches can sound unexpectedly lovely. Particularly attractive is the presence of distinct timbres from drum to drum, arising from different relationships between the air column resonances and the membrane resonances.

Tube drums call for specialized mountings, somewhat different from other drums, because of the need to hold a large number of small drums. The drums need to be spaced so that each tube's lower end has open air around it — otherwise the sides of neighboring drums will interfere acoustically. One way to make such a mounting is to create something like a table with a plywood top, and cut appropriately spaced holes, using a circle cutter, to accommodate the tubes. For this to work you need to have something along the outside wall of each tube near the top to catch on the rim of the hole when the tube is slid in. Whatever holds the drumhead on might do perfectly well for this purpose (with some added padding between mount and board if needed). With balloon drums, it may be that all it takes to catch and hold the tube is the edge of the balloon membrane, partially rolled up along the side of the tube. Alternately, several rounds of rubber bands stretched around each tube at the mounting point may serve the purpose. Such relatively lightweight systems can work because balloon drums sound best played gently, with lightweight beaters.

Friction Drums

Friction drums are membranophones in which a stick-slip vibration is communicated, either directly or indirectly, to a drumhead.

Common among friction drums are instruments like the Brazilian *cuica*, in which the friction is actually against a stick attached to or pressed against a drum membrane. Usually, the player rubs the stick with a small piece of wetted cloth; alternatively, rosined or wetted fingers may be used. Varying the pressure that the stick brings to bear on the membrane varies the tension on the membrane, and thus alters the sounding frequency. Touching the membrane with a finger of the free hand also creates pitch changes and some unusual effects. The very best players can play surprisingly melodically. For most mortals, pitch cannot be controlled with any accuracy, but you can get wonderful groaning, sighing and laughing sounds that are at the same time both bestial and oddly human.

Plans for making a simple but effective cuica appear in Sidebar 7-5. Several systems for affixing the stick to the membrane appear in Figure 7-6.

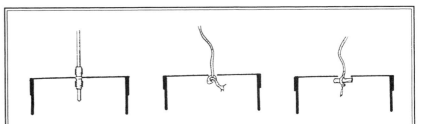

FIGURE 7-6: Friction drums — some methods for attachment of the rope or stick. The stick in the third drawing is taped and tacked on both sides of the membrane to prevent it from sliding out. Many other attachment methods are possible.

In some friction drums, a cord passing through a small hole in the center of the membrane and pulled taut serves in place of the stick.

It is also possible, though less common, to produce friction sounds through direct contact of the hand or mallet on the membrane. Some of these sounds are sighs and moans and groans, and some are steady in pitch, though not easily controlled. They lurk in drums everywhere, including the snare drums and tom toms of a normal drummer's kit. The best way to bring them out is through that miracle of modern synthetics, the superball mallet (see Chapter 5 for friction-mallet making). Try drawing a flexible-handled superball mallet across the head of an unsnared snare drum, or a tom tom. Observe the results when you excite different parts of the head, and when you hold the mallet handle with different degrees of firmness. Keep trying; it may take a while to get the knack.

Chapter Eight

RESONATORS AND RADIATORS

This is a special chapter devoted to systems that help to project the sound of instruments that would otherwise lack volume. The sections on resonance, radiation, phase relationships and impedance in Chapter 2 are also relevant to this topic, and readers may want to review them.

Acoustic sound radiators and resonators are of two main types: radiating surfaces and air resonators. Radiating surfaces include soundboards such as those used on guitars, violins and most Western string instruments, and membranes such as those used on banjos and most African and Eastern string instruments. Their job is to accept vibrational energy from an initial vibrating source like a string or a kalimba tine, and spread the vibration over a larger surface area. This allows them to drive the surrounding air more efficiently than the original source could have.

Air resonators include the air resonance tubes or chambers under marimba bars and drumheads, as well as the partially enclosed air chambers of guitars, violins and the like. (Notice that these soundbox instruments benefit from both types of radiation and resonance.) The job of air resonators is to pick up the vibration from the initial source, amplify it and then pass it on to the surrounding air through openings in the chamber. We covered the principles of air resonance in the aerophones chapter. We also discussed air resonators specifically in connection with marimbas and drums in their respective chapters. The current chapter will further our understanding of air resonance particularly as it relates to instruments with sound boxes.

Before discussing radiators and resonators in more detail, let me make brief note of one more form of acoustic sound reinforcement: sound reflectors. Particularly for unresonated free bar instruments such as marimbas, you can increase the effective volume and create a fuller tone by having a solid flat surface below the bars to reflect the sound. The distance from the bar to the reflecting surface is a key factor here: while a reflecting surface at a suitable distance will be beneficial, you'll find that at the wrong distance it can actually weaken the tone by causing cancellation. See Figure 4-6E for more on this.

We return now to the two main topics of this chapter, radiation and resonance. In practice these two terms overlap to some extent, but let us try to be clear about their separate meanings. Radiation, for our purposes, refers to the ability of a vibrating surface to drive the surrounding air, and thus project a sound. Resonance refers to the enhanced vibratory response of a body to driving frequencies at or near the body's natural frequencies. Thus, a well tuned resonator can take the input from a driver at the right frequency and respond with an especially generous vibration of its own. Then, if the resonator also happens to be an efficient radiator, it will project the sound with enhanced power.

SOUNDBOARDS AND SOUND CHAMBERS — BACKGROUND AND THEORY

Two qualities are needed if something is to work well as a sound radiating surface: it must be able to move a lot of air when it moves, and it must be able to respond generously to its driver (string, kalimba tine, or whatever). The first requirement can be met if the radiator has a lot of surface area. The conditions for the second requirement are more complex — we'll go into more detail later — but in general, the radiator should be light in weight relative to the driver, and not immutably fixed in place. At the same time, in order that the vibrations can spread throughout the radiator rather than simply dissipating locally at the point of input, the radiator must have a degree of rigidity.

You can achieve extensive surface area with minimal mass by giving the radiator the form of a thin sheet. But thin materials usually lack rigidity. There are several ways to increase a sheet's rigidity without too much increase in mass. One is to space reinforcing struts along the surface, as is done with piano soundboards. Another is to arch or curve the surface, as is done with violins. Still another is to stretch the material, as is done with banjos. And yet another is to use some innately light, rigid material, such as styrofoam, as is done with a couple of unconventional instruments described in this book.

Radiating Surface Area Requirements

How large should the radiating surface area be for a given application? Here are some guidelines.

Small surfaces do not project long wavelengths well. A common rule of thumb is that, for good projection, a radiating surface should be greater in both dimensions than half the wavelength of the lowest frequency it is intended to project. In actual musical situations, however, additional factors come into play, and there can be no hard and fast rule. A soundboard of modest size will reproduce low frequencies, but with poor volume. In some cases the sound may seem loud but, like an undersized loudspeaker, the radiator may be projecting primarily the higher frequency components of a complex timbre.

To achieve better low frequency response at manageable size, most low-frequency instruments, like the string bass, use an enclosed resonating chamber as part of the body that supports the soundboard. This enriches the low end by adding a generous amount of low-frequency air resonance to the mix. The enclosure also helps isolate out-of-phase vibrations from the back of the board. (I will talk more about these effects as we go along.)

Given that it is impossible to formulate simple rules on the subject, the best advice I can give regarding radiating-surface area size is to study existing instruments and make comparisons. A few selected examples: The lowest note on a string bass has a wavelength of over eight meters, while the soundboard is typically something over a meter high, and a little less wide. That is well short of satisfying the "half-wavelength rule," but the bottom part of the bass tone is aided very substantially by the air resonance coming out of the f-holes. Still, acousticians have suggested that the ideal size for the bass, were it not impractical, would be considerably larger. A grand piano, whose longest wavelengths are half again as long, has a soundboard more than twice as large, though without the same sort of air resonance enclosure. It does a respectable job on the low notes, although much of the volume derives from upper partials more than a strong fundamental. Meanwhile, upright pianos try to project the same frequencies with a much smaller soundboard — and do a very poor job of it in the bass (an effect also due to the shortened string length). At the opposite extreme, the smaller, lighter soundboard on a mandolin responds well to the high frequencies and projects them without difficulty for a clear, bright tone.

Phase Relationships

We have seen that waves coming from the front and back surfaces of a soundboard are out of phase and likely to cancel to some degree as they spread. This is especially true for the wider-spreading low frequencies. For a simple board of modest dimensions with no enclosure, this effect is quite pronounced, leading, in many cases, to a rather anemic sound. For larger boards the effect is somewhat reduced, as the waves don't reach around as much.

One way to prevent cancellation is to isolate sounds from the back of the board by enclosing the back entirely. Make the whole thing like a sealed box, with the soundboard as one side. Many speaker cabinets are designed this way, to isolate the out-of-phase waves from the back of the speaker. With musical instruments, the trouble is that the restricted air inhibits the vibration of the board. More often than not, you end up losing more than you gain.

An in-between approach is to only partially enclose the box. The violin soundbox, as an example, is almost entirely enclosed but for the f-holes. A great deal of air travels in and out of these holes, effectively communicating the out-of-phase vibration to the front of the violin, like it or not. Violin makers actually encourage this, because they like the tone quality of the air resonance from within. The resulting cancellation is somewhat mitigated, due to the fact that the air resonance reinforces most strongly different frequencies from those that the soundboard surface projects best. The blend is subjectively richer in timbre than either the direct soundboard surface sound or the air chamber resonance sound alone.

This discussion has focused on the out-of-phase front and back soundwaves. But, as always, the situation is more complex. Soundboards rarely vibrate in a simple back-and-forth motion. They flex in many modes simultaneously, with some parts of the soundboard thrusting forward while others move back. As a result, there are multiple out-of-phase vibrations coming off the front of the soundboard alone, not to mention the back, Acousticians have been developing increasingly sophisticated understanding of these sound-board vibration patterns, but the task of applying the knowledge to soundboard design is a daunting one. Members of the Catgut Acoustical Society have been in the forefront of studies in this area; see back issues of their journal for more information.

Mass and Rigidity; Impedance

Impedance relationships are another important element in the operation of sound radiators. The initial vibrator that drives the vibration — the string, kalimba tine, or whatever

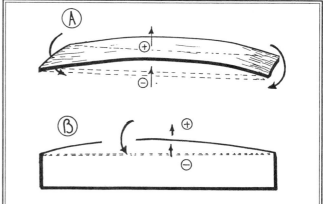

FIGURE 8-1: A. Phase relationships, and air movements that result in cancellation, in a flat soundboard as it flexes in the course of vibration. As the board flexes upward, it creates a compression above and a low pressure area below. But the higher pressure above immediately spreads around the board, equalizing pressure on both sides. This effect undermines the board's effectiveness as a radiator, especially for the wider-spreading low frequencies.
B. The same for an enclosed sound chamber with a sound-hole.

— is typically relatively high in impedance at the point where the driving takes place, concentrating a lot of vibrational energy in a small but strong vibration. The air into which the vibration is ultimately to be directed is a low impedance medium, carrying widespread, low-energy vibrations. Soundboards are intermediate in impedance; they serve to make the conversion.

To fulfill its intermediate role, the soundboard must not be so heavy and rigid that the initial vibrator cannot drive it effectively. Nor should it be so light or flimsy that overdriving takes place and the driver's energy is dissipated too rapidly. With especially heavy drivers, it may be hard to find a support system sufficiently strong and heavy to handle the driver, yet responsive enough and with enough surface area to radiate effectively. In this case, it helps to add another intermediate level of transference: the driver can be supported by a massive and rigid mounting system that is in turn attached to a separate radiator made of lighter, thinner material.

There is no clear-cut rule as to the ideal relationship between the mass and rigidity of the driver and that of the radiator. The best suggestion I can make, once again, is to observe and learn from existing instruments. A case study may help:

Kalimba tines are not usually massive, but they are generally quite rigid, and therefore relatively high in impedance, especially at their point of mounting. They demand a fairly rigid and heavy soundboard as a result. Most kalimbas use 1/8" to 1/4" hardwood soundboards, as opposed to the softer, lighter, springier ones used in most string instruments. But notice also that it is not unusual for kalimba players to use a three-tiered system. In this case, the tines are mounted on a rather heavy soundboard — perhaps a single fairly thick board. The heavy board alone provides a good, solid mounting for the tine, but is only so-so as a radiator (too thick and massive to move generously, and not enough surface area). But it in turn is held against the inside of a hemispherical gourd or calabash, so that the vibrations are transmitted to the gourd. The gourd has the requisite thinness, lightness and rigidity of a classic sound radiator, and it does a fine job, amplifying the volume and bringing out the lower frequencies.

To sum up: Light initial vibration sources, like small strings, often do well simply by directing their energy to a lightweight radiating surface. Heavier drivers require heavier mountings and radiators. Substantially heavier drivers benefit from having intermediary stages, such as mounting on a heavy framework attached to or held against a lighter but more extensive sheet radiator.

Transmission of Vibrational Energy

In most musical instruments the sound resonator and radiator mechanisms are attached directly to the drivers. Transmission of the vibration over long distances is not a concern in these cases. But it is actually quite remarkable how easily and efficiently vibrational energy can travel, given a medium without too much damping. Imagine that you create a high-impedance vibration in one location — a vibration which is scarcely audible because it doesn't radiate efficiently to the air — and send it through a network of rigidly connected bars, to where it feeds into an efficient radiating surface at some distant location. A listener will then hear the sound

FIGURE 8-2: Signaling device.

clearly emerging from the distant radiator. (The best examples of intelligent use of mechanical transmission in musical instruments can be found in the instruments of the Baschet Brothers in France, some of which are described in Chapter 4, "Idiophones," and elsewhere in this chapter.)

Here are guidelines for efficient mechanical transmission of sound vibrations over long distances:

The transmitting medium should have little internal damping, or there will be dissipation along the way. You might be surprised at how well wood does, but hard metals do better, especially over long distances. Wires pulled taut can also do well. All connections and joints must be solid and fast, both for efficient transmission and to prevent rattling. The vibrational energy should be in the form of high-impedance, longitudinal vibrations.

Here is an example of musical mechanical transmission, in the form of a fanciful signaling device. Imagine you have a friend living in the apartment building next to yours, with her window across from yours ten feet away. You find a lightweight, twelve-foot wooden pole, and stick it out your window, reaching across and touching her window with a light pressure (as in Figure 8-2). You take a tuning fork, bonk it on your knee to start it vibrating, and then hold the handle end-on against your end of the pole. The tuning fork is fairly quiet for you, being a poor radiator by itself. But to your friend, the tuning fork tone coming off the inside surface of her window sounds clearly. You can start and stop the tone on her end effortlessly, by touching and un-touching the fork handle to the pole even as the vibration sustains within the fork. This enables you to create a code: long-short-short means "meet me in the foyer," short-short-long means "hide — the landlord is on his way up the stairs to collect your rent;" etc. Alternatively, you could create a sort of remote musical instrument by holding tuning forks of different pitches against the pole to play melodies.

MORE ON PARTICULAR RADIATOR AND RESONATOR TYPES

We'll now move from general to specific information about systems and materials for resonators and radiators.

Wooden Soundboards and Sound Chambers

For lightweight soundboards such as those used on guitars, the violin family, mandolins and so forth, the traditionally preferred wood is spruce. The quality of commercially sold spruce has deteriorated in recent decades. Spruce of excellent quality, however, can often be found in the form of old piano soundboards, which can often be salvaged from piano repair shops or junk yards. On the other hand, some contemporary makers now swear by cedar or redwood. Pine has sometimes served, but is considered less effective. The best soundboard blanks are quarter-sawn, meaning that the broad surface of the board is roughly perpendicular to the growth rings of the tree. You can identify quarter-sawn wood by the close, straight pattern of the grain. High-quality plywoods are sometimes used as soundboards for their durability and workability, especially in applications calling for large, thin boards where splitting would otherwise be a problem.

For sound chamber backs and sides the woods are less critical. Despite a lot of folklore on the subject, any strong, hard wood will do. Maple is often used; so are various tropical woods, favored for their density as well as beauty.

Each of the standard instruments has its traditional sound chamber shape. One could ask, do those instruments *have* to be shaped that way to work right? It is true that the best instruments represent the culmination of a tradition. No one is likely to make a truly fine instrument without paying attention to lessons from past makers. Yet it is surprisingly easy to make a soundboard and sound chamber that do at least a decent job without following traditionally prescribed shapes. As long as the relationships involving impedance, enclosed air volume and surface area are not too far out of line, most sound chamber shapes are reasonably effective. So, if you wish to make an experimental instrument in an unconventional shape, you can feel free to explore without fear that some immutable law of sound chamber design will doom your efforts. A look at some of the unlikely shapes that have been used in historical instruments will confirm this. With that in mind, here are some general guidelines on sound chamber shape.

The approximate resonant pitch of the air chamber is important to the sound, determining as it does which frequency ranges will be most enriched. That resonance is jointly determined, as with any other vessel, by the volume of the chamber and the size of the openings. This means that even after you have built a sound chamber, you can alter its air resonance with only minor surgery, by enlarging or reducing the size of its sound holes. Just putting a piece of tape over part of the *f*-hole of a violin, it has been found, can make a big difference for the better, if a slight lowering of the air resonance happens to be what that particular violin needs.

Traditional sound chamber shapes are often quite elaborate and curvy. The curves help rigidify the sides — an effect which helps to strengthen the box and reduce damping. They may have some value in reducing the likelihood of standing waves and resulting wolf tones in the soundboard. (Wolf tones are tones which are distorted in pitch or tone quality, or disproportionate in volume, resulting from exaggerated resonance at a specific pitch in the instrument body.) But if

you can achieve the strength and rigidity you want without adding excessive mass, it remains possible to make decent-sounding instruments with straight sides. Parallel sound chamber walls, in theory, might lead to unwanted standing waves in the enclosed air; in practice, however, the standing waves problem in most instrument-sized rectangular chambers doesn't seem to be serious.

It can help a wooden soundboard to deliberately weaken it around its periphery, near where the board joins the sides. This allows it to flex more readily, as if it were hinged rather than being held rigid at the edges. With violins this is done by cutting a groove near the edge all the way around, and inlaying a decorative strip (which, even if glued in, lacks the structural strength of the natural wood). Lately makers of some zither-like instruments have done well with "floating soundboards," which are not permanently attached to the sides at all, but held in place on spaced support blocks around the edges by the pressure of the strings on the bridges.

As part of the process of soundboard design, try to assess where and in what directions the initial vibrator will drive the soundboard. For example, consider the guitar: The bridge is positioned so that strings will drive the lower portion of the soundboard most effectively. Accordingly, the lower portion is large, with lots of surface area, and has a strutting pattern underneath designed to carry those vibrations through the entire region.

Whatever the instrument, thin soundboards generally need reinforcement to increase rigidity and help assure that the vibrations will spread throughout the board rather than being absorbed ineffectually at a too-soft point of input. It is common to place some extra reinforcement directly under the bridge, in the form of wider a strap of wood or larger struts, often extending and carrying the vibration to other parts of the soundboard. Long struts should not attach to the sides of the chamber where they would increase the rigidity of the joint between soundboard and walls; they should stop some distance short of the walls. (Remember, you want something closer to a hinged effect.) There's also the possibility of adding a soundpost, which is an upright support piece wedged snugly between the front and back of the chamber, at a point underneath one side of the bridge. These matters are discussed further in Chapter 9, "Chordophones."

Construction of wooden sound chambers by traditional methods is a rather involved business, especially if you get into bending the sides, and elaborate decorative techniques. But for simpler chambers, you can do well by following the above guidelines and trusting to your basic carpenter's instincts.

Gourd and Calabash

Many African, Indian and Middle Eastern instruments, including string instruments, kalimbas and drums, use gourd or calabash resonators. Such resonators work very much like wooden resonator chambers. They enclose a resonant body of air, and also provide surface radiation. If possible, the inside of the dried and hollowed gourd should be scoured with steel wool to provide a smoother, harder, more reflective inner surface. Gourds can be finished with wood paints or finishes. Remember that while calabash are surprisingly strong, gourds are fragile; with tensioned elements like strings, it is usually necessary to have other structural elements take the stress.

Some instruments use gourds or calabashes topped with a wooden or membrane sound board. The first step here is to open the gourd with a smooth, flat cut, and sand it perfectly level. This provides a gluing surface for the board, or an even surface for the membrane to pull over. Other instruments use gourds left more nearly whole, with a smaller hole made to remove the seeds and to serve as a soundhole. The gourd can be attached directly to a structural element like a stick or board that carries a set of strings.

Another approach is not to mount the gourd at all. A hand-held gourd pressed directly against a string mounted on a separate carrier will provide a solid stopping point for the strings, so that the length of string between the gourd and the bridge can still vibrate. You can thus use the gourd like a giant slide or bottleneck, as in "bottleneck guitar." At the same time, the gourd serves as a radiator/resonator for the strings.

Rigid Metal Sound Radiators and Sound Chambers

We will look at two types of metal radiators and chambers: rigid and flexible. I make the distinction and treat them separately because the two types behave very differently.

It is possible to make metal sound chambers and soundboards very much like the wooden ones just described. Wooden soundboards can be attached to chambers whose backs and sides are metal, with woody results. With metal soundboards, the resulting sound is quite different from wood because the metal has much less damping than wood. As a result, it has more pronounced frequency biases, ringing out its own natural frequencies preferentially. Such a sound radiator is likely to have strong wolf tones and dead areas, and may distort the behavior of the initial vibrators by feeding back its own frequency preferences. It also tends to reverberate more than wood after the initial vibrator has stopped — an interesting effect.

More successful have been metal sound radiators designed to function a little like speaker cones. We have encountered these in connection with the Baschet instruments mentioned earlier. A high-impedance vibration is directed to the radiator, usually through metal bars attached to the initial vibrating elements. The radiators are made light yet rigid, so that the entire radiator body moves with the impulses applied

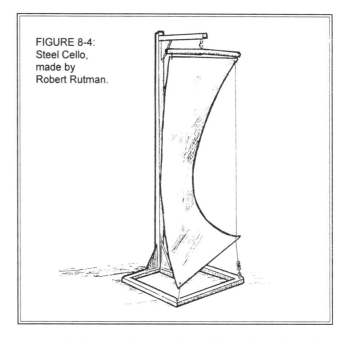

FIGURE 8-4:
Steel Cello,
made by
Robert Rutman.

to it. A simple cone shape works well (see Figure 8-3). The rod carrying the vibration can join the cone at the end point, which works well for strong vibrations, or along the seam at the side for weaker ones. (Side-mounting makes the cone less rigid in the direction of vibration, allowing for flex and altering the dynamics somewhat.)

These radiators don't have to be cone-shaped. If you work with other shapes, the key will be to find ways to add a few folds and bends to create lightweight configurations of adequate rigidity. Similar radiators have also been made of cardboard.

Flexible Metal Radiators and Resonators,

Freely mounted, flexible sheet-metal sound resonators are in a different world from the radiators we have discussed so far. Rather than simply reproducing only the vibrations fed into them, they add a generous dose of their own personality to the sound.

Such resonators are best made from sheets of stainless steel thick enough to have some body, but thin enough in relation to length and width to be floppy rather than rigid. They should be mounted in such a way that their vibrations are minimally damped, and they remain free to flex. Two effective ways to do this are suspension by cords and by resting on balloons. Sheet metal resonators typically require two or three balloon supports. (Round balloons set in small, bucket-like containers to prevent their rolling work well as feet.) The sheet alone, mounted that way, amounts to an amazing sound source in itself — give it a tap and listen to the resonances and echoes as they go on and on.

Things get a bit more complex when you add an outside vibration source. Figure 8-4 shows an instrument of a type made by Boston builder Robert Rutman, with a string approximately six feet long running corner to corner on a big, hanging stainless steel sheet. When you sound the string (normally by bowing), it starts vibrating at its natural frequency, and delivers that vibrational energy to the sheet metal resonator. The sheet metal picks up the vibration and sends it out into the room. But at the same time, the metal has its

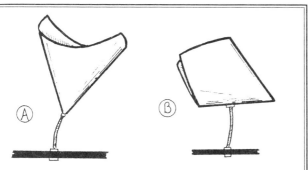

FIGURE 8-3: Baschet-style rigid cone radiators.

A. Attach the rod that carries the vibration at the point of the cone for strong vibrations.
B. Attach the rod at the side of the cone for weaker vibrations.

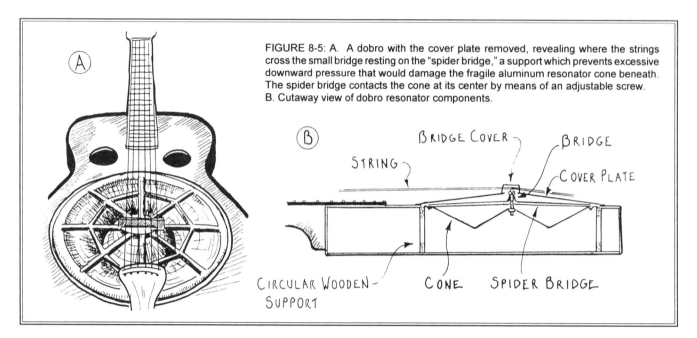

FIGURE 8-5: A. A dobro with the cover plate removed, revealing where the strings cross the small bridge resting on the "spider bridge," a support which prevents excessive downward pressure that would damage the fragile aluminum resonator cone beneath. The spider bridge contacts the cone at its center by means of an adjustable screw. B. Cutaway view of dobro resonator components.

own pronounced resonances and, to make matters more interesting, those resonances shift constantly as the metal flexes on its suspension cords. If the string or one of its overtone frequencies matches one of the sheet metal's resonances, the metal responds hugely. But as the radiator's resonances shift, it tries to bend the same vibrational impulse off to other frequencies, even as the string tries to sustain the same frequency. To some extent the metal frequencies feed back into the string and alter its behavior, even as the string continues to try to drive the resonator. The effect of all these interactions is a sort of thunderous rainbow of shifting resonances, and an instrument that plays the player as much as the player plays it.

Metal diaphragms (as opposed to free sheets) also lend themselves to shifting resonance sounds. One of the most wonderful effects, as people who have done a lot of dish washing should know, comes about when there is just a little water covering such a diaphragm (which just might happen to be the bottom of a lightweight cooking pot). As the water shifts and sloshes about, and especially when it only partially covers the diaphragm, the resonances bend wildly about. You can play a saucepan this way, striking the bottom with one free hand as you rock it about with the other, and listening to the bubbly bendy tones. If you were to introduce a steady-frequency vibration from some external source into the pot, you would get an outcome similar to the flexible sheet metal resonator effects described above — similar, that is, but with a lighter, subtler quality. This is the basis of the bowed rod instrument called the Waterphone, made and patented by Richard Waters — an instrument of extraordinarily beautiful sound (described in Chapter 4, "Idiophones"; see Figure 4-14). Richard Waters and others have also used water-modulated metal resonators with strings, metal tongue drums, and other instrument types.

One More Metal Form: Resophonics

Have you ever looked underneath the face plate on a dobro or National steel guitar? These instruments employ a unique system for sound radiation, devised in the 1920s by John Dopera and his brothers. Their primary goal, apparently, was to create a louder guitar in those pre-electric days. Some of their instruments were indeed quite loud, and they also have a distinctive tone quality for which they remain popular to this day.

Dobros and their kin look much like guitars, though the body may be made of either metal or wood. Unseen beneath a decorative cover plate in the middle of the dobro's face is a shallow cone of thin aluminum (see Figure 8-5). The instrument's bridge rests on a support piece connected to the apex of the cone, so that the string's vibrations are transmitted to the cone. The cone is designed to serve as the instrument's main resonator, functioning, in Dopera's conception, like a loudspeaker cone. In practice, the wooden or metal body of the guitar, as well as the resonances of the air chambers, contribute significantly as well, and the resulting sound is a composite. The term "resophonic" has been used to describe the system (which, in its entirety, is a bit more complex than the description here implies). In addition to guitars, people have made successful resophonic mandolins, banjos and other instruments.

Membranes

The most common form of string instrument sound radiator in Africa and much of Asia and the Middle East is membrane, usually in the form of animal skin. Because of their lightness, membrane resonators produce a loud sound of relatively brief duration, giving plucked strings something of a percussive effect. There is a characteristic membrane-resonator tone quality, often featuring strong partials in a mid-upper range and usually not rich in lower frequencies. This is in part due to the fact that membrane resonators are not usually very large. Those on some Eastern spike fiddles are only six inches or less across — and still they play quite loudly. Refer back to Chapter 7, "Membranophones," for information on different membrane types, their preparation, mounting, tensioning and so forth.

A special sort of membrane radiator is that used on the Stroh Violin, invented by Charles Stroh around 1900 and manufactured during the first quarter of this century. (Stroh cellos, guitars, mandolins, and so forth were sold as well. They are now quite rare.) The Stroh Violin was originally conceived for use in gramophone recording, replacing traditional violins which lacked the power to record well in the days of purely mechanical (pre-electrical) sound recording. The advantage of the Stroh Violin lay in its producing a highly directional sound that could be aimed right into the sound-collecting horn of the recording apparatus.

The instrument consisted of a stick-like neck and body, with no sound chamber (see Figure 8-6). The vibration at the bridge was transmitted through a mechanical connection to a small diaphragm mounted at the narrow end of a metal horn that opened out toward the side of the instrument. The movement of the diaphragm set the adjacent air in motion, and the vibration was directed out through the horn.

There is another valuable form of membrane sound radiator — one we have touched on several times already but have not described as such. It is inflatable bladders, such as ... balloons. I will add just a few more notes here on this topic.

Balloons make good radiators because — well, what can you think of that has more surface area and less weight? In many instances balloons are the one thing light enough to accept and radiate vibrations from bodies that are too light and weak to drive any other sort of radiator. They are so light and yielding that they can often be attached directly to the

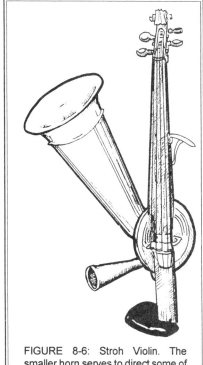

FIGURE 8-6: Stroh Violin. The smaller horn serves to direct some of the sound back to the player's ear.

most active parts of vibrating bodies without significantly damping the vibration. You can even press a balloon-radiator against a vibrating string without immediately killing the vibration, if you press it fairly near one end where the impedance is relatively high. You get a characteristic balloony tone, short in duration, but not unappealing. The Baschet Brothers have made and concertized with balloon guitars, in which a relatively heavy, durable balloon replaces the entire sound box. A special sort of minimal balloon guitar framework holds the strings under tension and supports a bridge which is pressed directly against the balloon (see Figure 8-7).

Balloons are not the only sort of inflated bladder radiator. Years ago there were crude bowed string instruments made with an inflated pig's bladder wedged between a single string and a stick that supported it. For a more readily available bladder that is stronger and stiffer than balloons (and tends to damp things more heavily), there are inflatable beach balls.

Styrofoam

It may be inelegant, but it is hard to match styrofoam as a sound-radiating surface. Styrofoam radiators can be amazingly efficient, which is to say, loud, and they seem to reproduce the vibration patterns of the initial vibrator in a fairly unbiased fashion. Styrofoam comes in all kinds of shapes and forms, and for many instrument types you can work with found forms. The throwaway pieces used for shipping electronic equipment often serve musical purposes well. The widely available styrofoam ice chests also work well as radiators. Styrofoam sheets are often available at hobby and crafts shops in various sizes and thicknesses. Closed-cell types (with smooth surface) are preferable for sound radiation to open-cell types. If your purposes call for a specific shape that you cannot find or create from available materials, consider forming your own. Styrofoam-like foams, made primarily for use in home insulation, are available either as a two-part liquid mix or as a fluffy liquid compressed in a spray can. You can squirt the stuff into a mold shaped according to your needs and it will dry rigid and light. See Sidebar 8-1 for further ideas on styrofoam radiators.

Other Radiator Materials

Any number of other materials can serve as sound-radiator surfaces as long as they have the required blend of rigidity and lightness in combination with generous surface area. Plastics have been used; so have various papers and cardboards, and accordion-folded, fan-like arrangements of cloth or paper made rigid by coats of polyurethane. Direct contact with table tops, floors and walls sometimes does a decent job for high-impedance sound sources like music boxes that don't

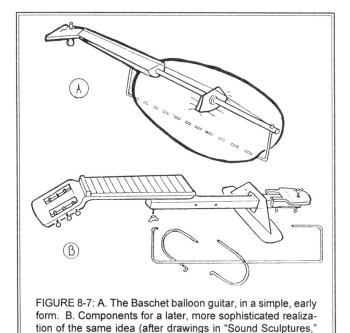

FIGURE 8-7: A. The Baschet balloon guitar, in a simple, early form. B. Components for a later, more sophisticated realization of the same idea (after drawings in "Sound Sculptures," unpublished manuscript by Bernard & François Baschet).

A SIMPLE STYROFOAM-RESONATED STICK ZITHER, AND FURTHER POSSIBILITIES

The drawing on the right below shows a styrofoam ice chest zither that you could make in not much more time than it takes for the glue to dry. It will sound best with steel strings (steel guitar strings or piano wire) set at fairly high tension. You can give it as many strings as you wish or have room for, set to to whatever tuning you wish. (Read more about strings and string scaling in the next chapter.) You can sound the strings by plucking or strumming, and you can use a slide, as in slide guitar, to provide a wider selection of pitches. The tone is bright and attractive, and surprisingly loud.

But since the resonator is easy to make, perhaps you will want to try something more ambitious with the rest of the instrument than a simple resonated board zither. There are many possibilities — for instance, I have had good luck with a series of styrofoam guitar-like things in various sizes and pitch ranges, with varying numbers of strings, and some unconventional fretting patterns. The design I favor consists basically of a stick with a styrofoam picnic cooler attached at each end (removable for storage and transport), as shown in the second drawing.

These styrofoam radiators provide very little in the way of air chamber resonance, and as a result they don't have the bass fullness that air resonance provides. Partially covering the cooler, as by fastening on the cooler lid with an appropriately sized sound hole punched in it, still does not yield a richer air resonance. For the air resonance to take effect, you need a soundboard or something similar flexing in and out relative to the rest of the chamber, creating an air pumping effect through the soundhole. With the styrofoam coolers, the entire box moves as one, and there is no pumping effect. Let this be a design

challenge for someone reading this: can you come up with some way to combine the extraordinary radiating properties of styrofoam with the resonance of a well-functioning air chamber?

For anyone who decides to make a styro-guitar or other more complex styro-string projects, Chapter 9 will provide additional information on various facets of string instrument design.

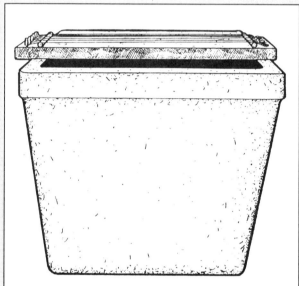

Styrofoam zither. The instrument shown here is nothing more than a piece of board with strings glued across the top of an inexpensive styrofoam picnic cooler. Tuning pins anchor the strings at one end; nails or screws at the other; dowels or metal rods serve as bridges.

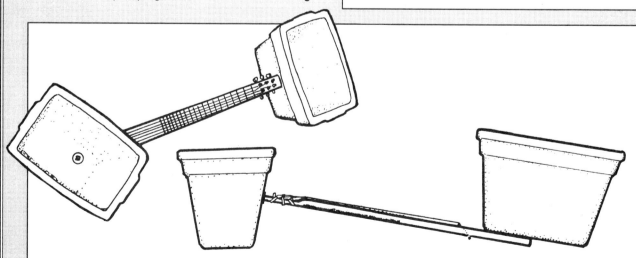

Styrofoam guitar. This is llittle more than a fretted six-string stick zither with styrofoam coolers stuck to the ends. The coolers can be glued in place or held in place by screws and large fender washers (making them rotationally adjustable and removable for transport and storage). The challenge in making this instrument is making the fretted neck strong enough that it doesn't flex and curve upward under string tension. For more on this, see Chapter 9, "Chordophones."

STRINGS WITH TUNED AIR RESONATORS

The drawing below shows a string instrument using a tuned air column for added volume and resonance. The instrument has two string segments and two notes, tuned to the air column's fundamental resonance pitch and to its next available overtone, the third harmonic at a 12th above (recall that stopped tubes resonate odd-numbered harmonics only). The two strings are actually one string divided at 3/4 of its length by a center bridge, yielding a string length ratio of 3:1 for the two tones a twelfth apart.

The tuned air resonator is a section of 4" plastic pipe mounted in a hole through the board that serves as the body of the instrument. The end of the tube is covered with a plastic stopper. These stoppers, sometimes called "test caps" or "knock-out plugs," are available at hardware stores.

The trick to making an instrument like this is creating the mechanism that allows the string to drive the air within the tube. This design uses a rocking bridge of hardwood, a little like that of a violin (which you will learn more about in the coming chapter). As shown in part B of the drawing, the bridge drives the plastic stopper, and this drives the air.

The plastic tube, at the suggested length of 18",

should have an air resonance fundamental frequency just below F3. You can check it by tapping it or blowing over the edge of the open end. The longer string segment will be tuned to F3. As you use the tuning pin to bring it up to pitch, you will hear the unmistakable increase in power as the string and air column come into coupling. The short string segment should also ring out, at C5. If the interval between the two segments is not an accurate 12th, shift the position of the middle bridge or the small bridges at the ends to correct it.

The tone of the instrument, aside from being more powerful and full-bodied than other strings, will reflect the stopped tube's overtone pattern, with the odd-numbered harmonics prominent and the even ones quieter.

Naturally, you can change the dimensions here to obtain different pitches. But the unglamorous truth is that we have just built a rather large instrument with only two notes. You could increase the range by building a tuned set, but the size problem would be compounded. I have sat down with pencil and paper a few times to see if I could come up with some configuration that would allow me to fit more pitches in a smaller space, but have not come up with anything really satisfactory. Any ideas?

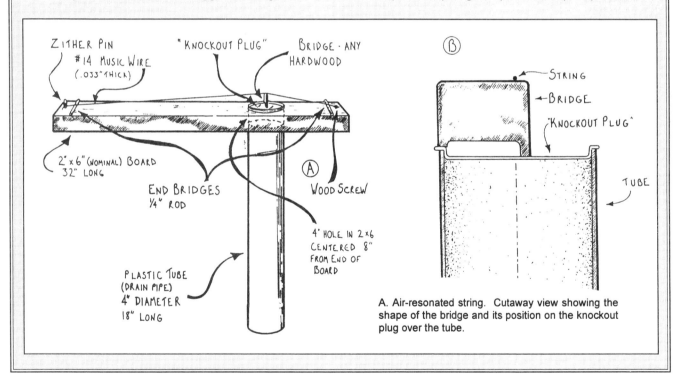

A. Air-resonated string. Cutaway view showing the shape of the bridge and its position on the knockout plug over the tube.

radiate well on their own.

Tuned Air Resonators in Unusual Applications

Marimba-like instruments, as we have seen, frequently use attached air resonators tuned to enhance specific pitches. Although it is not common, tuned air resonances can serve in many more applications. In the Indonesian bamboo chimes called *Angklung*, for instance, sections of bamboo are cut to a particular shape that allows the enclosed air column to reinforce the idiophonic pitch. Some bells are tuned for air resonance as well, either using the enclosed air or an attached external chamber. Back in Chapter 4 I described a simple and effective method for making a tubular chime which is its own self-contained air resonator, illustrated in Figure 4-6M. You can even use tuned air resonance chambers in connection with strings. Sidebar 8-2 describes such an instrument.

Chapter Nine

CHORDOPHONES

In this chapter we will cover the many forms that string instruments can take, and the acoustics of strings themselves. We won't have to spend much time on resonators and radiators for strings, having just covered them in the last chapter.

STRING INSTRUMENT FORMS

As with previous chapters, we will start with a look at a simple prototype instrument, in order to derive from it some sense of the essential elements of string instruments. For our model we will use a board zither of a sort that you could make in minutes from a piece of wire and some wood, as shown in Figure 9-1. Start with a 1" by 6" board, 3 feet long. Put a moderately heavy wood screw into the board near each end, leaving the head a quarter inch above the surface, and run a wire, pulled reasonably tight, from screw to screw, attached securely at each end. Now take two 6"-long pieces of wood an inch or so thick — a half-round shape would be ideal — and slide them under the string, pushing one piece firmly toward each end. This raises the wire from the board, and at the same time puts the string under increasing tension as the wood pieces approach the ends. When the string is tight enough, you can play the zither by plucking the string. Bring out a range of pitches by holding a glass bottle against the string at different points to vary its effective vibrating length, while plucking with the free hand.

What are the vital components of this string instrument?

1) The string.

2) A rigid structure to hold the string, which at the same time serves as:

3) A sound-radiating body, since a string in itself is a poor radiator of sound. In the current example, the board provides the structure and also serves as a sound radiator (though not a very powerful one).

4) A string tensioning mechanism. In this case, the process of sliding the wood pieces beneath the string provides the tension. The wood pieces also serve as:

5) Bridges; meaning, something to support the string at the end points of its vibrating length, and to transmit its vibration to the body of the instrument for radiation.

6) Some means for getting a range of pitches out of the instrument. In this case, the bottle in the player's hand serves the purpose.

7) Means to excite the string into vibration. That is provided, once again, by the player who plucks the strings.

These are the basic components of our model string instrument. The same functional elements appear in string instruments in general, but in a variety of other forms. As we proceed through this chapter we will study each of these functions in its own right. But before going to that level of detail, let us look at some of the ways that these components can all be put together. There are several possible configurations for strings and their carriers, and there is an agreed-upon terminology to describe those arrangements.

Zithers

Zithers are string instruments in which the strings are parallel to the sound table, and there is no separate neck. ("Sound table" can denote either a soundboard or the equiva-

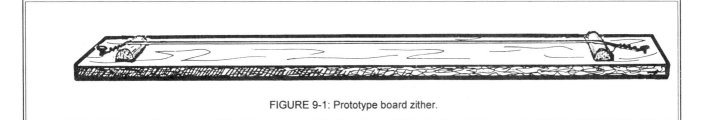

FIGURE 9-1: Prototype board zither.

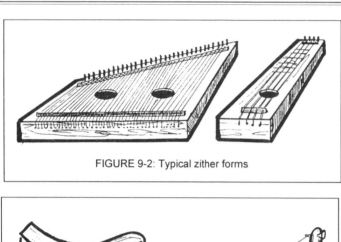

FIGURE 9-2: Typical zither forms

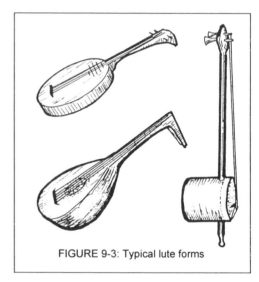

FIGURE 9-3: Typical lute forms

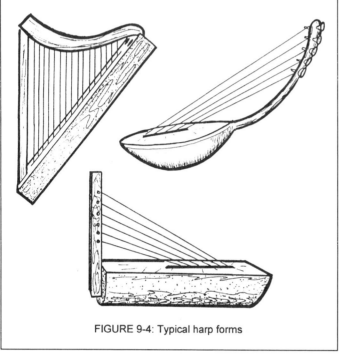

FIGURE 9-4: Typical harp forms

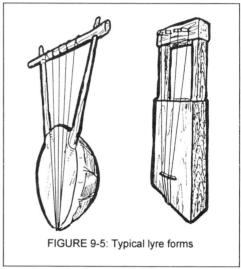

FIGURE 9-5: Typical lyre forms

lent in a membrane.) In addition to our board zither prototype, hammer dulcimers are zithers; autoharps are zithers; mountain dulcimers are zithers; qanun are zithers. By this definition, pianos and harpsichords are zithers too. With some exceptions, zithers are not designed to yield more than one pitch from each string, and so, in order to provide many notes, most have many strings. With the strings running right across the soundboard, it is normal to have the strings anchored to hitch pins or tuning pins set in heavier wood near the periphery of the board. Then, to communicate their vibration to the board, the strings pass over a low bridge near each end, crossing the board some distance in from the edge. There may be additional taller bridges mid-string as well, dividing each string into two or more vibrating segments. A few zithers, like Appalachian mountain dulcimers, are fretted or otherwise allow for varying the sounding lengths of the strings.

Lutes

Lutes too have strings running parallel to the sound table, but with a separate neck. The strings cross or are attached to a bridge that communicates the vibrations to the soundboard. Guitars, violins, shamisen, mandolins, and ouds, among many, many others, are lutes — not to mention the specific European instrument that claims the name "lute" as its own. The separate neck means that the strings' vibrating lengths can easily be altered by pressing them against the neck, pinching them, or simply exerting finger pressure against them in mid-air. Each string thus yields many notes, and so, unlike on most zithers, a few strings can produce a wide range.

Harps

Harps are instruments in which the strings rise at an angle from the sound table. This means that the strings pass through an open space to some sort of beam or bowed neck above. In the most basic forms there is no means for altering vibrating length, so, like zithers, harps usually have many strings capable of one note each. Where the strings attach to the sound table, extra reinforcement is needed, so there usually is a narrow board running on the inner and/or outer side of the sound table, along the line where the strings join.

Several African instruments, often labeled as harp-lutes, have lute-like necks — some even have multiple lute-like necks — but strings that join the soundboard with a harp-like angle of incidence.

Lyres

Lyres have strings parallel to the sound table, but rising, harp-like, through an open space to a yoke or cross bar above.

BASICS OF STRING VIBRATION
and STRING SCALING

We turn now to the individual components in string instruments, starting with the primary element, the strings. A common sense definition of a musical string might go something like this: a musical string is a long, thin strand of material which is stretched taut between two fixed points. It should be non-rigid, yet strong enough so that it can be stretched fairly tightly without breaking or permanently distorting. Ideally it should be cylindrical in shape — that is, circular in cross section, and uniform in diameter over its length.

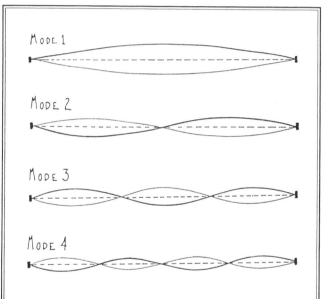

FIGURE 9-6: The first four modes of vibration for a stretched string. The frequencies and resulting pitches relative to the fundamental are given in the following chart. Mode 5 and higher modes produce tones continuing up the harmonic series.

Mode #	Frequency Relative to Mode 1	Interval Relative to Mode 1
1 (fund.)	f_1	(Unison)
2	$2f_1$	8ve
3	$3f_1$	12th
4	$4f_1$	Two 8ves

The frequency ratios and intervals given in the chart are ideal, and apply only for uniformly cylindrical strings of negligible rigidity.

There are several possible modes of vibration for strings, but the transverse modes are the ones of primary musical significance. The first several transverse modes are diagrammed in Figure 9-6, and their frequencies given. Notice that the overtone series is harmonic. The harmonic relationships actually hold only for a theoretically ideal string, but with modern commercial strings set to reasonably high tensions, the actual results usually come out very near to the ideal.

Three factors in interaction are primarily responsible for determining a string's vibrational frequencies. They are vibrating length (L), tension (T), and linear density (D). Linear density is the mass of the string per unit of length (M/L), and for most practical purposes you can think of it as a function of string diameter. The three variables are related to frequency as follows:

$$f \propto 1/L$$
$$f \propto T$$
$$f \propto 1/\sqrt{D}.$$

(The symbol $\propto$ indicates proportionality and can be read as "is proportional to.")

In other words: 1) greater string length yields lower pitch; 2) greater linear density yields lower pitch; and 3) greater tension on the string yields higher pitch. Sidebar 9-1 discusses further the physical properties of strings.

String Scaling

The term "string scaling" refers to the art of deciding just what sort of strings will bring out the best in an instrument. Pianos, harpsichords and harps, for instance, have a great many strings covering a wide range. They demand careful planning regarding string diameters, materials and overwindings. Good string scaling is equally important for small fretted instruments, even though they have fewer strings. People who work in string scaling and design have developed highly refined approaches, using precise formulas, and in recent years looking to computer programs. (One such program, which is commercially available, is listed in Appendix 1.) We will attain no such refinement here, but I will try to indicate some of the variables involved. What follows here is concerned primarily with string lengths, tensions and weights; more on choice of stringing material can be found in Sidebar 9-2.

The most important variables in scaling for a given string are linear density, length, and intended pitch. (Linear density is defined as the string's mass per unit length. It depends upon diameter as well as the material and makeup of the string.) The idea is to find the best values for length and linear density for the string to have appropriately high tension, at the string's intended pitch. The question of string tension may seem a bit abstract — most string instrument makers and players never actually measure their string tensions. (There are ways to do so, but they're not very convenient.) But string tension affects both tone quality and playing "feel" (perceived response under the fingers) in ways that are very much observable, even without measuring in pounds or kilos. In addition to being optimized for individual strings, it is

PHYSICAL PROPERTIES OF STRINGS

The "Basics of String Vibration" section of the main text describes string vibration patterns in a general way. Here now are some of the subtler factors affecting string tone for different stringing materials.

Internal damping refers to the degree to which vibrational energy is dissipated as heat in the material of the string itself. A high degree of internal damping leads to poor sustain and dullness of tone. Strings made of softer materials tend to have greater internal damping.

Rigidity, which is present to some degree in all strings, causes detuning of the string's harmonics. For a narrow string under high tension, the problem is insignificant. With thicker, more rigid strings, the higher overtones become increasingly sharp in pitch. The timbral result depends on the material of the string: for metal strings, excessive rigidity usually gives rise to a jangly tone and an apparent drop in pitch after the initial sounding. For strings of softer materials it usually leads to a duller tone and diminished sustain.

Tensile strength is the measure of how much stress a string of a given diameter can withstand without breaking. A related concern is *elasticity*, the measure a material's ability to endure stress short of the breaking point without stretching permanently out of shape. These two factors determine how high you can set the tension for a given string without it breaking or becoming misshapen.

What could loosely be called "stretchiness" is another important consideration. ("Elastic modulus" or "Young's modulus" are physicists' terms for the measure of this property.) Strings made of easily stretched materials do not drive soundboards as forcefully as unstretchy ones. They also tend to be high in internal damping. Stretchable strings have one advantage: strings set at low tension, when plucked forcefully, start out at a higher pitch initially and then stabilize at a lower pitch. (The same happens at higher tensions, but so slightly as to be negligible.) Stretchy strings, however, are less subject to this effect and so can be used at lower tensions. This was once an important consideration, but has become less so since the invention of overwound strings.

important that the tension be uniform, or nearly so, across all of an instrument's strings. This helps ensure that the strings will be in agreement in timbre and "feel," or at least reflect gradual transitions in these areas. In practice, it's not always feasible to have equal tension all across, as doing so would require either excessive lengths or excessive diameters in the bass. Some decrease in tension toward the bass is a common compromise.

Standard stringing materials are available in closely graduated sizes. (See Sidebar 9-2, part 2.) This allows the builder to find just the right diameter to yield the right tension at the desired length and pitch.

Extremes to be avoided in string scaling:

1) Strings that are too long and thin produce a weak fundamental; they also may not be sufficiently massive to drive a soundboard well.

2) Strings which are too short and fat tend to be rigid, making their overtones inharmonic.

3) Strings set at too high a tension break easily; and

4) Strings set at too low a tension suffer pitch drop after plucking and don't drive the soundboard strongly.

While high tensions are generally preferable, as a practical matter, some safety margin is needed between the string's intended pitch and the string's breaking point. A rule of thumb is that the breaking point of the string should be at least a whole tone or three semitones higher than the intended pitch of the string. But this recommendation can be taken with a grain of salt. Much lower tensions can be acceptable, and are actually desirable for string materials such as nylon which stretch and distort at tensions well below the breaking point.

At the lower end of the range, another consideration comes into play. To achieve lower pitches you need strings of greater mass, which generally means strings of greater diameter. But the larger the diameter the greater the rigidity, which causes inharmonicity. To get around this, string makers have come up with several ways to increase mass with minimal increase in rigidity. One is to use stranded wire. A string made up of many fine strands twisted or braided together has all the strength of a solid string of comparable weight, but far less rigidity. Another is overwinding. Overwound strings have a core of very strong thread or wire, wrapped over its entire length with coils of another wire. You are probably familiar with overwound strings as the lower three or four strings on guitars, all the strings on electric and most acoustic basses, those of the lower ranges on the piano, and so forth. The core provides the tensile strength. The overwinding provides a great deal more mass, but adds relatively little rigidity. The lowest strings for piano and some bass strings actually have multiple layers of overwindings.

In planning how to string a new instrument, you can get a good start by looking at existing instruments of similar size and range. This will give you a general sense of what to expect in terms of suitable materials, lengths, diameters and tensions. You can proceed from there by trial and error, simply by trying out different string sizes on the intended instrument. To do this you will need the following items in good supply: 1) strings of the desired material in finely graduated diameters; 2) common sense plus some familiarity with string instruments; and 3) patience.

For those who prefer more advance planning, here are some further guidelines. With many-stringed instruments like piano and harp, the ideal is to have both diameter and length gradually increase from string to string for progressively lower pitches, so as to keep

The number of materials that can serve for musical strings is limitless, ranging from dental floss to massive electrical power cables that sing in the open wind. I have been told by arachnid acquaintances that nothing is more harmonious than a perfectly proportioned web, although my own ears are too coarse to hear. I will not enumerate all possible string types here, but in the coming paragraphs I will touch on those that have been most important in instrument making. Consult Appendix 1, "Tools and Materials," for information on where to get what. Let us begin with ...

Metals

Metals that have been used for musical strings include high- and low-carbon steels, iron, various brass alloys, copper, zinc, tungsten, and silver. At one extreme are materials of high tensile strength, high rigidity and low internal damping. These characteristics lead to a bright sound, and they make for a string that is especially effective at high tensions and in the upper registers. At the opposite end of the scale are softer materials, having a rounder sound and some advantages in the lower registers.

The modern favorite for metal strings is high-tensile-strength, high-carbon, spring-tempered steel, variously called music wire, piano wire, or zither wire. It is the most durable of available stringing materials, and is able to withstand the highest tensions. Its internal damping is the lowest and its tone is the brightest. It serves well for high-pitched strings at high tension, and is also a common choice as a core wire for overwinding. The chart on the following page gives the standard sizes for piano wire, including both numbers by which they are designated and the diameter in thousandths of an inch.

Steel is subject to rust. For applications where moisture is a potential problem — in particular, for outdoor musical installations — stainless steel wire may be better.

Iron was the preferred material for metal strings for centuries before steel came to dominate. It has lower tensile strength and higher internal damping than steel, and its tone is rounder and less bright. Harpsichords strung with traditional iron strings do not have the aggressive, jangly sound of modern harpsichords strung with steel music wire — think about that the next time you find yourself trying to sort through the upper partials in somebody's steel-string continuo.

Brasses, bronzes and copper similarly have less tensile strength than steel, with more internal damping and less brilliance of tone. Though not as widely used as they once were, brass strings still appear on some instruments and remain available as music wire.

For overwinding wire, tensile strength is less important, though hardness remains a consideration, as well as resistance to rust and tarnishing. A wide range of metals can be and have been used, as has nylon.

Strings for instruments using electric guitar-style electromagnetic pickups require ferrous metals. Once again, steel is most popular.

Gut

Animal intestine, one of the oldest string materials, is now rarely used, having been to a large extent superseded by nylon. The exception is in early instruments for which historical authenticity is important. There is a popular, often-debunked notion that gut strings are made of catgut. Actually, sheep gut seems to be most common, while other types, such as mountain goat gut, have also been used. There is a traditional process of cleaning, drying and preparing the guts which is too repulsive to detail here. Individual strands of dried gut are very thin, and gut strings of various thickness are made by twisting different numbers of strands together. The thinnest mandolin string might be just two strands, while the largest bass string would use something over a hundred. In tone, gut strings are weak in the partials and strong in the fundamental, giving them a darker, more subdued sound than metal strings. Gut strings hold tunings poorly, because they are sensitive to changes in humidity. But they stretch and distort under tension less than nylon. Some people prefer the tone of gut to nylon, especially in the upper registers.

Nylon

Nylon strings sound fairly similar to gut, and are now used almost everywhere that gut once was. Nylon possesses both flexibility and high tensile strength, but it is subject to stretching and distortion over time. There are several types of nylon, and a particular variety chosen for its strength is used for musical strings. Monofilament nylon line is most common, but some overwound strings use an aggregation of nylon thread for the core.

Silk

Because of its strength and suppleness, silk has long been a standard stringing material in the East, and occasionally in the West. Silk strings are made from an aggregation of silk threads held together by braiding or twisting. Silk strings are stretchier than either gut or nylon. Like gut, silk is in the process of being superseded by nylon, even among players of kotos and other traditional silk-string instruments, for reasons having to do both with strength and affordability.

Other Materials

A partial list of less common materials that have been used for musical strings includes horsetail, leather thongs, animal veins and sinew, various sorts of rope and twine, and natural vegetable fiber from various vine-like plants.

SIDEBAR 9-2 (Continued): Standard sizes for Music Wire

Size	Dia.	Size	Dia.	Size	Dia.
4/0	.006"	9	.022"	16 1/2	.038"
3/0	.007	10	.024"	17	.039"
2/0	.008"	11	.026"	17 1/2	.040"
0	.009"	12	.029"	18	.041"
1	.010"	12 1/2	.030"	18 1/2	.042"
2	.011"	13	.031"	19	.043"
3	.012"	13 1/2	.032"	19 1/2	.044"
4	.013"	14	.033"	20	.045"
5	.014"	14 1/2	.034"	20 1/2	.046"
6	.016"	15	.035"	21	.047"
7	.018"	15 1/2	.036"	21 1/2	.048"
8	.020"	16	.037"	22	.049"

and the odd harmonics (which have an antinode there) will be strong. In some instruments, like most plucked lutes, it is the player who decides where to pluck. For others, such as most keyboards, the question of where to inject the energy is one of the maker's design decisions. For what it's worth, the point of input for pianos (where the hammer strikes) is typically between 1/9 to 1/7 of the string length from the bridge, yielding a fairly even balance of lower harmonics.

2) Equally important are the breadth and hardness of whatever provides the impulse. A pluck with a narrow, hard plectrum, or a strike with a narrow, hard hammer, will excite the upper harmonics much more than a pluck or strike from something soft and broad.

tension and tone quality more or less constant across the range. There is no accepted standard rate of change for the two variables; different instrument designers over the years have used different formulas. But as a very rough guideline, an increase in string length by a factor of 1.77 per descending octave, coupled with an increase in diameter by a factor of 1.13 should produce good-sounding results. These rates of change will yield a slight decrease in tension toward the bass end. (The foregoing numbers are based, by the way, on measurements from the upper middle ranges of a well made modern harpsichord.) In practice, a 1.77 increase in length per octave is impractical for many instruments, and so a lesser length increase offset by a greater diameter increase might be in order, especially in the bass range.

With instruments like guitars and violins, the lengths of all the open strings are the same. In this case, if one string is to sound an octave lower than another at the same tension, its linear density must be greater by a factor of four. This corresponds to doubling the thickness *if* material of the same density is used for both strings. I have taken a few minutes to investigate some sets of classical guitar strings to see where they come out on this question. It turned out that they adhered fairly closely to the ideal, coming up just a little short of the expected increase in mass, compensated by the usual slight reduction in tension in the bass.

SOUNDING THE STRING

How many different ways are there to excite a string? Many. But first, some basic principles:

1) The point at which you inject the energy into the string makes a big difference in the resulting tone. Plucking, striking or bowing near one end tends to excite lots of high harmonics; doing it nearer the middle yields a rounder tone. Modes of vibration having a node at the point where the energy is injected scarcely respond, while modes with antinodes near the injection point are excited most strongly. For instance, if you pluck a string at its mid-point, the even numbered harmonics (which have a node there) will be weak,

Plucking

Plucking amounts to displacing a string to one side and releasing it. It can be done with fingers or fingernails, or various sorts of plectra, or picks. The best plectra for most purposes are moderately hard, but not too rigid (as always, there are exceptions: some instruments traditionally are played with fairly hard, rigid plectra). In the past, hand-held plectra were made of tortoise shell, which has the right blend of hardness and flex. Plastics are more common now. You often can make a passable plectrum from common throwaway plastic items. The shape of the end of the plectrum (the plucking part) is important, since it determines the width of the plucking surface. The plectra in harpsichords traditionally have been quills — quite narrow — and this partly explains the harpsichord's rather bright sound.

Bowing

Bowing involves sounding a string by friction, exciting a stick-slip vibration. Violin-type bows are not the only things that can induce a string to join in this particular dance, and so bows take a variety of forms — some of them rather un-bow-like. Bows and their construction were discussed in Chapter 5, "Beaters, Scrapers and Friction Makers."

Striking

Most people are familiar with the hammers that strike piano strings, so there's no need to describe them here. Smaller hammered instruments, like hammer dulcimers, generally use a smaller, lighter, harder hammer, producing a light, bright tone (see Figure 5-1H). You can produce attractive hammer tones on strings with other sorts of light, hard beaters or sticks as well. One of the nice things about hammering by hand is the effect of bouncing the hammer on the string, producing a rapid tremolo.

Hammering On, and Striking with Tangents

The clavichord is an early keyboard zither with a different sort of hammering action. The arm that strikes the string is fronted with a small metal blade, called the tangent. It does not bounce off and leave the string to vibrate freely; instead it remains in contact with the string, and in so doing defines one end point of the string's vibrating length. The energy of the tangent's blow is enough to set the string into vibration (though not very strongly — clavichords are quiet instruments). The action is described later in this chapter in the section on keyboards.

A string-sounding technique very much like this can also be used in hand-played fretted instruments. The player brings down one of the left hand fingers (normally used for fretting, not for plucking) rapidly and forcefully on the string, hammering it against the nearest fret. The fretted instrument player's jargon for the technique is "hammering on." With acoustic instruments, because the hammered tone would otherwise lack volume, the technique is used in conjunction with plucking: the hammer-on follows a pluck in such a way that the energy from the pluck is carried over to the new pitch. With amplified instruments like electric guitar, it is possible to develop a playing style entirely around hammering on. Since you don't need the right hand for plucking, you can devote all ten fingers to hammering on, and the fretted instrument suddenly takes on a keyboard-like quality, both in terms of physical gesture and, in the hands of an experienced player, in the nature of the music as well.

The Chapman Stick is an instrument designed by Southern California builder Emmet Chapman specifically for a two-handed hammer-on technique. It looks like little more than an extra-wide fretted guitar neck, with no separate body. It has ten strings, with electric-guitar-style pickups, and is played with a neck strap in a position similar to a guitar. Another hammer-on instrument has been designed by John Starrett, to take the hammer-on idea closer to its logical, keyboard-like conclusions. The StarrBoard, a 32-string zither with pickups, rests on a table in front of the player, showing a checkerboard grid with the strings running toward the player and 24 frets running crosswise. John Starrett has also developed an acoustic version of the instrument, quiet in tone but playable.

Serrated Scrapers

Rarely, strings have been played using serrated sticks or large combs. Although the motion is similar to bowing, the sounding principles are not — there is no stick-slip, just the percussing-plucking effect of the serrations. You can get a variety of tones this way, generally pretty noisy, but sometimes noisy in interesting ways.

Wind

Aeolian harps are string instruments sounded by wind blowing over the strings. Traditionally, they take the form of a simple zither that can be set out on a window sill on a breezy day. Any string instrument, in fact, will sing if a strong enough wind crosses it at the right angle. The sound is eerie and beautiful, as the air currents excite a shifting array of harmonics. The tones tend to be sustained, gently rising and falling, sometimes hovering at a single pitch and sometimes sweeping rapidly across a range of harmonics. Sidebar 9-3 contains aeolian harp design information.

Makers have experimented with aeolian harps in diverse configurations. Many recent efforts, for reasons I have never understood, involve really huge constructions with extraordinarily long string lengths. The result is a subsonic fundamental and, in the hearing range, a general wash of indistinguishable microtonally close overtones. With strings of more conventional length, you get overtones within the hearing range bearing meaningful harmonic relationships, and the effect is more musical.

Aeolian harps remain mute if the winds are not strong enough or the wind direction is not right. You can make a more responsive but coarser-sounding wind harp by using ribbon-strings (strings in the form of flat bands). Bands of metal can be amazingly loud, but harsh in timbre.

There were some piano-like instruments made in the 18th and 19th centuries, with strings sounded by jets of compressed air, the most famous being the *anemocorde* made by Johann Schnell in 1789. At least one modern re-creation of the idea has been attempted, with, according to the builder (Japanese engineer Akio Abuchi), promising enough results to merit continued effort.

A very few chordophones use breath-blown strings, notably the gora and the lesiba, both originating in southern Africa. The blown portion of the string in these instruments is an attached segment of flattened quill, which is more responsive to the air stream.

You can also make wind-driven chordophones which depend not upon the movement of surrounding air, but rather upon the movement of the instrument through the air. Such instruments must be small and light enough to be swung or waved about. Once again, flat strings produce more sound than round ones. Large, flat rubber bands do the job quite nicely. They can be stretched over a minimal framework such as a cross shape, which can then be whirled or waved through the air.

Electromagnetism

One more way to set musical strings into vibration is through electromagnetism, using an arrangement which is basically an electromagnetic pickup operating in reverse. Electric guitar pickups respond to the movement of a steel string across the magnetic field of the coil contained in the pickup. This generates an alternating current in the coil that is analogous to the string's pattern of movement, and that electronic signal is sent to an amplifier and speaker. You can reverse the process by sending a heavily amplified alternating current pattern to a pickup, speaker driver, or other device which will serve as an electromagnet. When the electromagnet is held close to a steel string, it will drive the string. If the frequency of the signal sent to the electromagnet doesn't approximate any of the string's natural frequencies, the string doesn't respond much, but if there is a match, the string shows a generous resonance response, with gradually increasing amplitude.

You can work with this idea in several ways. One is to set up one electromagnet over each of a set of tuned steel strings, and use frequency generators to send the appropriate frequency to the electromagnet for each string. This is what Stephen Scott and Alex Stahl did with their "Bowed Pianos" in the mid 1980s. Another is to use a pickup in the conventional manner to pick up a string's frequency, send it to an

Lately people have been making aeolian harps in every imaginable shape and form, but the traditional aeolian harp, despite the name, is a simple box zither. The key to aeolian harp making lies not in the acoustic design of the zither, but rather in creating an optimal configuration for catching the wind, and in finding a good windy place to put the zither. The simplest harp or zither will sing beautifully if the wind catches the strings right. So the first step in making an aeolian harp is deciding where you want to put it. The best place, other than a windy mountain top, is a vertical sliding pane window that can be closed down over a zither lying flat on the sill, leaving just enough space for the wind to rush over the strings. (It helps to open some doors or windows on the opposite side of the house.) You can make the zither just long enough to fit on the sill. But if your windows swing open like a shutter, design the zither to stand upright, so that the window can once again be closed to the point where it just leaves room for the zither and a rush of air.

A typical aeolian harp is a rectangular box zither about 5" wide and 3" high (these dimensions are variable), and as long as the window sill. (Long strings are usually more responsive to wind than short ones.) The sides and back can be made of wood, 1/4" or 3/8" thick, while the soundboard can be made of something thinner (see the drawing). The end pieces should be thicker, say 1", for anchoring the tuning pins. You can use zither pins for tuning, and wood screws to anchor the strings at the opposite end, and any small rod-like pieces for the bridges at the string ends (refer back to Sidebar 2-1 for procedures on setting up strings, pins and bridges). The number of strings varies from harp to harp, but it helps to have quite a few, like 8 or 10. The traditional tuning is to have several different gauges of string, but all tuned to the same note.

This ensures that the tones you get from all the strings will be harmonically related. Many older aeolian harps have a tilted wooden baffle over the soundboard, designed to concentrate and direct the wind over the strings (as shown in the drawing, part B).

For a surprisingly loud tone try using flat, thin metal bands under tension, rather than conventional round strings. Boy, can they roar. The sound is coarse and growly, quite different from the delicate sound of round strings in the wind. Flat strings are hard to accommodate with the usual string tensioning systems; try instead the wedged-bridge approach to string tensioning shown in Figure 9-8.

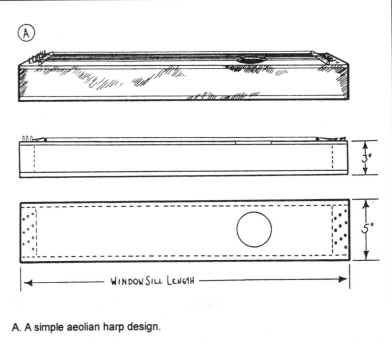

A. A simple aeolian harp design.

B. Many traditional aeolian harps have a baffle designed to catch the wind and direct it over the strings. Sometimes, unlike the design shown here, the soundboard may be level, and the baffle sloped.

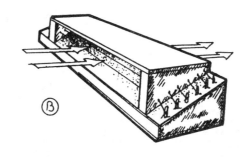

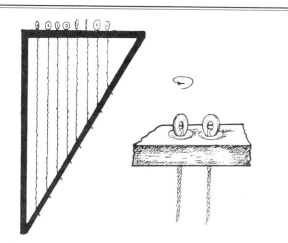

FIGURE 9-7: Twist-tensioning for strings. As described in the text, the string, consisting of two strands twisted together, is tensioned and tuned by varying the amount of twist. The string must be anchored at the lower end by some means which prevents rotation. At the upper end, the string is looped over a washer. The washer seats over an oversized hole with a brass grommet lining the rim. The hard steel of the washer digs into the softer brass of the grommet enough to prevent slippage; yet it is easy enough to turn the washer by hand to adjust the tuning. Two potential problems: 1) If the instrument design calls for strings that are very close together, you will have to use small grommets and washers closely spaced, making the tuning process a bit more awkward. 2) The washer that holds the string may not provide a perfectly immobile anchor, and this may damp the string vibration to some extent.

amplifier, and then back to another electromagnet held near the string, to perpetuate the sound. This is the idea behind the electric guitarist's sustain-enhancing device called the E-Bow.

STRING TENSIONING MECHANISMS

All of the string instrument body types described earlier call for some means to hold the strings at high tension, and to adjust that tension for tuning purposes. This calls for a strong, dependable, and minutely adjustable mechanism. The bridges wedged under the strings appearing on the prototype board zither from the start of this chapter comprise one of the simplest possible approaches. Many other approaches can be and have been used, including various kinds of adjustable

tie downs, turnbuckles, and so forth. The three most widely used and dependable methods are tuning pins, tuning pegs, and tuning machines. The hardware or materials for all three are readily available; see Appendix 1 for sources. Alternatively, you can make your own tuning pegs of hardwood, especially if you have a lathe. Miscellaneous notes:

Tuning pegs, turned from hardwood stock, usually appear on lutes, such as violins. They are the least dependable of the three preferred methods. They slip easily, and they wear, and when they wear they slip even more. Peg dope, a resin made to increase their grabbing power, helps. Tuning pegs are made with a slight taper, so that they become more snug as you push them in further. The holes they go in must be shaped accordingly. While violin headstocks may look delicate, it is important that the wooden body in which the peg sits be strong and solid hardwood.

Tuning pins are most often used in many-stringed instruments, such as pianos and other keyboard instruments, harps and zithers. They likewise must be set in a substantial hardwood body and carefully sized holes. The lower part of the body of the pin has tiny threads of very slight pitch, which ensure that the pin doesn't pull out. Standard piano pins are designed to fit a 3/8" pre-drilled hole. They are actually slightly larger in diameter, ensuring a snug fit; in fact, they are made in a range of very slightly increasing sizes, so that a pin can be found to fit tight even in a worn hole. Smaller pins, sold as zither pins, are usually made for a 3/16" hole, with actual diameter just slightly larger. Tuning pins can be turned with any adjustable wrench, but tuning wrenches made specifically for the purpose are not expensive, and are much preferable.

Tuning machines, such as appear on guitars, are the surest of tuning mechanisms, and also the most expensive. Their worm-gear mechanism prevents slippage, and, by setting a low gearing ratio, makes fine adjustments easy. Some tuning machines are individually mounted; others come in sets of three, four or six on a mounting bracket designed for use on particular instruments.

While the three methods just mentioned are most common, other string tensioning systems are possible. Figure 9-7 shows a simple system that I recently came up with (simple enough that I won't take inventor's credit, since I'm sure someone must have thought of it before). For this tuning mechanism, the instrument's strings are comprised not of a single strand of musical string, but of a double strand twisted together. (The idea of using multiple strands twisted together

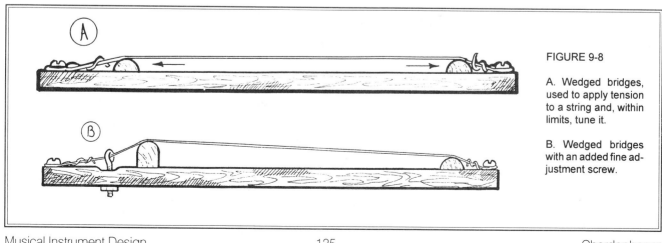

FIGURE 9-8

A. Wedged bridges, used to apply tension to a string and, within limits, tune it.

B. Wedged bridges with an added fine adjustment screw.

has been in use for centuries, since it has other advantages independent of the current discussion.) It's easy to make the two-strand twist by forming the string as a loop, pulled tight, anchored at the ends, and twisted by rotating one of the end-anchors, as the figure shows. To increase tension on the string, and thus adjust the tuning, one simply increases the amount of twist by turning the anchor. The resulting tunability is as dependable and as finely adjustable as the worm gears on a tuning machine, but you can create this mechanism out of common components at negligible cost. Because of its configuration, the twist-tune system is best suited to harps and lyres.

A few more notes on the wedged-bridge string tuning method discussed earlier. The farther you push the wedges toward the string ends, the more they stretch the string, and the higher the pitch (the increase in tension outweighs the effect of increased string length). To make wedged bridges or any similar approach more fine-tunable, consider adding a tension-adjusting screw or turnbuckle somewhere between one of the bridges and the string end-point (see Figure 9-8).

BRIDGES

For most string instruments, the strings need some means to communicate their vibrations to a sound table, as did the wedged bridges on the prototype zither. To fulfill its function well, a bridge must deliver the vibration in a way that really gets the sound table going. Bridges serve a second essential function by providing a hard, defined end-point for the string's vibrating length. The form of the top of the bridge, where the strings make contact as they pass over it, is important in this connection. The shape should not allow buzzing. Narrow rounded shapes work well; they also reduce wear on the string. Flat or angular shapes at the string crossing create problems. A slight notch at the crossing point can provide a seating to keep the string from moving laterally on the bridge as it vibrates.

There are several different types of bridges, with distinct physical and acoustic characteristics. Let's look at some examples.

Tall Bridges

With the term *tall bridge*, I refer to bridges like those used in members of the violin family; those ornately carved things rising high above the arched soundboard. I start with them because their action illustrates some important ideas. Figure 9-9 shows the arrangement of the bridge, strings, and elements of the body in a violin.

The bow moves perpendicular to the string, creating a transverse motion (right and left in the orientation of the picture). The left foot of the bridge rests directly over the sound-post, an upright pillar wedged firmly between the front and back of the instrument. This prevents the left foot from moving much, except to pivot. The right foot, meanwhile, is directly over the bass-bar. The bass bar stiffens the soundboard at this critical point and, extending across most of the length of the board, spreads any input far and wide. But it does not immobilize the board as the sound-post does. Thus, when in the course of vibration the string makes a rightward movement, the bridge pivots on the solidly anchored left foot, and pushes down on the right foot, forcing a whole portion of the soundboard downward. This makes for strong surface radiation from the right half of the front face of the soundboard, with minimal out-of-phase motion from the left half of the front face. It also compresses the air within the chamber, driving the air resonance and effectively pumping a pulse of air out through the violin's *f*-holes,

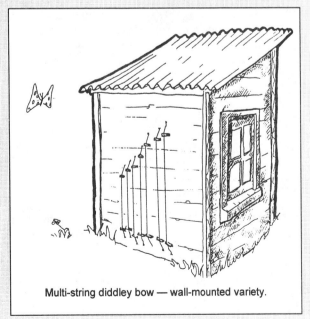

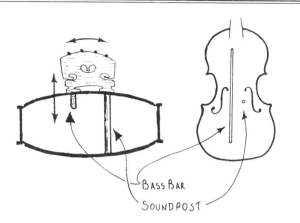

FIGURE 9-9: Components of a violin-type tall bridge. The arrows show the predominant direction of string movement, and the direction in which the bridge drives the soundboard as a result of the pivoting action.

BASS BAR
SOUNDPOST

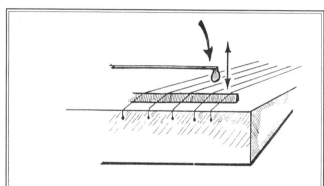

FIGURE 9-10: The direction of impulse for hammered zithers such as piano and hammer dulcimer is the right direction for direct communication to the soundboard.

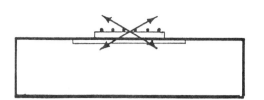

FIGURE 9-11: The direction of impulse for plucked lutes such as guitars is quite variable from one stroke to another, but for most plucks the impulse is at an oblique angle, making for somewhat inefficient transmission to the soundboard.

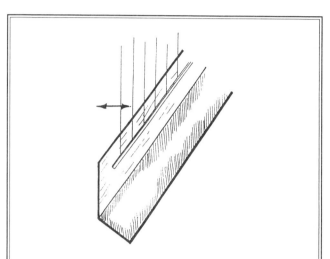

FIGURE 9-12: The direction of movement at a harp string-band, given the direction of a typical pluck, communicates the vibration to the soundboard quite efficiently.

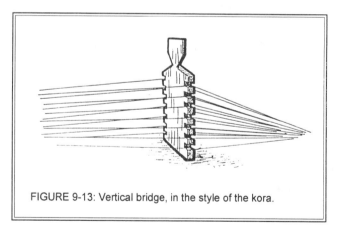

FIGURE 9-13: Vertical bridge, in the style of the kora.

again without much out-of-phase movement from the other half of the board. When the string swings back the other way, the reverse actions follow. The surface radiation off the soundboard and the air resonances coming through the violin's *f*-holes emphasize different frequency ranges, and the two combine for an attractive composite tone.

The height of the bridge provides leverage for its rocking action. A little more subtle is the effect of the elaborately carved shape of the bridge. The shaping modifies how the bridge delivers different frequencies to the soundboard. The standard design somewhat diminishes the transmission of high frequencies. People with expertise in these matters can modify an existing bridge, or carve a new bridge, to alter the tone of a violin in deliberate ways.

Low Bridges

Low bridges are used in most plucked lutes and zithers. They lack the sophisticated mechanics of the violin family, but they do the job. With hammer dulcimers, pianos and harpsichords, the direction of impulse to the string is not lateral, as it was with the bowed strings, but vertical — directly toward or away from the soundboard (Figure 9-10). This is the ideal direction for driving the soundboard, so no pivoting action is called for.

With plucked lutes, the plucking impulse is usually more at an angle, somewhat off perfectly lateral, but nowhere near perpendicular to the soundboard, as shown in Figure 9-11. This makes for less efficient transmission. It is one of the reasons why plucked lutes tend to be quiet, but the slow transmission may also allow them a bit more sustain. It is tempting to try to get better volume out of a plucked instrument like a guitar by plucking in the perpendicular direction. You can do this with very small amplitudes, but at large amplitudes — obtained by pulling the string straight out from the guitar and releasing — the string bangs into the frets and fingerboard. There is not enough room to vibrate in that direction. So try this: loosen the lowest string of a guitar enough to slide a block of wood between the string and fingerboard beside the nut, raising the string an inch and a half or so above the fingerboard. Retighten it. Now you can pluck perpendicular to the soundboard without snapping against the frets. You may be surprised at the difference this makes. The string sound is louder than it is in the normal configuration, and the tone richer in the bottom. Now pluck the same string laterally. What an anemic sound, by comparison! Designing a guitar or other plucked lute for vibration perpendicular to the soundboard, however, would be easier said than done, especially since guitar playing typically involves several different strokes with different plucking directions.

Harp bridges

That guitar experiment illustrates at least part of the reason why harps are efficient sound-producing instruments. Unlike a guitar, the natural direction of pluck in the harp's normal playing position sets the string vibrating nearly perpendicular to the soundboard (Figure 9-12). Harps, for this reason, can be

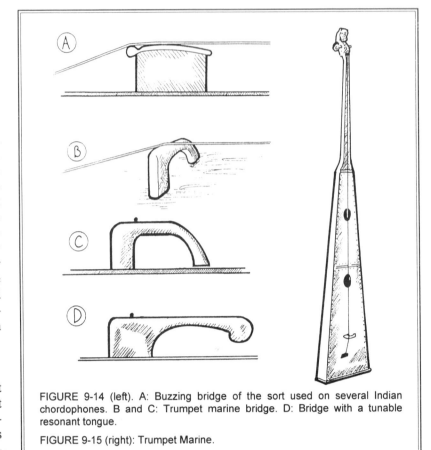

FIGURE 9-14 (left). A: Buzzing bridge of the sort used on several Indian chordophones. B and C: Trumpet marine bridge. D: Bridge with a tunable resonant tongue.

FIGURE 9-15 (right): Trumpet Marine.

made louder than guitar-like instruments, though with the rapid delivery of energy, they tend to have more rapid decay.

Vertical Bridges

The kora, and a lesser-known instrument from west central Africa called *mvet*, use upright bridges designed to hold the strings in a vertical line above the soundboard or string carrier. Such a design works for instruments which will be plucked, harp-like, in the direction perpendicular to the soundboard or carrier, and it has many of the acoustic as well as ergonomic advantages of harp-like arrangements.

Buzzing Bridges

Some bridges are designed not simply to transmit vibrations faithfully from string to soundboard, but to add distinctive new elements to the sound in the process. The best known of these are the extraordinary buzzing bridges found on several lutes from the Indian subcontinent, including rudra vina, tamboura, and sitar. Instead of providing a discrete edge to define the end of the string's vibrating length, these bridges have a very slightly raised stopping point, with a gently curving plateau of ivory, antler or bone in front, typically about an inch wide (Figure 9-14A). The string buzzes gently against the surface as it vibrates, producing the characteristic shifting blend of very prominent high harmonics. Sometimes a thread is introduced between the string and bridge to fine tune the harmonic buzz. In addition to its striking sound quality, the effect increases the string's perceived volume and sustain. The gentle slope is called *jawari*, and shaping it to

just the right contour for the desired tone is a subtle business. If you don't have an experienced maker to guide you through the process, you can still make some progress by trial and error. Some people have managed to create an effect like that of the jawari using slightly re-shaped sections cut from metal conduit. Alternatively, consider purchasing a bridge ready-made for one of the Indian instruments. Incidentally, it is easier to get good results with this sort of bridge on longer strings.

A different sort of buzzing bridge has been used in a few European instruments, the best known being the trumpet marine. The trumpet marine is a tall, skinny instrument, as shown in Figure 9-15, with a single string played entirely in harmonics by means of a bow, sometimes also having a set of unplayed strings concealed within the body designed to vibrate in sympathy. As shown in Figure 9-14 B and C, the main string passes over an uneven two-legged bridge, held in place by the string's pressure. One of the bridge legs is a tiny bit short, so that when the string pressure holds the main leg firmly against the soundboard, the other leg does not quite touch. When the instrument is bowed, that leg rattles against the board. When everything is adjusted right, the resulting tone is surprisingly rather like that of a quiet trumpet. Here is how the adjustment works: The string passes not over the middle of the bridge, but more toward the side with the main leg, as shown in Figure 9-14C. Sliding the bridge sideways a short distance in the direction of the short leg causes the string to pull in the opposite direction, slightly lifting the short leg, or at least reducing downward pressure on it. The resulting tone becomes harsh. Sliding the bridge the opposite way increases downward pressure on the short leg, forcing it against the soundboard and stopping the buzz. The trumpet tone arises somewhere in between.

Buzzing bridges of the trumpet marine type work best with bowing rather than plucking. Bowing introduces a steady stream of vibrational energy at a more or less constant level, allowing you to adjust the bridge for optimal response at that level. You can also try adjusting the bridge for a more raucous tone, including one in which the octave below the string fundamental makes an appearance. Whatever the quality of the buzz, it has the effect of increasing perceived loudness.

Tuned Bridges

Like almost everything on God's earth, bridges have their own internal resonances. These are generally too high to have any impact on the bridge's functioning. But you can deliberately build lower-frequency resonances into bridges, and tune them to the tonal regions you wish to enhance. One way to do this is by fashioning the bridge in a shape that includes a tongue protruding to one side of the bridge's main body, as shown in Figure 9-14D. The effect, if the coupling between the string and bridge is right, is quite pronounced. Depending on the configuration, you can obtain an unusually full, round tone, or a slightly reedy quality. The tuning relationship is not extremely precise; with a given bridge configuration you can hear the effect strongly over a range of pitches covering maybe a third or fourth — meaning that you can use the effect on a fretted string within a certain limit. You can tune the bridge's resonance by sliding the bridge to one side or the other and altering the string's point of contact on the bridge, just as described above for the trumpet marine. Tuned bridges work with plucked strings, but are more effective with bowed strings.

Further Considerations in Bridge Design

Some bridges are glued in place on the soundboard, with the strings actually tied to them, so that the bridge serves doubly as a bridge and a string anchor. Classical guitar bridges are made this way. With most other string instruments, the strings pass over the bridge and are anchored somewhere farther down the line. The bridge is then held in place against the soundboard by the pressure of the strings. With non-glued bridges you can adjust the position of the bridge for optimal sound or for intonational purposes. The mechanics of transmission are somewhat different in the two cases. Glued-on bridges serving also as string anchors undergo a lot of stress, and sometimes pull up. To reduce that likelihood, they must have a large surface of contact with the soundboard and be very strongly glued.

Some bridges, like violin bridges, are shaped to stand on two feet. Footed bridges are most common on arch-topped instruments, in part because having feet eliminates the need for a large undersurface fitted to the contour of the soundboard. Glued-on bridges should be flat-bottomed rather than footed, to provide the maximum adhesive surface.

Many zithers have one or two middle bridges in addition to those at the string end, dividing each string into shorter, independently vibrating segments. Middle bridges must be higher than the end bridges, so that the string presses down on the middle bridge as it passes over. A single additional bridge at the string's center point yields two equal string segments having the same pitch. Whichever side is initially sounded, sympathetic vibration between the two half-strings will enrich the tone. A bridge at the 2/3 point gives a string length ratio of 2:1 for tones an octave apart, providing an increased pitch range as well as some sympathetic resonances. There are many other options, multiplied further if one adds two middle bridges. On some oriental zithers, each string has its own small, separate center bridge, allowing for different bridge spacings from one string to the next. These movable bridges often take a two-footed A-frame shape. If the bridges are not glued down, but held in place by string pressure, they can be moved about to achieve different tunings.

The positioning of the bridge on the soundboard is important to the efficiency of vibration transmission. Locations at or very near the edge of the soundboard may be too rigid for the bridge to drive effectively. Some potential bridge locations, on the other hand, may be too weak to support the pressure of the strings. The positioning of struts on the underside of the soundboard affect strength at any given location, as well as the effectiveness with which vibrations introduced at that location are dispersed through the board. Another factor to consider: many soundboard shapes (guitar and violin are good examples) have recognizable vibrating regions within the overall shape. Different bridge locations will drive different regions more or less effectively. If a particular region of the soundboard, such as the large lower portion of a guitar, is essential to a good sound, then be sure to locate the bridge so as to drive that region most effectively.

PITCH CONTROL MECHANISMS FOR CHORDOPHONES: MULTIPLE STRINGS

It is time now to talk about the methods available for getting a range of notes from string instruments. The prototype board zither from the start of this chapter used a slide, like a Hawaiian guitar. That is but one of many options; here are more.

The most direct way to obtain many pitches from a string instrument is to have many strings to choose from, tuned to different pitches. This works well for plucked or hammered instruments like harps, harpsichords, pianos, and most zithers. Problems arise for bowed instruments, if all the strings lie flat in a plane. Then the bow can't get at them individually (unless you use a very small, rotating-wheel-type bow). To get around the problem, many-stringed bowed instruments

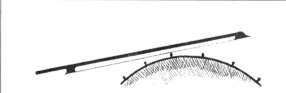

FIGURE 9-16: A curved bridge allows for bowing of individual strings on many-stringed bowed instruments.

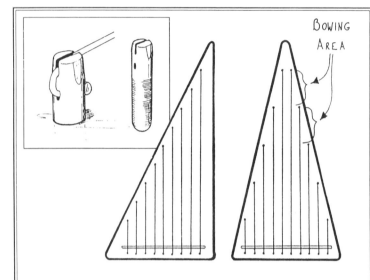

BOWING AREA

9-17: Two variations on a flat bowed-zither design. Each string is individually accessible to the bow in the region just beyond where the neighboring string ends.

Inset: Detail of the pin-bridges often used in such instruments. A string with a ball-end goes through a hole in the pin-bridge and loops over the top, where it rides in a groove in the top of the pin. These pins can be fashioned from standard zither pins by cutting off a bit of the top and cutting a groove in the top of the shortened pin.

usually have the strings arranged in a "curved plane" to allow for tangential bowing of individual strings (see Figure 9-16). Some builders have mounted strings all the way around the perimeter of a cylinder-shaped resonator to allow bowing all around and maximize the space available for strings. Some have even put the cylinder on a rotating bearing.

Figure 9-17 shows another approach that allows a player to selectively bow individual strings on a many-stringed zither. Instruments of this sort, commonly called *bowed psalteries*, have the strings arranged so that each extends slightly beyond its neighbor, leaving a small portion of its length accessible to the bow. To make this work, you need small, unobtrusive individual bridges for each string at its exposed end. The little bridge usually takes the form of a metal pin shaped much like a tuning pin, but with the string passing in a groove over the top. It can be made from a standard tuning pin by cutting a bit off the top to shorten the pin, and using a hacksaw to cut a groove across the top to hold the string in place.

Un-fingered bowed instruments have a lovely, light and fine tone, because the absence of the damping finger allows the upper harmonics to ring out and allows the string to continue ringing with each note after the bow has left it. The fine edge to the tone is especially prominent with bowed psalteries due to the necessity of bowing near the end of the string, preferentially exciting the upper partials.

Historical note: despite the ancient-sounding name, the idea for the bowed psaltery seems to be a modern one, first appearing in Germany in the 1930s.

Keyboards

Another approach to sounding-string selection for many-stringed instruments is the keyboard. We discussed keyboard layouts in Chapter 3, but we did not talk about keyboard mechanisms. Keyboards can be made to control hammering mechanisms, as with pianos, or plucking mechanisms, as with harpsichords, or hammer-on mechanisms, as with clavichords, and even bowing, aeolian and electromagnetic mechanisms, as with a number of intriguing but lesser-known instruments.

Keyboard-controlled hammer mechanisms (pianos) have two important advantages: unlike plucking mechanisms (harpsichords), they allow for wide variation in dynamics, and unlike hammer-on mechanisms (clavichords) they can be loud. But the mechanisms involved in creating an effective piano action are extremely complex, with about fifteen moving parts per key in modern piano actions. There are two main reasons for the complexity: 1)The sound is poor if the hammer is held rigidly; it must instead be rapidly "thrown" at the string (swinging freely on a pivot) so as to strike it in free-fly, and then bounce off. 2) You need a damper — a soft pad that comes down on the string when the key is released to stop it from continuing to ring. Standard piano actions (of which there are many variations) do no make the damper mechanism of a piece with the hammer mechanism, so an additional set of moving parts are required to operate the dampers.

Harpsichord actions are simpler. There is a plectrum (called the quill because that is what harpsichord plectra were originally made of) mounted on an upright rising from the far end of the lever that is the key. On the same upright, there is a damper above. At rest position, the damper rests on the string, while the plectrum waits just below it. When the front of the key is depressed, lifting the upright, the damper comes off the string and the quill rises to pluck the string. The only difficulty lies in the fact that there must be a pivot mechanism allowing the quill to fall back out of the way rather than plucking again on the way down.

But by far the simplest keyboard action is that of the clavichord. Just one moving part — the key itself! The clavichord's lever action is shown in Figure 9-18. With this action, the player can impart pitch bends and vibrato by varying pressure on the key after the initial strike (causing the tangent to bend the string upward slightly, altering the tension).

The attack of the tangent actually creates two potential vibrating string lengths — one on each side. The string segment on one side is prevented from sounding by a damper, usually in the form of a piece of soft cloth woven under and over the strings. This gives another happy result: As long as the tangent is in contact with the string, it defines a string segment that is free to vibrate un-damped. When the tangent drops away, that segment again becomes part of the whole string, to be immediately damped by the cloth on the far end. So — as with the piano, but with a far simpler mechanism — the clavichord string sounds as long as the key is depressed, and stops the moment it is released and the tangent drops.

Unlike other keyboard string instruments, clavichords can be made to produce more notes than they have strings. In fact, you can make a one- or two-octave clavichord with

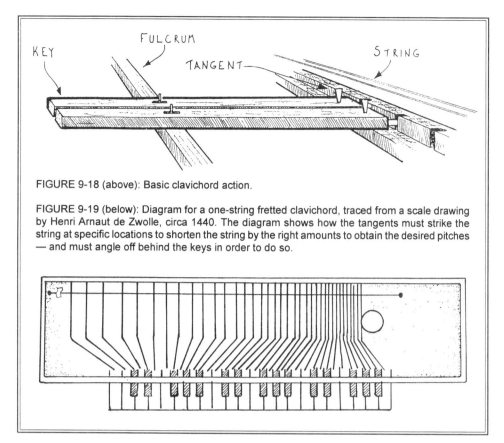

FIGURE 9-18 (above): Basic clavichord action.

FIGURE 9-19 (below): Diagram for a one-string fretted clavichord, traced from a scale drawing by Henri Arnaut de Zwolle, circa 1440. The diagram shows how the tangents must strike the string at specific locations to shorten the string by the right amounts to obtain the desired pitches — and must angle off behind the keys in order to do so.

just one string. You do this by arranging to have the tangents of all the keys strike at the appropriate place on the single string to produce all the notes (see Figure 9-19). Or you can have an intermediate number of strings each producing two or three or four notes. The disadvantage of this approach is that you cannot get two notes simultaneously out of one string, so any two notes produced by the same string cannot sound together. The multiple-notes-per-string approach in clavichords is called "fretting."

To produce the intended pitch, the tangent must dependably strike at the right point along the string. As shown in Figure 9-19 the back sides of the key levers may need to be offset at an angle, rather than extending straight back from the front of the key, to land the tangent in the right place. The angling makes it more difficult to create a smoothly operating lever. Most clavichords have guides at the far end of the key lever, as shown in Figure 9-18, to keep the tangent in line. The situation is less exacting in un-fretted clavichords, because with them you can use the tuning pins to tune each string to the desired pitches even if the tangent's striking locations are not ideal.

How about a bowed-piano keyboard mechanism? In the approach most often suggested, there is continuous bow, in the form of a band of bowing material running between two pulleys like tractor treads. Pressing a key lifts one end support for an individual string, to bring the string into contact with the bow. This attractively simple mechanism allows for some control of timbre and dynamics, even some vibrato, through key pressure. But despite several attempts over a period of centuries — the first known suggestion of the idea is in the notebooks of Leonardo da Vinci — the notion has never caught on.

Autoharpitude

Finally, one last rather clever and, to my mind, underrated sounding-string-selection method. The autoharp is a zither incorporating a selective string damper mechanism, apparently invented in Germany and first patented in the U.S. in 1882 by a German immigrant named Zimmermann. A set of anywhere from three to nine or more bars crosses over a soundboard with two or three dozen strings. Each bar is spring-mounted so that it can be pressed down onto the strings. On the underside of the bars are several damper pads, spaced out in such a way that when a given bar is pressed down, the dampers stop all the strings except those required to sound a particular chord. Each bar has its pads arranged to allow a different chord to sound. You play the zither by strumming across all the strings, while pressing different bars to bring out the desired chords. While the instrument is seemingly designed very narrowly for accompaniment in the form of block chords, good players have shown that it has a distinctive sound and a great deal more potential than the basic concept would imply. Some fancy versions have mechanisms for changing the damper positions, or modular extra bars to increase the range of chords available.

MORE PITCH CONTROL MECHANISMS: STRING LENGTH & TENSION

We have been looking at ways to select the string that sounds from among the set of strings on a multiple-string instrument. Now we turn to ways to get different pitches from a single string. The primary factors controlling string pitch, as we saw earlier, are length, tension and linear density. You can't very well change a string's density for each new note of a melody, so that leaves tension and length as the two manipulable factors. Of these, string length is the more manageable and by far the more common method, so we will start with it.

You can shorten the effective vibrating length of a string, causing it to vibrate at a higher frequency, by "stopping" it somewhere along its length — that is, pressing it directly with a finger as with violins, or pressing it against a fret as with guitars, or holding a slide or bottleneck against it. With unfretted instruments like violins, it is the player's job to know where to stop the string — where to place the finger, which is to say, how much to shorten the vibrating string length — in order to get any desired pitch. With fretted instruments like the guitar, it is the maker's job to place the frets in the right locations along the neck. Sidebar 9-5 contains the information you need to calculate string stopping points and fret placements. Alternatively, you can work out your stopping points by experimentation/earwork/trial and error, or by copying the string stopping points (e.g., the fret placements) from an existing instrument of identical string length.

Now on to specific string-stopping methods.

Fingering, Fretlessly

By fingering, I refer to any method for shortening a string's effective vibrating length by pressing it with a finger. The problem with fingers is that they are soft, and with direct contact they damp a string's vibration considerably. That is why most plucked string instruments have frets: the fret forms a hard, well-defined barrier to the string's vibrating length, so that the finger does not touch the active part of the string. Most fingered string instruments that don't have frets are not played by plucking. Instead, they inject an ongoing stream of mechanical energy into the string to ensure its continued vibration. In other words, they are (for the most part) bowed instruments.

This is not to say that fretless fingered instruments are never played by plucking. With the violin the plucking technique (called pizzicato) yields a brief tone of very rapid decay — an attractive effect, but one which is generally used sparingly. With more massive strings, the greater kinetic energy allows a fuller tone in spite of the damping. That makes pizzicato on a string bass more viable, and in fact people do it all the time. Plucking the strings on a fretless guitar falls somewhere in between — you get a rather damped tone, but more sustain than a pizzicato violin.

With some eastern fiddles, the player fingers the string unaided, in mid-air as it were. He or she presses it off to one side with the fingertip or, for a harder edge, the fingernail, or else pinches it between thumb and forefinger. This technique yields a great flexibility of pitch, as you can press or pinch the string anywhere, and bend it freely to alter tension. Pitch control for such instruments is demanding; they are hard to play in tune, and good players train for years. The flexibility in pitch and timbre makes them well suited to melodically oriented and intonationally sophisticated musical styles. The necks of such fiddles, naturally, do not need fingerboards. They often take the form of a turned wood pole rising from the body.

Most western bowed string instruments have fingerboards against which the player presses the string to stop it. This makes intonation a bit surer, as the string doesn't flex as freely and the player can memorize pitch locations on the fingerboard. You can even place visual pitch markers there, which is useful in realizing unusual tunings.

The art of neck and fingerboard design and construction lies in the spacing between the fingerboard and strings, commonly called the "action." If the strings are too high off the fingerboard, the instrument is hard to play. Also, the strings stretch considerably in being pressed far down, which increases tension and throws off the tuning. If the strings are too low, they rattle and buzz on the fingerboard. The ideal is to have the strings as low as possible without buzzing at the nut end, but incline them very slightly upward toward the bridge. The greater the expected amplitude of vibration, the higher the action must be, which suggests a need for higher action at greater string lengths. Fingerboards for bowed instruments typically are made straight. Bowed instrument nuts and fingerboards must be arched from side to side, to reflect the arched bridge and positioning of the strings that allows tangential bowing. The best guideline you will find for neck action is to study existing well-made instruments with string scalings similar to those of whatever instrument you may be considering making.

Frets

Frets are the small metal ridges that cross the necks of most plucked stringed instruments, and some bowed instruments. The player presses the string against the fingerboard just behind the desired fret, so that the string presses against the fret to provide a hard string-stopping point. Fretted bowed instruments have a brighter tone than their unfretted relatives, and longer ring time after the bowing stops (an attractive effect almost entirely absent on unfretted bowed instruments), but they offer less freedom for subtle pitch inflections. The notes on fingerboard action from the preceding paragraph apply to fretted instruments as well as unfretted, with these additional notes: while many fretted instruments have straight fingerboards, in other cases, including many guitars, the fingerboard is given a very slight curvature over its length, as if the tension of the strings had caused it to bow. This allows for slightly closer action at the highest frets. Aside from such deliberate curvature, any warpage, valleys or humps will lead to buzzing and difficulty in playing. Most steel string and electric guitar fingerboards are made with a slight lateral arching as well, to facilitate barring (a certain type of guitar fingering).

The locations of the frets on an instrument neck determine what the available string-stopping points will be and, as a result, what pitch relationships will be available. Very nearly all the commercially made fretted instruments in the West are set to 12-tone equal temperament. But as an individual maker, you can set your frets to whatever scale relationships suit your fancy, or you can use movable frets. Sidebar 9-5 tells how to plan your fret placements.

Frets have been made of glued-on strips of metal, wood, bone, or ivory. Cord has also been used, such as the same gut used for strings, tied in one or two loops around the neck. The standard modern metal frets are cut from commercially available fret wire, which has a special cross-section shape for the purpose (see Figure 9-20) and is available in a range of sizes.

Western instruments use low frets, so that the player can press the string over the fret and hard against the fingerboard without undue string stretching and pitch distortion. On many Eastern instruments the frets are made high, for the opposite effect: with room to press the string farther in toward the neck behind the fret (or greater ease in bending it sideways, as is more common), the player can realize more varied intonational inflections. Sitar frets, for instance, take the form of high, curved bars arching over the neck.

Sitar frets also have the great advantage of being movable, so that the instrument is not locked into a single intonation system. Moveable frets can also be made using cords tied around the neck, and a variety of other movable fret mechanisms have been designed.

There is a lot to be said for the freedom that fret-movability affords. But the matter of non-standard intonation in fretted instruments is a complex one. Imagine that you make an instrument with the frets spaced out along the neck so as to produce a particular scale — one with unequal intervallic spacings — for a certain string tuned to a certain note. Those same fret spacings under adjacent strings tuned to other notes will yield a transposition of the scale. In effect, each string will be fretted so as to play in a different key. This problem

---

Sidebar 9-5   LOCATING STRING STOPPING POINTS

This sidebar outlines principles for determining locations for string instrument frets to obtain particular intervals. Essentially the same principles can be applied in determining string stopping points for non-fretted instruments as well — e.g., fingering points along the neck of a violin for particular pitches, or tangent striking points for a fretted clavichord.

The basic rule is that, other things being equal, vibrating frequency is inversely proportional to string length. This means that the ratios between the active string lengths determined by the fret locations should correspond to the inverses of the desired frequency ratios. To see how this works, imagine that you want to place frets under a string, spaced so as to produce a basic just major scale at frequency ratios 1:1, 9:8, 5:4, 3:2, 5:3, 15:8, 2:1. For simplicity's sake, assume an open string length of one meter, with the open string pitch serving as the tonic and first degree of the scale. Where then should you place the fret to get the second degree at 9/8 times the fundamental frequency? Following the inversion rule, the calculation is: first fret location = 8/9 x 1 meter = 88.9 cm. Place the fret so that this is the distance from the fret to the far bridge. The location for the second scale degree, at 5/4 the open string frequency, is at a point 4/5 of the open string length, or 80 cm from the bridge. You can calculate the remaining fret locations in a similar manner. (But — important! — see the comments at the end of this section for offsetting factors.)

Notice that I haven't said anything about specific frequencies here. The actual sounding pitches will be determined by the tuning of the open string. But the pitch *relationships* established by the fret placements will remain true regardless of the tension (within reasonable limits).

In practice, fretted instruments are not often set to just tunings, in part because of problems associated with unequal fret spacings described in the main text. Most contemporary fretted instruments are set to the standard 12-tone equal temperament. Other equal temperaments can work too, as long as the number of tones per octave isn't too large. With equal temperaments, as discussed in Chapter 3, the frequency increases with each scale step by a constant factor. (Sidebar 3-1 gives values for the constant factors for a range of equal temperaments.) In keeping with the inverse proportion rule, the frets must be placed so that each successive fret shortens the active string length by the inverse of that factor. Thus, to locate the frets for 12-tone equal temperament on a 1-meter string, you proceed as follows:

The 12-equal scale factor (from Sidebar 3-1) is = 1.05946; its inverse is $1/1.05946 = .9438$.
Starting with the open string at 100cm —

1st fret located $.9438 \times 100.0$ cm = 94.38 cm from the bridge.

2nd fret located $.9438 \times 94.38$ cm = 89.08 cm from the bridge.

3rd fret located $.9438 \times 89.08$ cm = 84.08 cm from the bridge.

And so forth, through as many frets as you wish. This will yield the familiar pattern of progressively closer frets going up the neck one sees on guitars and mandolins and such. Similar patterns will appear when you apply the inverted factors for other equal temperaments, but the actual spacings will be different.

Important: These fret locations represent a theoretical ideal. In practice one must take into account an increase in tension due to the slight stretching of the string when it is pressed down to the fret, pulling the pitch slightly sharp. Correct for this by offsetting the fret to allow a slightly longer vibrating length. If the string is already in place, you can incorporate the correction into the original calculation by this method: Find the stopping location at which the string produces a true octave when pressed down to the fingerboard. (You can determine when the octave is true by comparing the fingered pitch to the harmonic tone generated by lightly touching the string at its midpoint and plucking.) The fingered true octave location will be a little short of the actual string midpoint. Double the active string length at this true-octave stopping point to get a slightly long "corrected" total string length, and use the corrected string length in place of the actual string length for your calculations.

Another approach some makers have used — simple and convenient if a little less precise — is "the rule of 18." Place the frets so that each successive fret shortens the sounding string length by 1/18th relative to the previous fret. This gives a result very close the twelve-equal factor with a small correction built in.

Finally, if the bridge on the finished instrument is not glued in place, but is movable, then you can easily compensate for fretting tension effects by adjusting the bridge location after the instrument is completed. If, for instance, the pitch is a bit sharp at what should be the octave fret, move the bridge a bit farther away, thus increasing the overall string length. Fine tune the bridge location as necessary to bring the frets in tune.

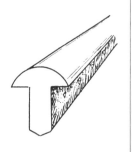

FIGURE 9-20: Fretwire. The lower part of the fret is tapped snugly into a slot cut in the fingerboard (the tangs along the side help hold it in place). The upper, rounded part remains above the fingerboard, and provides the stopping surface for the string.

Cutting the slots for the frets is precision work; one essential in the process is to use a saw that cuts a slot just wide enough to hold the fret snugly (available from lutherie supply houses). Alternatively, you can, within limits, adjust the width of a coping saw's kerf by gently hammering the teeth to reduce their offset, thus reducing the width of the cut. Filing the blade to narrow the kerf still more may be necessary as well. Poorly fitting frets can be made more secure by gluing.

doesn't arise for equal temperaments. With the fret spacings even and equal, you get the same set of available pitches and pitch relationships on any string tuned to any of the scale degrees. That is why fretted instruments are more amenable to equal temperaments than unequal tunings.

What to do, then, if you want to realize an unequal tuning on a fretted instrument? One solution is to add more and more frets to accommodate every desired note for every string. That quickly becomes a problem as the frets get too close together to play properly — it turns out that frets closer than about 1/4" are more or less unplayable — and, furthermore, playing such an over-fretted instrument gets confusing. Another approach is the use of *fretlets* — short frets that don't cross the entire neck, but lie under only one or two strings. They allow for different fret spacings under different strings. This is a more workable approach, but it, too, can be confusing and difficult to play.

One more possibility is to give up the idea of unequal tunings and work instead with higher-order equal temperaments. This approach is ideal as long as the number of tones per octave isn't too high. 19-equal guitars, many of which have been made, have proven to be quite musical. Above about 24-equal, for guitar-sized instruments, the fret spacing begins to get too small and the instruments become unplayable.

Slides

A slide is any heavy, hard, hand-held object which can be touched to a musical string to stop it without having to press it down behind a fret or against a fingerboard. The mass and hardness of the object provide a defined stopping point, so the string rings as clearly as if it were fretted. The most common slides are short, thick steel bars, or the necks of bottles broken off and with the sharp edges filed away so they can conveniently be worn on a finger. Any number of other objects can do as well. Slides have flexibility far surpassing frets. You can place the slide at any point along the string, or you can slide it along the string producing a continuous glissando. A few string instruments, like pedal steel guitar, Hawaiian guitar, and some dobros, are made specifically to be played with slides. Just as often slides are used as a special

effect on instruments that are normally fretted. In fact you can use a slide on virtually any musical string.

A serious limitation is that you can't very well use the slide to stop adjacent strings at different stopping points. It is awkward to make the slide cross one string at, say, the equivalent of the 7th fret, and simultaneously cross another string at the 9th. If you wish to play two strings in harmony, you are limited to pre-tuned intervals between the strings. Pedal steel guitars, widely used in country and western music, get around the problem by means of a string-tension-control mechanism that allows the player to change the intervals between the strings on the fly. (That's what the pedals are for.)

A lot of builders with an interest in alternative tunings use slides with their string instruments because of the freedom of pitch slides offer. A common approach is to make an instrument with the neck marked off beneath the strings to show the stopping locations for various intervals and scales. You can get quite elaborate with this, indicating different scale patterns and interval types in different colors, and creating in the cumulative effect quite a work of art. The late Ivor Darreg, a San Diego builder and intonational theorist, specialized in multi-sided board zithers (electrically amplified) with banks of strings on each side, all colorfully marked off for different scale types.

Overtone Selection

You can also draw different pitches from a single string by selectively bringing out different overtones. Since strings behave harmonically, this yields a coherent set of scale relationships as you move on up the series. But how can you get one overtone to sound without all the others?

The trick, well known to string players, is to pluck or bow the string while using the other hand to touch it lightly at a nodal point for the overtone that you wish to bring out. This immobilizes the lower modes of vibration that would normally be active at that point, while still allowing the higher mode having a node there to come through almost like a new fundamental. You can enhance the effect by plucking at or near an antinode for the same mode (Figure 9-21).

Harmonic tones are often used as a special effect on conventional instruments. There are relatively few string instruments made to play exclusively in harmonics. One such is the trumpet marine, the unlikely string instrument mentioned earlier for its unusual buzzing bridge. While trumpet marines had but one or two strings, some contemporary harmonic instruments have many. They fill the gaps in the

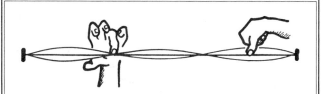

FIGURE 9-21: Isolating string harmonics: touch at a node and pluck near an antinode of the desired mode of vibration.

lower part of the series where the pitches are widely spaced, and also invite attractive sweeping effects across the strings. One of the most extraordinary harmonic instruments — both in conception and in sound — is the harmonics guitar with center bridge described in Sidebar 2-1.

You can get clearer, more accurately tuned harmonics and a more complete range (extending farther up into the series) working with relatively long, thin strings.

Tension Control

It is very difficult to control string pitch accurately through tension variation. A seemingly small change in the position of whatever it is that tugs on the string can produce a very large change in pitch, and it is hard to demarcate the range of motion with any accuracy. Most existing tension-controlled string instruments are pretty wobbly in pitch, and prone to a ubiquitous glissando that becomes tiresome.

Pedal steel guitar is perhaps the most highly developed tension chordophone. Several in the family of Indian folk instruments known as *ektars* employ the idea, as does the Vietnamese *dan bau*. The American washtub bass is another example. There are few other tension-controlled strings with any broad currency, but a number of experimental builders have explored the idea in various forms.

Tension variation may also be used as a subsidiary pitch-control mechanism on string instruments having other primary means of pitch control. An example of this is string bending during playing, which increases tension on the string and raises the pitch. Blues guitarists do this; so do players of a wide array of eastern instruments, both bowed and plucked. The "whammy bar" on many electric guitars is perhaps the most familiar mechanical subsidiary pitch-control mechanism.

TUNINGS AND STRING LAYOUTS

We spoke about tunings and pitch layouts in Chapter 3. At this point I will add a few considerations as they relate specifically to chordophones.

There is a reason why the open strings on a violin are normally tuned a fifth apart, while those on a string bass are a fourth apart. On lutes in general, the tunings of the open strings reflect the interval one can most conveniently finger on one string before moving to the next. On the short neck of the violin it is easy to cover a fifth in the first position, and then move to the next string to continue the scale. With the bass, the longer string scale means that greater reaches are involved in the fingerings, so the interval to be covered between strings is made smaller.

These conventions make a lot of sense, but you can also have fun with *scordatura*. Scordatura is the term used for unorthodox tunings of the intervals between the strings, and the fun comes because unorthodox tunings lead to new musical patterns that would be unlikely to arise in the standard tuning. The tuning configuration that you choose goes a long way toward establishing what sort of music comes most naturally to the instrument.

On harps and zithers, it seems unlikely that the strings should ever be arrayed in any pattern other than an ascending scale, but as we saw earlier with the kora, more imaginative

patterns can be musically fruitful. It has long been a fantasy of mine to make a big zither with many, many strings, laid out in separate sub-groups with varying numbers of strings. There would be movable bridges available to shove under the strings, making it possible to alter lengths to make all kinds of tunings feasible within the different groups. I would set some string groups to chordal sets, and others to scale or melodic sets, none of them necessarily in ascending order. There would be melodic sequences to be effortlessly brushed at any time, and some quasi-melodic, perhaps highly dissonant clusters. I would expect to move the bridges around and alter the tunings frequently, either for exploratory purposes or to provide the vocabulary for a particular piece or musical style. Why am I telling you this particular fantasy? To convey, in fairy tale form, a certain sense of the effect of tuning and layout in many-stringed instruments, and the role these factors have in creating an instrument's musical vocabulary.

A related matter: many string instruments use pairs of strings, or groupings of three, spaced so closely that they are naturally played together as one. The idea is to increase volume and enrich the tone emanating from a single pluck. Frequently with double or triple courses (as such multiple-string arrangements are called) all the strings of each course are tuned to the same pitch, as in pianos and mandolins. Sometimes one is tuned an octave above another, as with the lower four double courses of 12-string guitars.

A more potent approach was advanced by the irrepressible Ivor Darreg. He set as many as six or eight strings in a single course, tuned to relationships derived from traditional organ registrations. For certain stops on a big church organ, when you press down a single key, you get many pipes sounding not only the pitch normally associated with the key, but a number of additional pitches based in the main tone's overtone series. The result, with a well-designed registration, is a terrifically grand composite tone, sounding clear and unified in pitch with little sense that this is in reality several different tones. Darreg's Megalyra instruments, with similar registrations but in strings, possess the same grandeur.

UNORTHODOXIES

To close this chapter, let me describe a few musically interesting unorthodox string types.

Coiled Springs

Most people are familiar with some of the acoustic properties of springs, because most people have at one time or another sproinged a stretched spring and enjoyed the highly reverberant sound. A long, not-too-thick coiled spring can be set up to function much like any other musical string. Spring-strings concentrate high mass in a short length with relatively little rigidity. Their volume tends to be low, because their stretchiness prevents them from driving soundboards forcefully. But, being made of steel, they can work with electromagnetic pickups or contact microphones. Some spring-strings yield a recognizable pitch, but more often the fundamental for stretched springs of any size is subsonic. Springs also manifest audible longitudinal modes quite prominently. The composite sound quality is highly inharmonic and noisy, but innately interesting.

Ribbon-strings

Another unorthodox string type is flat, ribbon-shaped strings. Metal strapping material, magnetic recording tape, flat rubber bands and many other ribbon-like materials will behave as musical strings when stretched taut between two points. Their shape alters vibrating behavior in that they are not uniformly free to flex in all directions. It would appear that they should vibrate harmonically in the direction they are free to vibrate. But, for various reasons, inharmonic overtones and dual fundamentals sometimes appear, especially with shorter lengths of rigid materials like metal banding.

Ribbon strings with their wide flat surface have greater wind resistance. How much this inhibits vibration is difficult to estimate. But it has the positive effect of allowing the vibrating string to move more air by itself, making it possible to have a soundboard-less string instrument, albeit a quiet one. And, conversely, ribbon strings are also far more responsive to air currents, making all kinds of wind-activated string instruments more feasible.

Idiochords

An idiochord is an instrument in which the string is actually part of the body of the instrument, as with, for example, a strip of fiber raised from the surface of a length of bamboo or raffia stalk, but left attached at the two ends (Figure 9-22). Two small slivers of wood or bamboo are wedged under the lifted fibers and shoved toward the ends, in this way both raising the strip of fiber and tightening it. The end of the bamboo section may be wrapped with twine or wire to prevent the raised strip from running to the end and disconnecting entirely. The strip of fiber thus raised and tensioned functions as a string, while the hollow body of the stalk serves as a resonator.

Instruments built upon this principle exist in many parts of the world. A common elaboration is to bind several small idiochord zithers together to form what is called a raft zither. The tone of a well made instrument, while never very loud, can be clear and string-like, with well defined pitch. The thickness and shape of the fiber string are important determinants of tone quality. Thick strings, being more rigid, will produce a more inharmonic, percussive and short-sustaining

FIGURE 9-22: Idiochord zither. This particular instrument is a Bamboolin, by the Jamaican maker Lascelles Brown, following a design by his father Jonathan Brown.

tone. Thin strings will produce something closer to a familiar string tone. (You may be surprised at how thin you can trim the fiber before it becomes too weak.) Fiber strings which are rectangular in cross section, as opposed to square or round, will produce a dual fundamental. The direction of pluck will determine which of the two tones dominates. The wider and flatter the string, the greater will be the interval between the two fundamentals. For many purposes the dual fundamental will be considered a flaw, yet the effect is attractive in its way. You can cultivate it if you wish, tuning the interval by modifying the string's cross-sectional shape.

Strings with Deliberately Irregular Distribution of Mass

I described earlier how the tuning of the harmonic overtones in strings depends upon the string being uniformly cylindrical over its vibrating length, so that the mass is evenly distributed. Knowing this, you can create strings with highly irregular overtones, which translate into unique and exotic tone qualities, by deliberately offsetting the distribution of mass along the string. There are several easy ways to do this to a conventional string. The most common is by the addition of weights, as John Cage did in his famous prepared piano experiments. The weights can be nuts and bolts screwed on tight, or drops of solder or glue, or alligator clips, or whatever else you can make stick. Another simple technique is to tie a heavy multiple knot in the string. And another is to start with an overwound string with a steel wire core, and remove the overwinding from a portion of the string's length, creating a string with two segments of differing linear density.

The tone qualities you can get this way are outrageous. Especially effective, in a bizarre sort of way, are such strings played over a fretted neck — something Cage didn't have the opportunity to try with the prepared pianos.

Conjoined String Systems

Imagine a string which, instead of having both ends attached to fixed anchors, has one end attached to the mid-point of another stretched string. What would this configuration sound like when plucked? How would the strings affect one another's patterns of vibration; how would the two behave together acoustically? Taking the question further, how would a complex system of several conjoined strings behave?

The results turn out to be quite interesting — unwieldy

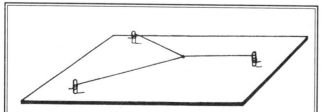

FIGURE 9-23: A three-string system, which can be formed by joining one string to a midpoint of another longer one and tightening it so as to pull the longer one into two angled segments.

Luigi Russolo, an artist and thinker identified with the Italian Futurist movement, conceived and built a number of remarkable instruments in the years between 1913 and 1921. The instruments were designed to realize Russolo's ideas concerning the creation of an art of noise, which he outlined in his work L'arte dei rumori. His conception of noise instruments incorporated the possibility of recognizable pitch within the context of highly irregular, inharmonic — in short, noisy — sounds. One recording of his instruments survives, but none of the instruments themselves survive. Information on their construction is available, with varying degrees of detail for different instruments, and reconstructions of some have been done in Europe and the U.S.

Most of them followed similar principles. A single main string was fixed at one end, and attached at the other to the middle of a membrane radiator mounted on a drum. The drum led directly to a large speaker horn, thus creating a membrane & horn arrangement not unlike a giant version of the Stroh Violin described in Chapter 8. Apparently the membranes on different instruments were treated with different substances to bring out different timbral qualities. The string was sounded by a rotating wheel, hurdy-gurdy-style. In some cases the wheel was rosined, for a stick-slip vibration, and in others it was notched or toothed, with the particular notching patterns eliciting different sounds. String pitch was controlled either by a tension lever or by a lever which controlled a heavy movable tangent. This entire arrangement was enclosed in a box, with only the large horn, the pitch lever, and the wheel-turning crank protruding outside and giving viewers something to wonder about.

---

in may ways, but intriguing, and sometimes quite beautiful. The plucked tone is generally a blend of many discernible pitches arrayed in nonharmonic relationships, a little like a large bell or gong. But unlike metal percussion, conjoined string systems are manipulable. By altering string lengths and tensions you can modulate the sound both timbrally and melodically.

The system described above, with the end of one string tied to the mid-point of another, functions as a system of three strings joined at the middle. The end-tied string pulls the other into an angle at the connection point, and the two resulting half-strings become quasi-independent (see Figure 9-23). This is the simplest of the many possible multiple-string configurations.

Conjoined string systems are hard to tune, because altering either the length or tension of any one segment affects some, but not others, among the several pitches that make up the composite tone. The interactions are multifaceted and complex. Yet a bit of noodling around is sure to yield any number of chance tunings of beauty or interest. You can create extraordinary effects by using a slide to play melodically on one of the string segments. This creates a mix of drone tones and changing harmonies of a sort no composer would ever dream up.

The peculiar tonal relationships of a single set of conjoined strings, present to some degree in every note played, grow tiresome before long. So it is worthwhile to create instruments having several differently tuned conjoined string sets.

Chapter Ten

SPECIAL EFFECTS

We now have studied the four primary acoustic instrument types. In this chapter we will look at tricks you can use to modify the sound of an instrument to create a special effect or tone quality. We will talk about ways to take simple sounds and make them more complex, in order to make them subjectively richer, or warmer, or spicier, or edgier, or more rhythmic and impulsive. This chapter is not oriented to any particular instrument type; many of the ideas presented here apply across the board to several types. We begin with —

CHORUSING AND BEATING EFFECTS

In Chapter 2 I discussed how, when two tones of close but not identical frequency sound together, interference patterns arise which the listener hears as a wavering of amplitude, called beating. You can hear this effect in piano notes for which the three strings are not exactly in tune, or in imperfectly tuned 12-string guitars or mandolins, with their double string courses. Some slight detuning is not necessarily bad with these instruments, as it does subjectively create a slightly fuller sound. But it is not part of the accepted style, and the intent of the person who does the tuning is usually to get the strings precisely in tune. On the other hand, in gamelan orchestras in the island of Bali, the makers create the effect deliberately, building the metallophones in detuned pairs, to be played in unison. The result has been described as a "shimmering" effect. Chorusing effects are especially effective with sustaining wind instruments. Many old-time harmoniums have stops,

such as the one lovingly called "Vox Humana," that bring two banks of reeds into play. Two separate reeds, nominally tuned to the same note, sound for each key that is depressed. The two are never really in tune, and the resulting slow beating is quite pronounced. Accordions, all but the smallest and humblest of them, do the same. One of my favorite sounds in the world is the highly irregular beating of a single melody line played on an old, poorly tuned accordion.

You can create the same effect in any instrument by using pairs of sounding elements. The closer the two tones are in pitch, the slower will be their beating. This means that you can control their beat rate by their relative tuning. It also means that you can create a sound with a continually varying beat rate by having their pitch differential vary slightly through time. This creates an attractive effect, one that is subjectively more natural sounding than beating at a steady rate. Electronic "chorusing" effects work this way, mixing the original sound with a waveringly detuned version of itself.

Double wind instruments, such as double fipple flutes or double ocarinas, have arisen in many parts of the world (see Figure 10-1). There is always a temptation to play polyphonic music with these instruments, but the loveliest sounds from them may come when you play the pair in unison, creating a single melody enriched by the two voices. Given the sensitive nature of wind instruments, the two voices are never quite precisely in tune, and the degree of detuning inevitably varies from note to note. The shifting beat patterns can be beautiful, especially with ocarinas in the lower ranges. I have made a

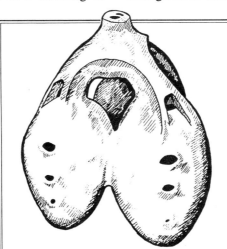

FIGURE 10-1: A triple ocarina of clay, made by Sharon Rowell. When you play the same melody on two of the chambers (not difficult to do), a chorusing effect deriving from everchanging beat rates between the two chambers creates a richer and warmer tone than that of a single ocarina.

double slide whistle in which both whistles are played as one, in near but imperfect unison, for a very distinctive sound.

You can get the same effect with strings (though it is less pronounced) by plucking while holding a steel slide at the mid-point of the vibrating length, and moving the slide slightly back and forth along the string. This causes the vibrating string segment on one side to wobble up and down in pitch as the opposite segment wobbles down and up. If you try this with something like a guitar, be sure to pluck on the side of the string away from the soundboard. (If you pluck on the soundboard side, the tone from the non-soundboard side will be too quiet to contribute to the effect.)

REVERBERATION & SYMPATHETIC VIBRATION

"Reverberation" refers to the lingering of a sound in the room after its original driving source has ceased sounding. Similar effects can be built into musical instruments themselves, independent of room characteristics. Many instruments are inherently reverberant. For instance, a harp's strings tend to pick up vibrations from one another, ring along with one another, and often continue to sound even after the original vibrating string has ceased. Other instruments have reverberant qualities due to the nature of their radiators and resonators.

For some instruments you may want to introduce more reverberation. The trick in doing this is to find some vibrating medium that will readily pick up the sound from the initial vibrator and vibrate in sympathy at the same frequencies. Several materials do this reasonably well.

Strings

Strings are an old favorite. Many instrument types, both Western and Eastern, employ extra strings intended only for sympathetic vibration. Sympathetic strings can work with instruments whose primary vibrating elements are strings, as well as idiophones of many sorts.

The most common approach has been to attach a relatively small number of strings, deliberately tuned for reverberation at specific pitches. This is done on the sitar, the European Viola d'Amour, and many others. Alternatively, you can attach a large number of strings which are not carefully tuned, under the assumption (justified by experience) that with enough randomly tuned strings, virtually any note you play will find a resonance in one or more of the strings. This latter approach is more work initially (more strings to be put on) and less work later (no careful tuning needed). It yields a satisfying wash of reverberance, with particularly fine, well defined high frequencies. The instrument called Prongs and Echoes, described in Sidebar 10-1, illustrates the idea in practice.

People sometimes use a piano with the dampers lifted for the same effect. Someone once told me how he had sat in a practice room playing trumpet, completely mystified when he seemed to hear someone in another nearby practice room also playing trumpet, and echoing his every note with uncanny accuracy. He was mystified, that is, until he realized that he had his foot on the damper pedal of the practice room's piano, and the ghost trumpeter was in fact the strings of the instrument right in front of him.

Springs

Coil springs make excellent reverberation devices, because a single spring can pick up and resonate a broad range of frequencies (in contrast to an individual string, which is quite specific in what frequencies it will resonate). This means that you can use one, two, or three springs, without any special tuning, for reverberation over the entire sounding range, where you would have had to use many strings. Their tone quality is not as good as strings, though. Their frequency biases tend to make for a recognizably "springy" sound.

The ideal spring is a long, thin, lightweight coil spring. It can be attached to the sounding body much like a string, under light tension. Like sympathetic strings, the spring may also provide an additional sound source in its own right.

Plates

Large, flexible pieces of sheet metal which are free to vibrate will also add a generous wash of reverb if given the chance. You get this effect, like it or not, any time you use a suspended or balloon-mounted stainless steel sheet as an instrument's primary sound radiator. The effect is more outrageous than subtle. Rigidly held metal sheets are less effective.

Air Chambers

Air-chamber resonance is effective as a reverberation device only at large scale — like room-size. Rather than building a room onto your musical instrument, it is easier to carry your instrument into an existing room with good reverberant qualities.

SHIFTING RESONANCE EFFECTS

We discussed shifting resonance effects in Chapter 8, "Resonators and Radiators," but because they create such unusual results, I want at least to mention them here. You can produce these effects only on instruments for which the driver and resonator/radiator are separate elements, such as strings and certain idiophones.

The idea is this: Many sound resonators and radiators have distinct frequency preferences, meaning that they respond to a greater or lesser degree depending on the frequency of the input from the driver. If these preferences are not fixed, but shift as the instrument is played, the sound takes on an iridescent quality, as different overtones within the original signal are emphasized from moment to moment. There are several ways to create shifting resonance effects, including the use of water-filled resonators and flexible sheet metal resonators. Both of these are discussed in Chapter 8.

You can also devise shifting resonance effects with air-chamber resonators. The best-known example of this is in vibraphones. Below each vibraphone bar is a tuned air-resonator tube. Between the bar and tube is a rotating baffle, driven on a spindle by a quiet motor. When the baffle is in a horizontal position it blocks any coupling between the bar and tube, and eliminates any resonance response from the tube. When it is in a vertical position, there is no blocking and full resonance is restored. The result is that as the baffle rotates, the tube resonance comes and goes, creating an oscillation in volume and tone quality.

In a related effect, many organs, including both pipe organs and small reed organs (harmoniums), use variable baffles, alternately blocking the soundwaves near the source or letting them pass freely into the room. The baffles are intended primarily as volume-control mechanisms, and on some of instruments the baffle position is controlled by a spring-loaded knee lever. Inevitably, the position of the baffle affects tone quality as well as volume. In addition to the intended crescendos and swells, the baffle mechanism can, if the baffle is not too large and unwieldy, be used to create wavering tremolos and similar effects.

RATTLES

By "rattles" I refer to any small thing that is loosely attached to a vibrating part of an instrument, so that it bounces against the vibrating body and adds its contact sounds to the

---

<u>Sidebar 10-1</u>　　　　　　　　　　PRONGS AND ECHOES

Here is an instrument designed to show off the reverberant effect of sympathetic strings. *Prongs and Echoes* (as I have called it) has a lot of strings, but the player doesn't play them. Instead, the strings are there to pick up and reverberate vibrations from another primary sound source. For that purpose, P&E has primary vibrators with the shortest, sharpest, most abrupt sound envelope I could come up with. The extremely short spring steel rods, mounted kalimba-style, create a sound that happens and is gone immediately, leaving behind the lingering wash of reverberant strings.

To make the Prongs & Echoes in keeping with the drawings shown here, you will need:

5 feet of hardwood board, 3/8" x 2¼" or thereabouts.

1/8" plywood or other suitable lightweight soundboard wood — two pieces of 12" x 14".

9" of hardwood 3/4" half-round.

Music wire in two or three small gauges (say, between #0 at .009" and #6 at .016") for a total of about 30'.

16 small tuning pins (zither pins).

16 small roundhead wood screws.

15 #8 x 32, 1/2"-long roundhead machine screws.

20" of metal rod or wire about 1/16" in diameter.

Spring tempered steel rod (also called "music wire") in four diameters: .025" (=.64mm); .032" (.81mm); .039" (.99mm);and .047" (= 1.19mm); one foot of each. If you can't get these exact sizes, get the nearest available. Use straight rods available in 3-foot lengths from hobby shops rather than the longer coils sold as musical instruments strings.

Construction Procedure: The drawings on the following page, augmented by your own construction sense, will give the basic information you'll need to make the instrument. The slowest and most difficult process will be cutting, bending, mounting and tuning the prongs. Figure D shows the basic mounting system. After pre-drilling the holes in the bridge, you can either use a tap to pre-cut the threads for the #8 screws, or you can simply screw the screws in directly, forcing the threads as you go, as you mount each prong. As part of the mounting and tuning process each prong will have to be cut to its total length. This length will typically be a little less than half the actual sounding length; precise measurement is not required, and after doing the first few you'll be able to estimate as you go. Be sure to clean up the cut ends at a file or grinder, since spring steel can leave wickedly sharp and jagged ends. After cutting, each prong will have to be bent to shape as shown in the figure. There is room on the bridge for two octaves with seven pitches per octave. The lowest note will be D_4, with a prong of .047" wire at a sounding length of approximately $1^5/_{16}$". The top will be D_6 with a prong of .025" wire, sounding length approximately 7/16". Within that range, you can tune as you wish. With these very short prongs, the tuning is exacting and difficult. The following chart indicates which wire sizes to use where.

Prong #	Pitches	Wire Diameter
1 - 3	$D_4 - F_4$	.047"
4 - 6	$G_4 - B_4$	.039"
7 - 11	$C_5 - G_5$	.032"
12 - 15	$A_5 - D_6$	.025"

Add the strings after the prongs. Run each string from its tuning peg, over the metal bridge at the edge of the soundboard, across the half-round bridge (between the prongs and screws wherever it falls), across the opposite metal bridge, and down to the corresponding anchoring screw. You can put any of the wire gauges anywhere on the instrument. The string tunings are completely random; just adjust each string to reasonably high tension. When all the strings are brought up to tension, the instrument is complete.

To play the instrument, pluck the prongs, kalimba style. Listen for the reverberation of the strings. I have found this instrument to work very well in ensemble, with a tone that cuts through easily, yet never crowds the mix. Use it to double melody lines played on other instruments for added punch and definition.

Needless to say, you needn't follow this plan to the letter in making the instrument. You can add more prongs to extend the range up or down a bit, or to fill in the missing chromatics. The 32 randomly tuned strings suggested here are about the minimum needed for good reverberation. In a similar instrument I built with 48 strings over a greater range of lengths, the overall reverberant tone quality is noticeably richer. A larger soundboard (but not a stiffer one) would also enrich the tone.

PRONGS & ECHOES (Drawings for Sidebar 10-1)

16 SCREWS, SPACED $^{15}/_{32}$" APART ON CENTER, STARTING 2½" FROM EACH END.

15 HOLES, SPACED ½" APART, STARTING 1" FROM EACH END, $^{9}/_{64}$" IN DIAMETER. (HOLES DRILLED OFF VERTICAL; SEE Ⓓ)

Ⓐ

Ⓑ

END BRIDGES STRAIGHT $^{1}/_{16}$" WIRE

MAIN BRIDGE ¾" HARDWOOD HALF-ROUND

3" d.

14"

6½"

9"

3"

16 ZITHER PINS

12"

Ⓒ

PRONG (RIGID MUSIC WIRE)

½" x #8 MACHINE SCREW

15°

$^{1}/_{8}$" PRE-DRILLED HOLE (FOR #8 SIZED SCREWS)

Ⓓ

15°

16 HOLES, SIZED $^{3}/_{16}$" (FOR STANDARD ZITHER PINS), SPACED $^{15}/_{32}$" APART ON CENTER, STARTING 2½" FROM EACH END.

Ⓔ

A. Prongs and Echoes, top view.

B. Exploded view showing box construction.

C. The lower end, showing the tuning pin hole spacing. The spacing for the wood screws at the upper end is identical.

D. Side and top views of the prong mounting system.

E. The finished instrument.

instrument's overall sound. But "rattles" may not really be the right word here, since it makes one think of rattly sounds. Well designed rattles can actually add a wonderfully light, delicate edge to an instrument's tone.

You can attach a rattle to any solid vibrating body, including strings, bars, tines, bells, and gongs, as well as secondary vibrators like soundboards. The effect of a well made rattle at its best sounds as an integral part of the overall timbre, perhaps highlighting selected upper partials. The effect can also add to the impression of loudness.

A well functioning rattle's contribution to an instrument's timbral mix ideally takes the form of harmonic overtones, even in cases where the initial vibrator's mix is itself non-harmonic. The reason this is possible has to do with the restricted nature of rattling motions. The rattle's own vibrating pattern at the initial vibrator's fundamental frequency is "clipped" due to its confined movement, producing not a sine wave, but something closer to a square-wave pattern of vibration. The ear interprets this vibrating pattern as possessing harmonics.

Rattles on Strings

For a rattle to work well, there should be an appropriate balance between the mass of the rattling object and the strength and amplitude of the vibration of the initial vibrator at the point where the rattle is attached. A string, as an initial vibrator, is very light. The rattling object must be considerably lighter if its mass rests on the string. The ideal place for a string rattle is at a point near enough one end that the impedance is sufficiently high to drive the rattle, but not so near that the amplitude is too small to do the job. Typically (depending on the weight of the rattle relative to that of the string), you can find a good point at about 2% - 4% of the total string length — for a guitar string, for instance, between about 5/8" and 1" from the end.

There are probably many ways to attach a string rattle that will stay put near that ideal location; one practical approach appears in Figure 10-2A. The rattle shown here, made of very light gauge metal wire, adds a glittery effect to the string tone. Try attaching it to just the one or two highest strings of a many-stringed fretted instrument, to let melodies played on those strings stand out finely limned against the accompanying strings.

Another way to add a harmonic-enhancing rattle to string tone is through the use of buzzing bridges. Look back to the section on bridges in Chapter 9, "Chordophones," for details on these.

Rattles on Kalimba Tines

Some kalimbas have shells or bottle caps loosely tacked or tied to their sides or bodies. I have also found it to be effective to attach lightweight rattles directly to the tines themselves. As with strings, rattles on tines add a delicate silver lining to the tone. Kalimba tines are generally higher in impedance than strings, so they drive the rattles more effectively. This makes the business of positioning and fine tuning of relative masses less exacting. A kalimba tine rattle design, very similar to that suggested for strings, appears in Figure 10-2B.

Rattles on Free Bars

As with strings and tines, a rattle attached directly to a marimba bar can add a harmonic edge to the tone. (This is despite the fact that the bars and tines themselves have non-harmonic overtones, as discussed above.) Free-bar rattles also create an impression of greater loudness. They work well on both wooden and metal bars. Vibrating bars are generally massive enough that the weight of any reasonably small rattle will not noticeably affect their vibration, so the rattle can be attached wherever the amplitude is sufficient.

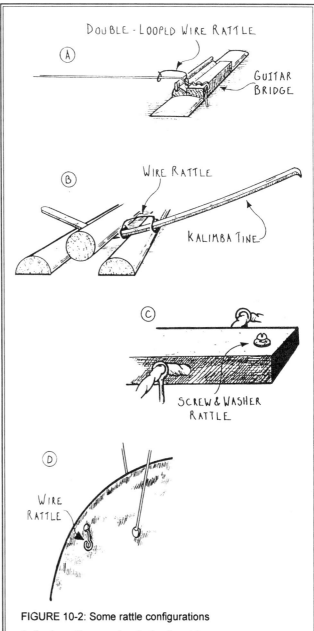

FIGURE 10-2: Some rattle configurations

A. A wire rattle on a classical guitar string.

B. A wire rattle on a kalimba tine.

C. A washer rattle on a marimba bar. The screw is screwed not quite all the way down over the washer, leaving room for rattling. You can fine-tune the rattle by adjusting the screw. An eighth turn can make the difference between a coarse, noisy sound, a fine, harmonic sound, or no rattle tone at all.

D. Wire rattle on a gong. Loops at the ends of the wire prevent it from jumping out.

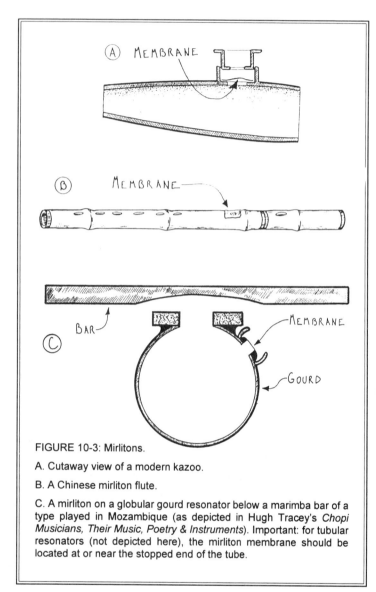

FIGURE 10-3: Mirlitons.

A. Cutaway view of a modern kazoo.

B. A Chinese mirliton flute.

C. A mirliton on a globular gourd resonator below a marimba bar of a type played in Mozambique (as depicted in Hugh Tracey's *Chopi Musicians, Their Music, Poetry & Instruments*). Important: for tubular resonators (not depicted here), the mirliton membrane should be located at or near the stopped end of the tube.

MIRLITONS

Think of a lightweight, non-rigid diaphragm in close proximity to a sound source. Such a diaphragm will tend to vibrate in sympathy with the sound source. If it simply reproduces the original pattern of vibration, its audible effect will be negligible. But sometimes, something about the diaphragm's anatomy or the way it is mounted will cause it to reproduce the original fundamental frequency with drastically altered timbral characteristics. Then the sound of even a very small diaphragm can make a big difference in the composite acoustic effect.

Instruments which use small attached membranes like this to deliberately alter an original sound are called *mirlitons*. The effect is not unlike that of a well designed rattle, injecting a distinct edge into the tone. The added edge may be coarse and noisy, or it may be thin, fine, and harmonic. And mirlitons are the perfect complement to rattles: while rattles work specifically on solid vibrating bodies, mirlitons work specifically with air resonances. The mirlitons most familiar in the contemporary western world are kazoos, which are made to modify the sound of the human voice (Figure 10-3A). But instrumental (non-vocal) mirlitons can be equally effective.

Mirlitons appear to produce their effect in either or both of two ways: 1) As the air causes it to oscillate, the membrane rattles against something. That something can be some hard thing in the middle of its path, or it can be the edges of its mounting. The resulting contact may make some noise, but more importantly it disrupts the membrane's vibration pattern. This creates the kind of clipping described earlier for rattles, adding a generous dose of high harmonics to the sound. 2) The membrane is unstretched and a little loose, so that instead of oscillating smoothly as a stretched membrane would, it flaps back and forth. Or it has a mildly convex or concave shape. When a threshold air pressure is applied, it buckles from one side to the other. The result once again is a clipped movement producing high harmonics.

Typical mirliton design involves a small membrane-covered hole somewhere along the body of an air chamber or air column. The hole may be anywhere from a quarter-inch in diameter to two or three times that. The membrane can be made of any light, thin material. Goldbeater's skin (which is a very fine, treated animal membrane), is one traditional source; various papers or fine parchments are another. Plastic wrap, cellophane, plastic grocery bags, onion skin, tin foil, and a number of more exotic materials have been used as well, with a preference for those that are thin, crisp, and reasonably water-resistant.

In mirliton flutes of the *ti-tzu* family in China (Figure 10-3B), the mirliton tone is not coarse like that of a kazoo, but extremely fine, lending a reed-like brilliance and a substantial increase in loudness. Mirlitons on air-column wind instruments such as this present special design problems. Because the membrane-covered hole must be along a tube which is at the same time determining the vibrating length and pitch of the instrument, the seal around the

Attaching directly to the surface of the bar near one end usually works well. Figure 10-2C shows a free-bar rattle design.

As mentioned briefly in Chapter 4, "Idiophones," you can create a rather different rattle sound — very raunchy — using pieces of paper attached near the end of the bar and overhanging the end. The paper adds some sound-radiating surface and also rattles against the bar end. If you are into Hendrix, you might like the effect. Otherwise you might hate it.

Rattles on Cymbals, Bells and Gongs

There is a kind of cymbal called a sizzle cymbal which has rivets passing loosely through holes around the rim. The thing really does sizzle. For bells and gongs too, you can used rivets or the equivalent, or even just one or more pieces of bent wire, running through a hole in the bell or gong (see Figure 10-2D). Depending on the original vibrating body, you might get an unpitched hiss, or you might get the kind of harmonic edge to a well defined pitch that we saw with rattles on other sound sources. Bells and gongs generally have the large mass and high impedance necessary to drive a rattle easily, but they don't always have great amplitude. Accordingly, rattles do best attached wherever amplitude is large.

membrane must be air-tight. Otherwise it will act just like a leaky pad on an orchestral flute. Part of the maker's art is to somehow make the diaphragm loose enough to buzz, yet firm enough not to disrupt the vibrating air column. This is immaterial with kazoos, where the pitch is determined by the singing voice, and the tube's length and degree of leakiness are unimportant.

Mirliton marimbas appear in central and southern Africa and in Central America. The bars have air resonators below, and mirliton membranes are set over holes in the resonators (see Figure 10-3C). Even at this remove from the initial vibrator, the mirlitons add the characteristic edge of high harmonics and a noticeable increase in loudness to the tone.

DAMPERS

Deliberately damped tones from sound sources that are normally allowed to ring can be appealing. The nicest effects seem to come about in connection with plucked strings. With just the right amount of damping the sound acquires a percussive quality, yet retains its sense of pitch. Some guitarists learn to achieve the effect by lightly touching the strings near the bridge with the fleshy side of the hand even as they pluck. An easier way is with a piece of foam rubber wedged between or beneath an instrument's strings. Normally the foam should be adjacent to the bridge — if it is closer to mid-string, the damping will be too much, and the tone reduces to a dull thud. On the other hand, a very light damper at selected mid-string regions can have the interesting effect of inhibiting lower harmonics more than higher harmonics having a node in the vicinity of the damper. This alters the relative prominence of the components in the overtone make-up, altering the tone quality in interesting ways. When the mid-string damper is very light and somewhat spread out, it may allow for fretting the strings within a limited range without losing the effect.

MOVING SOUND SOURCES AND DIRECTIONAL EFFECTS

The ears' directional sense, which allows one to recognize where sounds are coming from, is highly developed. Yet it is not often exploited in sound arts, even though the directional dimension within a sound composition adds depth and clarity. Near the end of Chapter 1, "Musical Sound Perception," I discussed some of the factors affecting directional perception.

There are several ways you can bring directionality into play as part of the aesthetic effect of instruments you design. One is simply to play in a highly reverberant room, where wall reflections envelop the listener from all sides. Another is to spread point-sound sources, each carrying different sounds, far apart. This is fairly easy to do with electronics where you can simply run wires to remote speakers. Some performers and composers have done wonderful work along these lines. Another use of directionality is to place several performers, each with their own instruments, at diverse points around a listening space. *Hocketing* is the technique, used by bell choirs, vocal groups, panpipe ensembles and others in diverse parts of the world, in which several players, each responsible for certain pitches and not others, work together in series to create melody. It is a great pleasure in its melodic-spatial effect as well as in its sense of social interlocking.

The German-American builder Trimpin has created extraordinary pieces involving computer-controlled, electromechanically played sound sources around the periphery of a room. The sound sources may be conventional instruments, new instruments of Trimpin's devising, or everyday noise objects, played by various mechanisms driven by solenoids under the command of a remote computer. The compositions often involve rapid, exquisitely timed sequences of events from the different points in the room, and the effect is unparalleled.

Within limits it is possible to build acoustic instruments with wide-ranging sound sources. Cathedral organs, with their banks of pipes spread across entire walls, are an example. One could also create remote playing mechanisms, or use the kind of highly efficient mechanical sound transmission to remote sound radiators described in Chapter 8, to spread far and wide the points from which an instrument's sounds emerge.

You can also create moving sound sources. Make a swinging trumpet by buzzing your lips into the end of a flexible hose and swinging the hose around your head as you play. Add a mouthpiece and some sort of flared bell at the end for improved tone and playability. You can also make a swinging harp (or bell harp, as it was once called), an instrument that actually achieved some popularity in the late 19th century. It was a zither, typically having sixteen courses of diatonically tuned strings, designed to be played while swinging at arms length. Or use hummers and bullroarers, described in earlier chapters, played by swinging on a cord around the head. And the list goes on.

With moving sound sources, listeners can experience the Doppler effect. The Doppler effect occurs when a sound source moves toward a listener, and the wave fronts coming off its surface are in effect crowded together, resulting in a shorter wavelength and a higher frequency. With a retreating sound source the reverse occurs. A whirled instrument will thus have a slight rise and fall in pitch for most observers as it alternately approaches and retreats.

A couple of other effects come about when sound sources spin rapidly on an axis. Picture a flat disk gong suspended from a single cord and made to spin rapidly as it sounds. The gong radiates its sound most strongly in the directions perpendicular to its flat surface; it does not radiate well to the side. For a listener in a given location, it is louder when it faces the listener; softer when it has turned edge-on at 90 degrees; louder again at 180 degrees, and so on. The listener hears a tremolo. The listener also experiences recurring phase reversals: the vibration coming from the front of the gong is precisely out of phase with that coming from the back. As the gong spins, the listener hears first one then the other. The sounds are identical, but reversed in phase, creating a subtle shifting effect.

Chapter Eleven

A FEW MORE THOUGHTS

I have filled this last chapter with ruminations touching broadly on musical instrument design. These reflections are concerned not so much with how one actually builds instruments as with how one thinks about instruments and their design. Some of these thoughts are practical and prosaic, and others are of no practical value whatsoever, unless you happen to work better against a backdrop of ideas.

First, some considerations of a utilitarian nature for anyone with an instrument-making habit:

There are big instruments, and there are small instruments. Big instruments take up a lot of space. If you persist in making big instruments, you will have storage problems. The closet fills up; the living room fills up; the kitchen fills up; etc. There is no cure for this, but there are a few things you can do for symptomatic relief: 1) Try very hard to build small instruments only. 2) If you have yard space, build instruments of weather-proof materials and keep them outdoors. 3) Make instruments that can be dismantled into storable parts, and reassembled. 4) Rent a warehouse.

One design concept is particularly helpful in making instruments smaller and at the same time more versatile. It is *modularity* (the term used by an advocate of the idea, Bob Phillips). Modular instruments are made with interchangeable components, so that an instrument can be configured for one musical purpose today and, by the removal of some parts and the addition of others kept on hand, configured for another musical purpose tomorrow. Most often this means that the instrument has a generous stock of sounding elements tuned to different pitches, but the instrument is only large enough to hold a subset of them at one time. Modularity has proven especially practical for marimba-type instruments, chimes and the like.

Adjustability is another valuable idea. Musical instruments are delicate devices requiring manufacture to fine tolerances. Because it is not always possible to know in advance the ideal settings for all the interacting parts on a given instrument, it is helpful to be able to adjust crucial settings after the instrument has been assembled, and

throughout its playing life. This applies to many, many facets of instrument design, from the location and height of a string instrument's bridge, to the orientation of the edge in a fipple pipe, to the distance of travel of a clavichord key, to the positioning of a flute pad, and so on indefinitely.

Unfortunately, it usually makes for more work in the construction process to build in adjustability at every turn. Further, adjustable components tend to be inelegant. And in many instances the addition of adjustable mechanisms is simply impractical. The common-sense approach is to try to assess, in an instrument's early design stages, where the tolerances are most sensitive for the proper functioning of the instrument, and then to consider in each case whether it is feasible to build adjustability in there.

A lot of musical instrument design, for those who are not simply reproducing standard instrument types, is imagination work. At the earliest stages in the conceptualization of a new instrument, try not to let yourself get locked into a particular way of thinking about the design. It is not unusual to persist in envisioning the finished instrument in a particular form, all the while remaining inexplicably blind to some slightly different approach which would yield better results. *The simpler the better* is a good rule, and when the simpler and better approach does come to you, you will find yourself saying, "but it's so obvious — why didn't I think of that before?"

In creative instrument making, you must expect to depart from the original plan now and then. Through the process of construction and trial you learn what works and what does not for a particular sound-making mechanism. For that reason, it is valuable to work initially towards the creation of a rough but functional prototype. From the prototype you can work toward more refined realizations of the idea. The best instruments come from makers whose results improve as they work through an idea, and then work through it again, and then work through it again. You can learn things from prototyping and modeling that you cannot learn any other way.

Does it matter what an instrument looks like as long as it sounds good? There is no right or wrong answer to that question, of course, but I will say this: Musical instruments are interesting to look at. People are attracted to them visually. The requirements of acoustic design give rise to intriguing forms, whether or not the maker deliberately makes design choices based upon a visual aesthetic. An instrument which looks beautiful, or even one which looks bizarre, has an appeal that makes people more inclined to listen with open ears. Makers do well to know this, and to cultivate and enjoy the visual aspect of their instruments.

What about names for newly created instruments? It turns out that, for whatever reason, people respond strongly to instrument names, and a good name may play a significant role in drawing interest to a particular instrument. Harry Partch came up with some wonderful ones, and it's worth noting that some of his best-remembered instruments are those with the most memorable names, and not necessarily those that were most important to his music. His *Spoils of War*, *Marimba Eroica*, and *Quadrangularis Reversum* come to mind.

And finally, a word on the question of control in musical instruments and musical sound. Musical instruments are designed to produce sound, and to do so in a fashion that can be controlled by the player. Typically this means that the player decides which pitches should sound when, and for how long. As a secondary matter, the player may also govern volume and, to some degree, timbre. Need this priority be accepted as given? Or could one have musical instruments in which timbre is primary, while pitch selection is secondary? Or, how about instruments in which microtonal pitch inflections are primary, while traditional scale degrees fall by the wayside? For that matter, how about a different concept of control, such that the ideal of the player's mastery over the instrument is replaced by one of creative interaction with the instrument?

The answer of course is that all these things are possible and are sometimes practiced, and sometimes yield beautiful and exciting music. Such music may call for a different sort of listening than the listening that goes with familiar musical styles.

I encourage you to keep a flexible attitude regarding control as you work with the wide variety of possible sources of musical sound. It will be tempting to turn each sound-generating system into a pitch-selection and rhythm-control device — after all, that is what most musical instruments are, and what most instrumental music is composed for. But it may be that to do so is to impoverish the sound. Try to let the instrument and its sound suggest their own music.

Now we have come to the end (but for the appendixes that follow). I hope that these pages have been valuable to you, and will continue to be. To all who put the information in this book to use, may your efforts be fruitful, and may they bring more music to the world.

APPENDICES

TOOLS AND MATERIALS

This appendix contains information on tools and materials that are useful in musical instrument making. A list of supply sources is at the end.

TOOLS

Tools and equipment for instrument making, or any other sort of shop work, may sometimes seem more a barrier than a door-opener. So, let me stress from the start that there is a great deal you can do using a minimum of tools. One of my favorite builders, whose instruments strike me as endlessly creative and enjoyable, works entirely with commonplace materials and just a few simple hand tools. Even for those who later learn to use special materials and advanced shop equipment, the early experience of working with hand tools is a vital one.

Professional makers of particular types of musical instruments use many specialized tools. We will leave those tools to professionals, and won't discuss them here. You can learn more about them from books and periodicals devoted to construction of specific instrument types. For most purposes, the tools most broadly useful in acoustic musical instrument making are the same tools that are standard in general wood and metalworking. They include various sorts of hand saws and/or power saws, sanders, drills and bits, vises, measuring devices, squares, clamps, wrenches, screwdrivers, files and rasps, planes, knives, snips, a radio for distraction, and so forth. Those more serious about metal work may get into welding and soldering equipment. Among special-purpose tools that might come in handy are tubing cutters. These come in various sizes, and allow quicker and cleaner work than hack saws. Very large, powerful bolt cutters can save hack sawing and filing time, and a motorized grinding wheel is also a time saver for certain jobs. Quartz tuners or other tuning equipment (discussed in Sidebar 3-2) and leaklights for wind instruments (discussed in Chapter 6) have a special place in some instrument building shops. For fuller discussions of shop tools, look to any of the widely available books

devoted to the topic.

Please use your tools and materials wisely. Follow safety instructions on tools and product labels; wear face or eye protection even in borderline cases where it doesn't really seem necessary; use a breather mask when doing dusty work or anything involving toxic fumes; and don't use power tools if you are tired or agitated.

Certain materials commonly used in musical instruments are toxic. Experimental instrument builders often use PVC plastic as an inexpensive tubing material. PVC fumes are toxic and carcinogenic, so any operations involving heating, sanding or cutting require a mask and good ventilation. Metal filing, grinding and soldering operations require similar precautions. The dusts from brass and aluminum are poisonous, and stainless steel yields hazardous gases when heated. Solder contains lead. Dusts from many tropical woods are either allergenic or to some degree toxic, as are those of some temperate softwoods such as redwood and cedar.

MATERIALS

This is an overview of some of the most useful among the many materials that can be employed in the making of musical instruments. I will start with a rundown of uses and properties of important raw materials, followed by a review of manufactured items or materials made specifically for musical instruments. Following that is information on a few particularly useful secondary materials. Toward the end of this appendix you will find notes on where to get what, including a list of suppliers for many of the materials discussed.

Woods

Hardwoods work well for marimba bars and tongue drum tops, sound chamber backs and sides, and any application calling for strength, density and durability. Traditionally, various tropical hardwoods, such as rosewood and ebony, have been considered the best woods for musical applications. The preferred tropical woods have greater density than most temperate hardwoods, not to mention richer colors. But with the increasing scarcity of tropical woods, it becomes imperative to consider the alternatives. Temperate hardwoods commonly used in instruments include maple, walnut, and cherry. Osage orange and black locust are two temperate woods comparing well to rosewood in strength and density.

Softwoods work well for soundboards and applications where strength and durability are less essential. The universal standard for soundboards is spruce, prized for its lightness and resilience, although top-quality spruce is getting rare. Some makers are partial to cedar or California redwood. Pine is an inexpensive alternative. Redwood, incidentally, makes surprisingly clear-toned xylophone bars.

Plywood musical instruments have a bad reputation, but plywoods have a place in musical instrument making, given their strength and versatility (not to mention availability and inexpensiveness), especially since musical instrument design so often calls for strong, thin surfaces.

I have always enjoyed working with non-commercial local woods. In my part of the United States we have bay, sometimes called laurel or pepperwood, a beautiful aromatic hardwood, but subject to pest infestation; madrone, a very hard whitish wood that is murder to season up without checking (splitting); tanbark oak, which finishes up very different from other oaks in grain and color; and the list goes on. In your region the list will differ, but is likely to be comparably extensive. Many non-commercial woods are non-commercial not because of problems with the wood itself, but for reasons having to do with the economics of availability, distribution, and demand. If you have the opportunity, it can be fun, rewarding, and sometimes frustrating, to work with such wood. Along the same lines, always keep an eye out for salvageable used wood. The quality of stock cut when the world was younger often exceeds that of anything commercially available today.

Metals

Steel

Steels are blends of iron with small amounts of carbon. They come in several grades, differentiated primarily by their carbon content and degree of work-hardening. For many musical applications, such as music wire, the highest grades of high-carbon, spring-tempered steel yield are often preferred. These are the hardest and strongest steels, with the least internal damping; they generally produce a very bright tone. For a rounder tone and less sustain, use a softer steel or use one of the other metals. Those softer steels are more commonly available — they're the stuff of steel reinforcement rods, metal conduits, threaded rods and household wires you see in hardware stores. For many musical purposes their warmer tone is be preferable. Stainless steel — a steel alloy containing chromium — can be made quite hard and is corrosion resistant, and so is good for outdoor purposes. For corrosion resistance in a softer, less expensive steel, use the commonly available galvanized steel, which is conventional steel with a coating of zinc.

Spring-tempered steel may be hard to find. You can get coils of music wire in a wide range of thicknesses from piano supply houses and some lutherie suppliers. (See Sidebar 9-2 in Chapter 9 for a chart of standard music wire sizes.) You can get 3-foot rods in thicknesses ranging up to a quarter inch, still sold under the name "music wire," at many hobby and crafts shops. You can also look to industrial metals suppliers for further options. As well, you can salvage spring-tempered steel, or only slightly softer tool steels, from a variety of sources: clock springs, Victorola drive springs, spatulas, putty knives, the teeth of long-toothed rakes, hack saw or coping saw blades, hand saw blades and circular saw blades.

Brasses, Bronzes and Copper

Brasses are alloys primarily of copper and zinc; bronzes are copper and tin. They are slightly softer than the hardened steels, with a slightly warmer tone. These metals serve for strings on some instruments, and they are the metals most often used for bells, chimes, and gongs, as well as metallophone bars in many parts of the world. Copper tubings are available in hardware stores; for other forms of copper, and for brasses and bronzes in general, look to metals suppliers and scrap yards. Find telescoping tubing for slides at some hobby shops.

Aluminum

Aluminum is softer still, and so produces the mellowest tone of the metals described here. Yet it can have excellent ring time. Thus it makes lovely chimes or free bars with relatively little clanginess. Look to metals suppliers and scrap yards.

Plastics, Synthetic Rubbers, Styrofoam

As a rule, plastics do not have especially desirable acoustic qualities, but they prove useful now and then. Some of the very dense, highly rigid new synthetics have been favored for making the bodies of electric guitar-type instruments. Plastics can also serve as wind instrument tubes and the like, where the shape, mass and reflectiveness of the material matters, but internal acoustic properties do not. Hard plastics are commonly used for respectably playable but inexpensive student models in woodwind instruments.

Lots of experimental and homemade wind instruments are made of PVC (polyvinyl chloride), for the simple reasons that PVC tubing is functional, inexpensive, fairly workable, and widely available in a range of diameters at hardware stores. On the downside, it is unattractive, doesn't clean up or take finishes well, becomes brittle if exposed to sunlight for long periods, and has toxic qualities mentioned earlier.

ABS (acrylonitrile-butadiene-styrene) plastic, available in tubes and other forms at many hardware stores, is superior to PVC in its internal acoustic properties (greater resilience), workability and appearance.

You will find a few other plastic tubings at the hardware store as well, some of which are softer and more flexible than ABS or PVC. Plexiglass and related plastics are more attractive, but quite a bit more expensive. Plexiglass is available in rods, sheets, blocks and tubing shapes from retail plastics outlets like Taps Plastics, as well as industrial suppliers.

For plastics in shapes not commercially available, consider clear epoxy resins in a two-part liquid form that you can cast in a mold.

Synthetic rubbers are useful as mallet heads and occasionally for other purposes such as padding or damping. We have already spoken of rubber balls, as well as various foam rubbers, and the liquid rubber coating called Plasti-dip, all commonly available. In addition, specialized industrial supply outlets may have liquid rubbers in a two-part mix, made to be poured into molds, or ready-formed in sheets or rods. They come in a graduated range of hardnesses.

Styrofoam is an extraordinarily effective sound-radiation surface material. Styrofoam can be cut with a hack saw or a styrofoam cutter, or you can shape it by sanding. (A styrofoam cutter is nothing more than a heated wire which easily swims through the material. You can purchase one at low cost, or make one using batteries and a stainless steel wire.)

Similar rigid foams are used for insulation in building construction and are available at hardware stores in spray cans or in two-part mixes. With these, you can make molds to fabricate your own styro-shapes.

Glass, Ceramics and Stone

Glass is especially effective used as an initial vibrator in friction instruments. It also makes a nice-sounding marimba bar. Being rigid and brittle, glass tubes work well for wind instruments. It is not particularly effective as a soundboard material. It is fragile and not easily workable, but it can be cut (in straight lines) and, within limits, ground. The most resonant glasses seem to be the high quality quartz glasses, often called crystal, followed by lead glass, then soda-lime glass (the most common type), and, least resonant, Pyrex.

In contrast, the clay from which ceramics are made is infinitely shapable, making it especially valuable for oddly shaped wind instruments. As an initial vibrator, as with marimba bars, chimes, bells and the like, the tone of ceramic is somewhat damped but still appealing. Ceramics have been used for string instrument bodies and even soundboards with acceptable, though not spectacular, results — but this calls for exceptional skills on the part of the maker. There are many different clay formulas and firing techniques which affect the material's resonant qualities.

Instruments using stone as the initial vibrating element are called lithophones. Many different sorts of stone marimbas and chimes have been made, as well as some stone whistles. The resonant qualities of stone vary substantially from one sort to another; most are extremely dull, while some, like travertine marble, and some slates and volcanic rocks, produce a fairly bright tone quality.

Natural Materials

Bamboo and Other Hollow Stalks

Bamboo is an instrument maker's delight. The wood of a good bamboo is hard and strong, yet springy, and the tubular shape suits many musical applications. The tone quality of the wood itself tends to be bright, with clear pitch.

There are several species of bamboo. Of the main families, those of the *Phyllostachys* family produce fine, strong, hard woods in large sizes; the *Arundinaria* family produces good woods in smaller sizes; and the *Bambusa* family generally produces inferior woods. The largest varieties are *Phyllostachys pubescens*, commonly called "Moso," and *Phyllostachys bambusoides,* with stalks reaching maximum diameters of 6" or 7".

Bamboo is very much subject to splitting with changes in humidity. Coat bamboo instruments inside and out with multiple coats of polyurethane or another moisture-proof finish to retard moisture loss and prevent splitting.

Arundo donax, the same cane reed that is used for making woodwind reeds, is also useful for flute making. There are many other light vegetable stalks that are hollow and suitable for making casual flutes and whistles.

You can order cut bamboo in large and small diameters from suppliers listed under "Natural Materials" at the end of this appendix. Smaller diameters are often available at garden supply outlets.

Gourd and Calabash

The word "gourd" refers to a whole family of vine-growing plants, but it is the hard-shell fruit of certain species that interests instrument makers. Gourds have been bred to grow in an endless variety of sizes and shapes, though dried gourds are light and somewhat fragile. The word "calabash" is sometimes used to refer to the same hard-shell fruits, but more properly it refers to the fruit of the calabash tree. Calabashes are roundish in shape, heavier than gourds when dry, and incredibly hard and strong. Gourds and calabashes are ideal for providing sound chambers and radiating surfaces for instruments like strings, kalimbas, and drums. The incredible variety of gourd shapes means that they can also be useful as wind instrument tubes or ocarina bodies.

Calabash trees do not grow in temperate zones, but gourds grow well through most of the world, and it is a great pleasure to grow your own if you have a little earth. To prepare a gourd for musical use, the green gourd must, after harvesting, be hung up to dry for several months. (If you are drying several, make sure they do not touch one another.) Then it can be cut open (where you cut depends upon the final form you want) and the seeds and loose fiber removed. The inside should then be scoured with steel wool to provide a smoother, harder, more reflective inner surface. Gourds can be finished inside and out with wood paints or finishes.

For sources of gourd seeds, as well as information on gourd culture and gourd craft, become a member of the American Gourd Society (P.O. Box 274, Mt. Gilead, OH 43338) and get their newsletter. You can order dried gourds from suppliers listed under "Natural Materials" at the end of this appendix, or from various sources advertising in the American Gourd Society's Newsletter.

Kelp

The seaweed known as giant bull kelp (*mereo cystis* or *macro cystis*) is one of the few materials in which you will find a natural conical bore for wind instruments. The weed, which grows to astonishing lengths in the ocean, dries to form a hollow tube of uniformly expanding diameter, and even obliges wind instrument makers by providing a bulb at the larger end which can be cut off midway to leave a small bell. The dried kelp tube is light and fragile, but fairly rigid. It is easy to cut and drill, but not strong enough in itself for the attachment of key levers and such. Even so, for those who live where they can get their hands on it, it is a delightful resource for an experimental wind maker.

Kelp can be found in great quantities washed up on the ocean beaches of the West Coast of North America, especially after a storm. Sometimes usable horns dry nicely on the beach, in exotic twisty shapes, and you can just collect them. Alternatively, you can harvest fresh kelp and sun-dry it yourself. The key to doing this is to keep the entire plant intact, from the bulb to the root, until dry. If cut or punctured, it will collapse upon itself, and rot, and stink. Dried kelp is very much inclined to re-absorb water, so as soon as the kelp is dry, give it several coats of a moisture-resistant finish like polyurethane. (To coat the inside you can plug the end and fill the horn with finish, then pour it out.)

Horn, Bone, Shell and Hide

These various animal materials are available from suppliers in the list at the end of this appendix, or you may be able to scrounge them from butchers, slaughterhouses, zoos, or ranchers.

Horns from the main species of domesticated livestock — cattle and sheep — have been used for wind instruments since before the start of recorded history. They possess a natural conical bore; they are both strong and workable; and they can be polished to great beauty. Cow horns range roughly from 12" to about 20", with a gently curved shape. Sheep horns cover a roughly similar range, but are curly. Some other animal horns, such as antelope and gazelle, have also been used.

Many animal bones are long and hollow, and can be used for flutes. Some makers have also made bone marimbas, which are more interesting for their concept than for their sound. Leg bones from domestic livestock can be had without contributing to the demise of wildlife species. Hollowed tusks from elephants and other species have served for conical wind instruments, but severe trade restrictions, with good justification, have made it almost impossible to obtain usable tusks.

Eggshells from larger birds can make good ocarinas and whistles. Ostrich eggs are especially good for egg craft of all sorts. A typical ostrich egg is perhaps five inches in diameter and as thick and strong as fine china, with a lovely dimpled surface. The shell can be drilled or ground without fracturing. Ostriches are widely domesticated; their eggs are available and are not under trade restrictions.

Small seashells make nice rattles. Among larger seashells, conch shells make beautiful, richly resonant trumpets, their spiraling bores having a naturally conical shape.

Tortoise shell and armadillo shell have been used for sound chamber bodies, though tortoise shell is under trade restrictions.

Natural animal hide is commonly used for drum membranes as well as skin-covered string instrument sound chambers. See the full discussion in Chapter 7, "Membranophones."

Secondary Materials

What follows is not an exhaustive list of secondary materials; think of it as a collection of useful odds and ends.

Adhesives, Fillers, Finishes: The usual epoxies, wood glues and such serve their accustomed purposes in musical instrument making. Flexible glues, water-soluble glues, and glues that will yield to heat are favored for certain purposes, because they can be undone later for repairs; they may be less prone to cracking when subjected to vibration; and they may allow freer vibration. A couple of special products worth highlighting: 1) Autobody filler, sold at autoshops everywhere, has a thousand uses. 2) Non-runny epoxies are available; their ability to stay put while drying is valuable in some applications. 3) Hot glue is not very strong and makes an inelegant joint, but it is quick and convenient for casual or temporary purposes. The glue is a plastic that comes in the form of sticks that are loaded into a hot glue gun. The cost of the gun is not prohibitive. 4) For wind instruments made of wood, dependably water-resistant glues are called for. Marine-grade adhesives such as Weldwood Resorcinol™ will serve. But avoid toxic adhesives where there will be oral contact.

Regarding varnishes and other finishes for musical instruments — there is a lot of folklore on this subject, much of it pretty silly in my view, especially regarding violin varnishes. I will avoid the controversy and simply say that conventional and widely available finishes work just fine in most musical instrument applications. One special case: mouthpieces for wind instruments must be left unfinished or else finished with something non-toxic. Options for wood include mineral oil, walnut oil, and mixtures of such oils with paraffin or beeswax. Such mixtures are sometimes sold at housewares stores as salad bowl finish.

Balloons: Useful in a million ways, as described in earlier chapters. Variety stores often only have balloons in small sizes, made with thin latex. Go to a party store or a toy store for a wider selection. Sometimes you can get giant weather balloons in surplus, made of a similar latex, but in sizes up to six feet in diameter.

Corrugated Tubing: Essential for corrugaphones. The stuff sold as hot water flex pipe doesn't work well. (The corrugations are too shallow.) Use the more deeply ridged gas-heater hose, available at hardware stores. Various plastic flexpipes also work as well or better, except that they tend to turn up in diameters too large for blowing. Corrugated plastic tubing is often available through surplus outlets.

Elastics: Latex rubber bands age badly, especially if stretched for a prolonged period of time. For long term applications, use elastic straps purchased from fabric stores, or bungee chords. They, too, do poorly under continuous stretching, but they outlast rubber bands. Surgical latex rubber tubing, available from medical supply stores, serves well in many applications. Where rubber bands are what you want, they can be obtained (sometimes on special order) in a great range of sizes from office supply outlets and sometimes from surplus outlets. Whatever the elastic material, many wraps of loosely stretched bands will perform better and outlast a few wraps of tightly stretched bands.

Foam Rubber: Useful for many applications in padding, sealing and insulating. Hardware stores and auto parts stores have adhesive-backed weatherstripping in a variety of densities, widths and thicknesses. For most applications in musical instruments, the dense, closed-cell neoprene weather stripping foams are much preferable to the softer open-cell foams that don't spring back after squashing. Larger foam pieces, like those used in mattresses and pillows, are available in various densities from various places you can find in the phone book. Industrial surplus places may have a variety of foams or solid rubbers in sheets of various thicknesses, often adhesive-backed.

Grease: Useful for lubricating and improving the seal on all sorts of sliding stoppers. Don't use margarine; use lithium grease, available as bearing grease from auto supply stores.

Inner Tubes: Useful either for elastics or as padding material. You can get used inner tubes from garages and bike shops.

Monofilament Nylon Line: Useful as musical instrument strings, imitation bow hair, and for other purposes. Use nylon intended for musical instrument stringing where possible; it is stronger and less stretchy. Otherwise, go to nylon fishing line. For large-diameter nylon, similar to the unwound gut bass strings of old, try weedwacker line, sold at hardware stores and sometimes available as surplus. For very fine nylon, as for bow hairs, use nylon thread, available at fabric shops and sewing centers.

Surgical Rubber Tubing: Soft latex tubing, useful for various padding, insulation and elastic strapping purposes; available from medical supply centers.

Velcro: A thousand and one uses. Available from fabric stores at high prices, or from industrial surplus places in quantity for much less.

SOURCES

Here are some ideas on where to get what. Send a large, self-addressed, stamped envelope when you write for catalogs or information from any of the vendors listed; that saves work for the vendor, and will get you a quicker response.

Local Sources

Neighborhood Retail Outlets: Hardware stores, fabric stores, auto supply stores, hobby and crafts shops, toy stores, music stores, and variety stores (K-mart) have many of the things instrument builders seek, at great convenience. Prices may be higher than what you'd pay via second-hand scrounging or discount mail order.

Lumberyards, Metals Suppliers, Plastics Outlets: These are basic sources for raw materials, but they don't always stock the specialty items that instrument builders crave.

Scrap Yards: Here you will find all kinds of metals. If you go searching for something in particular, it is a matter of luck whether you will find it. If you go there looking to be sonically inspired, you will be inspired.

Flea Markets, Pawn Shops, Junk Yards: Important sources for used and junked instruments which you can raid for parts. (Also, occasionally for fine instruments.) If you really get into the instrument-building habit, you will constantly have your eye out for such things, and develop a collection of junked instrument parts from which to draw as the need arises.

Specialty Music Stores

There are several stores specializing in unusual and hard-to-find instruments and accessories, and that do much of their business by mail order. Here are some of them:

Ali Akbar College of Music Store, 215 West End Ave., San Rafael, CA 94901

Andy's Front Hall, P.O. Box 307, Voorheesville, NY 12186

Anyone Can Whistle, A Catalog of Musical Discovery, Box 4407, Kingston, NY 12401

Earthshaking Percussion, 900 Moreland Ave., Atlanta, GA 30316

Elderly Instruments, 1100 N. Washington, P.O. Box 14210, Lansing MI 48901

The Folk Music Center, 220 Yale Ave, Claremont, CA 91711

House of Musical Traditions, 7040 Carroll Ave., Tacoma Park, MD 20912

Lark in the Morning, P.O. Box 1176, Mendocino, CA 95460

Mandala Percussion, 1390 South Potomac St., Suite 136-T, Aurora, CO 80012

Musicmakers Kits, PO Box 2117, Stillwater, MN 55082 (specializing in buildable kits for unusual instruments)

Piano Tuner Supply Houses, Lutherie Supply Houses

These are some of the companies specializing in materials used in string instrument building and repair, including woods, strings, and hardware:

Luthier's Mercantile, P.O. Box 774, 412 Moore Lane, Healdsburg, CA 95448

Stewart-MacDonald's Guitar Shop Supply, 21 N. Shafer St., Box 900, Athens, OH 45701

San Francisco Pianos, 657 Mission, San Francisco, CA 94105

Educational Music Supply Houses

The following outlets carry a wide range of musical merchandise and accessories at discount prices, aimed at school band music programs:

Interstate Music Supply, P.O. Box 315, 13819 West National Ave., New Berlin, WI 53151

The Woodwind and the Brasswind , 19880 State Line Road, South Bend, IN 46637 (they also have a percussion catalog)

Wind Instrument Manufacturers

For parts and accessories associated with wind instruments, you can go directly to the manufacturers, part of whose business is the sale of parts to band instrument repair technicians. Two leading U.S. manufacturers are:

G. Leblanc Corporation, 7001 Leblanc Blvd., Kenosha WI 53141-1415

United Musical Instruments, P.O. Box 727, Elkhart, IN 46515

String Manufacturers

For customized musical instrument strings (such as long, narrow wound strings not available as part of any standard instrument string set) you can buy or build your own string winding-machine, or you can contract with a string manufacturer, such as —

E. & O. Mari, Inc., 256 Broadway, Newburgh, NY 12550

For gut strings —

Donna Curry's Music, 1780 Fort Union Dr., Santa Fe, NM 87501

Drum and Percussion Supplies

For hardware and accessories —

Stewart-MacDonald's Drum Makers Supply, 21 N. Schafer St., Box 900, Athens, OH 45701

Universal Percussion, 2773 E. Midlothian Blvd., Struthers, OH 44471

The Woodwind & The Brasswind Percussion Catalog, 19880 State Line Rd., South Bend, IN 46637

For natural drumheads, pre-cut to various sizes, with or without hoops —

United Rawhide Mfg. Co., 1644 N. Ada St., Chicago, IL 60622

Mid-East Mfg. Inc., 808 E. New Haven Ave., Melbourne FL 32901

Natural Materials

Here are some sources for shell, bone, gourd and the like:

Boone Trading Company, 562 Coyote Road, Brinnon, WA 98320 (tusk, bone, shell, ostrich eggs, horn, turtle shell, etc.)

Tandy Leather Company has stores in cities across the U.S. and will also sell by mail. One store location is 116 W. 25th Ave., San Mateo, CA 94403 (long horn and steer horn)

Eastern Star Trading Company, 624 Davis St., Evanston, IL 60201 (with additional outlets in California, Florida & Washington) (bamboo)

The Gourd Factory, P.O. Box 9, Linden, CA 95236 (dried gourds)

Industrial Supply and Surplus

This company, which sells primarily to industry, has the most complete inventory of hardware items and raw materials you will find anywhere:

McMaster-Carr & Company, P.O. Box 4355, Chicago, IL 60680-4355

If you haven't browsed through the American Science & Surplus catalog, you're missing all the fun. An incredible potpourri of useless junk, much of which turns out to be just what you didn't know you needed.

American Science & Surplus (formerly Jerryco), 601 Linden Place, Evanston, IL 60202

Another surplus catalog, with more emphasis on electronics:

Herback and Rademan, 18 Canal St., P.O. Box 122, Bristol, PA 19007-0122

Software

Stringmaster, available from Mark Bolles, 1405 Little Leaf, San Antonio, TX 78247. This is a string scaling package, allowing you to calculate suitable string lengths, diameters, materials and tensions for different applications. For IBM compatible computers.

Just Intonation Calculator, available from Soundscape Productions, 1071 Main St., Suite 1, Cambria CA 93428. Performs a wide variety of calculations for composers and theorists in connection with just intonation, with internal sound for tuning reference and ear training. Also sends MIDI tuning dumps to many different types of synthesizers. For MacIntosh computers.

Microtonal MIDI Terminal, available from The Southeast Just Intonation Center, P.O. Box 15464, Gainesville, FL 32604. Just intonation calculations with MIDI synthesizer re-tuning capability. For IBM compatible computers.

FREQUENCY AND TUNINGS CHARTS

This appendix contains two charts designed to map out the territory of the audible sound spectrum. It supplements information in Chapter 3, "Tuning Systems and Pitch Layouts."

FREQUENCY CHART

The chart on the following two pages shows the pitch name, frequency, wavelength, and musical staff notation for frequencies within the hearing range. It uses several standards and conventions addressed in the following paragraphs.

Pitch Names

There is substantial agreement in western musical practice as to how to name the pitches within the octave, using the familiar note names C, C#, D and so forth. But distinguishing between like-named pitches in different octaves remains confusing. Quite a few systems have been used to give each pitch a unique label. The one given in the left hand column of this chart, using capital letters with subscripted numerals to denote octaves, has become the most commonly used among acousticians; it has been accepted by the American Standards Association; and it is the one we have used throughout this book. In the adjacent column the chart gives note names according to the Helmholtz system, since this system appears in widely used musical sources such as *Grove's Dictionary of Music and Musicians*.

Pitch Standards

The frequency of A above middle C is normally used as a benchmark for fixing musical pitches to a standard. Over the centuries the frequency of that A has ranged from below 400Hz to 455Hz and higher. The International Organization for Standardization has set the modern pitch standard at A=440Hz (1955; reaffirmed in 1975), and this chart is predicated upon that standard.

Just vs. Tempered Tunings

The chart presents frequencies for pitches in 12-tone equal temperament, despite calls from many thoughtful musicians to lessen the dominance of 12-equal. The reason for using 12-equal here is that it presents a familiar frame of reference, while the just systems in use are too diverse to allow for standardized presentation. (The scales chart following this one presents a better picture of just relationships.)

Sharps and Flats

To keep the chart to a manageable size, only the "natural" notes are given. Instructions for finding frequencies and wavelengths for the sharps and flats appear at the end of the chart.

Air Temperature

The wavelengths are accurate for typical room temperature conditions. Instructions for estimating wavelengths at other temperatures, including the slightly elevated temperatures typical in breath-blown wind instrument tubes, appear at the end of the chart.

COMPARATIVE TUNINGS CHART

Following the frequency chart is a comparative chart of tuning systems, showing how various musical scales compare to the most basic just intervals, to the familiar intervals of 12-tone equal temperament, and to one another. It contains the historical European quarter-comma meantone scale system; three raga tunings and blues intonations as representatives of tunings outside the European tradition; Harry Partch's "monophonic fabric" as a model of the work of a 20th-century theorist; plus a couple of higher-order equal temperaments.

The chart presents pitch *relationships* only. Intervals between pitches are shown, but actual frequencies are not specified. For comparative purposes, all the tuning systems are built over a common, unspecified root tone.

Each tuning appears on the chart as a ladder, with the pitches laid out in ascending order, spaced vertically according to interval size. Each tuning is given over a range of one octave. (The one-octave range is adequate if you assume that the same set of intervals are to be duplicated in other octaves. That is true of most tuning systems, though not all.) To help demarcate the tonal territory, horizontal reference lines cross the entire chart at heights corresponding to certain basic just intervals: the major second 9:8, the major third 5:4, the perfect fourth 4:3, the perfect fifth 3:2, and the major sixth 5:3. The pitch locations are marked by a short, bold horizontal line across the ladder. In cases where the scale degrees are flexible or ambiguous, the stippling within the ladder indicates the relevant pitch regions. The notations surrounding each scale degree are as follows:

1) For tunings based in just intonation, ratios appear to the left of each scale degree mark. The ratio represents the frequency of the given scale degree over the frequency of the scale's first degree. It is the number by which the frequency

Pitch Name (ASA)	Pitch Name (Helm.)	Frequency	Wave-length (cm)	Wave-length (inches)	
C_0	C"	16.352	2100.71	827 1/16	C_0: Bottom of the organ's 32' octave; lowest definite pitch on any standard instrument.
D_0	D"	18.354	1871.52	736 13/16	
E_0	E"	20.602	1667.34	656 7/16	20Hz: Approximate bottom of hearing range for someone with good hearing.
F_0	F"	21.827	1573.76	619 19/32	
G_0	G"	24.500	1402.06	551	
A_0	A"	27.500	1249.09	491 25/32	A_0: Standard piano's lowest note
B_0	B"	30.868	1112.81	438 1/8	
C_1	C'	32.703	1050.36	413 17/32	
D_1	D'	36.708	935.76	368 13/32	
E_1	E'	41.203	833.67	328 7/32	String bass low E
F_1	F'	43.654	786.88	309 25/32	
G_1	G'	48.999	701.03	275	
A_1	A'	55.000	624.55	245 7/8	
B_1	B'	61.735	556.41	219 1/16	
C_2	C	65.406	525.18	206 3/4	
D_2	D	73.416	467.88	184 7/32	
E_2	E	82.407	416.83	164 3/32	Guitar low E
F_2	F	87.307	393.44	154 29/32	
G_2	G	97.999	350.51	137	
A_2	A	110.00	312.27	122 15/16	
B_2	B	123.47	278.20	109 17/32	
C_3	c	130.81	262.59	103 3/8	
D_3	d	146.83	233.94	92 3/32	
E_3	e	164.81	208.42	82 1/16	
F_3	f	174.61	196.72	77 7/16	
G_3	g	196.00	175.26	68	
A_3	a	220.00	156.14	61 15/32	
B_3	b	246.94	139.1	54 3/4	
C_4	c'	261.63	131.3	51 11/16	**MIDDLE C**
D_4	d'	293.66	117.0	46 1/16	
E_4	e'	329.63	104.2	41 1/32	
F_4	f'	349.23	98.4	38 23/32	
G_4	g'	392.00	87.6	34 1/2	
A_4	a'	440.00	78.1	30 3/4	**A-440**
B_4	b'	493.88	69.6	27 3/8	
C_5	c"	523.25	65.7	25 27/32	
D_5	d"	587.33	58.5	23 1/32	
E_5	e"	659.26	52.1	20 1/2	
F_5	f"	698.46	49.2	19 3/8	
G_5	g"	783.99	43.8	17 1/4	
A_5	a"	880.00	39.0	15 3/8	
B_5	b"	987.77	34.8	13 11/16	

Two 8va

8va

in 12-Tone Equal Temperament

Pitch Name (ASA)	Pitch Name (Helm.)	Frequency	Wave-length (cm)	Wave-length (inches)	
C$_6$	c'''	1046.5	32.8	12 15/16	C$_6$: Highest normal note for trumpet
D$_6$	d'''	1174.7	29.2	11½	
E$_6$	e'''	1318.5	26.1	10 ¼	
F$_6$	f'''	1396.9	24.6	9 11/16	
G$_6$	g'''	1568.0	21.9	8 5/8	
A$_6$	a'''	1760.0	19.5	7 11/16	
B$_6$	b'''	1975.5	17.4	6 27/32	Bb$_6$: Bb sop. clarinet's highest note
C$_7$	c''''	2093.0	16.4	6 15/32	
D$_7$	d''''	2349.3	14.6	5 ¾	
E$_7$	e''''	2637.0	13.0	5 1/8	
F$_7$	f''''	2793.8	12.3	4 27/32	
G$_7$	g''''	3136.0	11.0	4 5/16	
A$_7$	a''''	3520.0	9.8	3 27/32	
B$_7$	b''''	3951.1	8.7	3 7/16	
C$_8$	c'''''	4186.0	8.2	3 7/32	C$_8$: Standard piano's top note
D$_8$	d'''''	4698.6	7.3	2 7/8	D$_8$: Piccolo's top note
E$_8$	e'''''	5274.0	6.5	2 9/16	
F$_8$	f'''''	5587.7	6.2	2 13/32	
G$_8$	g'''''	6271.9	5.5	2 5/32	
A$_8$	a'''''	7040.0	4.9	1 29/32	
B$_8$	b'''''	7902.1	4.4	1 23/32	
C$_9$	c''''''	8372.0	4.1	1 5/8	
D$_9$	d''''''	9397.3	3.7	1 7/16	
E$_9$	e''''''	10548.1	3.3	1 9/32	
F$_9$	f''''''	11175.3	3.1	1 7/32	
G$_9$	g''''''	12543.9	2.7	1 1/16	
A$_9$	a''''''	14080.0	2.4	0 31/32	
B$_9$	b''''''	15804.3	2.2	0 27/32	20,000Hz: Approximate upper limit of hearing range for one with good hearing.
C$_{10}$	c'''''''	16744.1	2.1	0 13/16	

8va

Two 8va

Three 8va

ADDITIONAL NOTES FOR THIS CHART

This chart contains data for natural notes only. To find the frequency of a sharp or flat, multiply the frequency of the pitch a semitone below by the 12-equal scale factor of 1.05946. To find the wavelength, divide the wavelength of the pitch a semitone below by the same factor.

The wavelengths given in this chart are based on a sound speed of 343.5 meters per second, which corresponds to typical atmospheric conditions at a temperature of 68 degrees Fahrenheit. At warmer temperatures the wavelength for any given pitch will be slightly longer, and at cooler temperatures it will be slightly shorter.

Temperatures within breath-blown wind instrument tubes are typically slightly higher. For such applications, multiply the wavelength values on this chart by 1%, for results corresponding to a temperature of 83 degrees Fahrenheit and a sound speed of 347 meters per second.

of the first scale degree must be multiplied to obtain the frequency of the higher degree in question.

2) For tempered tunings such as the equal temperaments, the ratio to the left of each scale degree mark is replaced by a decimal number between 1 and 2. Like the ratios, the decimal is the number by which the frequency of the first degree must be multiplied to obtain the frequency of the degree in question.

3) To the right of each scale degree mark is a number representing a cents value. The cents system is a widely used method for precise indication of musical intervals. It uses a basic unit called the cent, defined as 1/100th of a semitone in 12-tone equal temperament. The octave thus comprises 1200 cents. Aside from being useful in its own right as a calibrator, the cents value provides easy comparison to familiar intervals in 12-tone equal temperament. For example, you can recognize that a tone in some exotic tuning standing at 270 cents above the tonic is 30 cents (3/10 of a semitone) below the minor third in 12-equal, since by definition the 12-equal minor third is 300 cents.

4) For some of the tunings a scale degree name or number appears in a box to the right and below the scale degree mark.

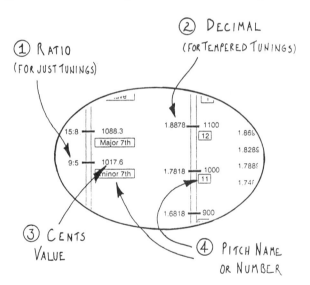

① RATIO (FOR JUST TUNINGS)

② DECIMAL (FOR TEMPERED TUNINGS)

③ CENTS VALUE

④ PITCH NAME OR NUMBER

The Tunings

Five-limit Just

Five-limit just intonation is usually considered to be the theoretically ideal intonational basis for music in the European tradition, and some other musical traditions as well. The designation "5-limit" refers to the fact that 5 is the largest prime number required in either the numerators or denominators to build the ratios of the tuning. (Roughly speaking, the larger the limit number, the more harmonically complex and potentially dissonant will the intervals of the tuning be perceived.) The sound or mood of an accurately tuned 5-limit is usually described as sweet and restful. A common form of 5-limit is presented here; other variations are possible.

Twelve-Tone Equal Temperament

Twelve-equal, dividing the octave into twelve equal steps, is the standard tuning in current Western music. It has found favor over other equal temperaments because it is the smallest

number of equal divisions per octave that does a fairly good job of approximating the important intervals of 5-limit just.

Quarter-Comma Meantone / 31-Tone Equal Temperament

Quarter-comma meantone, an unequal temperament of twelve tones per octave, was one of the widely used temperaments prior to the ascendance of 12-equal in the 18th century. The early unequal temperaments sought to achieve excellent approximations of just intervals in some keys, at the cost of poor approximations in some other keys (which were then avoided).

It happens that the mathematical operation used to generate quarter-comma meantone, if carried a bit further, can generate something indistinguishably close to 31-tone equal temperament. Thus, quarter-comma meantone can be considered to be a subset of 31-tone equal temperament. For that reason, 31-equal and quarter-comma meantone are presented on a single axis on the chart here. The cents values and scale degree multipliers given are correct for 31-equal except on the twelve meantone degrees, where the correct meantone values are given. The two differ by no more than a little over a cent.

Nineteen-Tone Equal Temperament

Nineteen-tone equal temperament has been cited as a practical option for moving to higher-order equal temperaments, since it approximates just intervals nicely, and can be accommodated using keyboard layouts and notational systems close to the familiar forms used for twelve-equal.

Monophonic Fabric (Partch's 43)

Harry Partch set forth this 11-limit scale as his most comprehensive tonal resource. For the reasoning behind his choice of intervals, read his *Genesis of a Music*.

Blues

Blues is an exotic and very subtle approach to intonation as long as it is played on an instrument that allows full intonational expression. It has provided a major counterbalance to the predominance of 12-equal in European and American music of this century. Blue tonalities often use sliding pitches; minute tonal inflections have musical meaning; and pitches can be hinted at (through bending) without actually being sounded.

North Indian Ragas

Dr. David Courtney of Sur Sangeet Services in Houston, Texas, provided the pitch data given here for three selected North Indian ragas. He obtained the data through a set of computer-based samples used in conjunction with intonational evaluations by trained Indian musicians.

Ragas are more than scale systems. Each raga has diverse musical and extra-musical associations, which of course are not reflected on the chart.

The pitch set associated with a particular raga may have five, six or seven tones. Frequently, however, the tones are not discreet, but represent only something like a resting point in a broader pitch region through which the tone can slide. In some cases, as with the *Suddha Kalyan* on the chart, an entire region may be one of sliding pitch, with no recognizable resting point at all. As with the blues, the flexible tones within the ragas are indicated on the chart as gradations rather than fixed points.

COMPARATIVE TUNINGS CHART

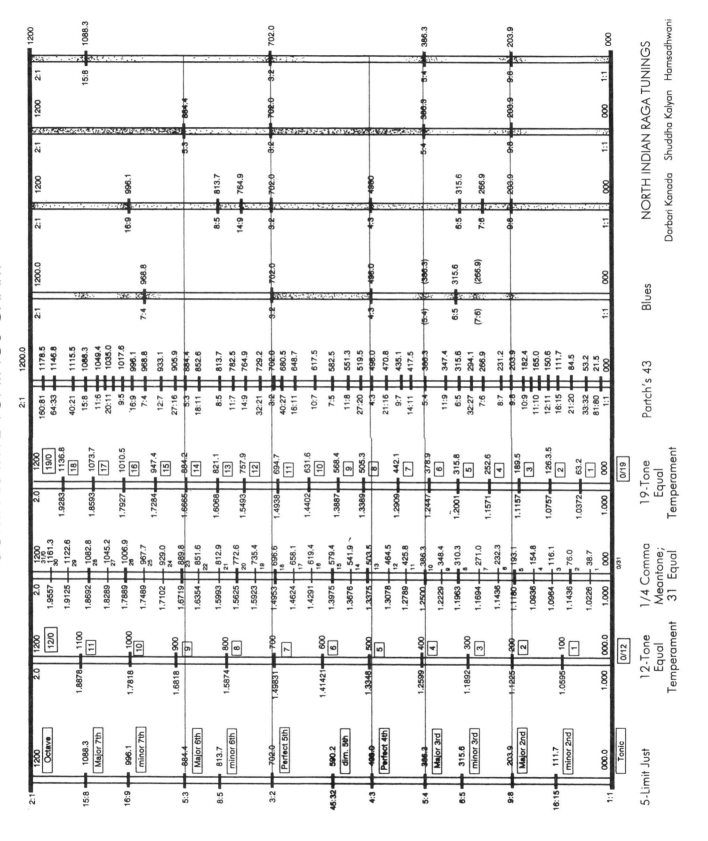

Appendix Three

AMPLIFICATION, MICROPHONES AND TRANSDUCERS

There is much to be said for letting quiet instruments be quiet, and simply learning to listen. Still, there are occasions when quiet instruments need amplification if they are to be heard. There are three steps in the electronic amplification of acoustic sound instruments. 1) As raw material, you have the sound of the instrument — vibrations in the body of the instrument or the air it encloses, which are radiated into the atmosphere. The first step is to take the movement patterns of these vibrations and convert them into analogous patterns of alternating voltage. That is the job of the *transducer* — the microphone or pickup. 2) Step two is to take the patterns of alternating voltage, called the *signal*, and make them stronger — amplify them — without distorting the pattern. This is the job of the amplifier. 3) Finally, the amplified electronic signal must be converted back into sound in the air. This is the job of the loudspeaker. Through the electromagnetic effect associated with the movement of current in a wire, the amplified signal drives the speaker cone in a pattern of movement that, ideally, replicates the original vibration. The speaker, in turn, drives the surrounding air.

Stages two and three — the amplifier and speaker — are generally the province of commercial electronics manufacturers. In most cases all the instrument maker does is to try to get hold of decent equipment. But in stage one — converting the physical sound into an electronic signal — the instrument maker has some real choices. Let us consider the options. Discounting some exotic technologies that remain on the horizon, there are three practical possibilities.

AIR MICROPHONES

By "air microphone" I refer to the standard microphone, which you place in front of a sound source to pick up the sound. The mic responds to the same vibrations in the atmosphere that the ear does, converting them into minute fluctuations of voltage. There are several types of microphones with different mechanisms for picking up and converting atmospheric vibrations, the two most widely used

being condenser microphones and dynamic microphones. Condenser microphones tend to have a brilliant tone with well-defined transients, working particularly well on plucked string instruments, percussion, and other sounds that benefit from precision, clarity and definition. Dynamic microphones tend to give a warmer feeling and do well with voices, many wind instruments, and other sounds that benefit from a sense of fullness or richness of tone. Dynamic microphones as a rule are also less expensive and more rugged than condenser mics.

Some microphones, called omnidirectional mics, respond equally to sound from all directions. Others, called cardioid mics, are designed to pick up preferentially sounds from sources located in front of the mic. All mics, but especially omnidirectional mics, are prone to feedback. Feedback occurs in any amplification system when the output finds its way back into the input and cycles through again, only to be picked up by the input again. With microphones, for instance, the sound from the speakers is picked up by the mic, re-amplified and sent to the speaker again, only to be picked up by the mic once more, creating a vicious circle that results in unwanted squealing or whistling from the speaker. Cardioid mics can be aimed away from the speakers, mitigating the feedback problem to some degree.

Advantages of air microphones:
Air microphones can be used with any audible sound source.
Of all the available transducer types, a top-quality microphone yields the most accurate and natural-sounding reproduction of the original sound as the ear hears it.

Disadvantages of air microphones:
Air mics aren't very selective; they pick up whatever extraneous sounds are present in the surrounding air along with the sounds of the intended instrument.
It is difficult to build an air mic into an instrument. For the best sound they usually need to be held on a separate stand in front of the instrument (more on mic placement in a

moment).

Air mics, as mentioned before, are prone to feedback. Mic placement and orientation can help control the problem, but this can inhibit the player's positioning and movement.

Tips for using air mics:

Microphone placement is an art and a science; sound technicians make a lifetime study of it. But as the maker of an instrument, you have the advantage of having a good sense of which aspects of the instrument's sound you wish to emphasize or balance, and where along the body those sounds emanate most strongly. For instance, on a plucked string instrument with a soundbox, you have the air resonance from within the soundhole, the plucking noise coming directly from the strings, and the tone coming off the front of the soundboard. All play a part in a full, yet bright and well defined composite tone. Don't tape a small air mic inside the soundhole (as is sometimes done); you will get too much air resonance for a boomy, muddy tone. Place the mic in front of the face where it can pick up all the components, angling it slightly this way or that to emphasize different components according to your taste. Alternatively, in some cases you will find that a more natural sound comes not from a close mic, but a more distant mic positioned to pick up a natural blend of the instrument's sound components, along with some room reverberation. (Distant miking has the disadvantages, however, of picking up more extraneous noise and producing a weaker signal.) If circumstances allow, do both: use a close mic for clarity and a distant mic for balance and added room resonance.

Feedback is not a big problem in the recording studio, because it is not necessary to boost the volume to high levels in the recording chamber. It is more of a problem in performance situations demanding high volume. To minimize feedback problems, avoid positioning mics too close to speakers, and aim directional (cardioid) mics away from them. Watch out for solid walls that will reflect speaker sound directly back at the mics. Use equalization (electronically filtering selected frequency ranges) to reduce the effects of disproportionately strong resonances at specific frequencies in the room or in the instrument itself.

CONTACT MICROPHONES

Contact microphones take advantage of the piezo-electric effect. Piezo-electric crystals are chemical structures which respond to changes in pressure by producing a tiny fluctuation in electric voltage. Subjected to a vibratory movement, they produce an alternating voltage which is, ideally, analogous to the vibratory pattern. This signal can be sent to an amplifier and speakers just like the signal from a microphone. The piezo-electric contact mic is attached directly to the body of an instrument so that it can respond to the vibratory movement. It can be attached permanently or stuck on temporarily.

Notice that acoustic sound in the atmosphere, such as a listener in the room would hear from the unamplified instrument, is not part of the equation here. What gets amplified is the vibration pattern at some specific location in the solid material of the instrument, not the sound in the air. In instruments for which air resonance has a role to play, the

air resonance tone is lost on the contact mic. So is the blend of sound radiating from different parts of the instrument's surface. As a result, contact mics tend to have a sound which, speaking subjectively, is unnatural and (to this critic's ear) not especially appealing. Various tricks have been used to compensate. These include placing multiple contact mics at carefully selected locations, using compensatory electronic equalization or other electronic signal processing to recreate a more natural sound, and using contact mics in conjunction with air mics.

Advantages of contact microphones:

Contact mics are convenient and unobtrusive, since they can be attached directly to an instrument, or simply built in. They are conveniently compact, too.

Contacts mics are far less subject to feedback than air mics. They can feed back, however, especially when attached to soundboards, as they often are. (The sound from the speaker drives the soundboard, where the contact mic picks it up once again to complete the feedback loop.) The problem lessened considerably when the contact mic is attached to something heavier than a soundboard.

They can be used for instruments having strong vibrations in the body, but which don't radiate well to the surrounding air. In fact, they can be used in place of soundboards or other sound-radiating mechanisms, simplifying the instrument design and construction process considerably. Designing an instrument this way — e.g., designing a string instrument with a rigid body but no soundboard — can allow for longer sustain in sounds such as plucked strings, since energy need not be dissipated in radiation to the air.

Disadvantages of contact microphones:

They can't be used very well with aerophones, since they need some solid vibrating body to attach to. In instruments with solid vibrating bodies but air resonance as well, they pick up the body sound but miss the air resonance entirely.

They tend to yield an unnatural and often unattractive sound.

While contact mics pick up relatively little unwanted room sound, they may produce an exaggerated and disconcerting response to any unintentional knocking or scraping on the body of the instrument.

Tips for using contact mics:

The key question for any given instrument is where to attach the contact mic. It should not be attached where it will inhibit the initial vibration. This generally means that it must be attached where impedance is high enough that the vibration will not be significantly affected by the added weight. Thus, for string instruments it cannot be attached directly to the string, but may be attached or built into the bridge, or somewhere on the soundboard, or even at the headstock or along the neck. For heavier initial vibrating bodies such as chimes or marimba bars, where the impedance is high to begin with, it may be acceptable to attach the contact mic directly to the initial vibrator. In special cases where you wish to bring out a particular mode of vibration or de-emphasize another, and you can locate the nodes and antinodes on the vibrating body, then you should attach the contact mic as near as possible to an antinode (point of maximum vibration) for the desired modes, and as near as possible to nodes for the unwanted ones. In most cases, however, the situation is not so clear cut, and then experimentation is the key. Apply the contact mic at different points, play, and listen. Consider using two or more at different locations and mixing their signal. This leads to varying degrees of cancellation between out-of-phase signals, but you may get lucky and find just the blend you want.

ELECTROMAGNETIC PICKUPS

Electromagnetic pickups are the sort used on electric guitars. More generally, they can be used in any application where the vibrating body is of a ferrous metal, which is to say, any metal that is responsive to magnetism. In addition to steel strings, electromagnetic pickups have been used with the steel tines of kalimbas, various sorts of chimes or forks in electric pianos, and so forth. They work on the principle of magnetic induction. Movement of a magnet near to a loop of conducting wire will induce a tiny current in the wire. Electromagnetic pickups contain windings of a great many loops of fine copper wire wrapped over a bar magnet, so that the movement of magnetic materials in the vicinity alters the magnetic field and induces a current in the coils. If the movement is, say, that of a vibrating string, the induced current will be an alternating current in a pattern analogous to the vibratory movement. This signal can then be sent to an amplifier and speaker for a sound corresponding to the initial vibration.

As with contact mikes, what one ultimately hears from the pickup is not a reproduction of a sound in the air. It is a direct transduction of the string's movement. Radiation from the instrument to the atmosphere plays no significant role; air resonance plays no significant role; and the acoustic properties of the body of the instrument play a relatively small role.

Electromagnetic pickups are subject to electromagnetic interference from outside sources, which adds an unwanted hum to the tone. The hum can be greatly reduced by using two coils wired together a certain way. These dual-coil pickups are called "humbucking" pickups. Their tone tends to be fuller and darker, while single-coil pickups are clearer and brighter in sound.

Advantages of electromagnetic pickups:
While their tone quality is quite different from that radiated to the air by an acoustic instrument, electromagnetic pickups give a relatively undiluted transmission of the initial vibratory movement, often resulting in a subjectively pure sound that can be appealing.

Feedback problems with electromagnetic pickups are minor. At the same time, in some applications electromag-

netic pickups allow for a relatively controlled form of feedback that can be cultivated to good effect.

Electromagnetic pickups pick up almost no unwanted sound, responding exclusively to the movement of the instrument's intended initial vibrating elements.

Electromagnetic pickups can be conveniently and unobtrusively mounted on the instrument.

By positioning the pickup at different locations relative to the vibrating body, you can emphasize different modes of vibration, and obtain a variety of tone qualities. By using multiple pickups in different locations, you can make these different timbres available at the flick of a switch.

As with contact mics, electromagnetic pickups can be used with instruments which radiate poorly to the air, and can make radiation systems such as soundboards unnecessary. Without the need to dissipate energy through radiation, such instruments can be designed for longer sustain in sounds that would otherwise decay rapidly (e.g., plucked strings).

Disadvantages of electromagnetic pickups:
They work only with initial vibrators of steel or other ferrous metals.

They do not reproduce the instrument's natural sound as radiated into the room. Acoustic qualities of the body of the instrument and air resonances are largely lost.

ADDITIONAL NOTES

All three of the transduction methods described here produce a very weak output signal commonly called "mic level." (One exception: some electromagnetic pickups may produce a signal substantially stronger than typical mic level.) Mic level signals must initially be sent to a pre-amp, which boosts them to a higher level of signal strength referred to as "line level." The line level signal is then sent to the main power amp. Most amplifiers have pre-amps built in. An amplifier's input jacks labeled "mic" will route the signal through the pre-amp. Those labeled "line" or "tape" (along with a few other designations) are intended for signals already at line level and are wired to bypass the pre-amp.

Very few home builders attempt to make their own contact mics or air microphones; they buy them from electronics manufacturers. Some electric instrument builders do like to make their own electromagnetic pickups, particularly in cases where the size and shape of commercially available pickups isn't suitable for the intended instrument. Pickup winding by hand is a time-consuming task, and it is difficult to produce results as good as even modestly priced commercially made pickups. For more on pickup winding, look to one of the books on the subject, such as Donald Brosnac's *Guitar Electronics for Musicians*.

MORE ON AIR COLUMNS, TONEHOLES AND WOODWIND KEYING MECHANISMS

This appendix contains technical information on wind instruments and their construction, with an emphasis on calculation of air column lengths and their frequencies, tonehole sizing and placement, and tonehole keying mechanisms for woodwinds.

CALCULATING EFFECTIVE AIR COLUMN LENGTHS & FREQUENCIES

To a first approximation, the wavelength for the fundamental resonance in a conical tube or an open cylindrical tube is twice the tube length. For a cylindrical tube stopped at one end, it is four times the tube length. (See Figures 6-14 through 6-16.) You can determine the frequencies and sounding pitches for these wavelengths by referring to the wavelength chart in Appendix 2. However, in practice, wind instrument tubes consistently behave as if they were slightly longer than they actually are. Some of the factors involved vary from player to player and cannot be quantified, while others are more predictable. The following paragraphs will help you to estimate actual effective lengths, given these secondary effects.

End Corrections

One reason wind instrument tubes behave as if they were longer than they actually are is that the standing wave within extends a bit beyond the open end. The amount of the extension varies with frequency and with the diameter of the opening. For practical purposes this *end correction factor* can be approximated in a simplified fashion as $l = 0.3d$, where l is the end correction and d is the tube-opening diameter. Thus, the approximate effective length of a tube open at one end is

$$L_e = L + .3d$$

where L is the actual tube length and L_e is the effective length. For a tube open at both ends, you need to apply the correction twice, which comes to:

$$L_e = L + .6d$$

Effects of Mouthpiece Cavities

On many wind instruments, the shape of the mouthpiece causes the overall tube shape to deviate from the ideal conical or cylindrical form. For instance, on conical brass instruments, where the apex of the cone should be, there is instead a definitely un-conelike appendage (the mouthpiece). You can minimize the ill effects of distortion of tube shape at the mouthpiece by thinking in terms of equivalent volumes. As shown in Figure 12-1, if the mouthpiece encloses the same total volume of air that the cut-off portion of the cone would have, then the overall air column will show resonance peaks at frequencies close to those that the complete cone would have. The desired tunings and overtone relationships will be roughly preserved. An imperfect missing-apex volume match can leading to serious mistuning in the upper frequencies.

To apply the same reasoning to cylindrical instruments, think of the length of additional cylindrical tubing that would have the same volume as the actual mouthpiece. The resonances of the overall air column will correspond roughly to the those of the basic tube with this equivalent-volume length added in place of the mouthpiece.

These equivalent volume calculations are most accurate at lower frequencies. At higher frequencies, where upper partials come into play, the situation is more complex.

In determining the mouthpiece volume to be used in finding these equivalencies, you may also need to take into account the fact that the elasticity of a reed or lips applied to the mouthpiece can cause the mouthpiece to behave as if it is larger than it is — in other words, the effective mouthpiece volume may be greater than the measured physical volume. The softer the reed or lips, and the greater their surface area over the mouthpiece air chamber, the greater is this effect.

Aside from equivalent volume considerations, a mouthpiece may still have its own independent higher frequency resonances, as the peculiarities of its shape enhance or inhibit specific frequencies. Small differences in mouthpiece shape make a big difference in overall instrument sound.

Irregularities in Air Column Shape, and a Remedy for Flat Upper Registers

Bulges or constrictions along an air column affect its resonance frequencies. The effects depend upon the size, shape and location of the irregularities. Figuring these effects out in detail is a rather subtle business, but we can make a couple of useful observations. First, let us note that a common perturbation is caused by the small cavities along a tube's length within closed toneholes (for instance, the little bit of extra space along the side of a clarinet tube under a closed key pad). While the specific effects on different resonances vary, the presence of closed toneholes above the first open hole will usually tend to lower the sounding pitch slightly.

Second, let's highlight one particularly useful air column irregularity effect. For various reasons, wind instruments have a tendency to be flat in the upper registers. You can counteract this problem by modifying the tube shape in a way that has a slight lowering effect on the lower frequencies, and progressively less effect on higher frequencies. This can be achieved through a slight taper toward the blowhole end. For example, an effective taper for a simple flute might be a gradual reduction in tube diameter starting at a point about 1/5 of the total tube length from the mouthpiece end and reaching a total reduction of about 10% by the time it gets to the stopper just beyond the blowhole (Figure 12-2).

TONEHOLE LOCATION AND SIZING FOR WIND INSTRUMENTS

It is difficult to use prescriptive mathematical methods to determine precisely the correct tonehole sizes and locations to produce particular pitches for tubular wind instruments. (Mathematical models do exist, but they aren't easy to apply.) But it is possible to arrive at acceptable approximate locations for desired pitches, and then to fine tune by adjusting the tonehole size. Chapter 6, "Aerophones," describes the process of fine tuning through hole-size adjustment. Here are guidelines for tonehole location, followed by guidelines for register holes.

Toneholes

Imagine that you want to know where to place a tonehole so as to produce a particular pitch in a tubular wind instrument. You can begin by making a preliminary location assessment based upon the simplifying assumption that hole diameter is to be as large as the tube diameter. Were this assumption true, it would mean that the hole could be located at the same point where the tube would be cut off to produce the same pitch. You can figure out where this point would be by either of the two ways described in Chapter 6: 1) If you know what absolute pitch you want, then you can calculate the tube length needed to produce the wavelength for that frequency. 2) If you are more concerned about relative pitch within the instrument than absolute pitch, you can figure it based upon the frequency ratio of the desired tone to the tone you're already getting from the full tube length, inverting the frequency ratios to get effective tube length ratios.

This tube cut-off location represents a very rough first approximation to the actual desired hole location, based on the unrealistic assumption that the tonehole diameter is so large as to equal the tube diameter. The actual location will be farther up the tube (toward the mouthpiece), by an amount which we will label C, short for tonehole Correction. Below is a list of factors to be taken into account in determining how large, approximately, C should be. The first three factors listed have the effect of lowering the sounding pitch below what one would predict based on the cut-off point calculation described above. You compensate for this lowering by moving the theoretical hole location upward on the tube (closer to the mouthpiece). The fourth factor has the effect of reducing the impact of the others; take it into account by reducing the amount of upward displacement you would other-

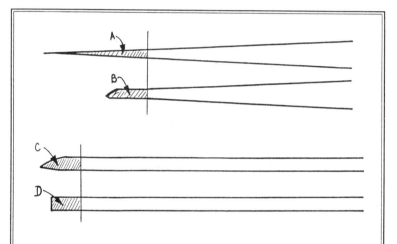

FIGURE 12-1: Equivalent volumes. For most conical wind instruments, the need for a mouthpiece at what would otherwise be the apex of the cone makes it impossible to have a true cone. One can achieve a fair approximation to the acoustic behavior of a true cone if the volume of air enclosed in the non-conical region created by the mouthpiece (region B) is roughly equivalent to the volume that would have been enclosed in the missing apex portion of the cone (region A).

The situation is similar for cylindrical tubes. The effective column length of a non-cylindrical mouthpiece (region C) approximately corresponds to that of a cylinder containing the same volume (region D).

Figure 12-2: In wind instrument tubes such as flute tubes, a slight taper toward the blowhole over 1/5 of the tube's length will lower the pitch of the lower tones, with progressively less effect on higher tones, thus offsetting the tendency to flatness in the upper registers.

wise have made. Here, then, are the factors. These effects are also laid out graphically in Figure 12-3.

1) *Smaller hole → larger correction.*

This is the most significant factor. A smaller hole lowers the pitch. To compensate, shift the theoretical location up the tube (toward the mouthpiece). How much to shift depends upon how much smaller than the main tube diameter the hole is to be. The smaller the ratio of the hole diameter to the tube's internal diameter at the hole location, the greater the hole's displacement toward the mouthpiece.

2) *Thicker hole → larger correction.*

The tube wall has some thickness, and the hole correspondingly has some depth. In addition, you might intend to build up the tube wall a bit to make a good seating for finger or key pad, making the hole deeper. That hole depth functions like a bit of additional tube length, lowering the pitch relative to the predicted value. End correction effects play a role here as well, making the air act as if the hole were slightly deeper than it actually is. To compensate, move the theoretical hole location up the tube by an amount slightly more than the hole depth.

3) *Many large closed-tonehole cavities above the first open hole → slightly larger tonehole correction.*

This effect is somewhat variable but, on balance, closed toneholes located above the tonehole in question tend to lower the sounding pitch slightly, if those closed holes are large and deep. Compensate by shifting the theoretical location up the tube slightly for those holes that will have closed toneholes above.

4) *Additional open toneholes below the first open one → smaller tonehole correction.*

When there is another open tonehole below the primary tonehole, the additional opening has an effect similar to making the primary hole larger. This counteracts the pitch-lowering effects of factors 1 - 3 above, so: where there will be additional open tone holes below the one in consideration, accommodate by reducing the upward displacement suggested by the other factors.

Where the primary hole is quite large — say over 75% of the tube diameter — the presence of additional lower open tone holes makes relatively little difference. But when the primary hole is small, the additional opening afforded by one or more open toneholes below is significant. This can be summarized in the following subsidiary rules:

a) *The smaller the primary hole, the greater the reduction of the tonehole correction factor due to additional open holes below.*

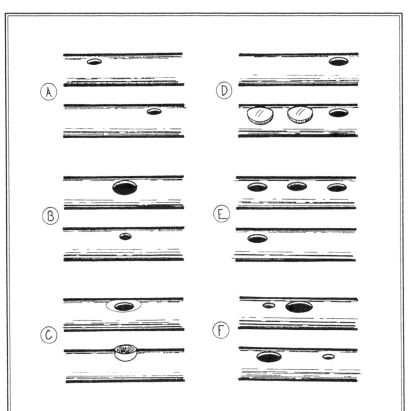

FIGURE 12-3: Effects of tonehole sizes and locations on sounding pitch.

The configuration in the upper drawing will produce the higher pitch in each pair but the last (which is a more complex situation — see explanation below). The mouthpiece is assumed to be to the left.

A. The closer to the mouthpiece a hole is, the higher the resulting pitch.

B. The larger a hole is, the higher the pitch.

C. The shallower the hole, the higher the pitch.

D. Covered toneholes above the first open tonehole have the effect of lowering the pitch slightly.

E. Additional open toneholes below the first open tonehole have the effect of raising the pitch.

F. The smaller the first open tonehole is, the more it will be affected by additional open toneholes below. The larger and nearer the additional open holes below, the more they will raise the pitch of the first open tonehole.

b) *The larger and/or nearer the additional open tone holes, the greater the reduction of the tonehole correction factor.*

A useful sidelight: While there are many advantages to large toneholes, small holes have the advantage that they make cross fingerings possible. Cross fingerings are fingerings which leave one open hole but cover the next, in order to obtain a slightly lower pitch. As indicated above, covering the next hole below the primary open hole doesn't have the required pitch-lowering effect if the holes are very large. Cross fingerings may seem awkward in a way, but they do allow a greater number of pitches with fewer holes than would be the case if each pitch demanded its own separate hole.

Even with the help of these rules, trial and error will continue to play a substantial role for most builders, along

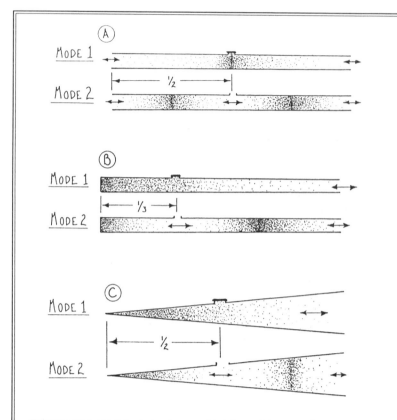

FIGURE 12-4: Register hole placement to bring out the second register in three basic tube types. Standing wave patterns for the first and second modes are shown for each tube type. Heavily stippled areas represent regions of maximum pressure variation; double-headed arrows within tubes represent areas of maximum movement and minimum pressure variation.

Important note: These placements apply when the tube's entire vibrating length is in effect. As described in the main text, when toneholes are opened along the tube, register hole placement should reflect the resulting shorter wavelengths within the tube, and so should be placed correspondingly closer to the mouthpiece.

A. Cylindrical tube open at both ends. Ideal register hole placement is at 1/2 of the tube length.

B. Cylindrical tube stopped at one end. Ideal placement is 1/3 of the way from the stopped end.

C. Conical tube. Ideal placement is at 1/2 of the tube length from the closed end.

better-than-nothing results in difficult situations, such as those with serious mouthpiece biases. The formulas are too complex for inclusion in this text. For more information see the booklet *Air Columns and Toneholes: Principles for Wind Instrument Design* by Bart Hopkin (distributed by Tai Hei Shakuhachi, PO Box 294, Willits, CA 95490).

Register Holes

A register hole usually takes the form of a small hole rather closer to the mouthpiece than the far end, which remains open the entire time the instrument plays in the upper register. There may be one all-purpose register hole on an instrument, or two or three on a single instrument, designed for different registers or different portions of different registers. Or, as is the case with flutes and recorders, one of the regular tone holes may double as a register hole.

Register holes work by inhibiting the lower mode of vibration that would normally dominate in the tube, allowing an upper mode to sing out as the predominant tone. Here's how: the register hole is located at a point of substantial pressure variation for the lower mode. When the hole is closed the air column vibrates normally, with that lower mode predominating. But when the hole is open, it creates a leak at a point where the periodic pressure build-up is essential to maintain the lower mode oscillation. The leak undermines the pressure build-up and inhibits the lower mode from sounding. Yet it has no such effect on any mode that happens to have a pressure node (point of minimum pressure variation) at that point. Higher modes meeting that description remain free to sound. The trick, then, is to locate the register hole at a point of substantial pressure variation for the lower mode(s) you wish to eliminate, yet near to a pressure variation minimum (a node) for the mode you want to bring out. Figure 12-4 shows the ideal locations for a register hole designed to throw the instrument into the second register for the three most common basic tube types.

Notice that the locations indicated in Figure 12-4 are ideal for a tube with no other open tone holes. If you open toneholes along the tube, you shorten the effective wavelength, moving all the nodes and antinodes farther up the tube. The register holes will then be misplaced. It seems to follow that you need a new, precisely located register hole for every note of the lower register. That would indeed be ideal, but real-world musical instruments get by with much less. When the register hole is slightly removed (but not too far) from the ideal location, it still has the effect of inhibiting the lower mode a good deal more than it inhibits the upper, and the air column remains more inclined to set up a strong vibration in the upper mode than the lower. And so a compromise position for the

with a generous dose of after-the-fact fine tuning through hole-size adjustment. Especially difficult are instruments in which strong biases at the mouthpiece distort the expected air column resonances. In such cases, end results often turn out to be very different from even the best predictions.

If your initial hole location estimates are good, you will end up with holes of roughly the same size on cylindrical tube instruments, or holes that uniformly increase in size for conical tubes. Instruments in which hole sizes vary in an irregular manner will be uneven in tone quality from one note to the next.

One final note: Formulas designed to yield exact hole sizes and location for specific pitches in wind instruments have been created by researchers including Douglas Keefe, John Coltman, and the late Arthur H. Benade. The best of these formulas yield good results in many situations, and register hole can usually be found which will be OK, though perhaps not great, over a substantial part of the range. Misplaced register holes cause a small amount of detuning; that's part of the compromise.

For a reasonable compromise location, place the register hole near the ideal location for some representative pitch near the middle of the range over which the register hole is to apply. This means moving the hole some distance up the tube (toward the mouthpiece) from the ideal whole-tube location suggested by the diagrams in Figure 12-4.

TONEHOLE KEYING SYSTEMS

When toneholes are too big or too far apart to be covered by fingers, keys are needed. Elements of a typical tonehole key are: 1) the head of the key, usually flat and round and slightly larger than the hole, made to close down over the hole; 2) the pad, covering the underside of the head and allowing the head to seal silently and leaklessly over the hole; 3) some sort of arm or lever, with the head at the end, which may incorporate a pivoting or fulcrum arrangement; 4) some kind of spring to keep the key open or closed (as the case may be) when not activated by the player.

The key must dependably come down squarely over the hole. Any tilting or misalignment virtually assures that there will be leakage. For this reason, the components of the key must be sturdy, well designed, and made to close tolerances. Tonehole key making in all but the most rudimentary applications is a difficult and exacting business; that is why casual home builders don't often get into it. But a casual builder may be able to equip an instrument with one or two simple lever-operated keys for out-of-reach toneholes. Some simple, home-buildable approaches to key-making appear in Figure 12-5, and the following notes provide further information.

On most woodwinds, holes that are to be covered with key pads (finger-covered holes too, sometimes) have their rims made level rather than following the curvature of the tube wall. This can be done either by making a flat raised rim around the hole or, with thick-walled tubing materials, by making a flat-bottomed concavity. The level surface allows a flat keyhead

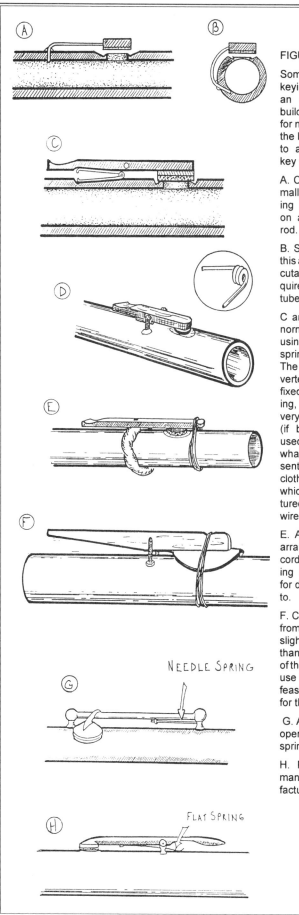

NEEDLE SPRING

FLAT SPRING

FIGURE 12-5

Some possible tonehole keying mechanisms, with an emphasis on home-buildable types. Notice that for most of these the rim of the hole must be made flat to accommodate the flat key and keypad.

A. Cutaway view of a normally open pad for covering large holes, mounted on a flexible spring steel rod.

B. Similar to A above, but this arrangement (shown in cutaway view, end-on) requires less space along the tube.

C and D. Two views of a normally closed system, using a clothespin-style spring beneath the key. The key pivots on an inverted U-shaped support, fixed to the tube by soldering, gluing, tapping into a very snug hole, using nuts (if bent threaded rod is used for the support) or whatever other means presents itself. In the inset: clothespin-style spring, which can be manufactured by hand from music wire.

E. A normally closed key arrangement using elastic cord, for use where the tubing material isn't suitable for drilling into or soldering to.

F. Curved key head, made from a section of tubing slightly larger in diameter than the outside diameter of the air column tube — for use in cases where it is not feasible to create a flat rim for the hole.

G. A key on a pivoting rod operated by a needle spring.

H. Flat spring, used on many commercially manufactured woodwinds.

and pad to cover the hole. You can achieve the same effect by starting with a square tube, which has level surfaces to begin with. An alternative to leveling is to shape the head of the key to follow the contour of the tube surface. Do this by using a circular cut-out section from a slightly larger diameter tubing for the head of the key, as in Figure 12-5F. This approach is more prone to leakage (being more exacting in terms of fit), but it may be the most practical method on wind instruments of extraordinarily large diameter.

About tonehole key pads: The softer the pad, the more readily it accommodates irregularities in the hole rim, and compensates for any misalignment in the angle at which the pad comes down over the rim, making for a leakless seal. But the surface of a soft pad also contributes to damping, and many soft pads of large surface area covering the holes undermine tone quality. You can purchase keypads ready-made in a range of sizes from woodwind manufacturers and band instrument repair places. Alternatively, you can make your own pads from leather, thin sheets of soft rubber or foam, or whatever else seems to serve the purpose.

Normally open vs. normally closed: You can make tonehole keys that automatically remain closed down over the hole until the player lifts them through the key action, or keys that remain open until the player presses them down. Choose whichever approach makes for easier fingerings. For remote keys, normally closed keys are generally easier to make, through a simple fulcrum-and-lever action. For keys designed to cover large holes falling directly under the fingers, it's easier to make normally open keys having no fulcrum as in Figures 12-5 A and B, which the player simply presses down to close.

Springs: Whether normally open or closed, some sort of spring must be in place to return the key to default position when it is released. Very stiff springs improve the seal on default-closed holes, but they make the playing action stiffer. The ideal is to use a moderately soft spring with perfect key alignment for a leakless seal. Commercial woodwinds often use needle springs — straight sections of spring-tempered steel wire (music wire), typically about an inch long, rigidly mounted at one end, with the other end pressing against a catch somewhere on the key lever to push it in the desired direction (see Figure 12-5G). Or they may use flat springs, as in Figure 12-5H. You may come up with a design in which coil springs do the trick, or one which uses clothes-pin-style springs (Figure 12-5C). For normally open keys, you may be able to have the arm which holds the key serve also as the spring, as in Figure 12-5A. An inelegant but workable approach is to use some sort of elastic banding to pull the key lever back one way or the other, as in Figure 12-5 E and F. If you do this, do not use rubber bands. Left under tension, they deteriorate rapidly. Use elastic cord or straps such as are sold at fabric stores, with many rounds of elastic under light tension rather than a few rounds under high tension.

Fulcrums and Pivoting Mechanisms: Many key designs use some sort of lever arrangement. Commercially manufactured woodwinds make extensive use of long pivoting rods, similar in concept to that shown in Figure 12-5G. This and other arrangements are not hard to work out on paper, but to make such tiny yet strong metal components with the required degree of precision is a daunting task for most people. So is the attachment of such mechanisms to the instrument tube as firmly as is necessary. Figure 12-5 A through F show possible key lever designs in a rougher, more homemade sort of style. If you're a tinkerer and junk collector you may be able to scrounge workable key lever hardware components from old instruments or other small mechanical items.

Compound Actions: On many commercially manufactured woodwinds, the keying actions are mind-bogglingly complex. They are designed so that a single action of the player's finger results in multiple tonehole actions up and down the instrument — press down one key, and several different holes open or close. Long pivoting rod actions like that shown in Figure 12-5G work well in applications like this, because you can arrange for arms extending out from different points along the pivot rod to fulfill various functions. Once again, the job of building such an action from scratch is a lot to ask of anyone but a skilled machinist in a well-equipped shop. One must admire the manufacturers who produce such fine mechanisms.

GLOSSARY

Absolute pitch   Pitch, in contexts where relationships or intervals between pitches are not important, but specific pitches as uniquely identified by rate of vibration are.

Aeolian   Adjective applied to musical instruments sounded by wind, such as aeolian harp and aeolian chimes. (In another usage, the term "aeolian mode" usually refers to the natural minor scale.)

Aerophone   Wind instrument.

Antinode   A point in a vibrating object which undergoes maximum movement or pressure variation for a given standing wave vibrating pattern.

Attack   The manner in which a sound begins.

Beating   A steady rise and fall in loudness that results when two tones of close but not identical frequency sound together.

Cancellation   When two out-of-phase vibrations counteract one another's effects so as to reduce the cumulative signal strength, they are said to cancel.

Chordophone   String instrument.

Chorusing effect   The subjectively richer effect of two or more vibration sources sounding together at approximately, but not precisely, the same frequencies.

Contact microphone   A microphone which responds not to vibrations in the atmosphere, but to vibration in a solid object to which the microphone is attached.

Damping   The diminishing of sound energy in a vibrating medium, through radiation or frictional losses.

Decay   The manner in which a sound diminishes after reaching maximum volume.

Displacement   The distance of a vibrating object at any given moment from its rest point or equilibrium position.

Driver   Any vibrating object which drives a vibration in another object or substance, as, for instance, a vibrating string drives its soundboard.

Edgetone   A vibration in the atmosphere created when a narrow air stream strikes an edge, as with flutes.

End correction   Sound waves in air column tubes behave as if the tube were slightly longer than it actually is. The end correction represents the difference between a tube's physical length and the slightly longer effective length of the air column.

Envelope   Usually, the characteristic pattern of rise and fall in a sound's volume over time. (May also refer to other sorts of patterns that can be represented on a graph.)

Equal temperament   A tuning system in which the scale degrees are equally (logarithmically) spaced. (Each successive step of the scale is the same interval above the preceding one.)

Ergonomic   Comfortable to use and well suited to the natural motions of the human body.

Fipple flute   A flute in which a narrow duct directs an air stream against an edge, as with recorders.

Formant   A frequency region that is favored in a resonating system. When different frequencies are fed into the resonator, any input frequencies which happen to fall in the range of a formant are resonated particularly strongly.

Frequency   The number of complete vibratory cycles per second in a given vibration. A sound's pitch is a function of its frequency — the more cycles per second, the higher the perceived pitch.

Frequency ratio   The ratio between two vibrational frequencies. This corresponds to the perceived musical interval between the pitches for the two frequencies, e.g., a frequency ratio of 2:1 corresponds to the interval of an octave.

Fundamental   Most musical sounds contain a blend of many frequencies. The lowest of these is the called the fundamental.

Its pitch is usually perceived as the defining pitch for the sound.

Harmonic A tone whose frequency is an integral multiple of a given fundamental frequency. Most musical sounds contain a blend of many frequencies including a fundamental and additional overtones; when the overtones are integral multiples of the fundamental's frequency, they are called harmonics. The fundamental itself is considered to be the first harmonic.

Harmonic series A series of pitches whose frequencies bear the relationship f, $2f$, $3f$, $4f$ …

Helmholtz resonator An air chamber which is not long and thin like an air column, but extensive in two or three dimensions (i.e., short and fat, or globular), open to the outside air through a relatively small opening.

Hertz Term used to designate frequency as measured in cycles per second, often abbreviated as Hz, e.g., 440 cycles per second = 440Hz.

Hocketing The practice of distributing a melody line among two or more players or singers, each of whom is responsible for some, but not all, of the pitches of the melody.

Idiophone Musical instrument in which the initial vibrating body is a solid, unstretched material.

Impedance Roughly, a measure of a vibration's concentration of energy, as manifest by how much force must be applied to achieve a certain amount of movement in the medium.

Inertia The tendency of any moving object to continue its motion in the same direction with constant speed.

Interval The musical relationship between two any pitches. Between a very high and a very low pitch, there is a large interval. Between two nearly identical pitches, there is a small interval.

Just intonation Any tuning system in which the intervals are based on frequency ratios.

Kalimba A lamellaphone, or plucked-prong instrument, of eastern, central and south-western Africa. In this book, the name is used generically to refer to hand-played plucked prong instruments of all sorts.

Longitudinal vibration Vibration in which the direction of displacement is along the same axis as the direction of wave travel.

Marimba Strictly speaking, certain types of kalimbas and certain African and Latin American xylophones, usually with resonators. More generally, it is often used to refer generically to free-end bar instruments of all sorts, and that is how it is used in this book.

Membranophone Musical instrument in which the primary vibrating body is a stretched membrane — i.e., a drum.

Mirliton A small membrane covering a hole in the side of an air column or air chamber, which adds a prominent buzz to the sound.

Mode of vibration Pattern of vibratory movement for a standing wave in an object or substance. Most vibrating objects are capable of many modes of vibration and manifest them simultaneously.

Natural frequency The frequency at which a body will vibrate if left alone after initial excitation, as, for instance, a string vibrates at its natural frequency after plucking.

Node A point in a vibrating object which undergoes no movement, or no pressure variation, for a given mode of vibration or standing wave vibrating pattern.

Organology The study of musical instruments, particularly from a historical and cultural perspective.

Overtone Most musical sounds contain a blend of many frequencies. The lowest of these is normally called the fundamental; the additional tones above it can be called overtones or partials. Overtones may or may not be harmonic, depending on their frequency relationship to the fundamental.

Partial Most musical sounds contain a blend of many frequencies. The individual frequencies can be called partials.

Phase In a steady-state vibrating pattern, phase refers to where in its vibratory cycle the vibrating body is at any instant. Given two vibrations of the same frequency, the two are said to be "out of phase" when at a given instant one experiences displacement in the opposite direction from the other. They are "in phase" when they experience displacement in the same direction at the same time.

Pitch The listener's sense of how "high" or "low" a musical sound is. It corresponds to vibrational frequency, with higher frequencies corresponding to higher pitches.

Radiation The transmission of sound energy from a vibrating medium to the surrounding atmosphere.

Register In wind instruments, the range of tones available when the instrument tube operates in a particular mode of vibration. Most tubular wind instruments have a fundamental register in which the air column's fundamental mode dominates the tone, a second register in which a higher mode comes to the fore acting as a surrogate fundamental over a higher range and, in some cases, a still higher third register. "Register" can also refer to a rank of organ pipes.

Register hole In wind instruments, a small hole relatively near the mouthpiece which aids in throwing the instrument into an upper register.

Relative pitch Pitch, in a context where absolute pitches as identified by their rates of vibration are not important, but the relationships or intervals between pitches are.

Resonance The especially strong response of any vibrating system to driver frequencies at or near the preferred natural frequencies of the system.

Resonance response curve A graph showing how the intensity of vibratory response varies over a range of frequencies for a given vibrating object or medium. The resonance response curve of a soundboard, for example, indicates how strongly the soundboard vibrates in response to different input frequencies from its driver.

Restoring force A force that works to return an object which has been displaced to its equilibrium position.

Reverberation The continued ringing of a sound in a room after the original source of the sound has ceased. It may also refer to a continued ringing in other vibrating elements such as attached springs or sympathetic strings.

Standing wave A wave in a medium of finite length which repeatedly reflects back on itself, developing seemingly stationary patterns as the cumulative result of the multiple reflected traveling waves. Standing waves are contrasted with traveling waves, in which the wave progresses through the medium, carrying wave energy to a distant location rather then repeatedly reflecting back on itself.

Stick-slip The mechanism by which vibrations are generated in bowed instruments, as well as other friction instruments and non-musical squeaks.

String scaling The science of selecting the best string lengths, diameters and materials for a given application.

Sympathetic vibration Vibration in a string or other vibrating element which comes not from being played directly, but rather from picking up vibrations from other vibrating elements at or near one of the sympathetic vibrator's natural frequencies.

Temperament A tuning system in which some of the ideal just intervals are deliberately detuned slightly in order to achieve more regular intervals between the pitches of the tuning.

Timbre Tone quality.

Transducer Something which converts a sound vibration from one medium to another; most often used in connection with microphones and pickups which convert vibrations in the air or solid media into patterns of changing voltage in an electric circuit.

Transverse vibration Vibration in which the direction of displacement is perpendicular to the direction of wave travel.

Traveling wave A progressive wave, which moves through its medium. All waves are in fact traveling waves, but traveling waves are often contrasted with standing waves, in which seemingly stationary patterns develop as the cumulative result of multiple reflected traveling waves.

Twelve-tone equal temperament The standard tuning system in Western music today, employing twelve equally spaced scale steps per octave.

Wave The cumulative effect of a series of small movements in a medium such as the air or a solid object, in which slight displacement of one particle causes a similar displacement of adjacent particles, giving rise to a series of displacements traveling rapidly through the medium. Sound, as perceived by the ears, is the result of a rapid series of waves in the atmosphere impinging on the eardrum.

Waveform The characteristic repeating pattern of change, either in pressure variation or in displacement, for a vibratory movement. Waveform is usually represented as a wavy line on a graph, plotting displacement or pressure change against time for a representative point in the vibrating medium.

Wavelength The distance between one wave front and the next. The longer the wavelength, the lower the frequency and the lower the perceived pitch.

BIBLIOGRAPHY

This bibliography includes selected English language works on general organology, texts on acoustics and intonation theory, and collections of instrument-making plans. It is not exhaustive in any of these areas.

This bibliography does not list works devoted to specific standard instruments, since the number of different instrument types and books would be unmanageably large. If you have an interest in a particular instrument, begin by looking it up in the *New Grove Dictionary of Musical Instruments* (available at large libraries), which is organized like an encyclopedia. Most of its articles contain bibliographies that can help guide your further research.

This bibliography also does not list books on the instruments of specific cultures. The world is too big, the books too many, and the field too rapidly changing to do a good job

of that here. Once again you can begin with general sources such as the *New Grove*, and follow the bibliographies.

In searching for further information on topics relating to musical instruments, keep in mind the periodical literature. There are newsletters or journals devoted to most standard instrument types, as well as many obscure types (jaw harp and musical saw, for example). You can find periodicals devoted to particular instruments by perusing the music section of *Ulrich's International Periodicals Directory* or similar sources to be found in the reference section of the local library. The only periodical devoted to new and unusual instruments of all sorts is *Experimental Musical Instruments*, edited by the author of this book, available from PO Box 784, Nicasio, CA 94946 ($24/year [$34 outside the North America] at the time of this writing).

General Organology

Baines, Anthony, *The Oxford Companion to Musical Instruments*. Oxford: Oxford University Press, 1992. Just under 400 pages, organized as an encyclopedia, with entries providing fairly detailed information on a broad range of western and non-western instruments. Less complete than the *New Grove* listed below, but far more affordable.

The Diagram Group, *Musical Instruments of the World: An Illustrated Encyclopedia*. New York: Facts on File, 1976. A browser's delight; beautifully illustrated, but far less detailed and complete than the *New Grove* listed below.

Marcuse, Sibyl, *Musical Instruments: A Comprehensive Dictionary*. New York: W.W. Norton Co., 1975. A dictionary of musical instrument names and terminology. Very complete for historical instruments (with virtually nothing on 20th century instruments), but the entries are very brief.

Sachs, Curt, *The History of Musical Instruments*. New York, W.W. Norton & Co., Inc., 1940. For many years an important scholarly resource, now somewhat outdated in both content and approach.

Sadie, Stanley, ed., *The New Grove Dictionary of Musical Instruments*. New York and London: MacMillan Press Ltd., 1984. In three volumes; organized as an encyclopedia. This is by far the most complete source for information on instruments of all sorts. Costs over $300.

Acoustics and IntonationTtheory

Backus, John G., *The Acoustical Foundations of Music*, 2nd edition. New York: W.W. Norton, 1977.

Banta, Christopher C., *Basic Marimba Bar Mechanics and Resonator Principles*. Pasadena: Creative Percussion Company, 1982. Design principles for vibrating bar instruments.

Barbour, J. Murray, *Tuning and Temperament*. East Lansing, MI: Michigan State College Press, 1951. The closest thing to a standard general reference in the field of intonational theory.

Benade, Arthur H., *Fundamentals of Musical Acoustics*. New York: Dover Publications, Inc. 1990. An essential, if fairly demanding and at times idiosyncratic, overview of the topic.

Benade, Arthur H., *Horns, Strings & Harmony*. Garden City, NY: Anchor Books, 1960. A simpler and friendlier view of musical acoustics compared to the previous listing.

Brosnac, Donald, *Guitar Electronics for Musicians*. Amsco Publications, 1988.

Doty, David, *The Just Intonation Primer: An introduction to the theory and practice of just intonation*. 1993. The best place to start for just intonation theory (Non-just scale systems, such as equal temperaments, are not covered.)

Fletcher, Neville H. and Rossing, Thomas D., *The Physics of Musical Instruments*. New York: Springer-Verlag, 1991.

A highly technical treatment, likely to be meaningful only to those with advanced training in math and physics.

Hall, Donald, *Musical Acoustics: An Introduction* 2nd edition. Pacific Grove, CA: Brooks-Cole Pub. Co., 1991. Designed as a college-level textbook. Accessible, lucid and practical throughout.

Helmholtz, Hermann, *On the Sensations of Tone*. New York: Dover Publications, 1954 (first published in 1885). Helmholtz' pioneering study of musical acoustics, with extensive appendices by translator Alexander Ellis, is still read as a foundational text today.

Hill, Ralph David, *Sounds of Just Intonation: Introduction to Nontraditional Harmony*. San Francisco: The Just Intonation Network, 1984. Available from the Just Intonation Network at 535 Stevenson St., San Francisco CA 94103. This package includes both a text introducing concepts of just intonation and two cassette tapes for hearing the sounds discussed.

Hopkin, Bart, *Air Columns and Toneholes: Principles for Wind Instrument Design*. Willits: Tai Hei Shakuhachi, 1993. Available from Tai Hei Shakuhachi at P.O. Box 294, Willits, CA 95490. Starts with a non-mathematical overview, then works its way through to a more technical approach.

Olsen, Harry F., *Music, Physics and Engineering*. New York: Dover Publications, Inc., 1967. A compendium of technical information.

Partch, Harry, *Genesis of a Music*. New York: Da Capo Press, 1974. Partch's account of the development of his musical ideas and instruments remains an important source for both intonational theory and practical acoustics.

Collections of Instrument Plans and Descriptions

Banek, Reinhold and Scoville, Jon, *Sound Designs: A Handbook of Musical Instrument Building*. Berkeley, CA: Ten Speed Press, Berkeley, CA, 1995. About fifty unconventional designs presented in accessible, readable style. First published in 1980, this is the classic text of the genre.

Baschet, François & Bernard, *Sound Sculpture: The Baschet Experience — Shapes, Sounds and People — 1945-1965* (unpublished manuscript, 1965); and Baschet, François, *The Art of Musical Fountains* (unpublished manuscript, 1989). The former is a colorful and anecdotal description of the Baschet brothers' sonic explorations during a seminal period — both entertaining and educational. The latter is a more abbreviated account of some later work.

deBeer, Sara, ed., *Open Ears: Musical Adventures for a New Generation*. Roslyn, NY: Ellipsis Kids, 1995. About fifteen musical instrument-making projects, along with other music-making ideas, from twenty familiar musical personalities ranging from Babatunde Olatunji through Pete Seeger to Tom Keith.

Ditrich, Will, *The Mills College Gamelan: Si Darius and Si Madeleine*. 1983; available from the American Gamelan Institute, Box A-36, Hanover, NH, 03755. Detailed descriptions and drawings of instruments created by Bill Colvig and Lou Harrison.

Het Apollohuis, *Echo: the Images of Sound*. Eindhoven: Het Apollohuis, 1987. A collection of essays and photo documentation of sound exploration occurring at the Dutch arts center, Het Apollohuis.

Francis, Lindo, and Trussell-Cullen, Alan, *Hooked on Making Musical Instruments*. Auckland: Longman Paul Ltd., 1989) About 50 simple instruments that can be made by children.

Grayson, John, ed., *Sound Sculpture*, and *Environments of Musical Sound Sculpture You Can Build*. Vancouver: A.R.C. Press [Aesthetic Research Center of Canada], 1976. A variety of essays and plans for sound exploration, culled from several builders.

Hopkin, Bart, *Making Simple Musical Instruments*. Asheville, North Carolina: Lark Books, 1995. Plans for about twenty-five instruments, most relating to familiar types but with lots of imaginative twists.

Jones, Claire, *Making Music: Musical Instruments in Zimbabwe Past and Present*. Harare, Zimbabwe: Academic Books (Pvt.) Ltd., 1992. Descriptions and construction information for about 30 Zimbabwean instruments, written for use in the schools.

Partch, Harry, *Genesis of a Music*. New York: Da Capo Press, 1974. In addition to its theoretical information, Partch's manifesto contains detailed descriptions and information on construction of his unique instruments.

Hunter, Ilene and Judson, Marilyn, *Simple Folk Instruments to Make and Play*. New York: Simon & Schuster, 1977. A collection of good, workable, simple children's instrument-making projects.

Roberts, Ronald, *Musical Instruments Made to be Played*. Leicester: Dryad Press, 1968. Plans for simple instruments both conventional and unconventional.

Sawyer, David, *Vibrations*. Cambridge: Cambridge University Press, 1977. Twenty-eight imaginative and unconventional designs.

Shepard, Mark: *Simple Flutes: Play Them, Make Them*. Willits: Tai Hei Shakuhachi, 1992. Available from Tai Hei at P.O. Box 293, Willits, CA 95490. Lucid description of the principles behind simple flute design.

Sloane, Irving, *Making Musical Instruments*. New York: E.P. Dutton, 1978. Detailed notes for making banjo, snare drum, Appalachian dulcimer, hardanger fiddle and recorder.

Walther, Tom, *Make Mine Music!* Boston: Little, Brown & Co., 1981. Instructions for about twenty-five instruments that can be made by children, along with activities and philosophical musings.

Waring, Dennis, *Making Folk Instruments in Wood*. New York: Sterling Publishing Co., 1979. Plans for about fifty instruments, some conventional and some unconventional; all of them enjoyable and beautiful.

INDEX

formants 4, 5, 10
Forster, Cris 50
frame drums 95, 96
Franklin, Ben 50
free bars 9, 10, 15, 16, 17, 29, 31-38,
    50, 143
      finding the nodes 34
      fundamental tuning 32
      mounting 37, 38
      overtone tuning 33, 34
Free reeds 70
French horn 70
frequency 1, 7, 8, 16, 21, 157, 167
fret placements 24, 132-133
frets 132
fretwire 134
friction devices 57, 58
friction drums 105
friction mallets 58
friction rod instruments 45
Fullman, Ellen 15
fundamental 3, 4, 10, 11, 18, 35, 36, 43,
    51, 167

G

gamelan 139
Genesis of a Music 28, 160
gesture 25, 28
glass 37, 47, 50, 153
glass harmonica 50
gongs 19, 37, 48, 50, 51, 52, 144, 145
Goodfellow, Robin 77
gourds 35, 153
guiros 53, 58
guitars 19, 20, 110, 129, 132
gut 121

H

hammer dulcimer 127
hammers 130
harmonic canon 26
harmonic overtones 4, 12, 17, 77, 134,
143
harmonic series 2, 3, 4, 6, 12, 14, 17, 70,
71, 72, 119
harmonicas 70
harmonics 2, 3
harmonics flute 77
harmonics guitar 12
harmoniums 70, 139, 141
harp bridges 128
harps 118, 127
harpsichords 127, 130
Hawaiian guitar 134
hearing range 1
Helmholtz resonators 35, 71
hocketing 145
Hornbostel, Erich M. von 30
horsetail hair 57, 58
Hsun 61
humbucking pickups 165
Hume, Ben 67
hummers 145
hurdy-gurdy 58

I

idiochords 136
idioglottal reeds 67
idiophones 29
impedance 19, 108, 109
industrial supply and surplus 151
inharmonic overtones 2, 3, 4, 6, 15, 37,
    41, 48

inharmonic partials 92
intonarumori 137

J

jaltarang 50
jaw harps 43
jawari 128
Jew's harps
    SEE jaw harps
jugs 65
just intonation 21, 22, 23, 77, 157

K

kalimba 7, 14, 25, 28, 40, 41, 42, 109,
    141, 143
kazoos 144
kelp 76, 153
kettle drums 96
keyboards 25, 27, 28, 130
keyed bugle 81
kora 28, 127, 128

L

labial reeds 69
lamellaphones
    SEE rods fixed at one end, kalimbas
lesiba 123
line level 165
lip-buzzed instruments 70, 81, 167
lithophones 153
log drums 43
Long String Instrument 15, 58
longitudinal vibration 15, 16
loudspeaker 7, 163, 165
low bridges 127
lutes 118, 127
lutherie supply houses 155
lyres 118

M

magstrip 80, 81
Mahillon, Victor 30
mallet handles 55
mallet heads 55
mallet overwraps 56
mallets 5, 55, 56, 57
mandolin 108
Manflower 60
maracas 2, 53
marimbas 29, 35, 144, 145
    SEE ALSO free bars
marimbulas 41, 42
mbira
    SEE kalimba
Meadows, Michael 46
Megalyra 135
membrane reeds 66, 68-69
membranes 14, 112
Membranophones 30, 91-106
metals 152
microphones 163
mirlitons 144
modes of vibration 11, 14, 15, 17, 18, 30,
    31, 32, 34, 36, 40, 50, 74, 93, 119, 170
modularity 147
monochords 24, 26
mounting systems 59, 60
mouthpieces 65, 66, 67, 70, 167, 168
moving sound sources 145
music boxes 40
music stores 155
musical glasses 50

musical saw 52
mvet 128

N

nail violin 46, 47
names for musical instruments 148
natural materials 151, 153
New Grove Dictionary of Music 177
ney 63
nodes and antinodes 12, 14, 16, 17, 24,
    30, 31, 34, 36, 40, 48, 50, 170
notched bow 58
nylon 121, 155

O

ocarina fingering 83
ocarinas 63, 139
orchestral chimes 37
organ pipes 75
oscilloscopes 24
outer air instruments 88
overtones 2, 4, 11, 14, 15, 35, 41, 43,
    51, 134
    SEE ALSO partials, harmonics

P

panpipes 63, 64, 77, 145
Partch, Harry 28, 148, 160
partials 2, 5, 17, 18, 32, 49, 92, 143
    SEE ALSO harmonics, overtones
pedal steel guitar 134
pellet drums 103
pendulums 7
pennywhistle fingering 83
percussion aerophones
    SEE plosive aerophones
phase relationships 18, 95, 108, 126,
    127, 145
Phillips, Bob 147
piano 19, 25, 107, 108, 127, 140
piano tuner supply houses 155
pianos 25
Pick-behind-the-bridge Guitar 12
piezo-electric effect 164
pin-bridges 130
pipe organs 66, 77, 141, 145
pitch 1, 2, 4, 11, 14, 21, 157
pitch layouts 25
pitch pipes 24
plastics 152
plate reverb 140
plectra 130
plexiglass 152
plosive aerophones 85
prepared piano 136
Prongs & Echoes 140, 141, 142
prototypes 77, 83, 147
PVC plastic 151, 152

Q

Quadrangularis Reversum 28
quarter-comma meantone 157, 160
quartz tuners 24

R

radiation 11, 19, 75, 107-116
rradiators 19, 20, 35, 36, 43, 47, 109,
    113, 117, 140
raga 157
rasps 53
ratios 1, 22, 23, 77, 157
rattles 53, 141
Reckert, Sascha 50